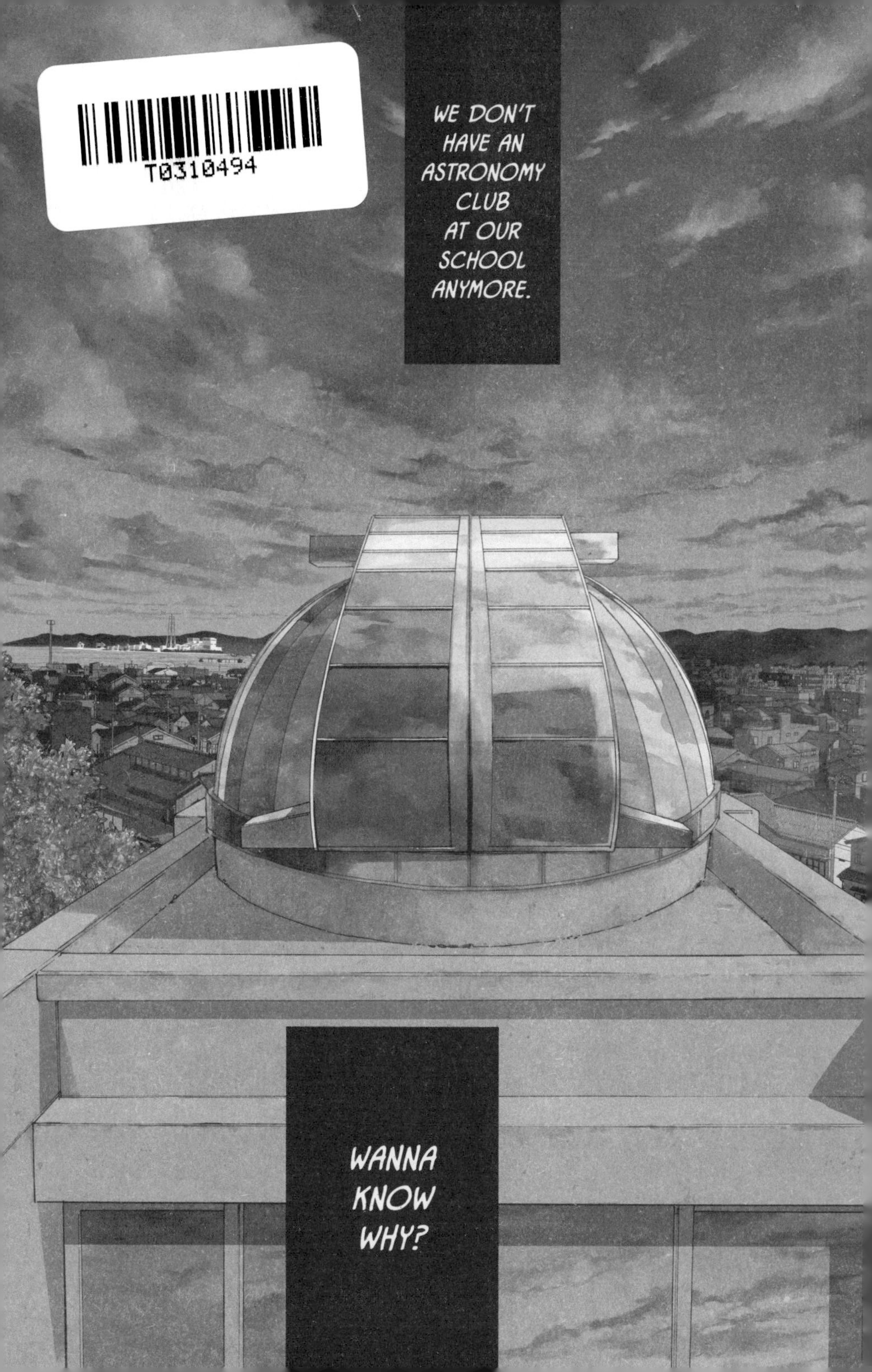
WE DON'T HAVE AN ASTRONOMY CLUB AT OUR SCHOOL ANYMORE.
WANNA KNOW WHY?

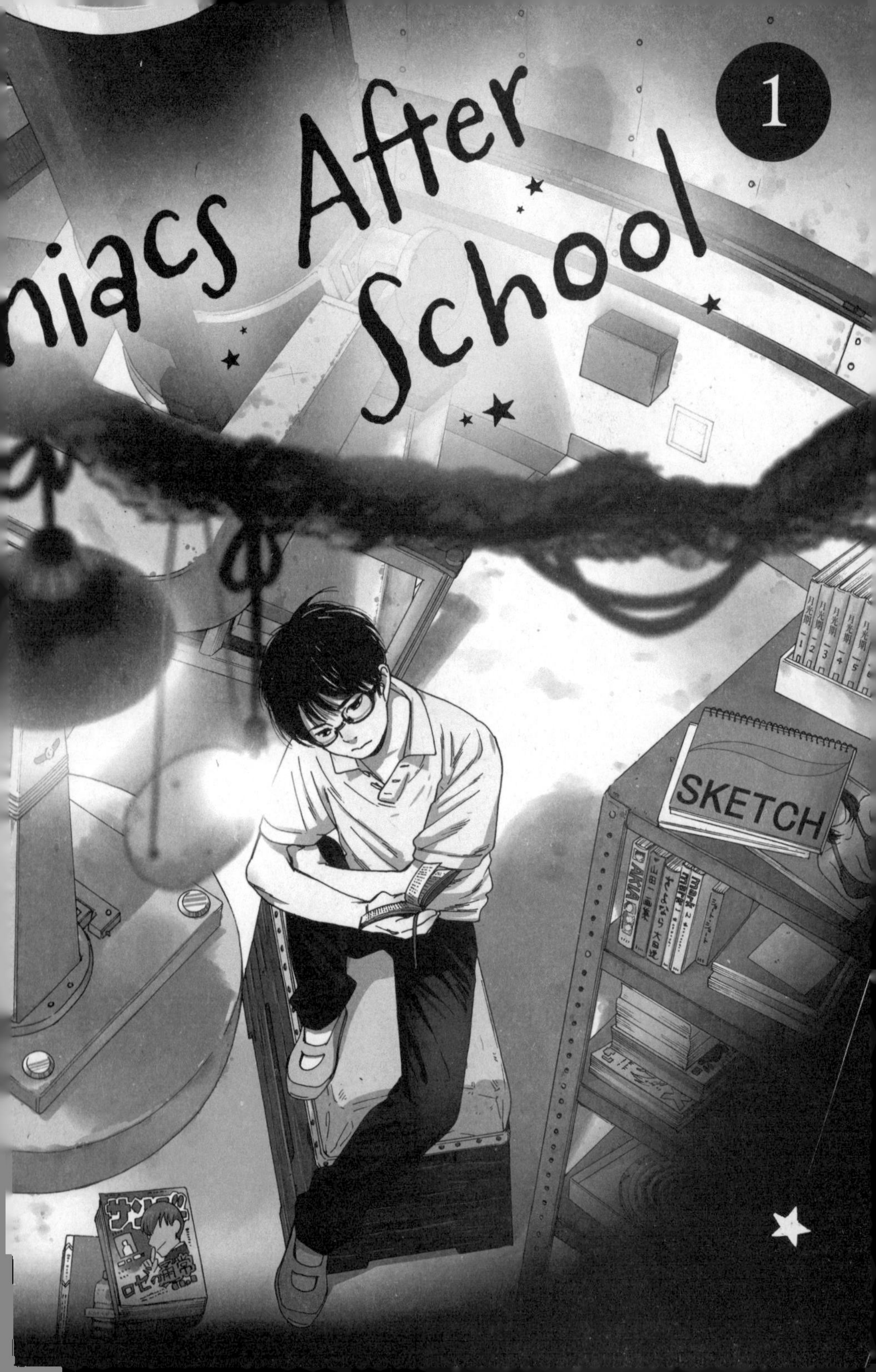
niacs After School
1
SKETCH

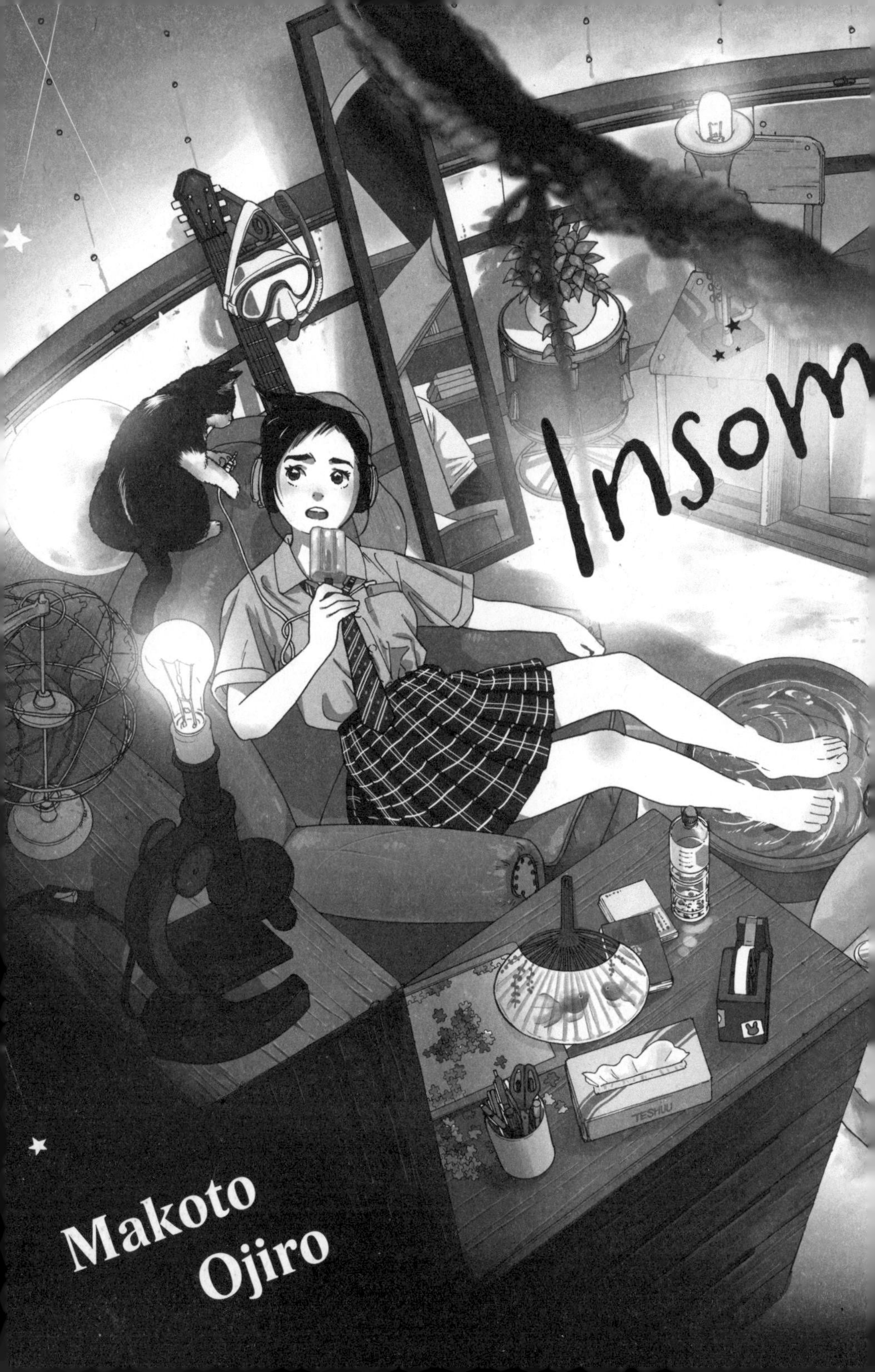
Insom
Makoto Ojiro
TESHUU

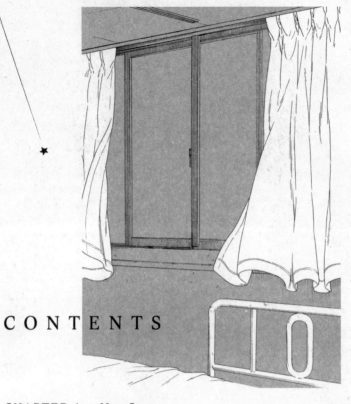

C O N T E N T S

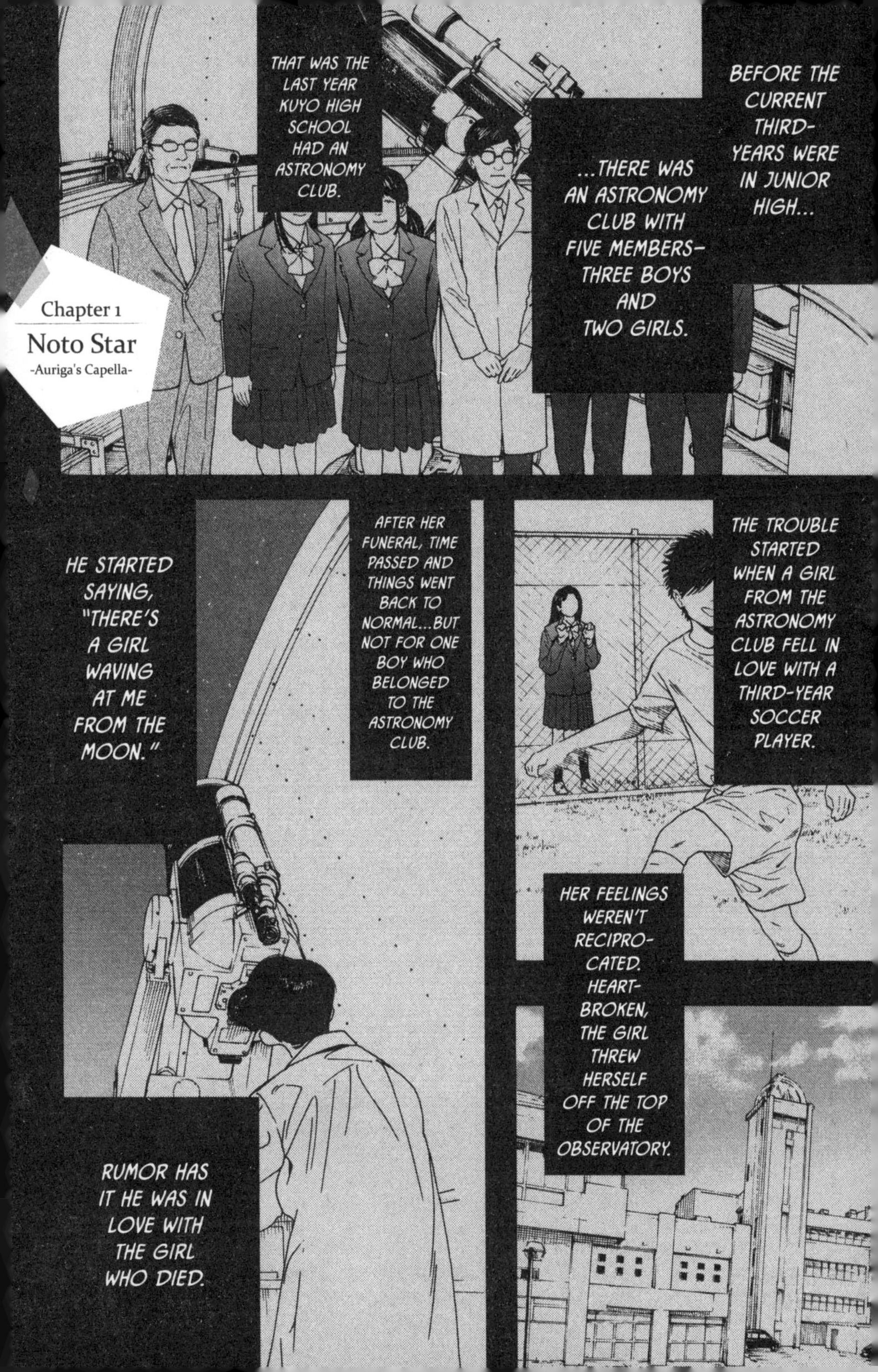
Chapter 1
Noto Star
-Auriga's Capella-
BEFORE THE CURRENT THIRD-YEARS WERE IN JUNIOR HIGH...
...THERE WAS AN ASTRONOMY CLUB WITH FIVE MEMBERS— THREE BOYS AND TWO GIRLS.
THAT WAS THE LAST YEAR KUYO HIGH SCHOOL HAD AN ASTRONOMY CLUB.
THE TROUBLE STARTED WHEN A GIRL FROM THE ASTRONOMY CLUB FELL IN LOVE WITH A THIRD-YEAR SOCCER PLAYER.
HER FEELINGS WEREN'T RECIPRO-CATED. HEART-BROKEN, THE GIRL THREW HERSELF OFF THE TOP OF THE OBSERVATORY.
AFTER HER FUNERAL, TIME PASSED AND THINGS WENT BACK TO NORMAL...BUT NOT FOR ONE BOY WHO BELONGED TO THE ASTRONOMY CLUB.
HE STARTED SAYING, "THERE'S A GIRL WAVING AT ME FROM THE MOON."
RUMOR HAS IT HE WAS IN LOVE WITH THE GIRL WHO DIED.

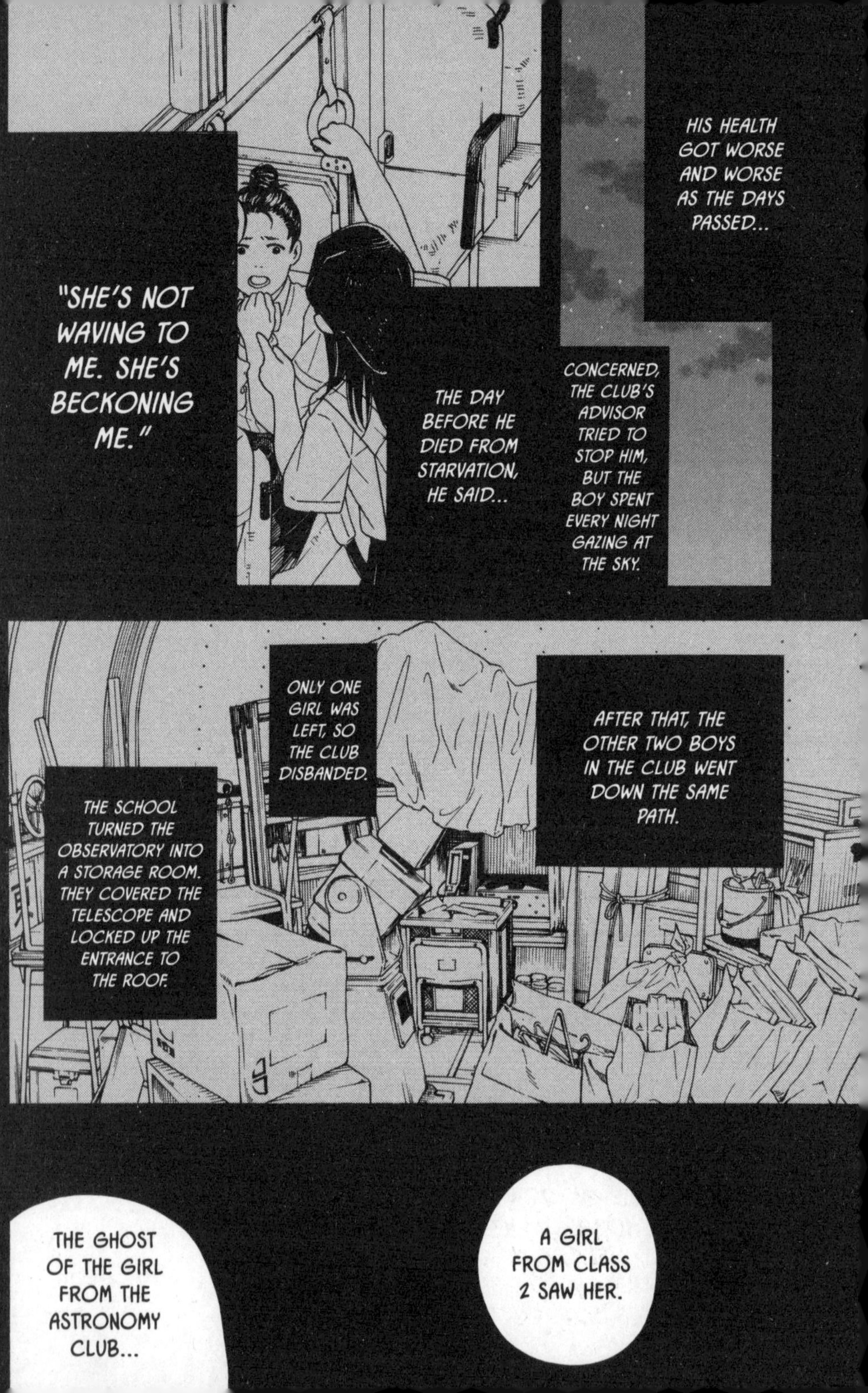
HIS HEALTH GOT WORSE AND WORSE AS THE DAYS PASSED...
CONCERNED, THE CLUB'S ADVISOR TRIED TO STOP HIM, BUT THE BOY SPENT EVERY NIGHT GAZING AT THE SKY.
THE DAY BEFORE HE DIED FROM STARVATION, HE SAID...
"SHE'S NOT WAVING TO ME. SHE'S BECKONING ME."
AFTER THAT, THE OTHER TWO BOYS IN THE CLUB WENT DOWN THE SAME PATH.
ONLY ONE GIRL WAS LEFT, SO THE CLUB DISBANDED.
THE SCHOOL TURNED THE OBSERVATORY INTO A STORAGE ROOM. THEY COVERED THE TELESCOPE AND LOCKED UP THE ENTRANCE TO THE ROOF.
A GIRL FROM CLASS 2 SAW HER.
THE GHOST OF THE GIRL FROM THE ASTRONOMY CLUB...

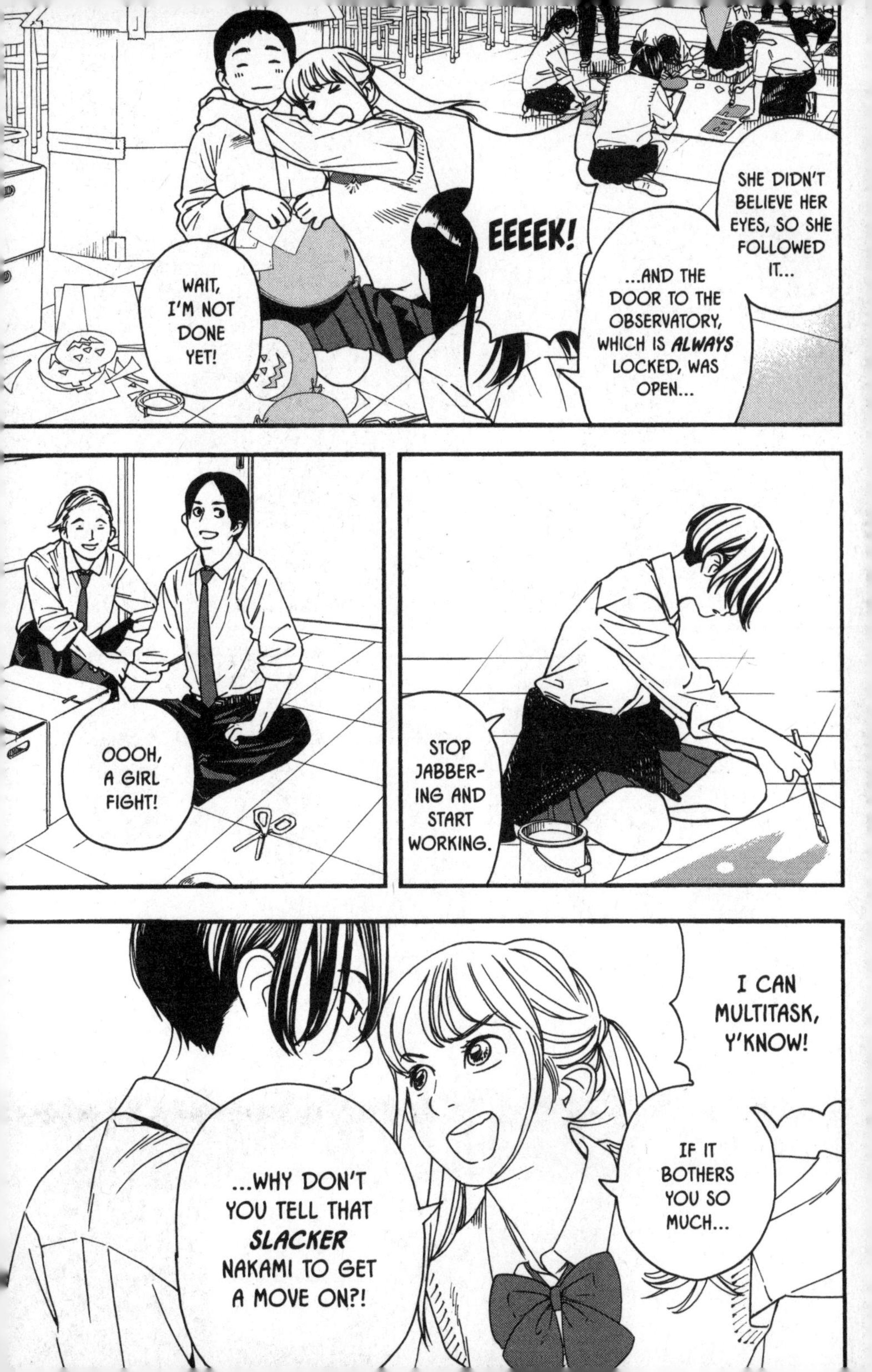
SHE DIDN'T BELIEVE HER EYES, SO SHE FOLLOWED IT...
...AND THE DOOR TO THE OBSERVATORY, WHICH IS *ALWAYS* LOCKED, WAS OPEN...
EEEEK!
WAIT, I'M NOT DONE YET!
STOP JABBERING AND START WORKING.
OOOH, A GIRL FIGHT!
I CAN MULTITASK, Y'KNOW!
IF IT BOTHERS YOU SO MUCH...
...WHY DON'T YOU TELL THAT *SLACKER* NAKAMI TO GET A MOVE ON?!

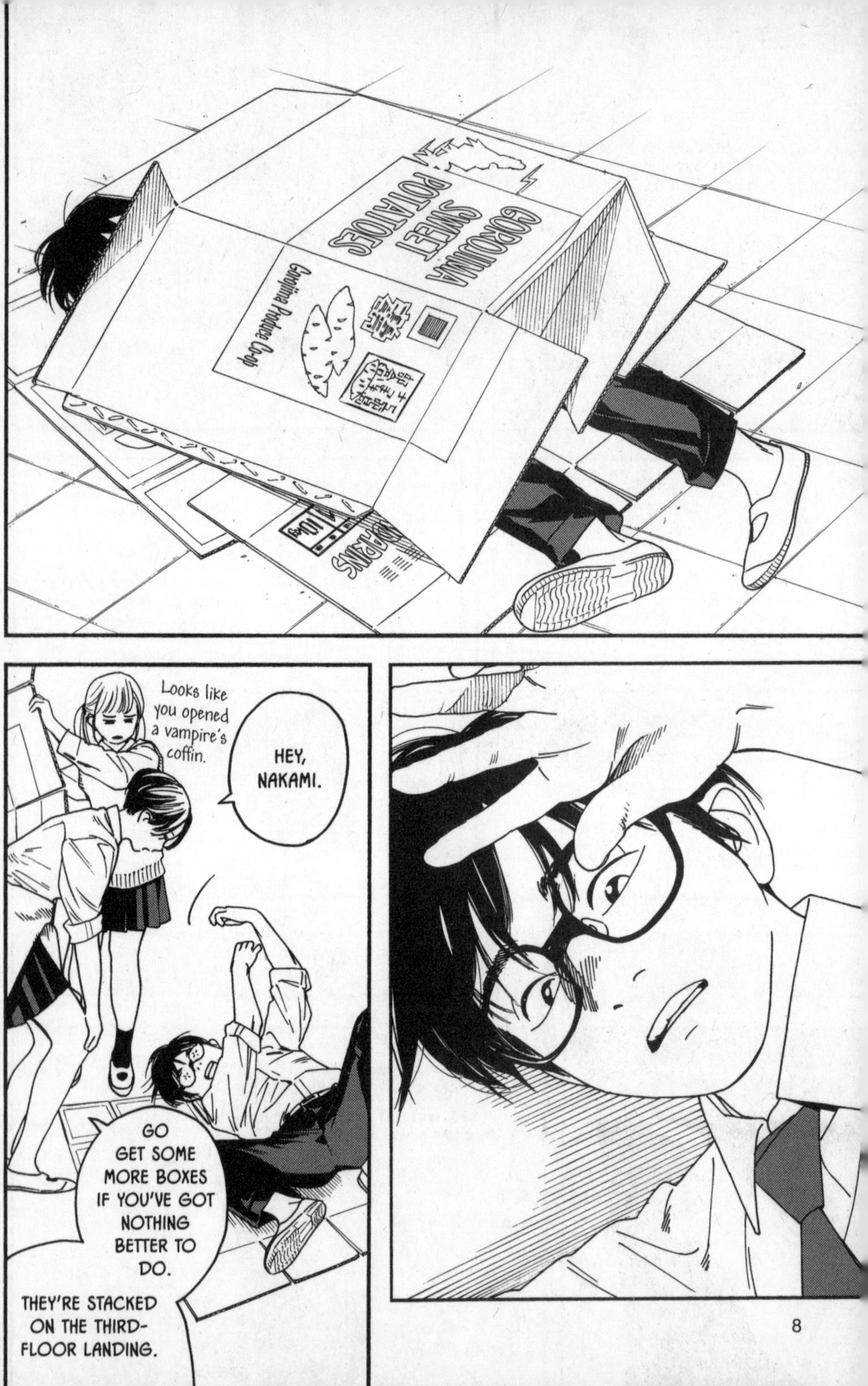
GOROJIMA SWEET POTATOES
Gorojima Produce Co-op
HEY, NAKAMI.
Looks like you opened a vampire's coffin.
GO GET SOME MORE BOXES IF YOU'VE GOT NOTHING BETTER TO DO.
THEY'RE STACKED ON THE THIRD-FLOOR LANDING.

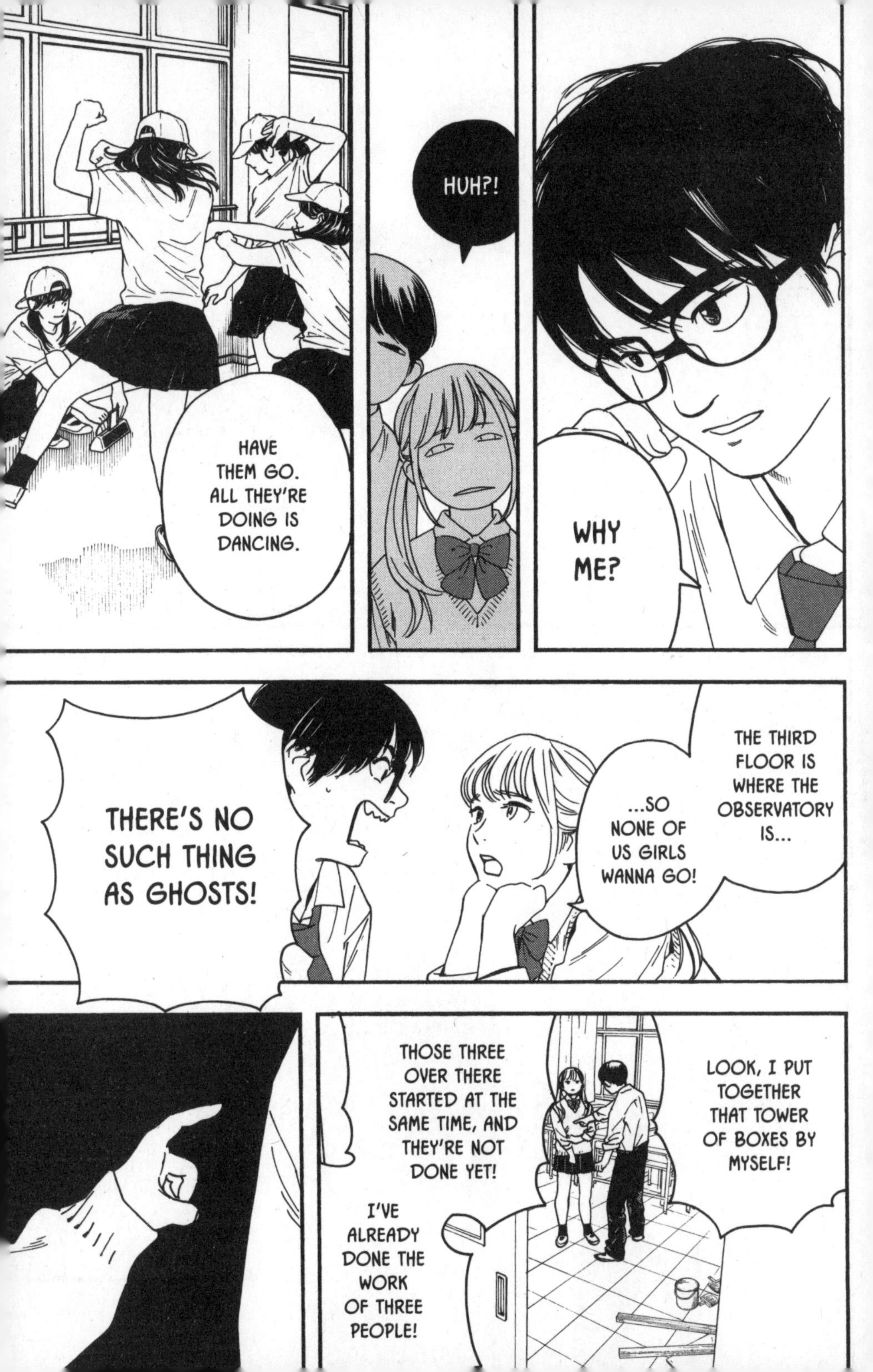
WHY ME?
HUH?!
HAVE THEM GO. ALL THEY'RE DOING IS DANCING.
THE THIRD FLOOR IS WHERE THE OBSERVATORY IS...
...SO NONE OF US GIRLS WANNA GO!
THERE'S NO SUCH THING AS GHOSTS!
LOOK, I PUT TOGETHER THAT TOWER OF BOXES BY MYSELF!
THOSE THREE OVER THERE STARTED AT THE SAME TIME, AND THEY'RE NOT DONE YET!
I'VE ALREADY DONE THE WORK OF THREE PEOPLE!

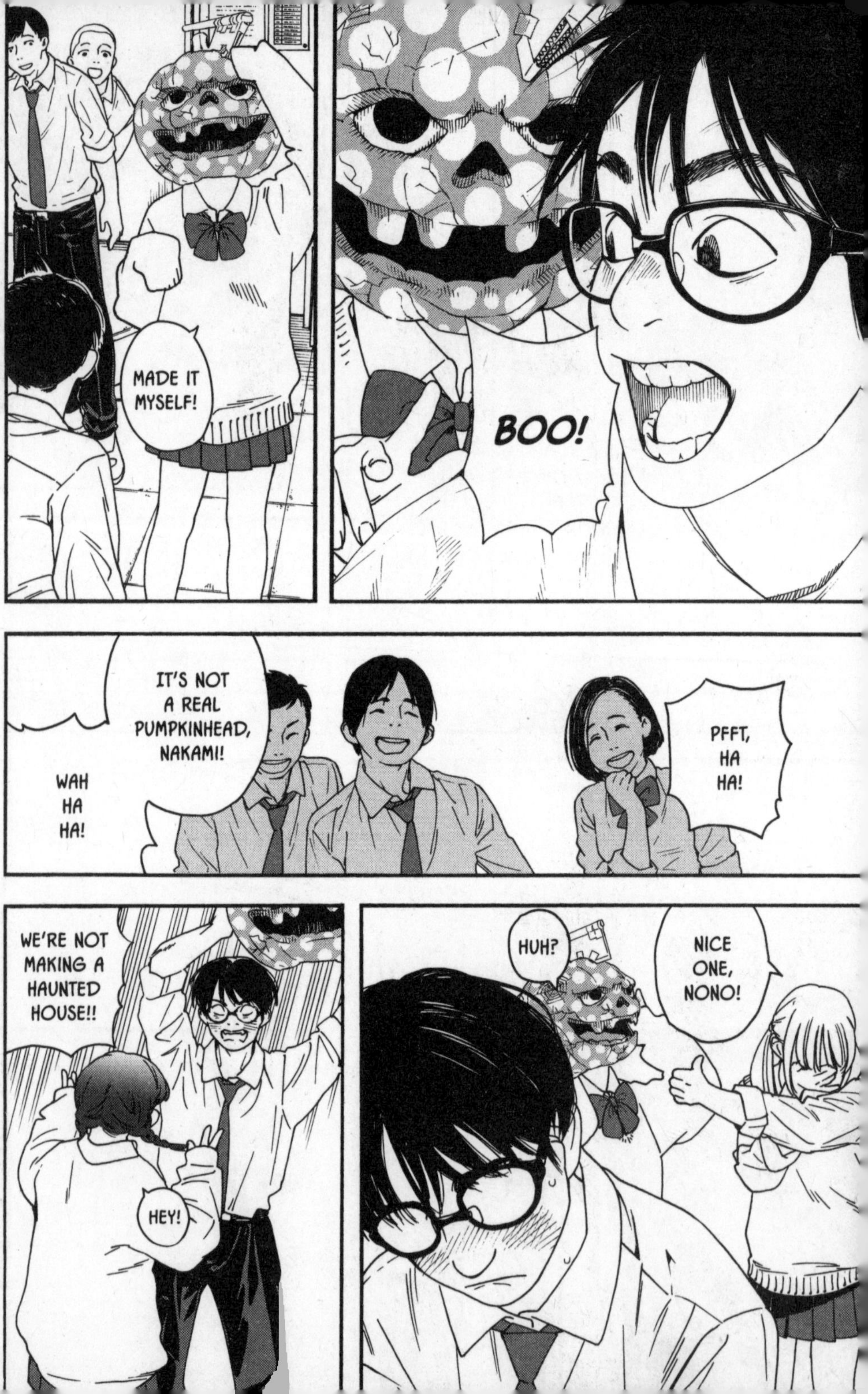
BOO!
MADE IT MYSELF!
PFFT, HA HA!
IT'S NOT A REAL PUMPKINHEAD, NAKAMI!
WAH HA HA!
NICE ONE, NONO!
HUH?
WE'RE NOT MAKING A HAUNTED HOUSE!!
HEY!

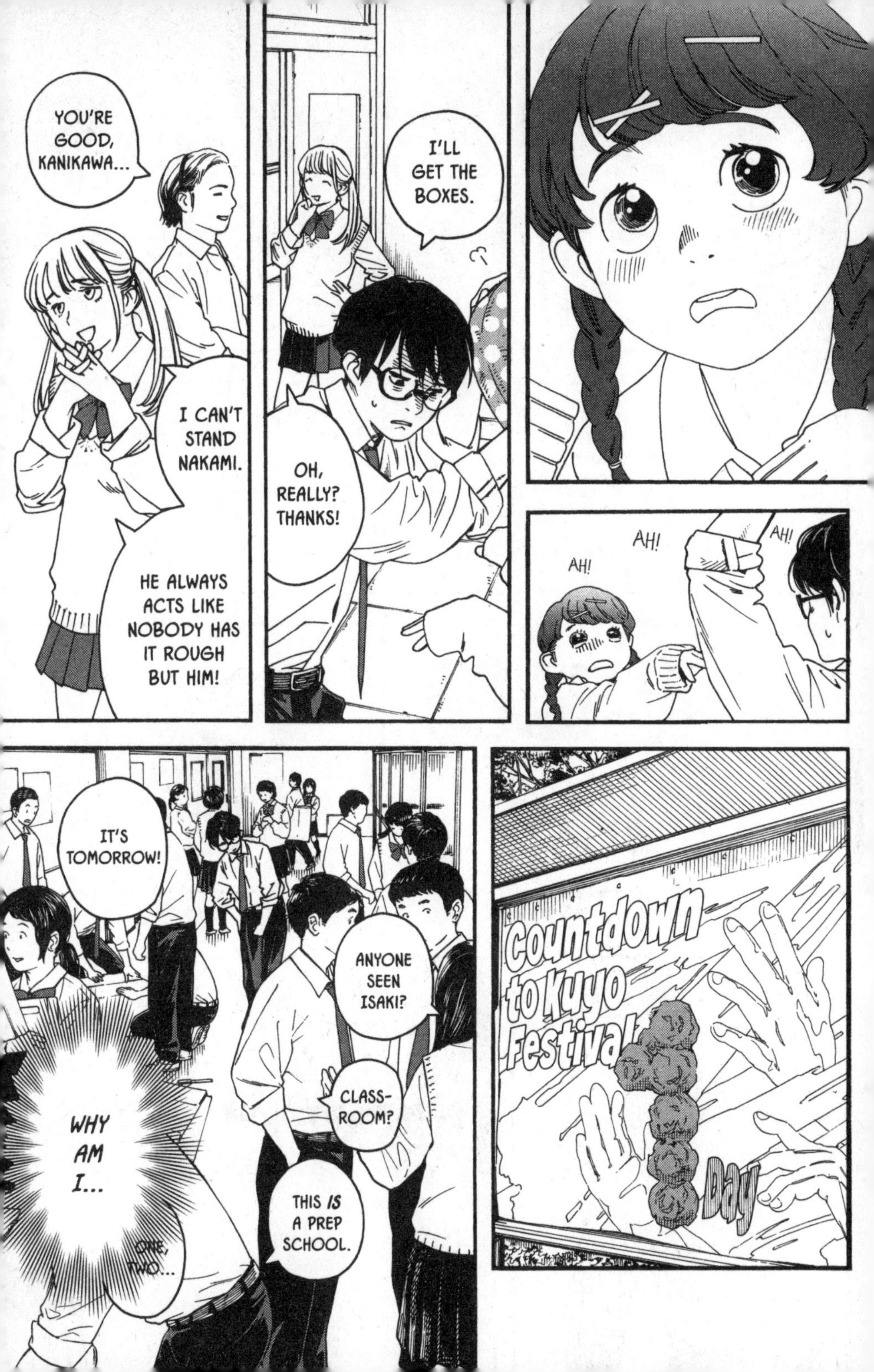
AH!
AH!
AH!
I'LL GET THE BOXES.
OH, REALLY? THANKS!
YOU'RE GOOD, KANIKAWA...
I CAN'T STAND NAKAMI.
HE ALWAYS ACTS LIKE NOBODY HAS IT ROUGH BUT HIM!
Countdown to Kuyo Festival
Day
ANYONE SEEN ISAKI?
CLASSROOM?
THIS *IS* A PREP SCHOOL.
IT'S TOMORROW!
WHY AM I...
ONE, TWO...

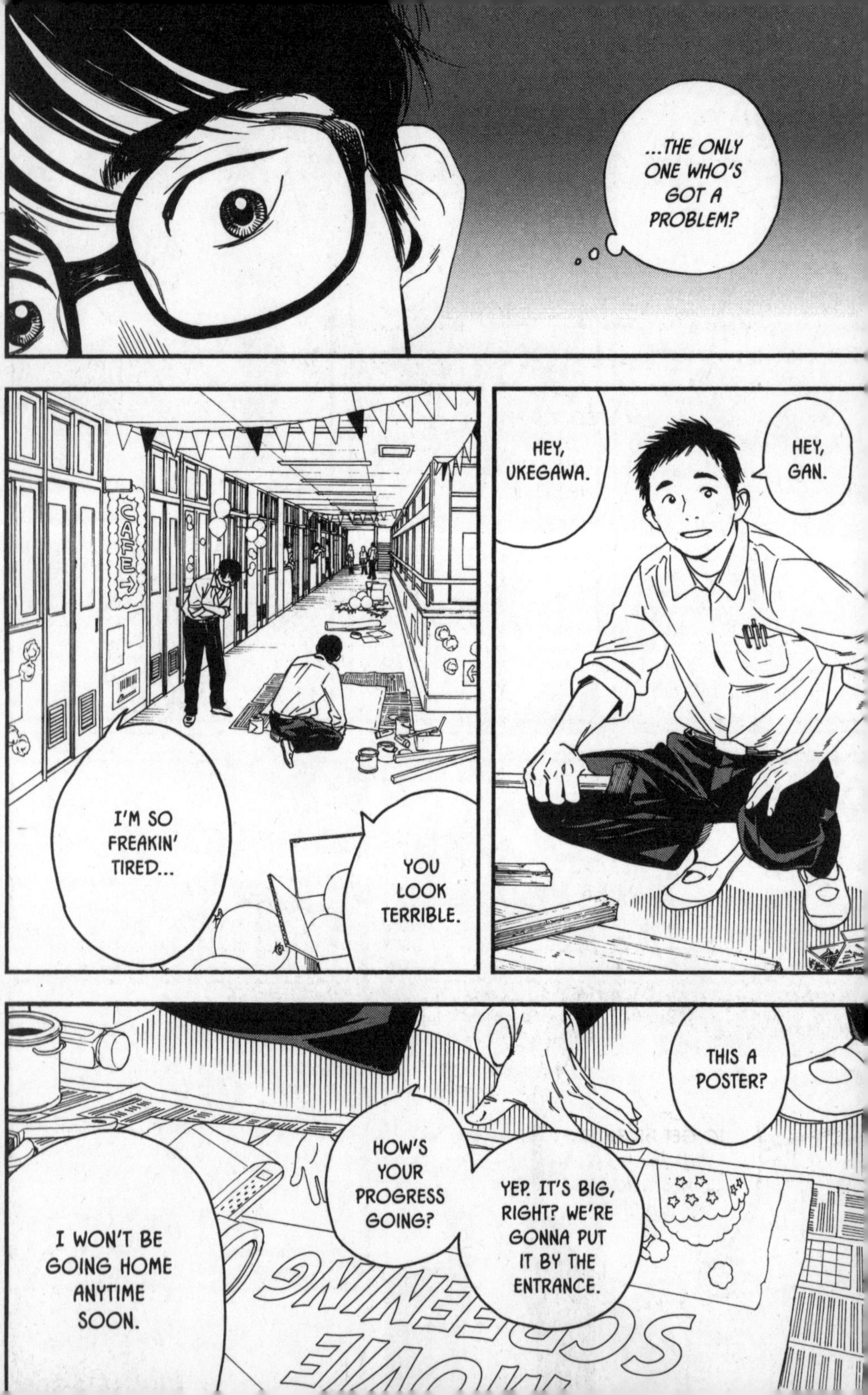
...THE ONLY ONE WHO'S GOT A PROBLEM?
HEY, GAN.
HEY, UKEGAWA.
YOU LOOK TERRIBLE.
I'M SO FREAKIN' TIRED...
THIS A POSTER?
YEP. IT'S BIG, RIGHT? WE'RE GONNA PUT IT BY THE ENTRANCE.
HOW'S YOUR PROGRESS GOING?
I WON'T BE GOING HOME ANYTIME SOON.

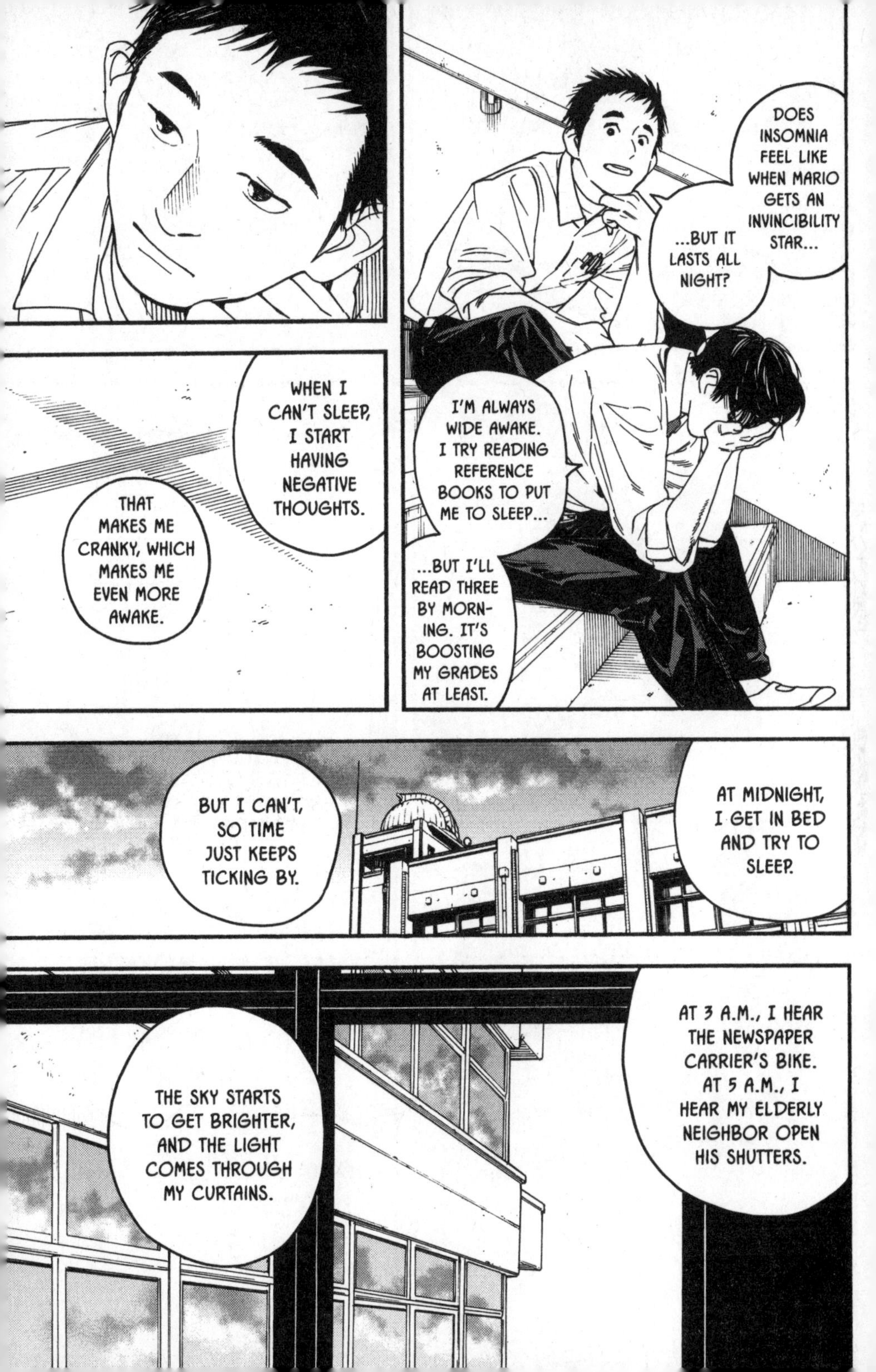
DOES INSOMNIA FEEL LIKE WHEN MARIO GETS AN INVINCIBILITY STAR...
...BUT IT LASTS ALL NIGHT?
I'M ALWAYS WIDE AWAKE. I TRY READING REFERENCE BOOKS TO PUT ME TO SLEEP...
...BUT I'LL READ THREE BY MORN-ING. IT'S BOOSTING MY GRADES AT LEAST.
WHEN I CAN'T SLEEP, I START HAVING NEGATIVE THOUGHTS.
THAT MAKES ME CRANKY, WHICH MAKES ME EVEN MORE AWAKE.
AT MIDNIGHT, I GET IN BED AND TRY TO SLEEP.
BUT I CAN'T, SO TIME JUST KEEPS TICKING BY.
AT 3 A.M., I HEAR THE NEWSPAPER CARRIER'S BIKE. AT 5 A.M., I HEAR MY ELDERLY NEIGHBOR OPEN HIS SHUTTERS.
THE SKY STARTS TO GET BRIGHTER, AND THE LIGHT COMES THROUGH MY CURTAINS.

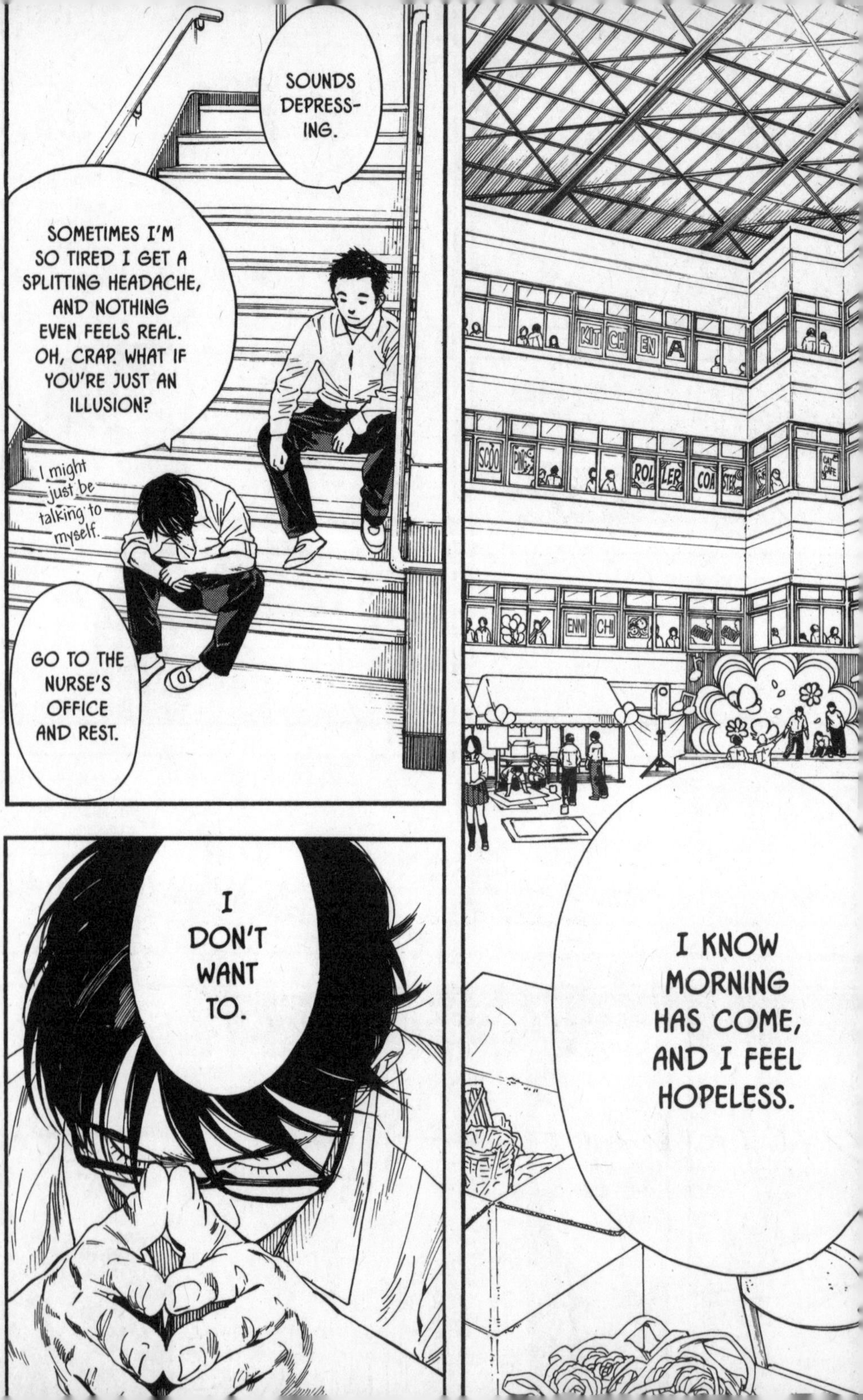
I KNOW MORNING HAS COME, AND I FEEL HOPELESS.
SOUNDS DEPRESS-ING.
SOMETIMES I'M SO TIRED I GET A SPLITTING HEADACHE, AND NOTHING EVEN FEELS REAL. OH, CRAP. WHAT IF YOU'RE JUST AN ILLUSION?
I might just be talking to myself.
GO TO THE NURSE'S OFFICE AND REST.
I DON'T WANT TO.

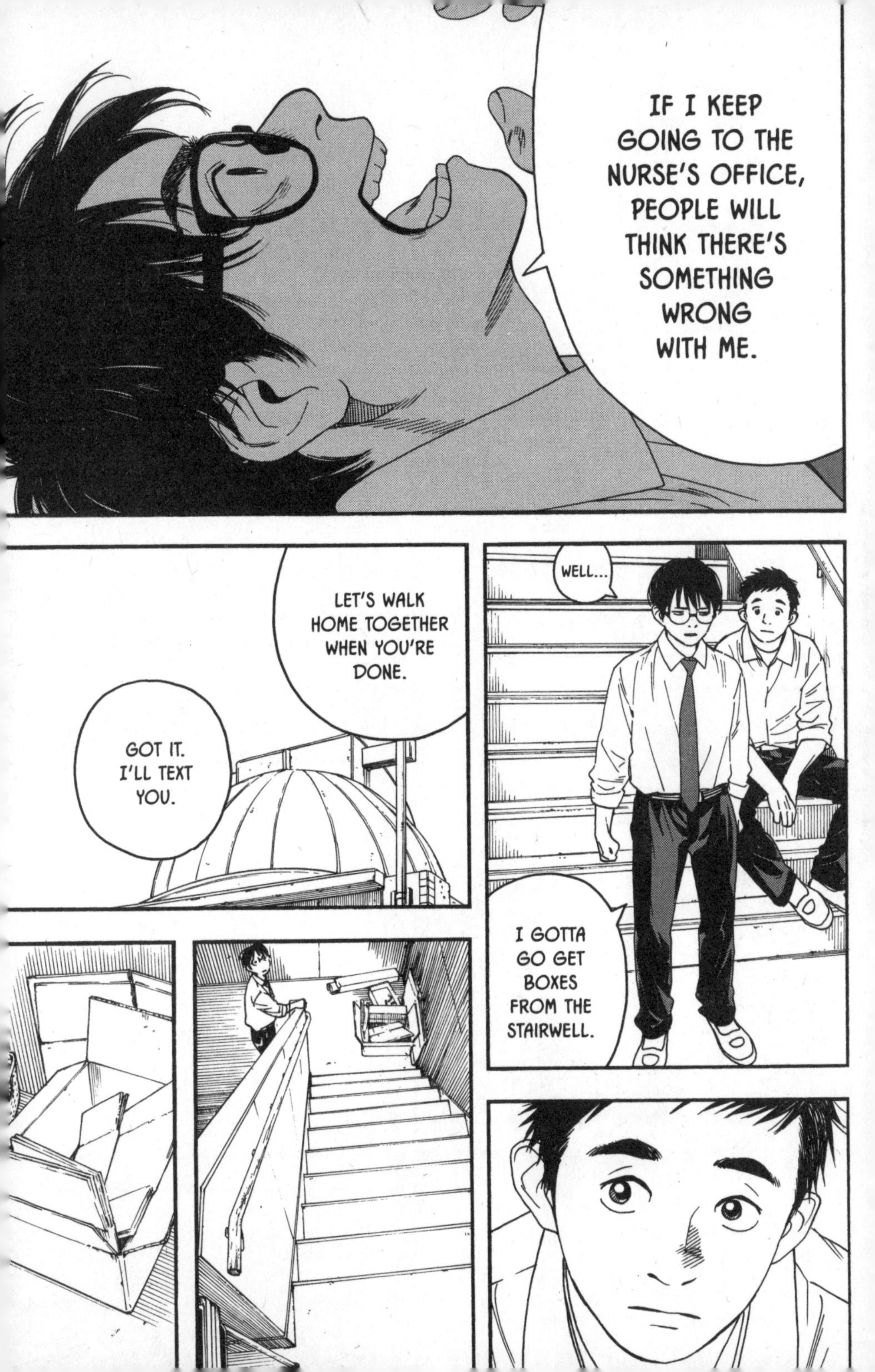
IF I KEEP GOING TO THE NURSE'S OFFICE, PEOPLE WILL THINK THERE'S SOMETHING WRONG WITH ME.
WELL...
I GOTTA GO GET BOXES FROM THE STAIRWELL.
LET'S WALK HOME TOGETHER WHEN YOU'RE DONE.
GOT IT. I'LL TEXT YOU.

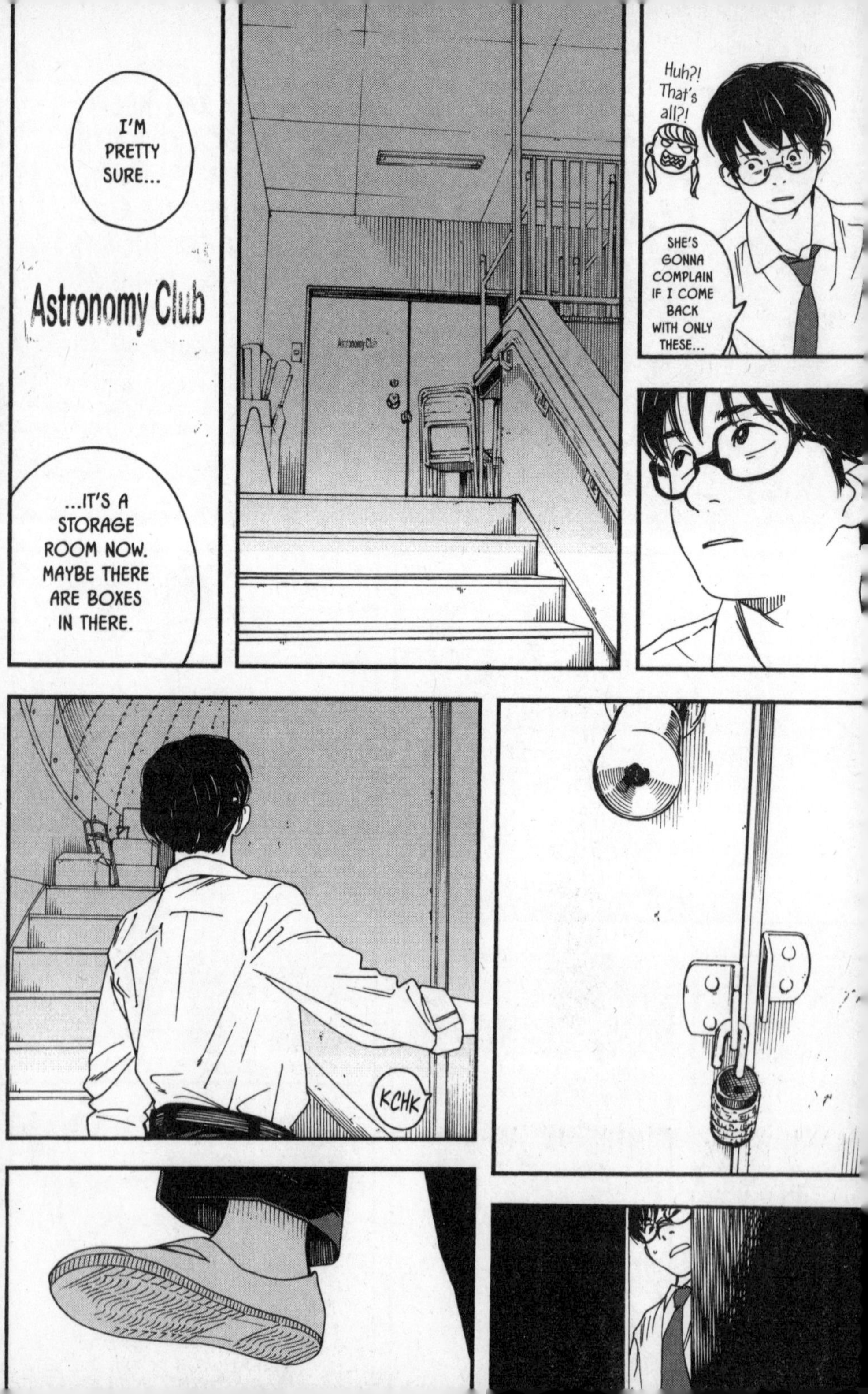

Huh?! That's all?!
SHE'S GONNA COMPLAIN IF I COME BACK WITH ONLY THESE...
Astronomy Club
I'M PRETTY SURE...
Astronomy Club
...IT'S A STORAGE ROOM NOW. MAYBE THERE ARE BOXES IN THERE.
KCHK

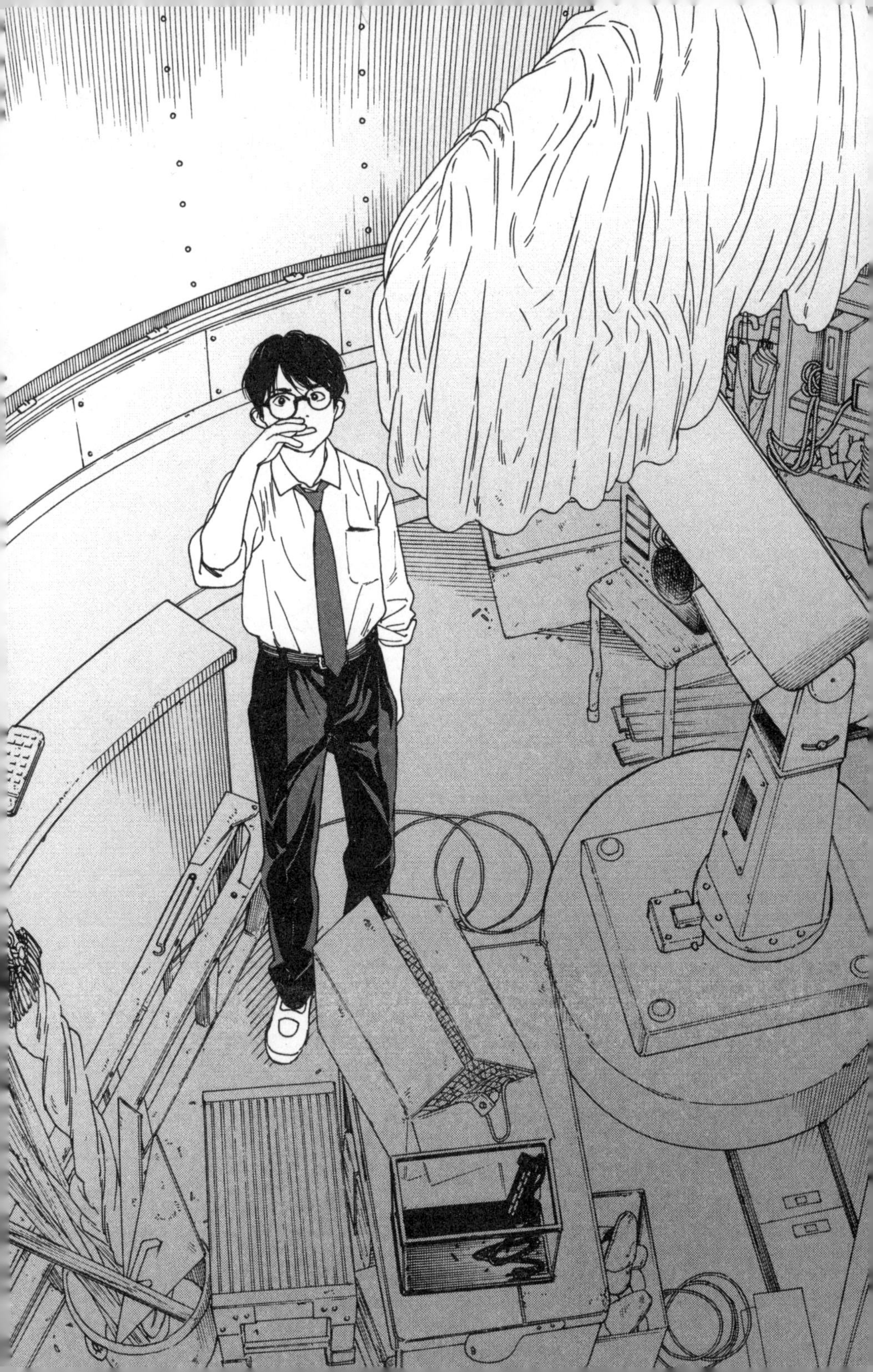

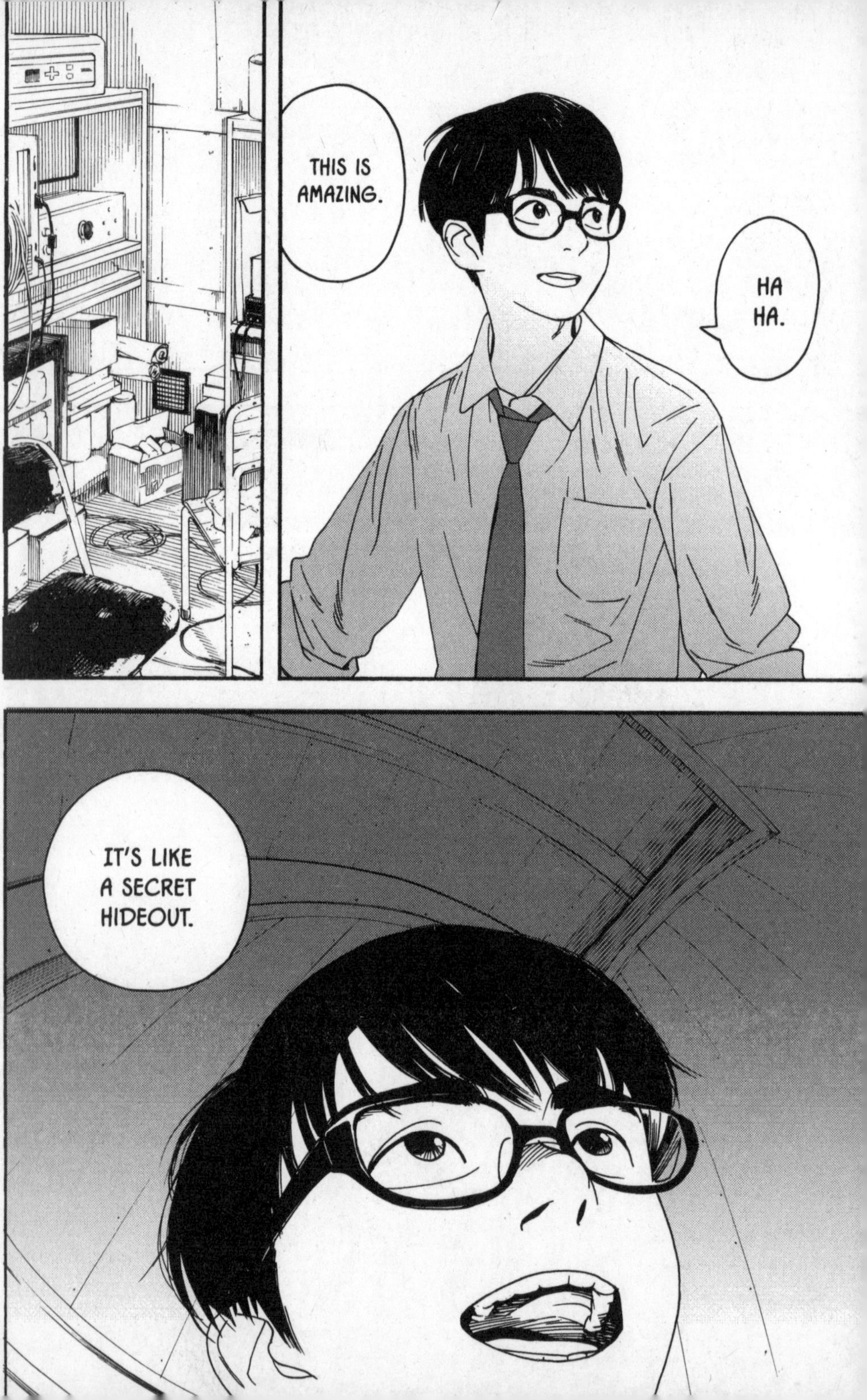
HA HA.
THIS IS AMAZING.
IT'S LIKE A SECRET HIDEOUT.

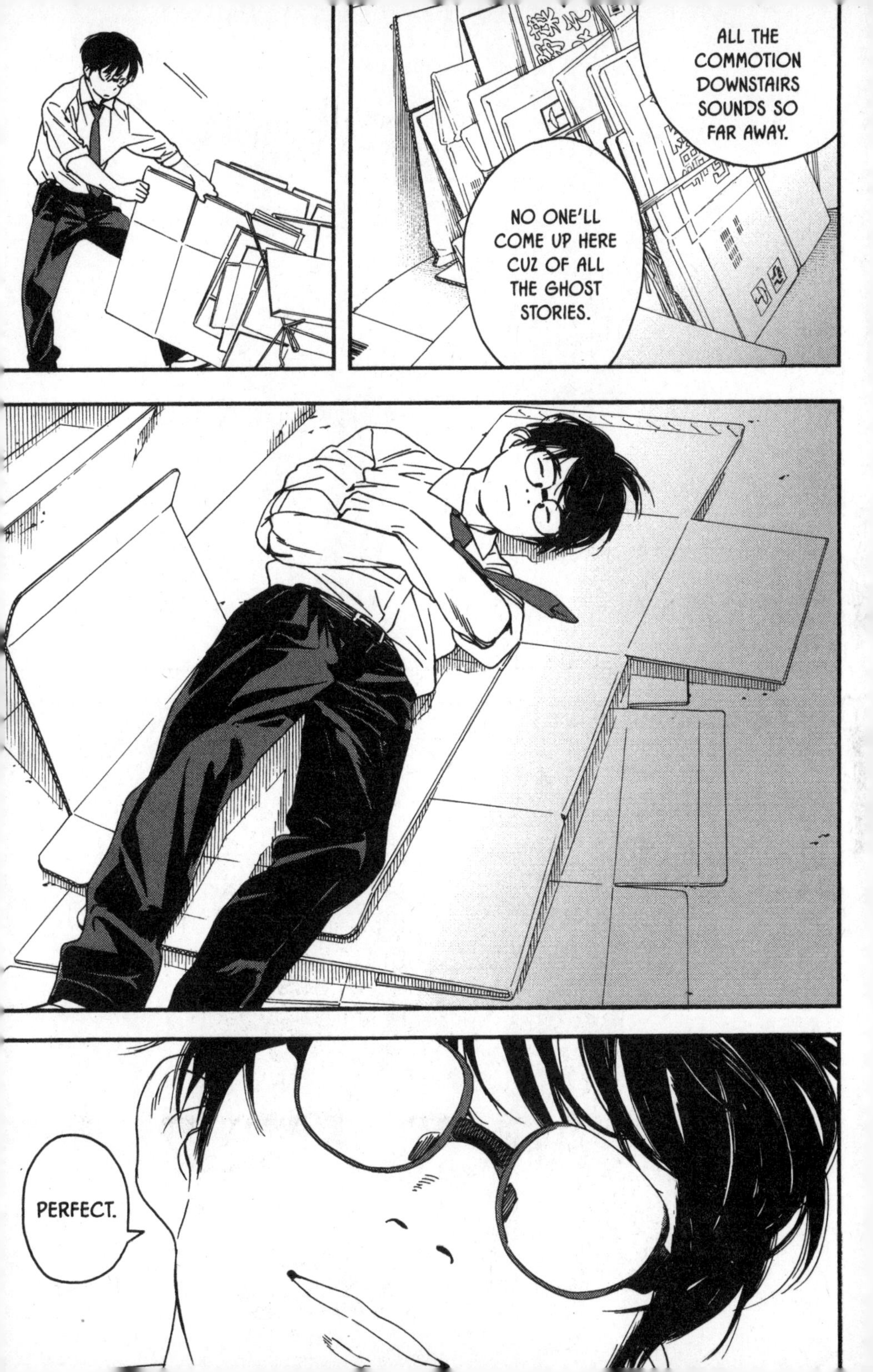
ALL THE COMMOTION DOWNSTAIRS SOUNDS SO FAR AWAY.
NO ONE'LL COME UP HERE CUZ OF ALL THE GHOST STORIES.
PERFECT.

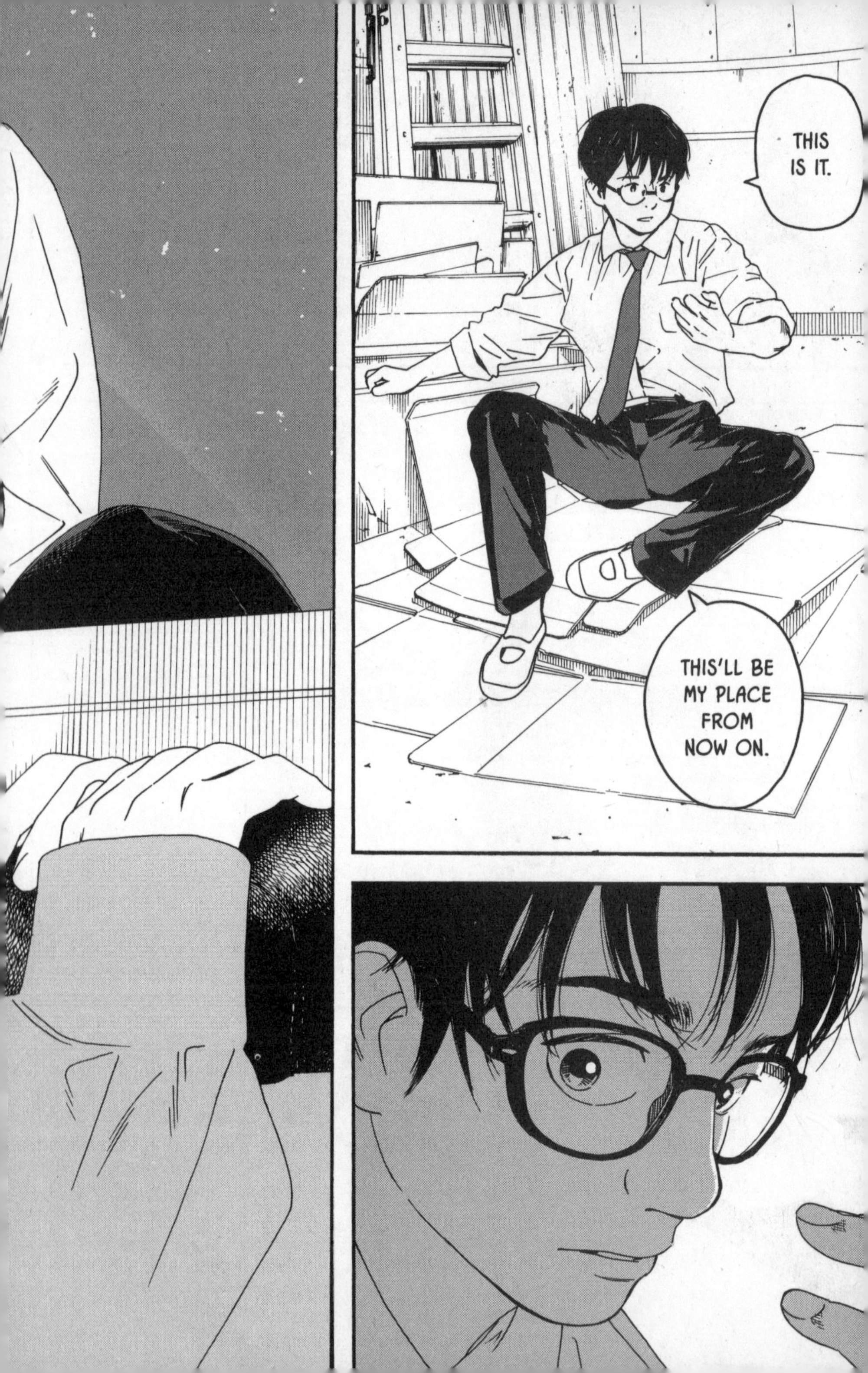
THIS IS IT.
THIS'LL BE MY PLACE FROM NOW ON.

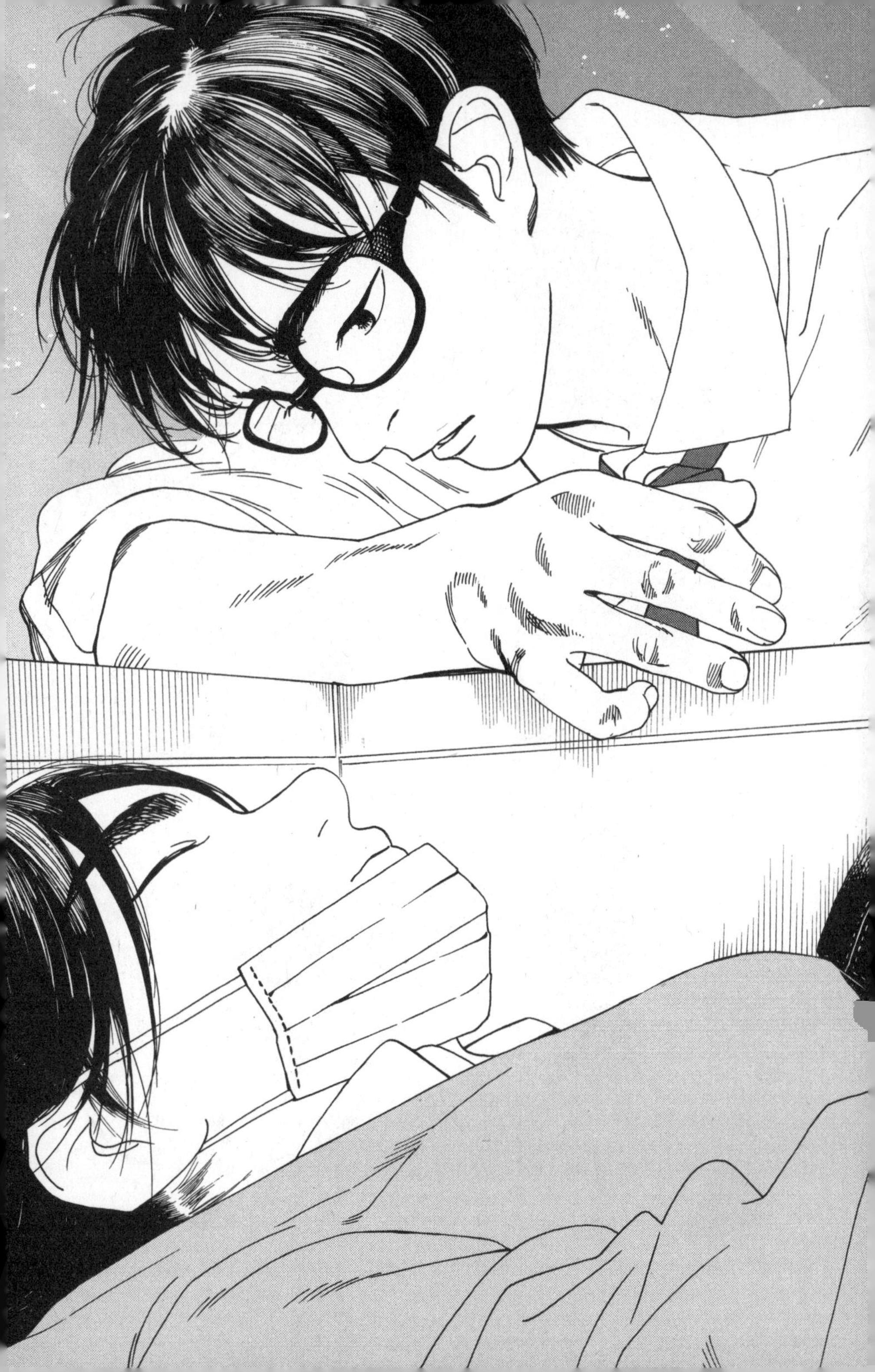

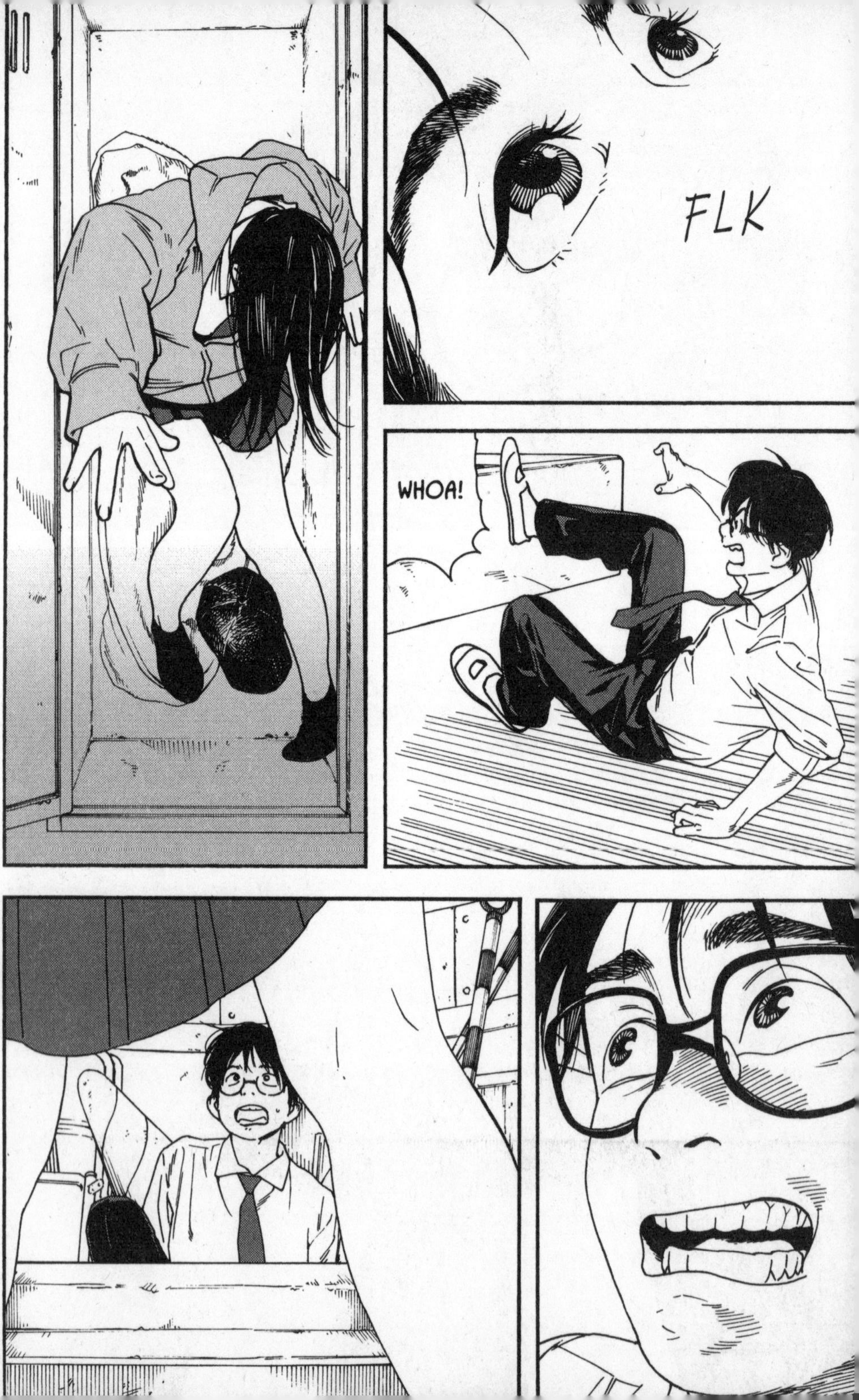
FLK
WHOA!

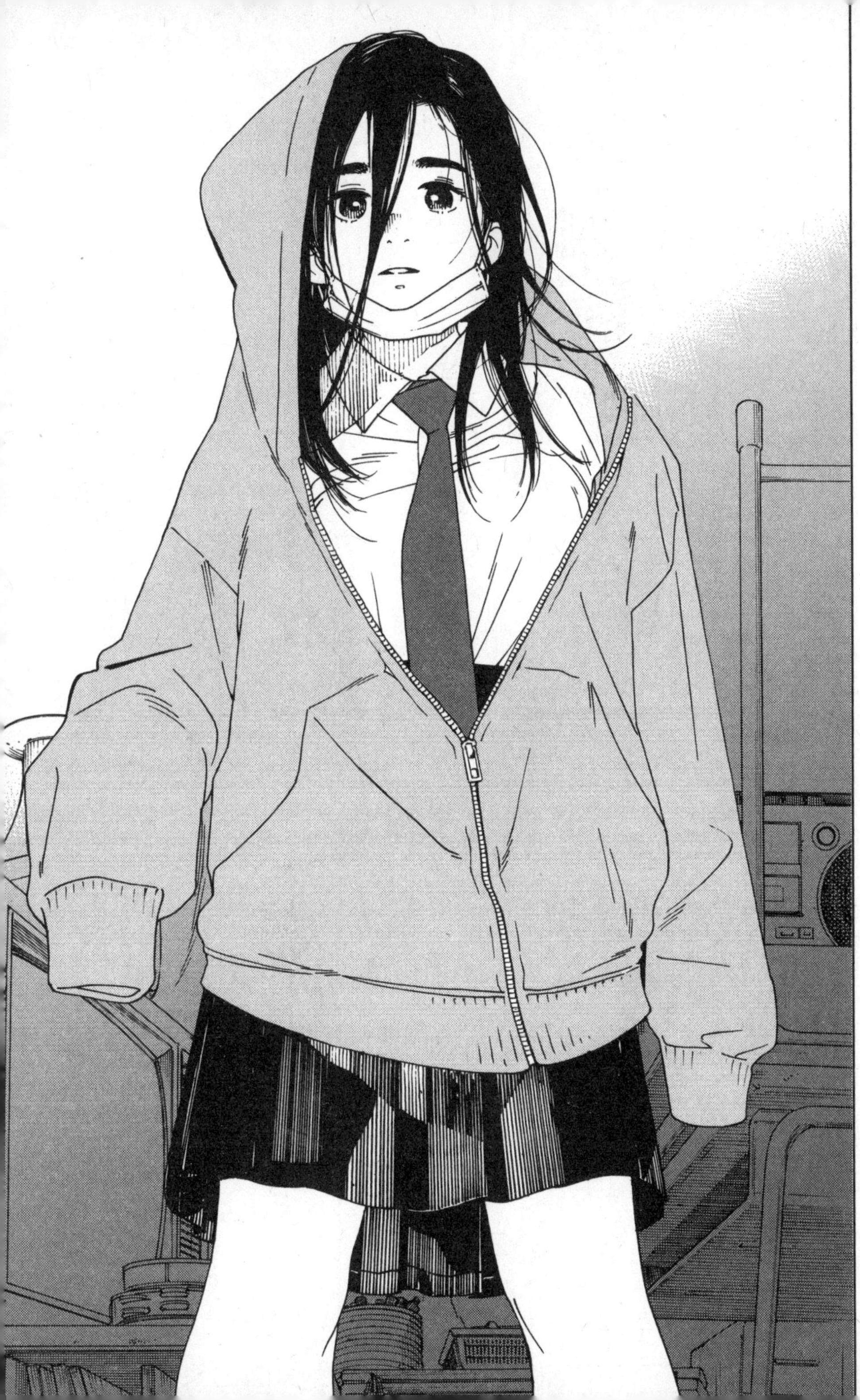

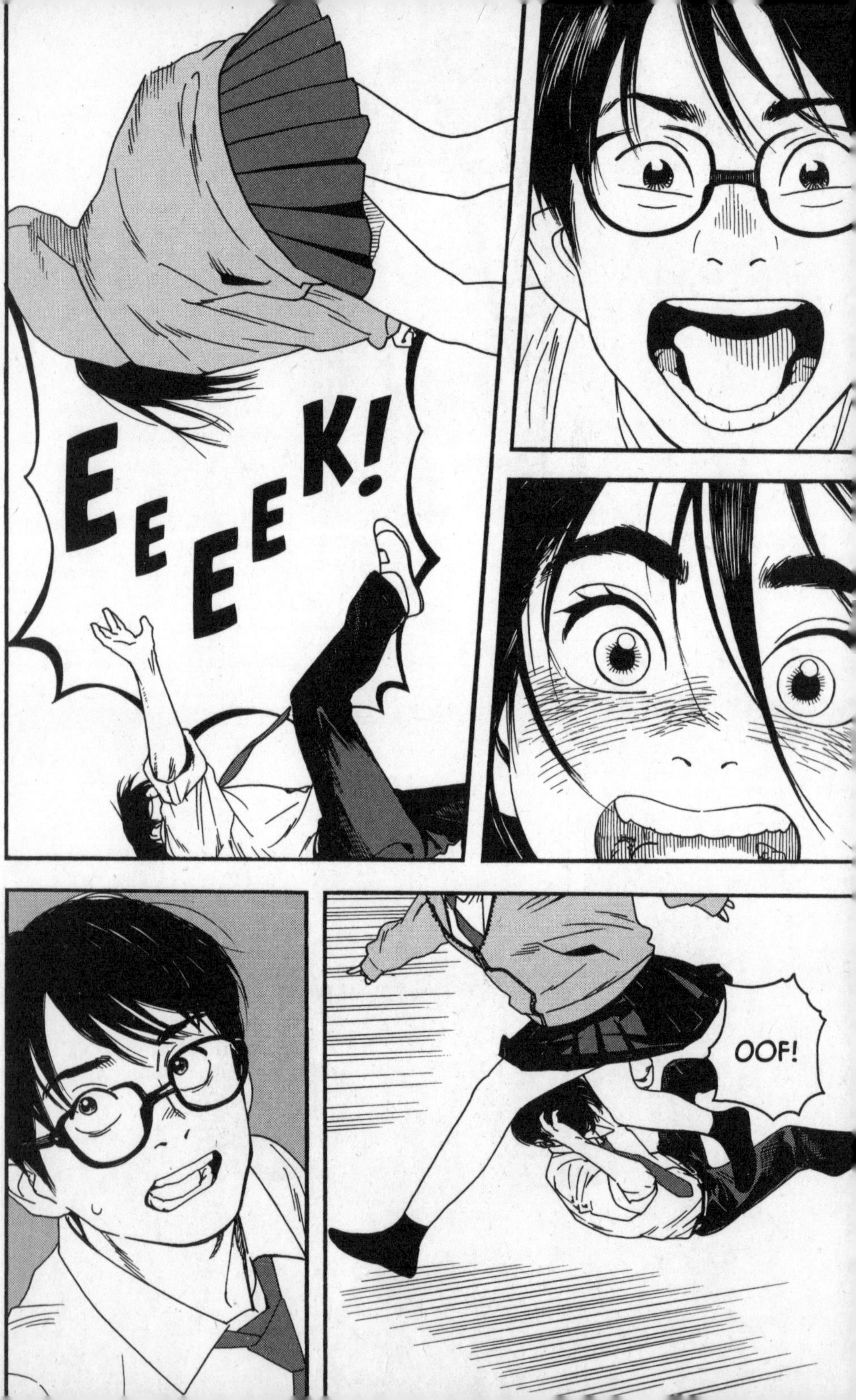
EEEEK!
OOF!

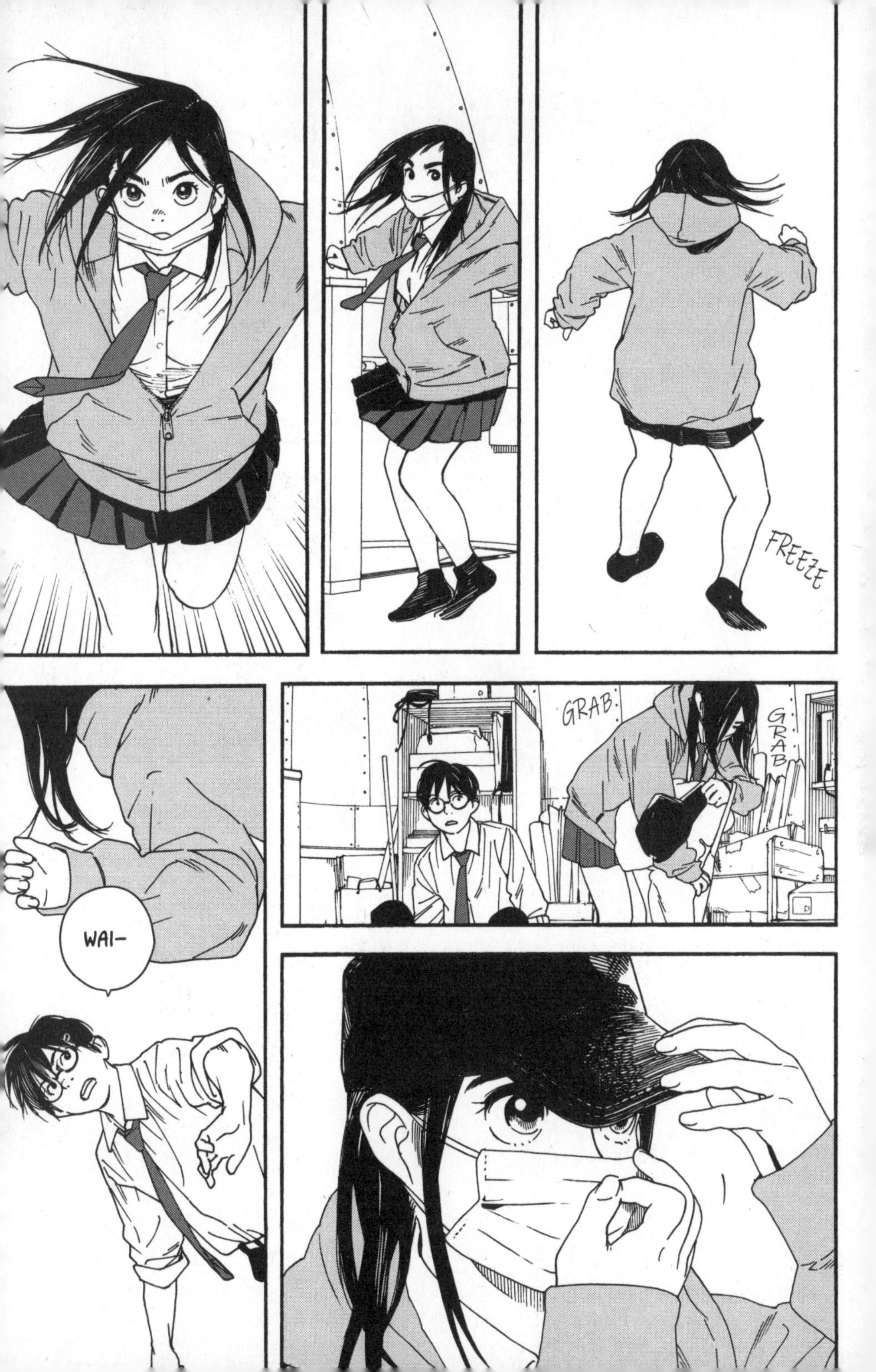
FREEZE
GRAB
GRAB
WAI-

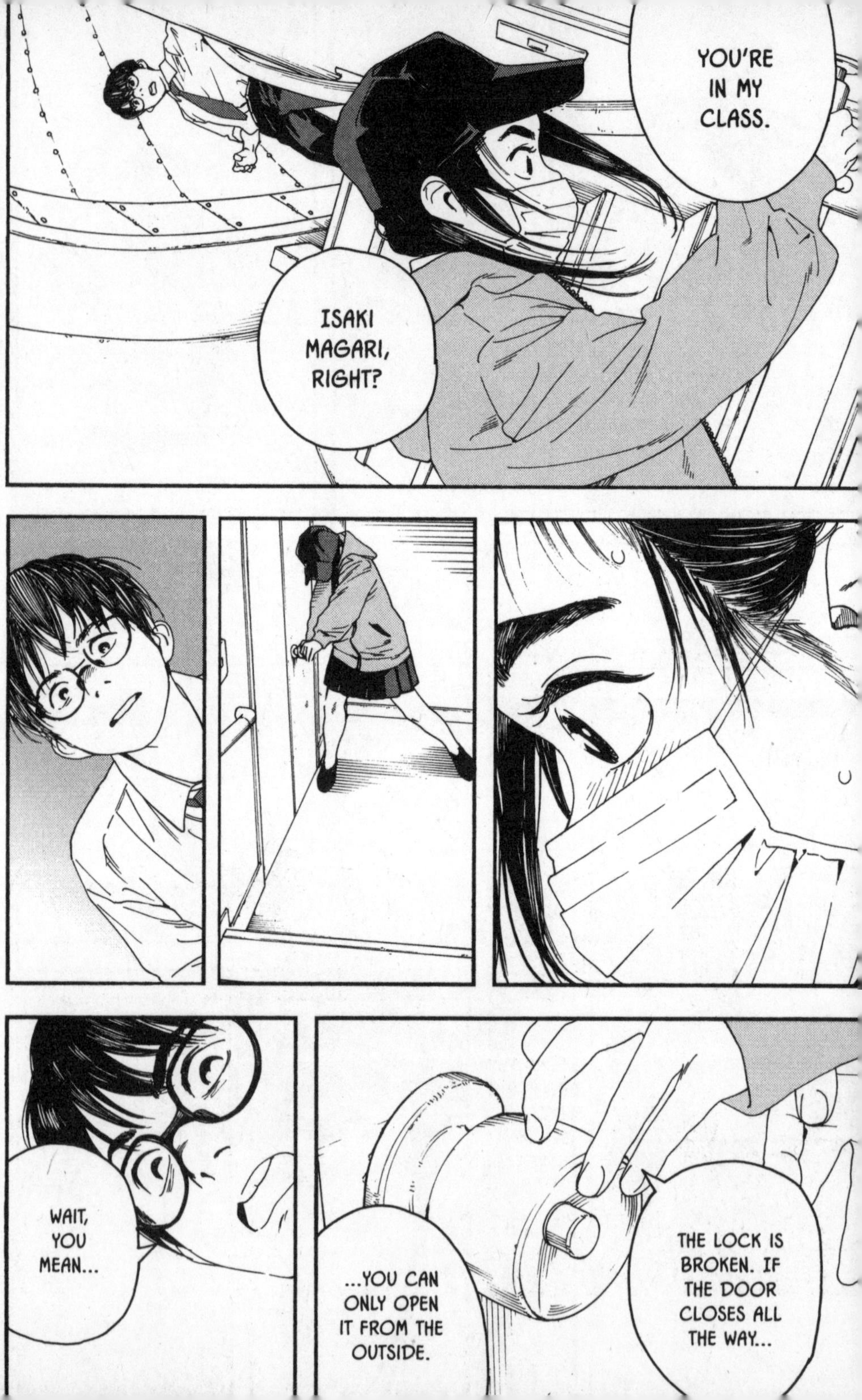
YOU'RE IN MY CLASS.
ISAKI MAGARI, RIGHT?
THE LOCK IS BROKEN. IF THE DOOR CLOSES ALL THE WAY...
...YOU CAN ONLY OPEN IT FROM THE OUTSIDE.
WAIT, YOU MEAN...

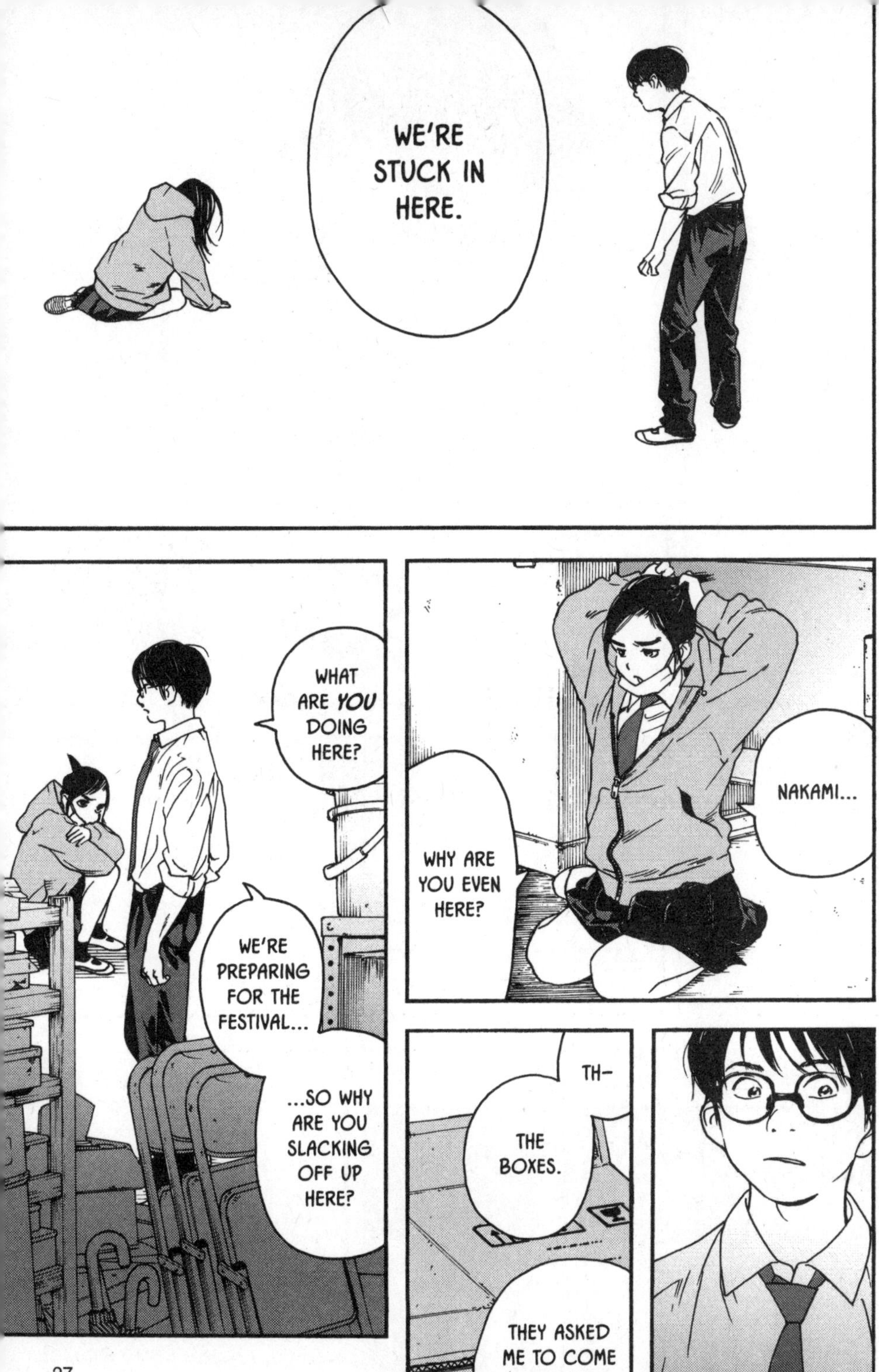
WE'RE STUCK IN HERE.
NAKAMI...
WHY ARE YOU EVEN HERE?
TH-
THE BOXES.
THEY ASKED ME TO COME GET THEM.
WHAT ARE *YOU* DOING HERE?
WE'RE PREPARING FOR THE FESTIVAL...
...SO WHY ARE YOU SLACKING OFF UP HERE?

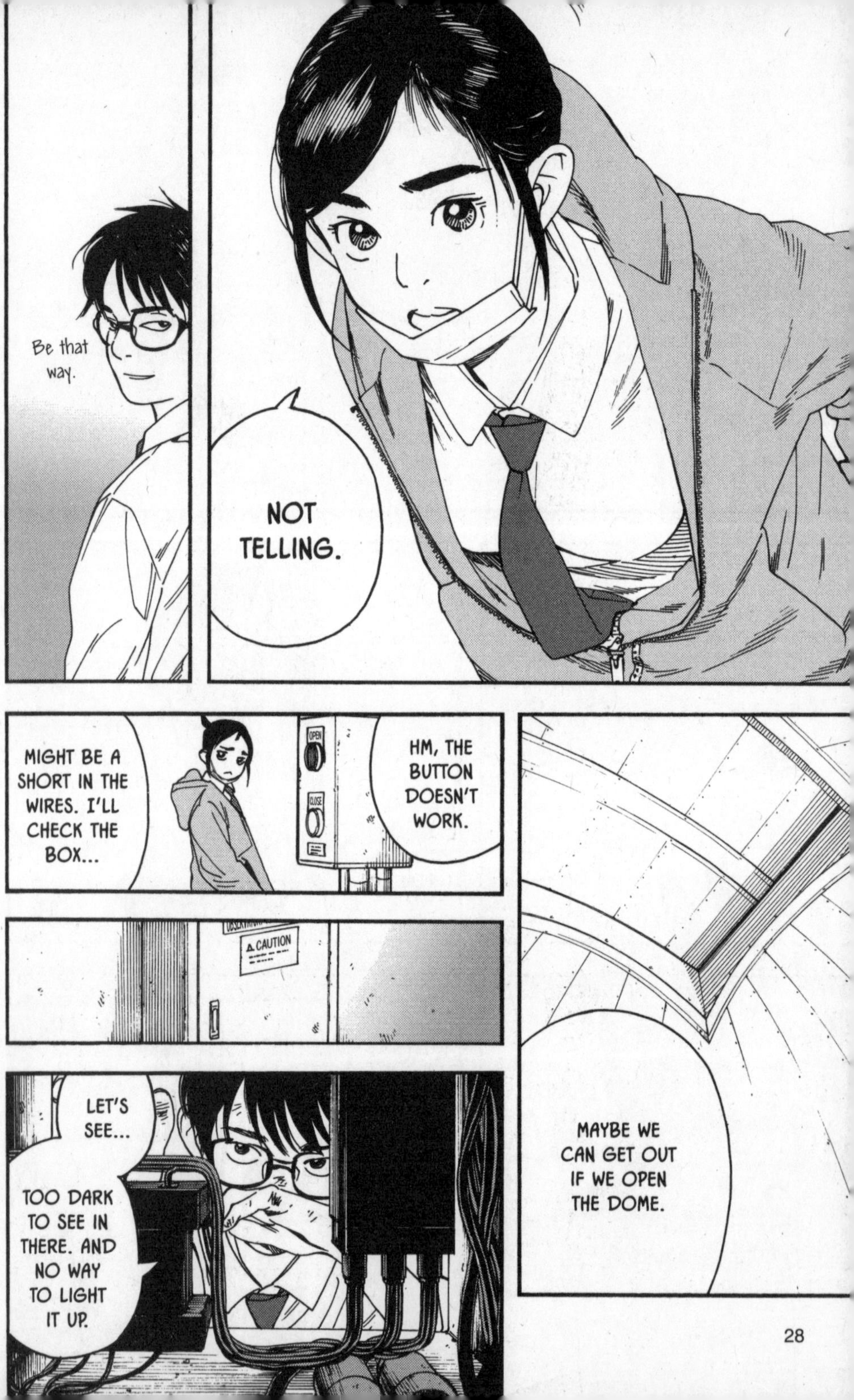
NOT TELLING.
Be that way.
MAYBE WE CAN GET OUT IF WE OPEN THE DOME.
HM, THE BUTTON DOESN'T WORK.
OPEN
CLOSE
MIGHT BE A SHORT IN THE WIRES. I'LL CHECK THE BOX...
CAUTION
LET'S SEE...
TOO DARK TO SEE IN THERE. AND NO WAY TO LIGHT IT UP.

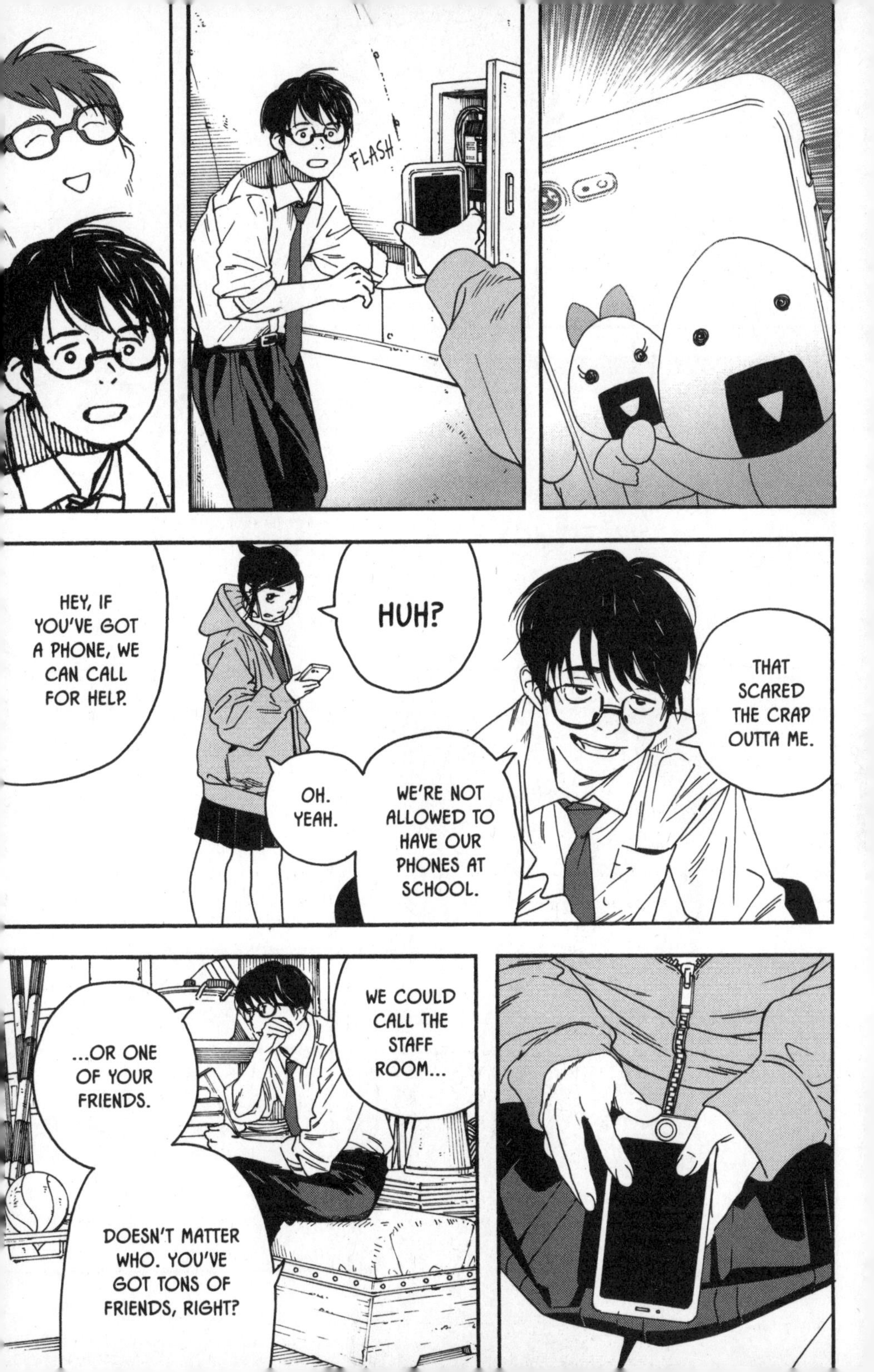
FLASH!
THAT SCARED THE CRAP OUTTA ME.
HUH?
WE'RE NOT ALLOWED TO HAVE OUR PHONES AT SCHOOL.
OH. YEAH.
HEY, IF YOU'VE GOT A PHONE, WE CAN CALL FOR HELP.
WE COULD CALL THE STAFF ROOM...
...OR ONE OF YOUR FRIENDS.
DOESN'T MATTER WHO. YOU'VE GOT TONS OF FRIENDS, RIGHT?

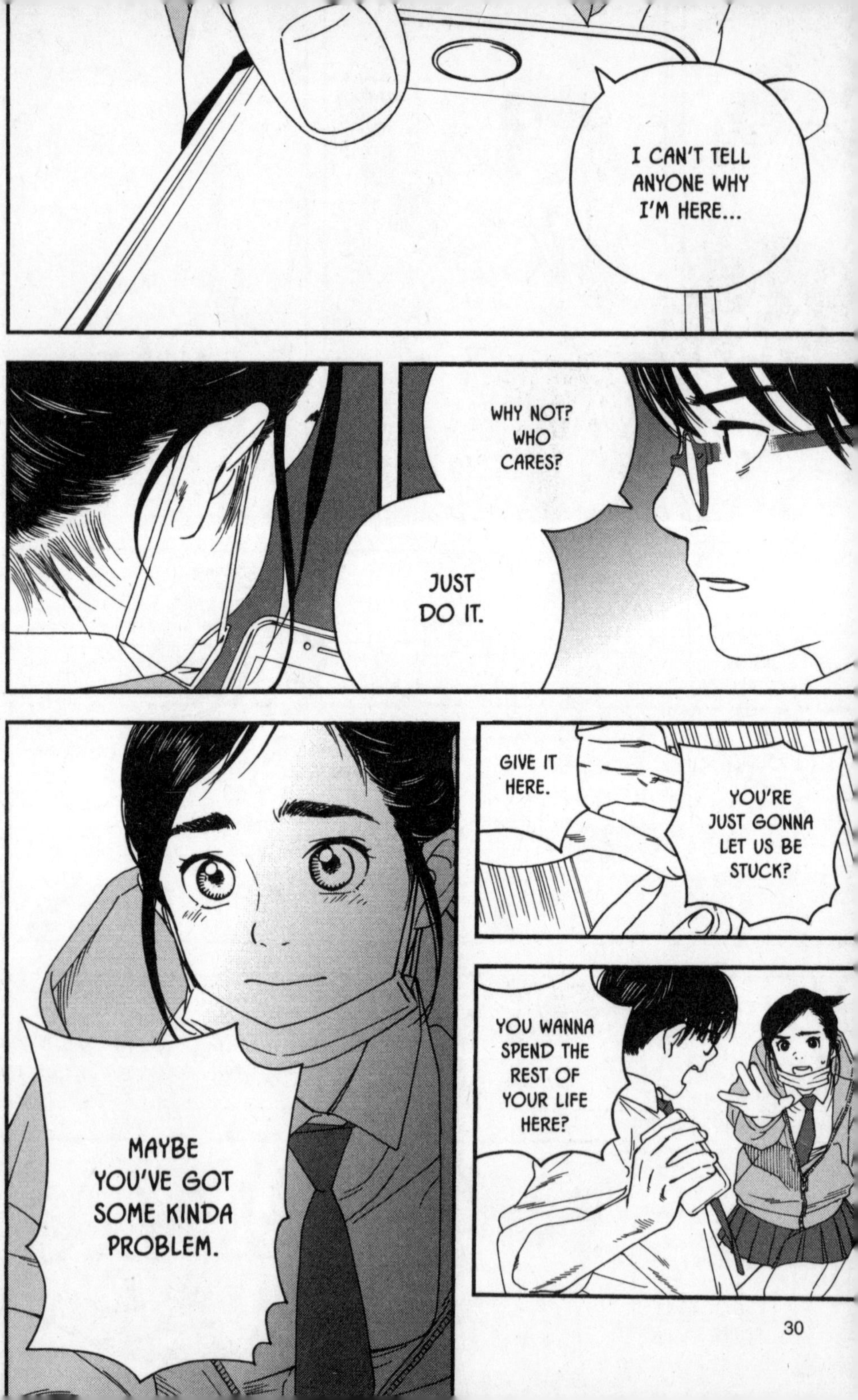
I CAN'T TELL ANYONE WHY I'M HERE...
WHY NOT? WHO CARES?
JUST DO IT.
YOU'RE JUST GONNA LET US BE STUCK?
GIVE IT HERE.
YOU WANNA SPEND THE REST OF YOUR LIFE HERE?
MAYBE YOU'VE GOT SOME KINDA PROBLEM.

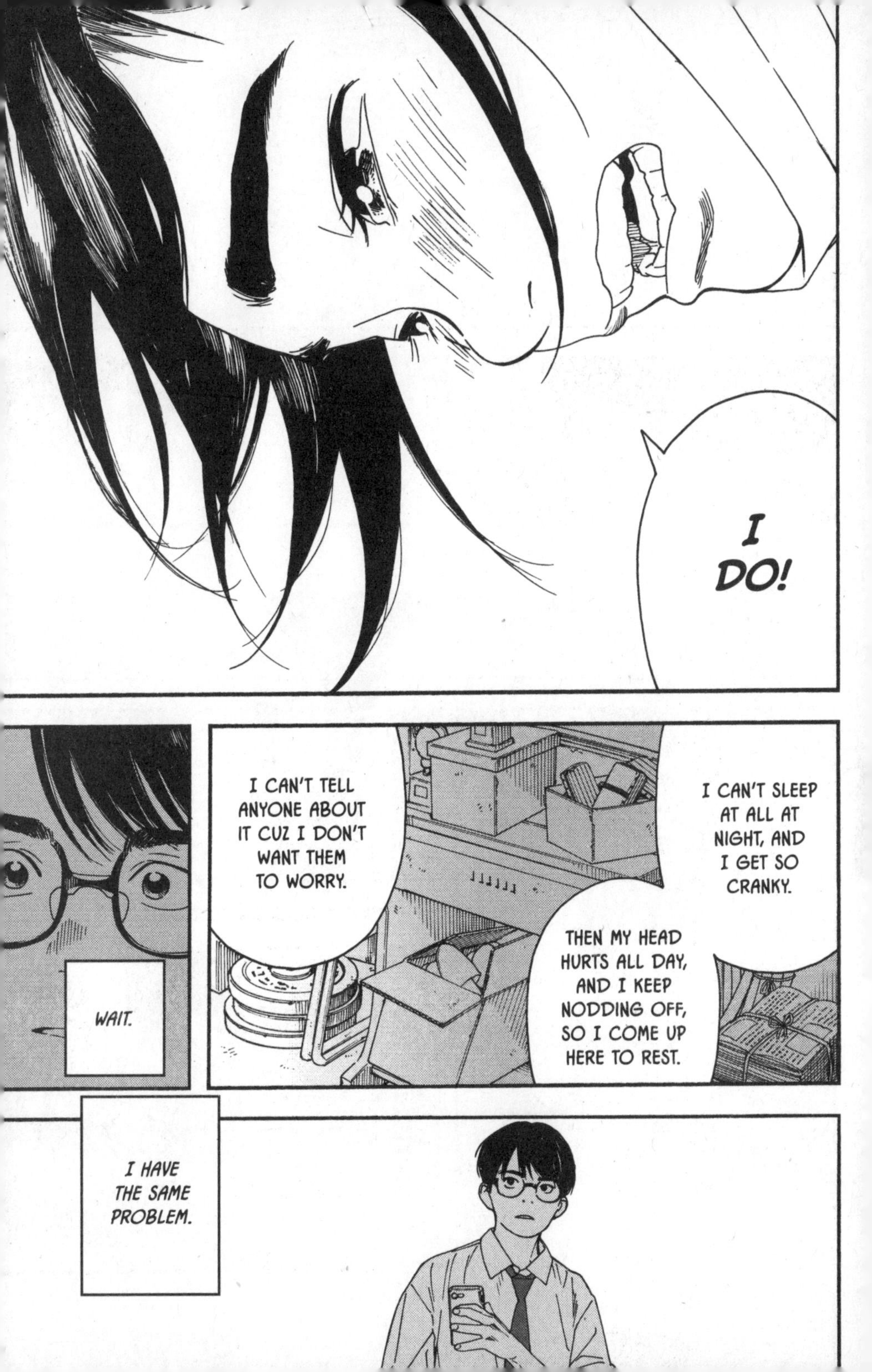
I DO!
I CAN'T SLEEP AT ALL AT NIGHT, AND I GET SO CRANKY.
THEN MY HEAD HURTS ALL DAY, AND I KEEP NODDING OFF, SO I COME UP HERE TO REST.
I CAN'T TELL ANYONE ABOUT IT CUZ I DON'T WANT THEM TO WORRY.
WAIT.
I HAVE THE SAME PROBLEM.

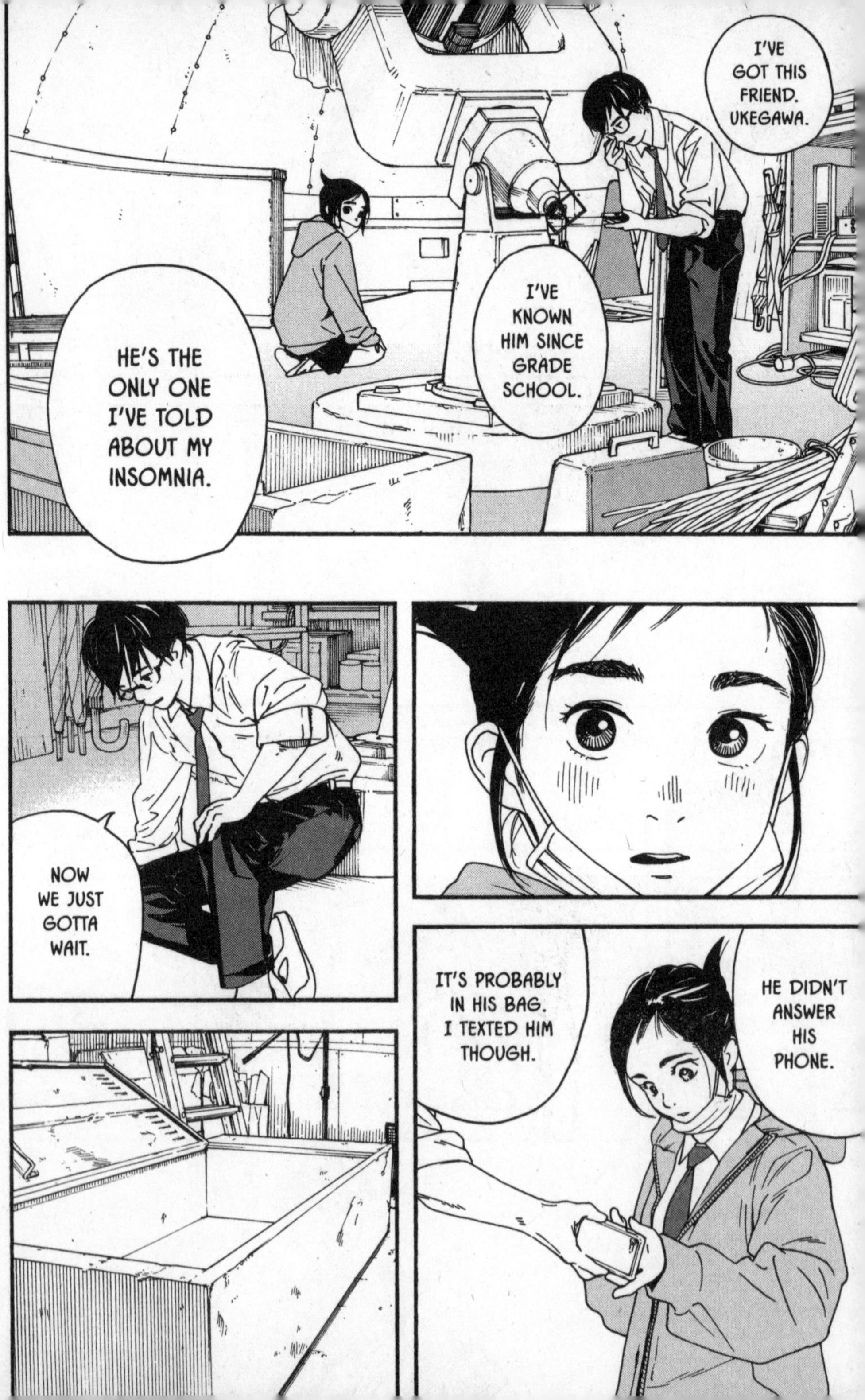
I'VE GOT THIS FRIEND. UKEGAWA.
I'VE KNOWN HIM SINCE GRADE SCHOOL.
HE'S THE ONLY ONE I'VE TOLD ABOUT MY INSOMNIA.
NOW WE JUST GOTTA WAIT.
HE DIDN'T ANSWER HIS PHONE.
IT'S PROBABLY IN HIS BAG. I TEXTED HIM THOUGH.

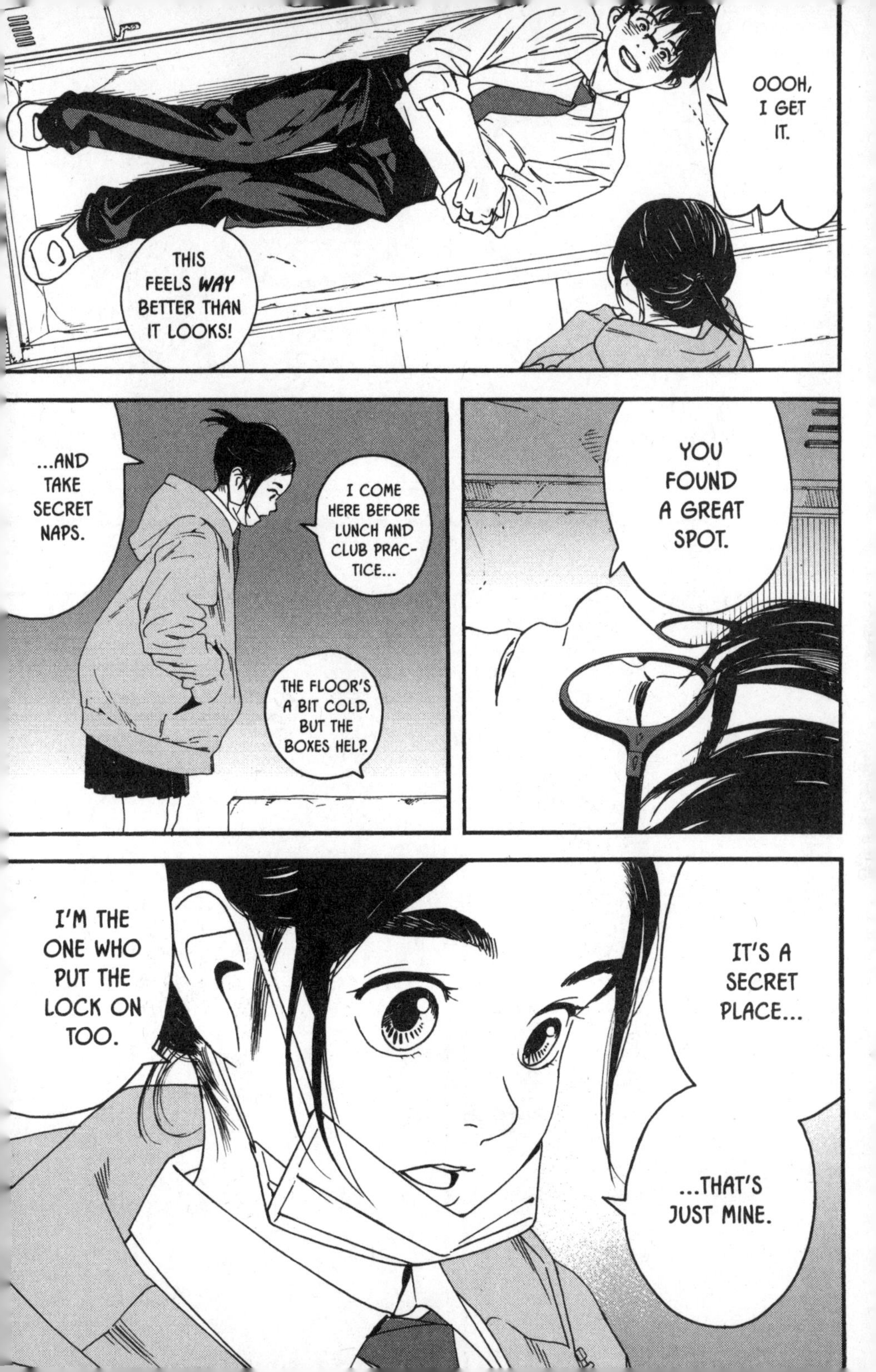
OOOH, I GET IT.
THIS FEELS *WAY* BETTER THAN IT LOOKS!
YOU FOUND A GREAT SPOT.
I COME HERE BEFORE LUNCH AND CLUB PRAC-TICE...
...AND TAKE SECRET NAPS.
THE FLOOR'S A BIT COLD, BUT THE BOXES HELP.
IT'S A SECRET PLACE...
...THAT'S JUST MINE.
I'M THE ONE WHO PUT THE LOCK ON TOO.

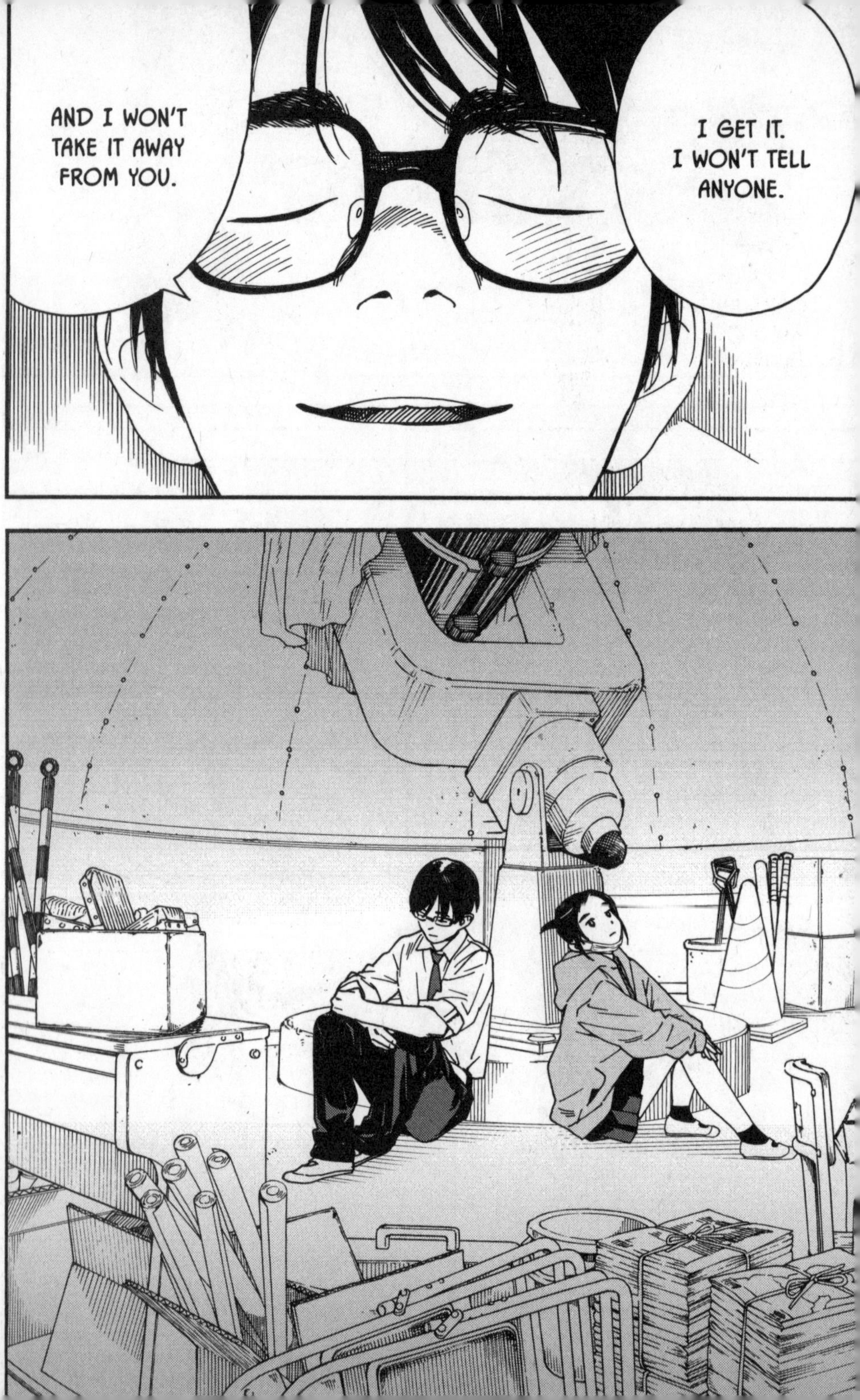
I GET IT. I WON'T TELL ANYONE.
AND I WON'T TAKE IT AWAY FROM YOU.

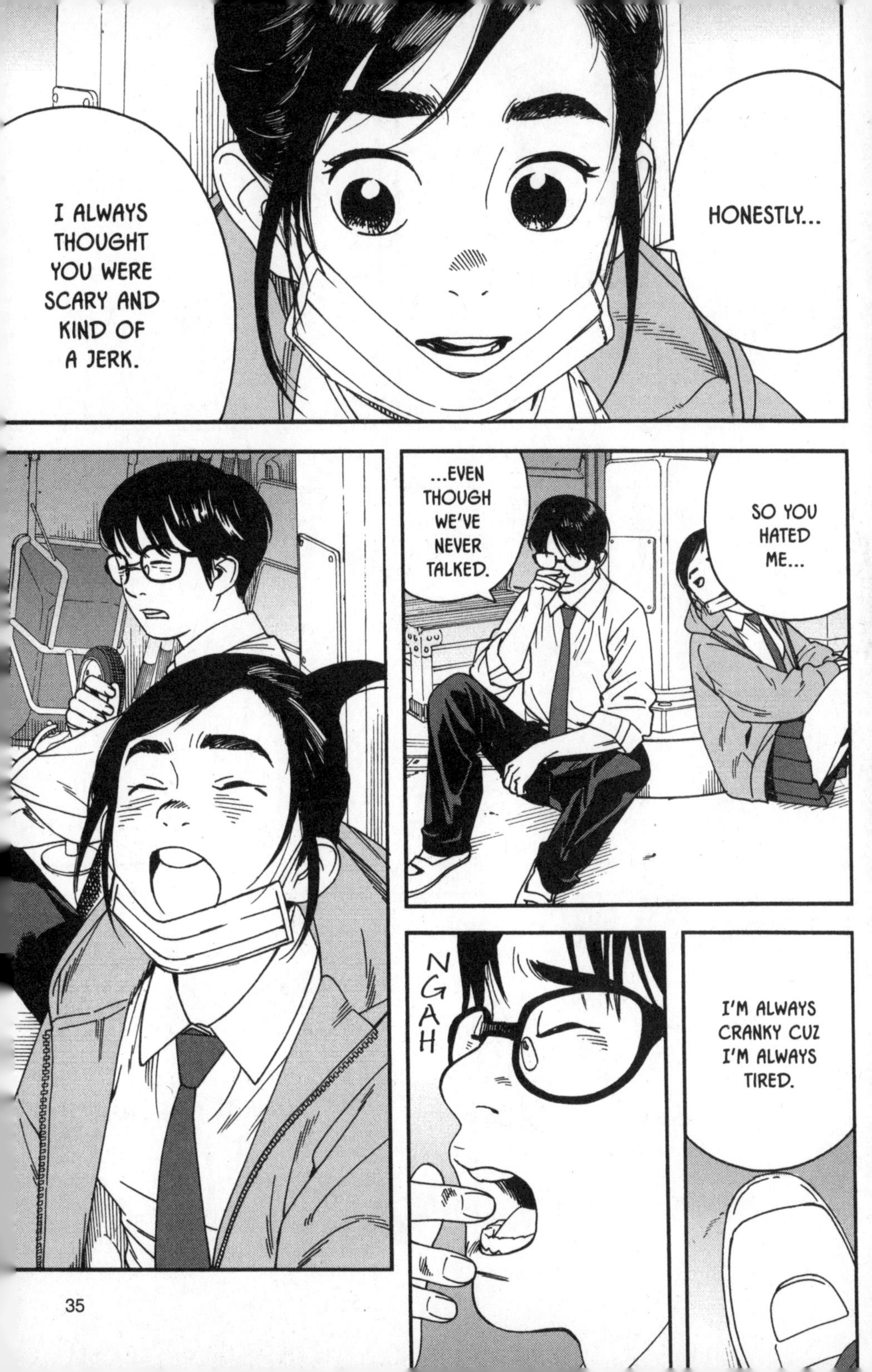
HONESTLY...
I ALWAYS THOUGHT YOU WERE SCARY AND KIND OF A JERK.
SO YOU HATED ME...
...EVEN THOUGH WE'VE NEVER TALKED.
I'M ALWAYS CRANKY CUZ I'M ALWAYS TIRED.
NGAH

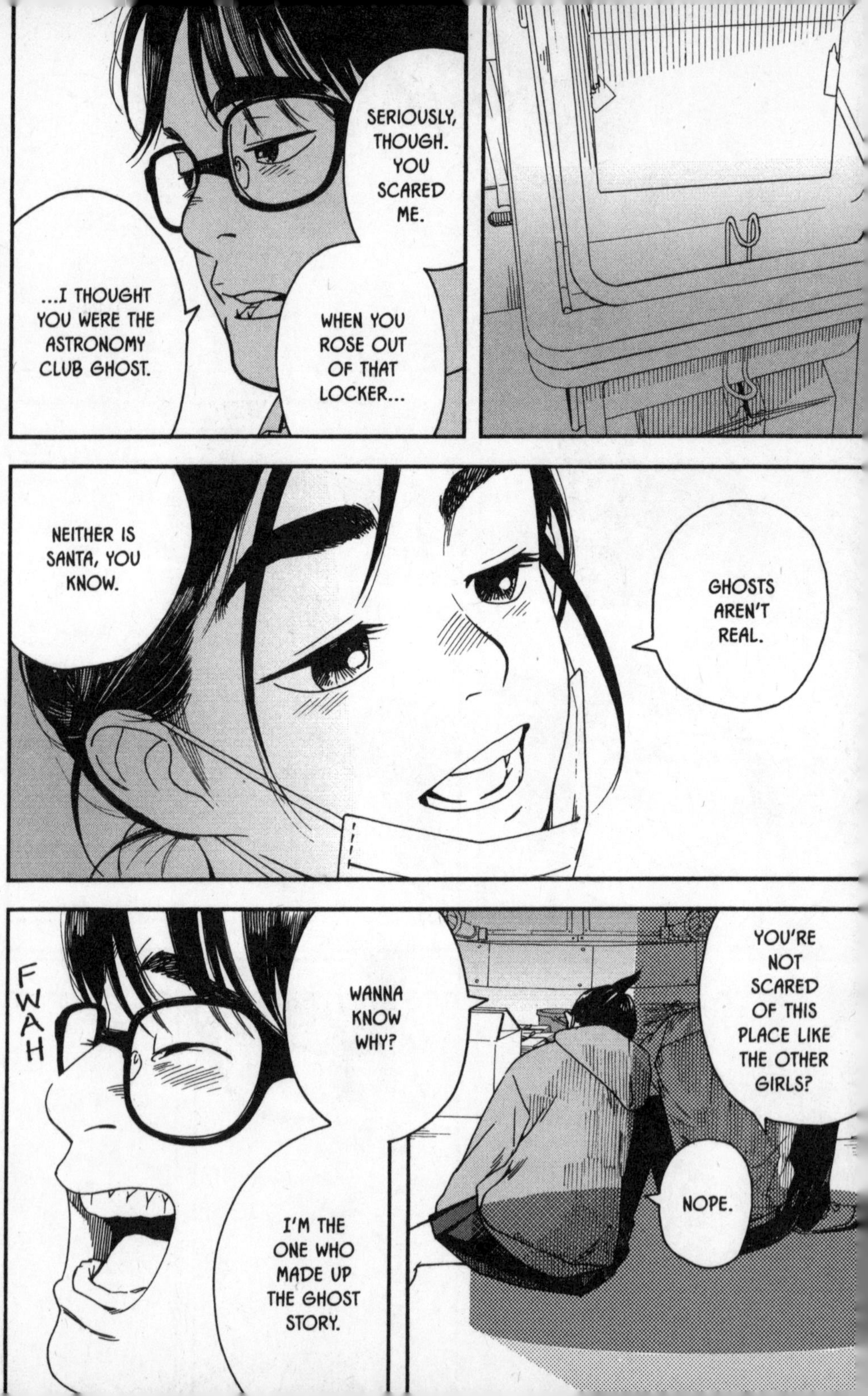
SERIOUSLY, THOUGH. YOU SCARED ME.
WHEN YOU ROSE OUT OF THAT LOCKER...
...I THOUGHT YOU WERE THE ASTRONOMY CLUB GHOST.
GHOSTS AREN'T REAL.
NEITHER IS SANTA, YOU KNOW.
YOU'RE NOT SCARED OF THIS PLACE LIKE THE OTHER GIRLS?
NOPE.
WANNA KNOW WHY?
FWAH
I'M THE ONE WHO MADE UP THE GHOST STORY.

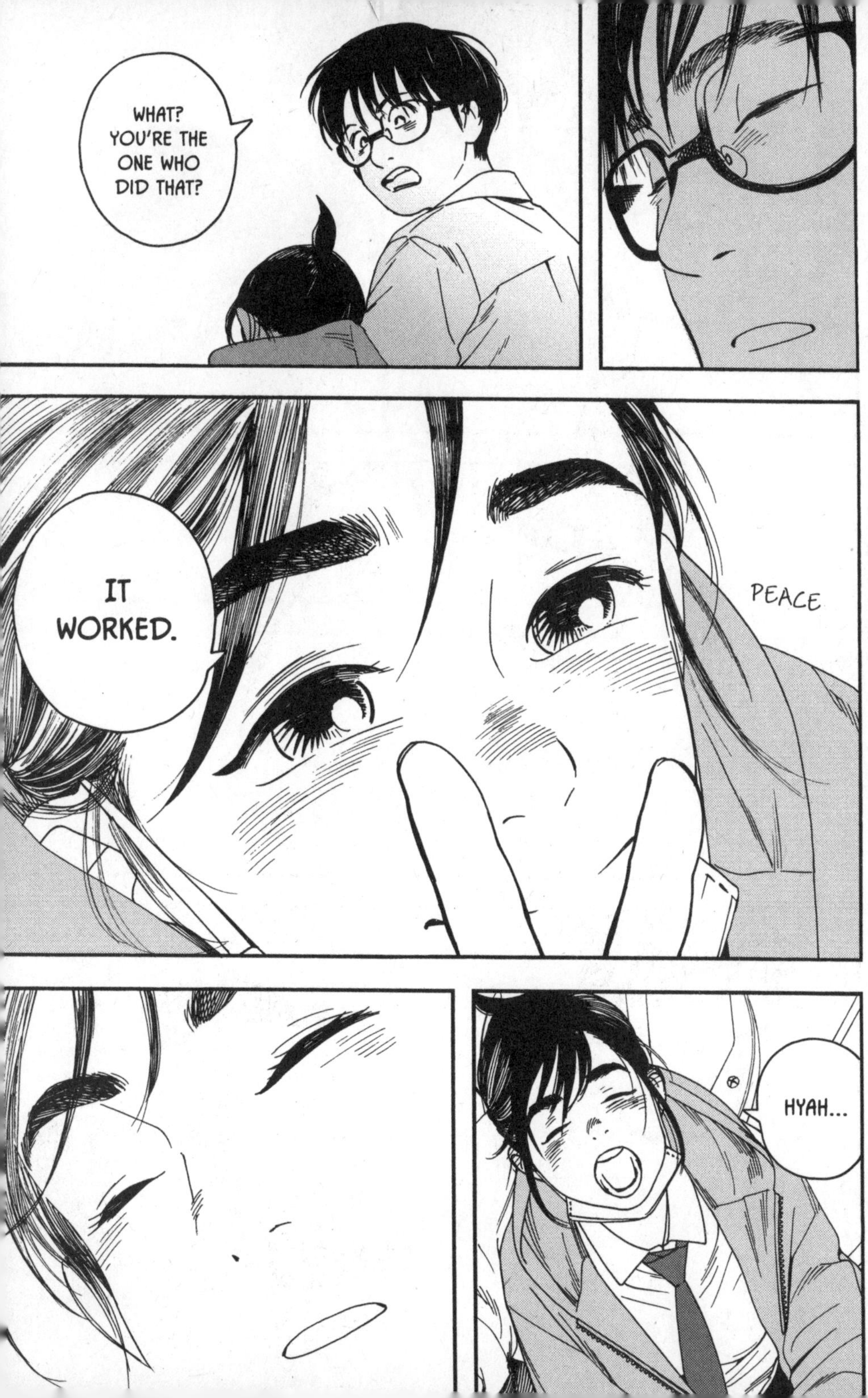
WHAT? YOU'RE THE ONE WHO DID THAT?
PEACE
IT WORKED.
HYAH...

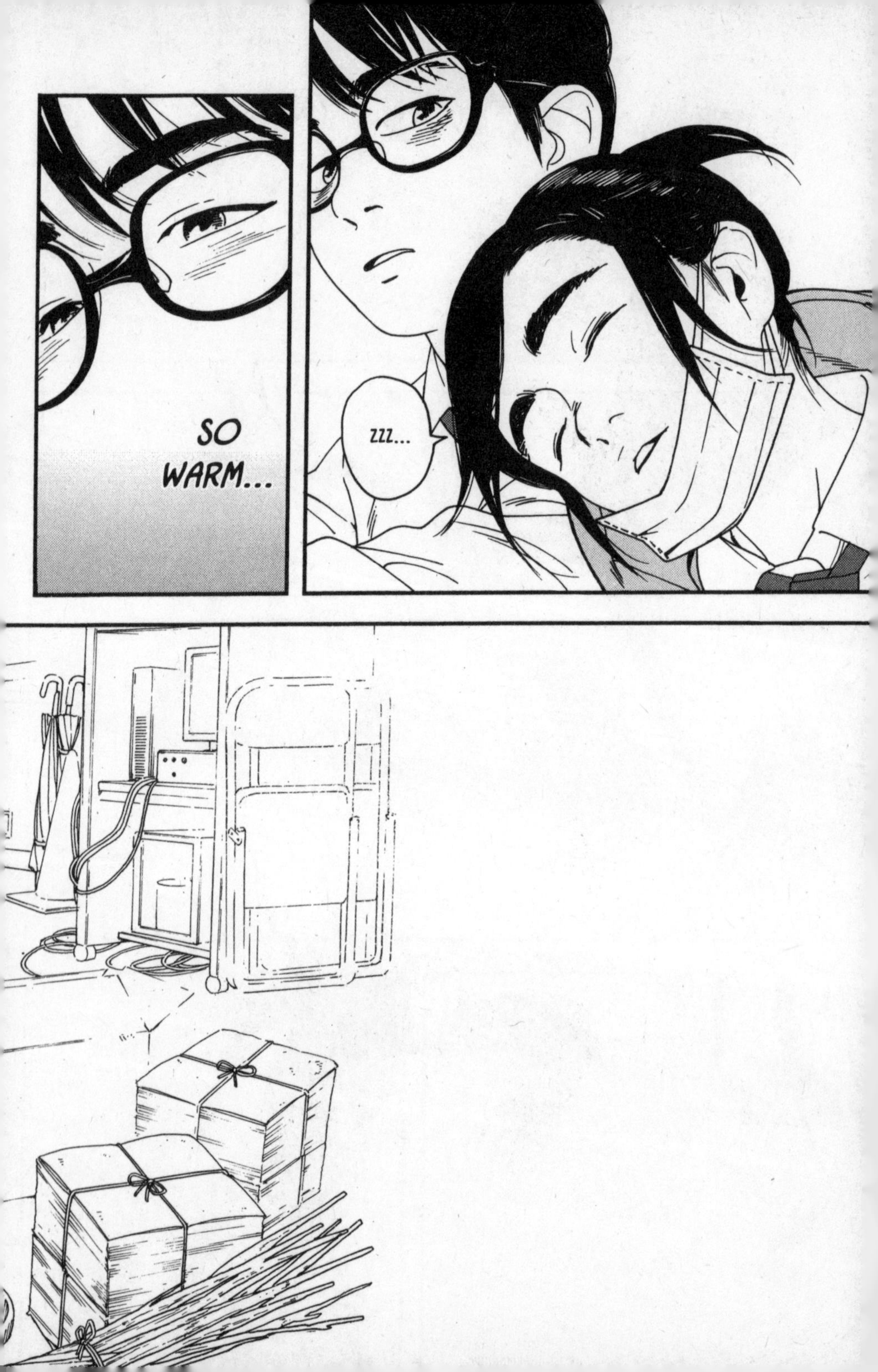
ZZZ...
SO WARM...

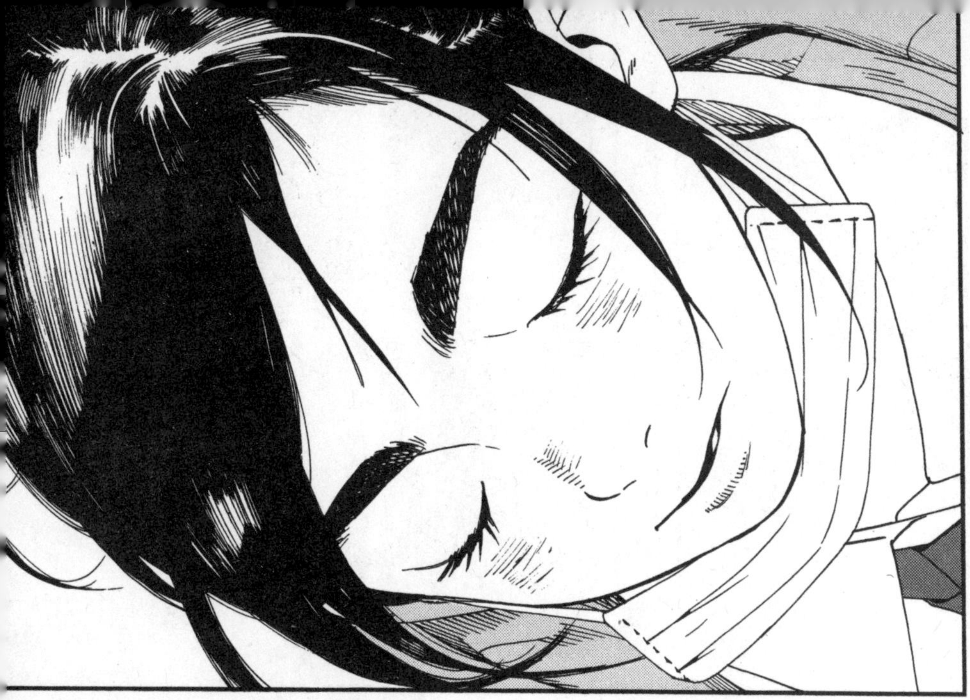
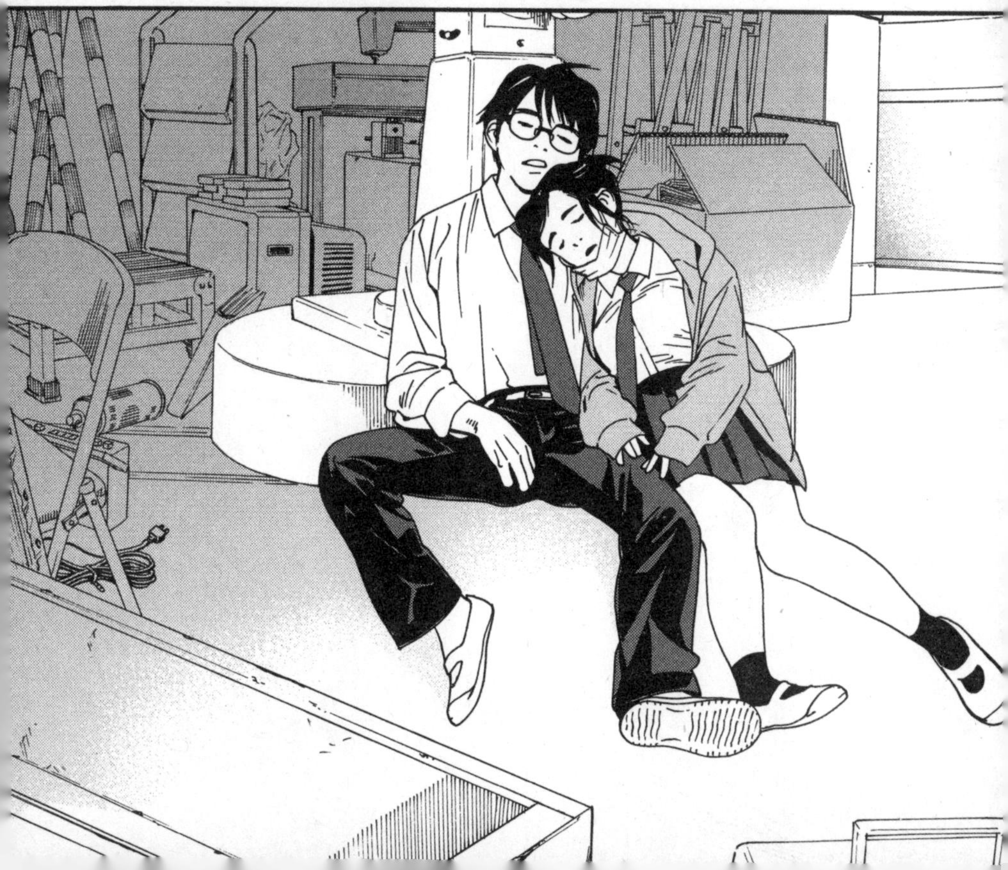

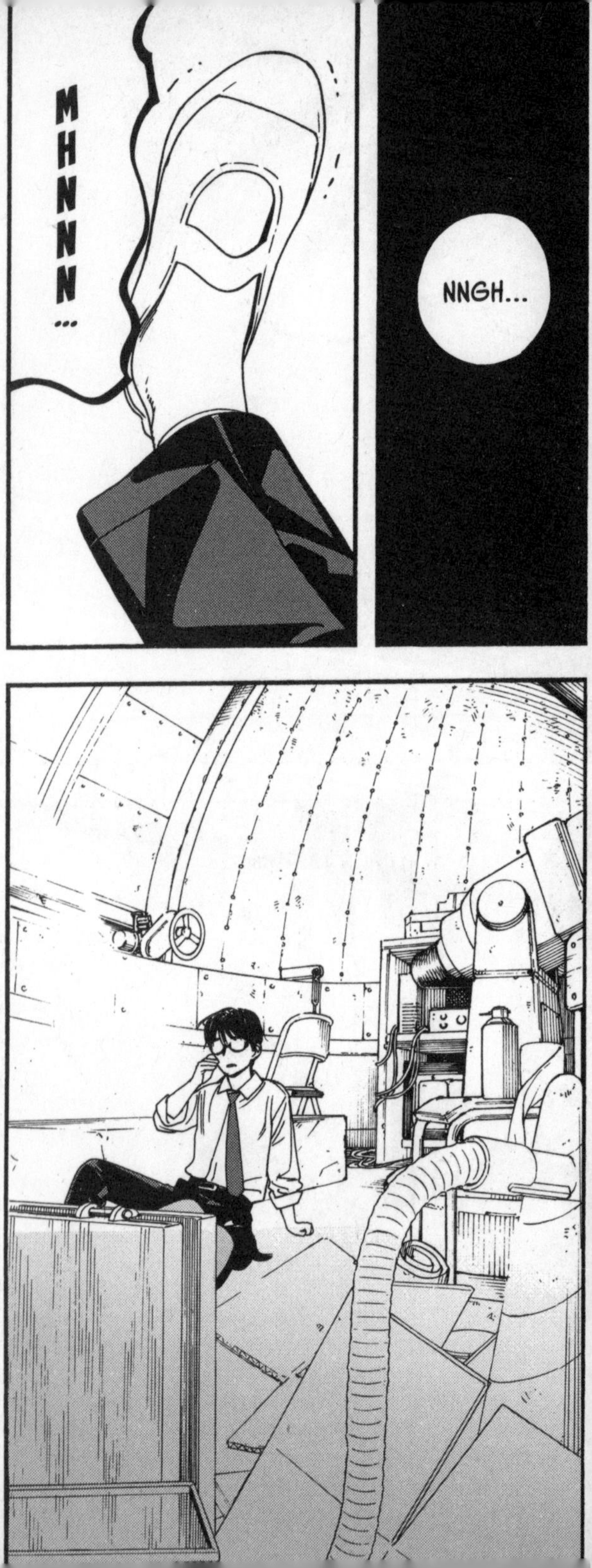
NNGH...
MHNNN...

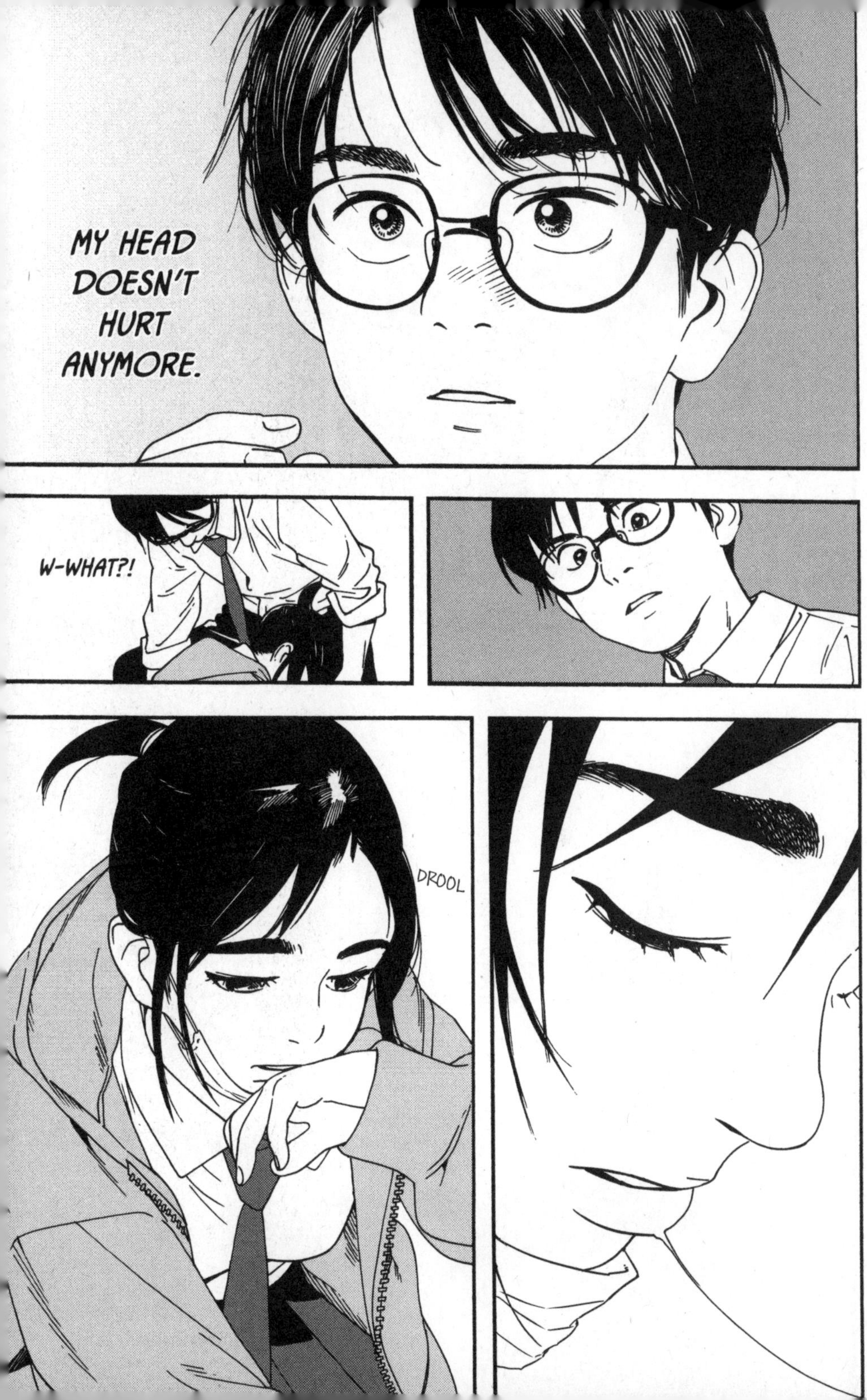
MY HEAD DOESN'T HURT ANYMORE.
W-WHAT?!
DROOL

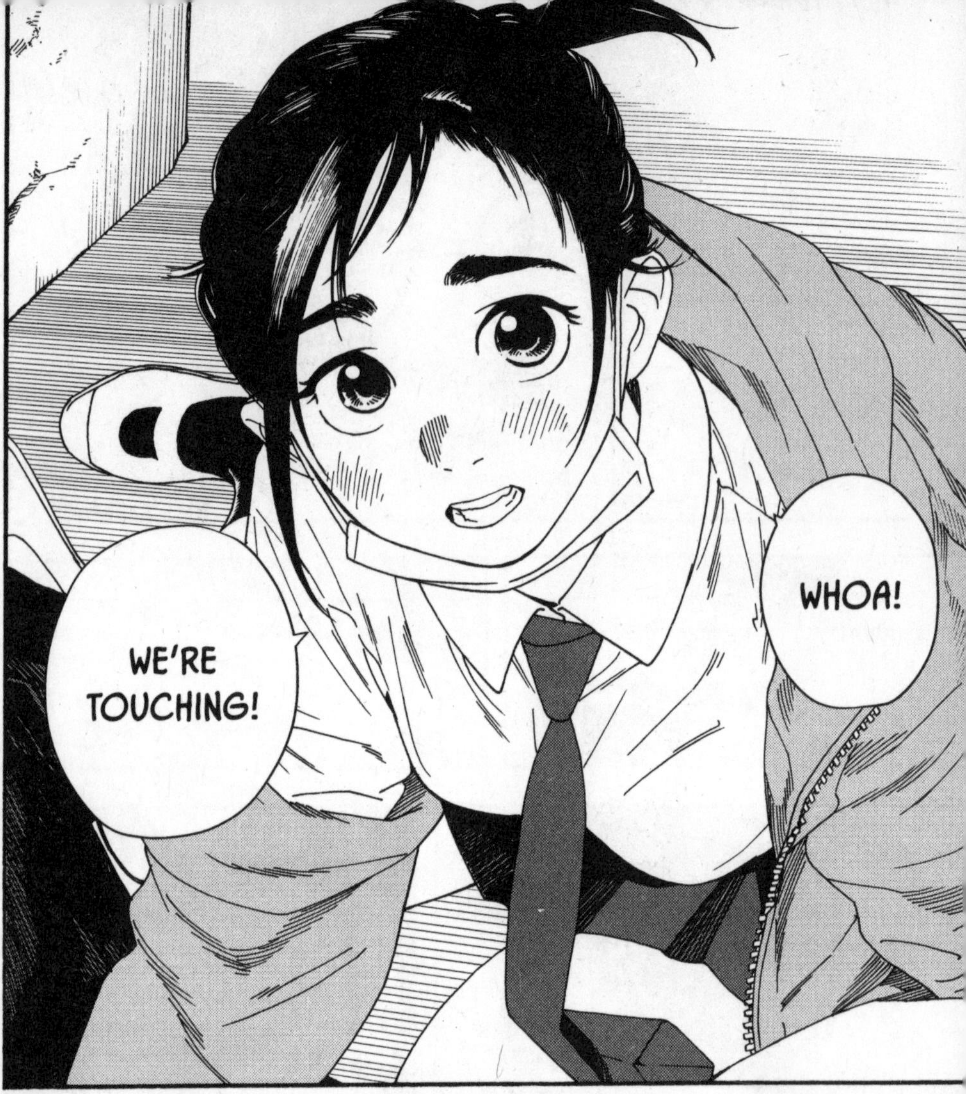
WHOA!
WE'RE TOUCHING!

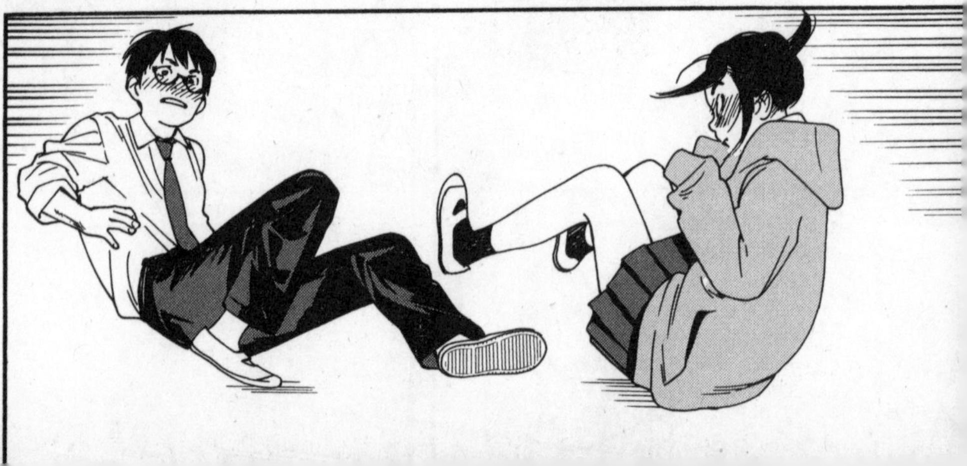

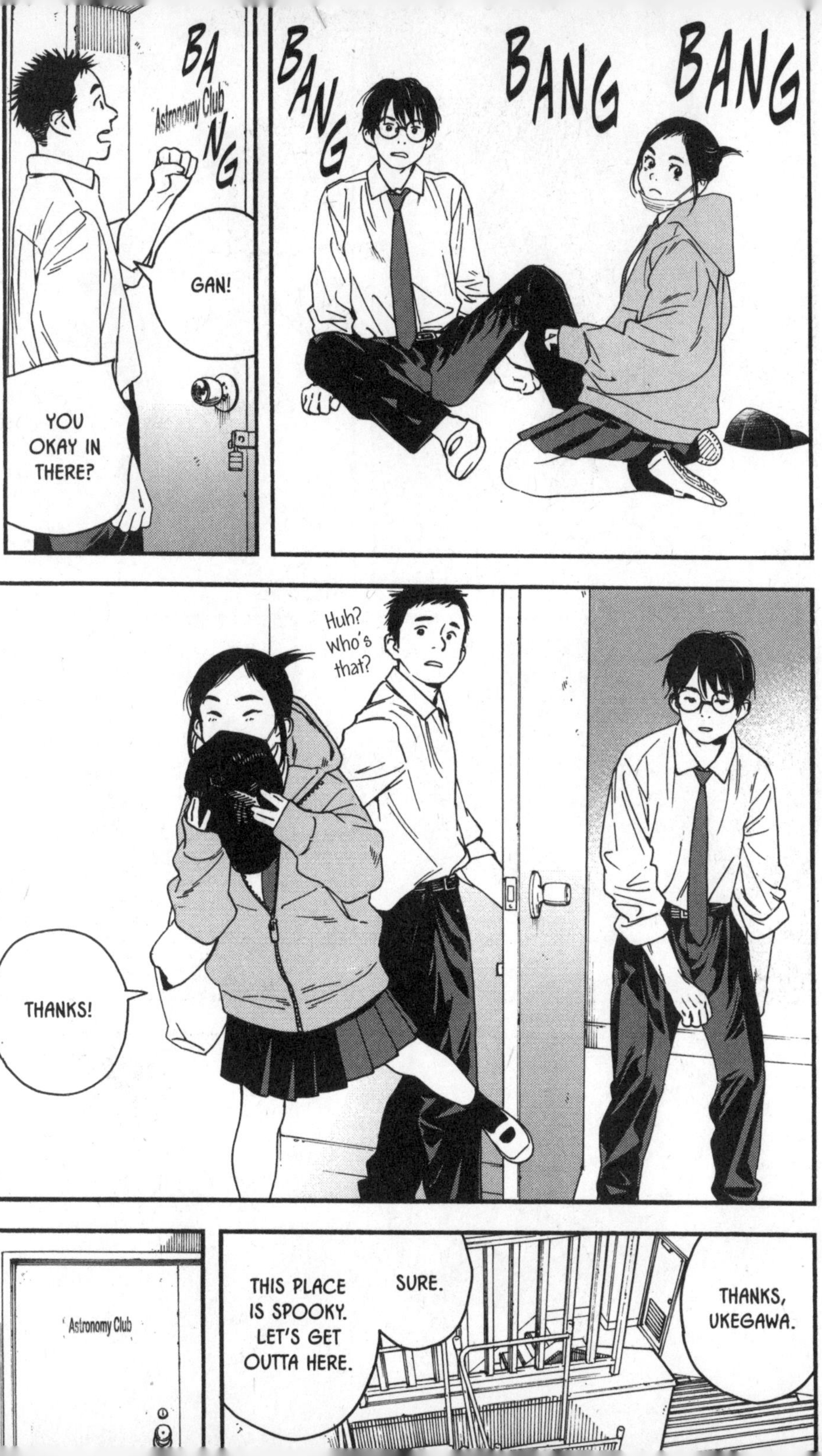
BANG
BANG
BANG
BANG
Astronomy Club
GAN!
YOU OKAY IN THERE?
Huh? Who's that?
THANKS!
THANKS, UKEGAWA.
SURE.
THIS PLACE IS SPOOKY. LET'S GET OUTTA HERE.
Astronomy Club

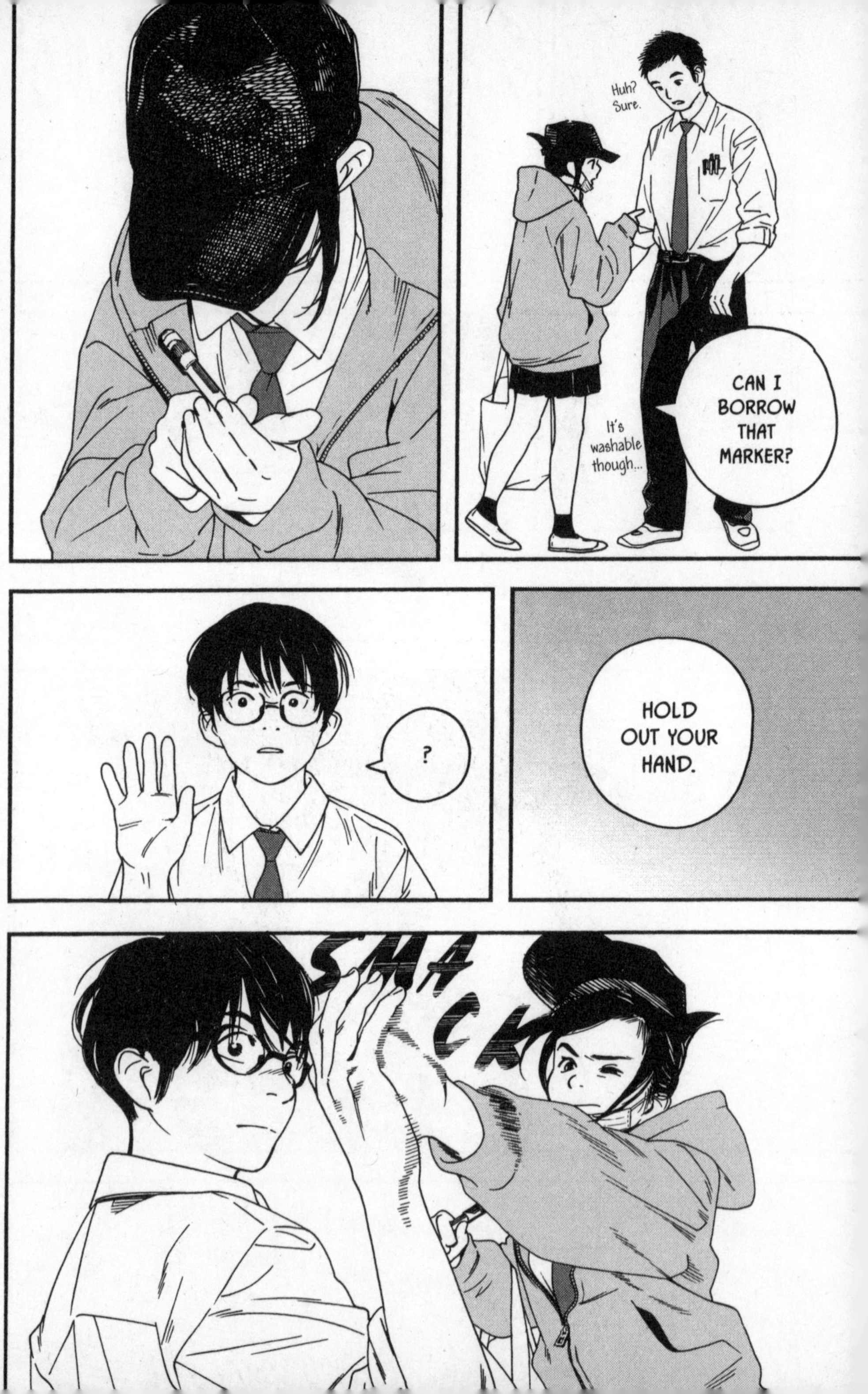
CAN I BORROW THAT MARKER?
Huh? Sure.
It's washable though...
HOLD OUT YOUR HAND.
?
SMACK

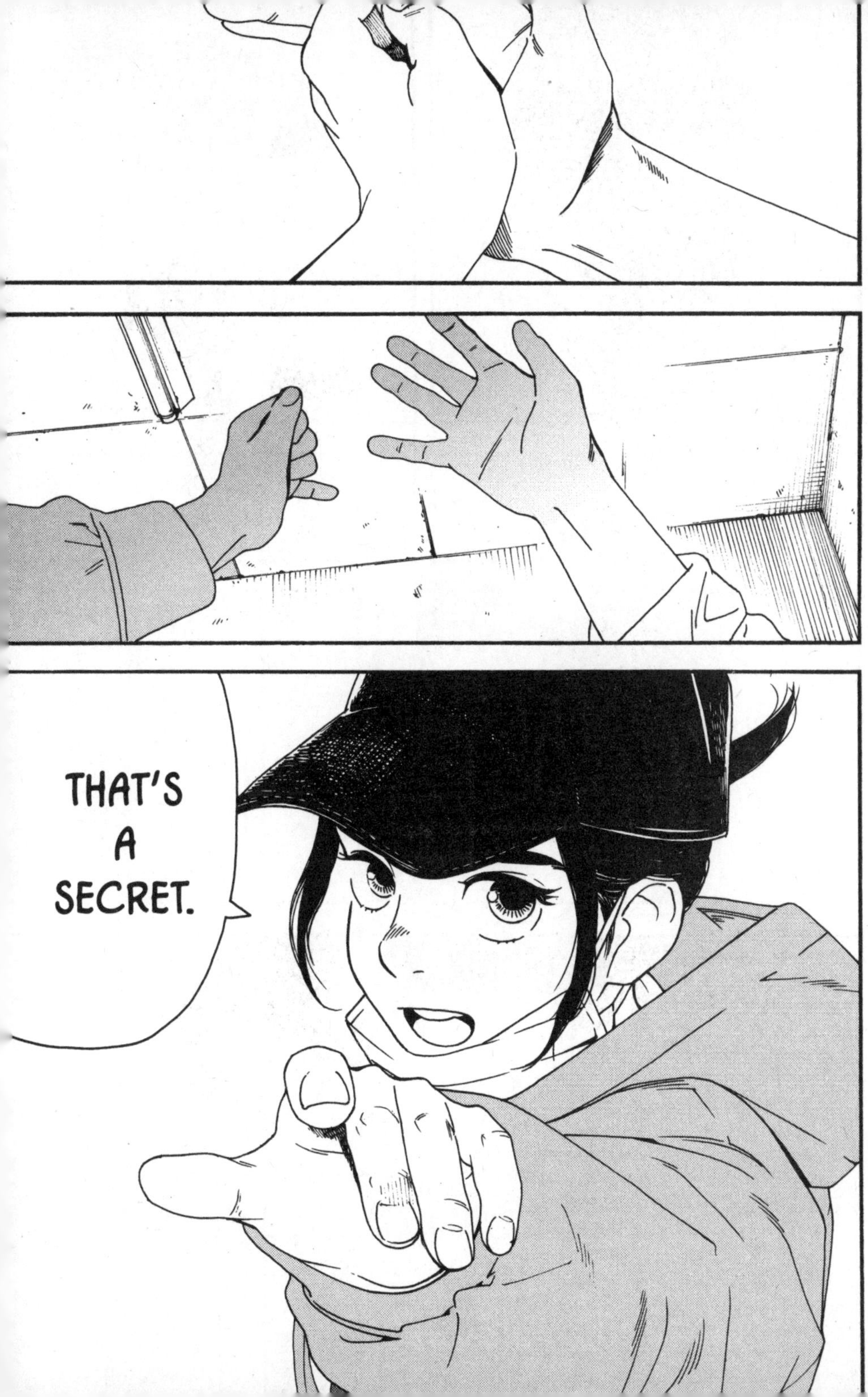
THAT'S A SECRET.

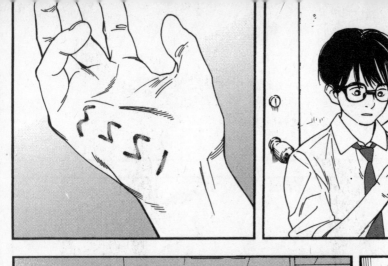

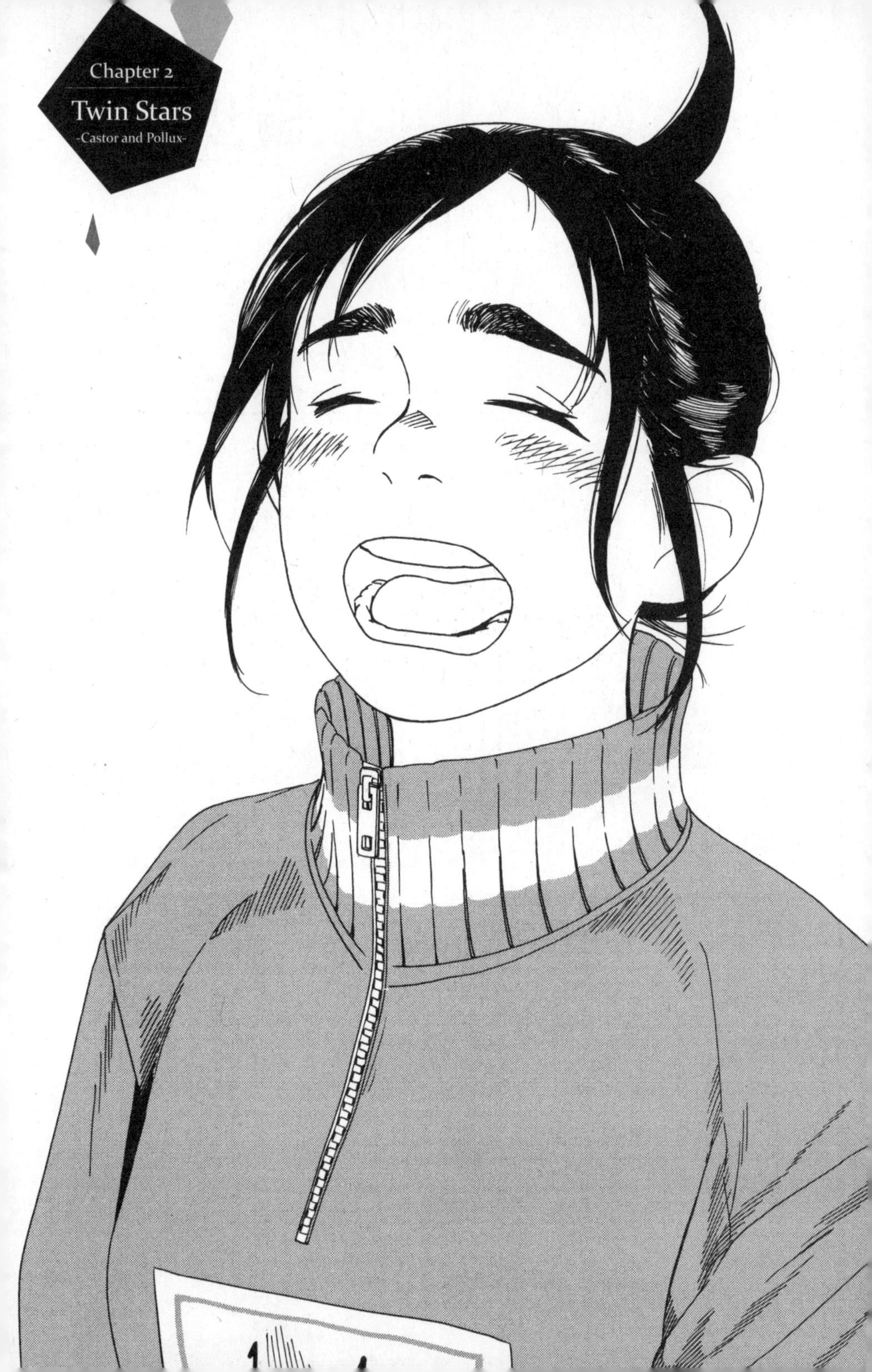
Chapter 2
Twin Stars
-Castor and Pollux-

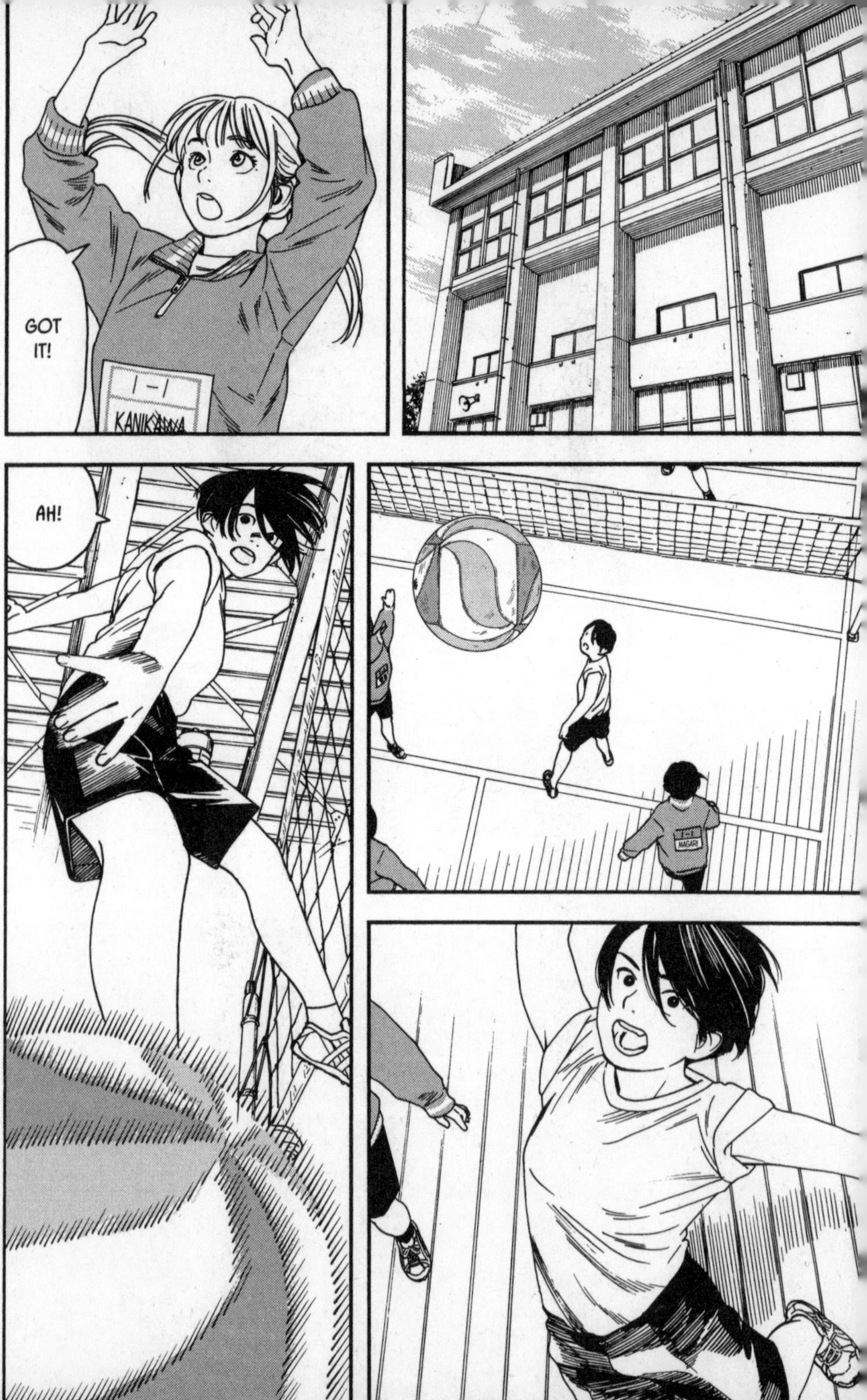
GOT IT!
1-1
MAGARI
AH!

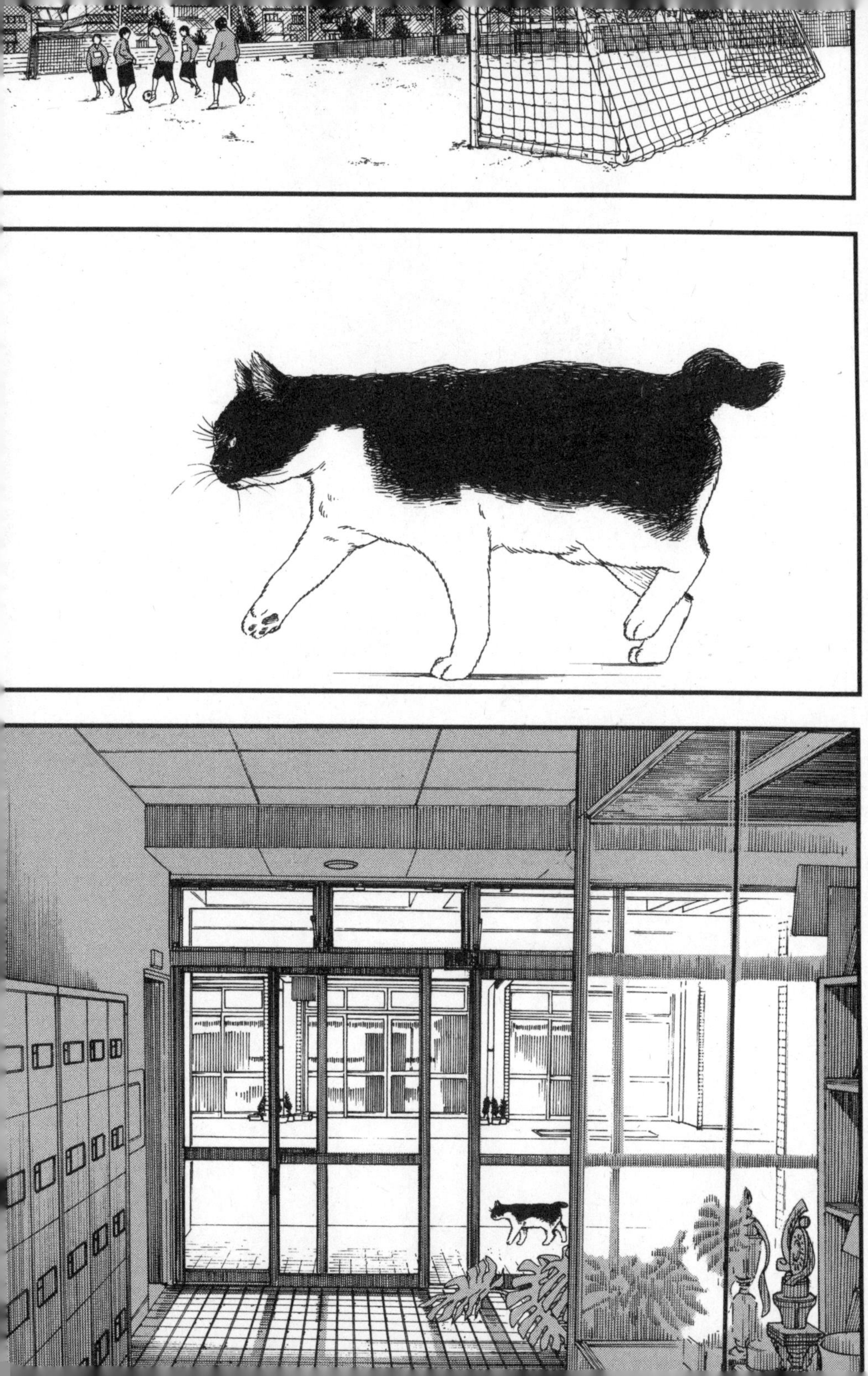

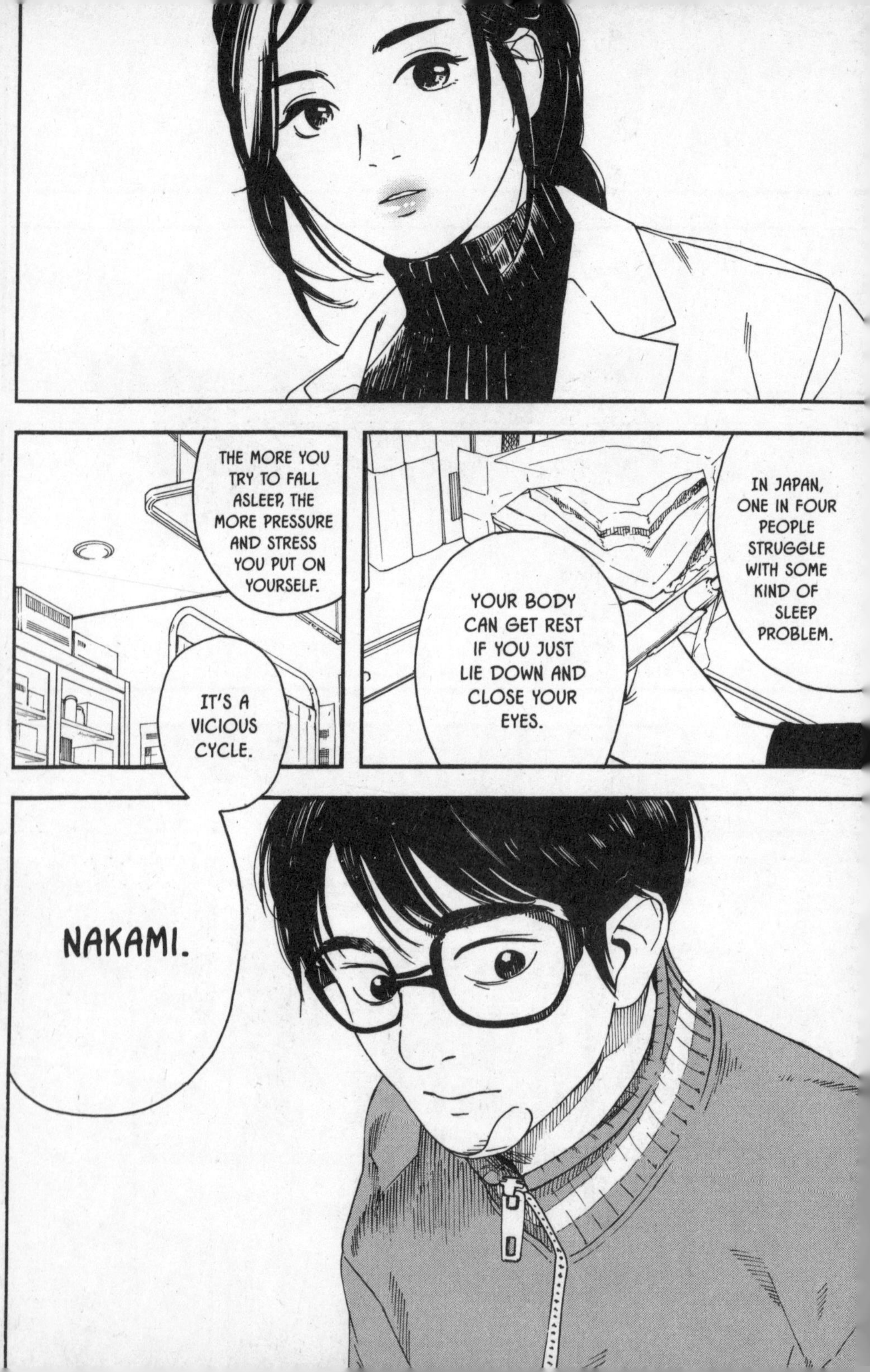
IN JAPAN, ONE IN FOUR PEOPLE STRUGGLE WITH SOME KIND OF SLEEP PROBLEM.
YOUR BODY CAN GET REST IF YOU JUST LIE DOWN AND CLOSE YOUR EYES.
THE MORE YOU TRY TO FALL ASLEEP, THE MORE PRESSURE AND STRESS YOU PUT ON YOURSELF.
IT'S A VICIOUS CYCLE.
NAKAMI.

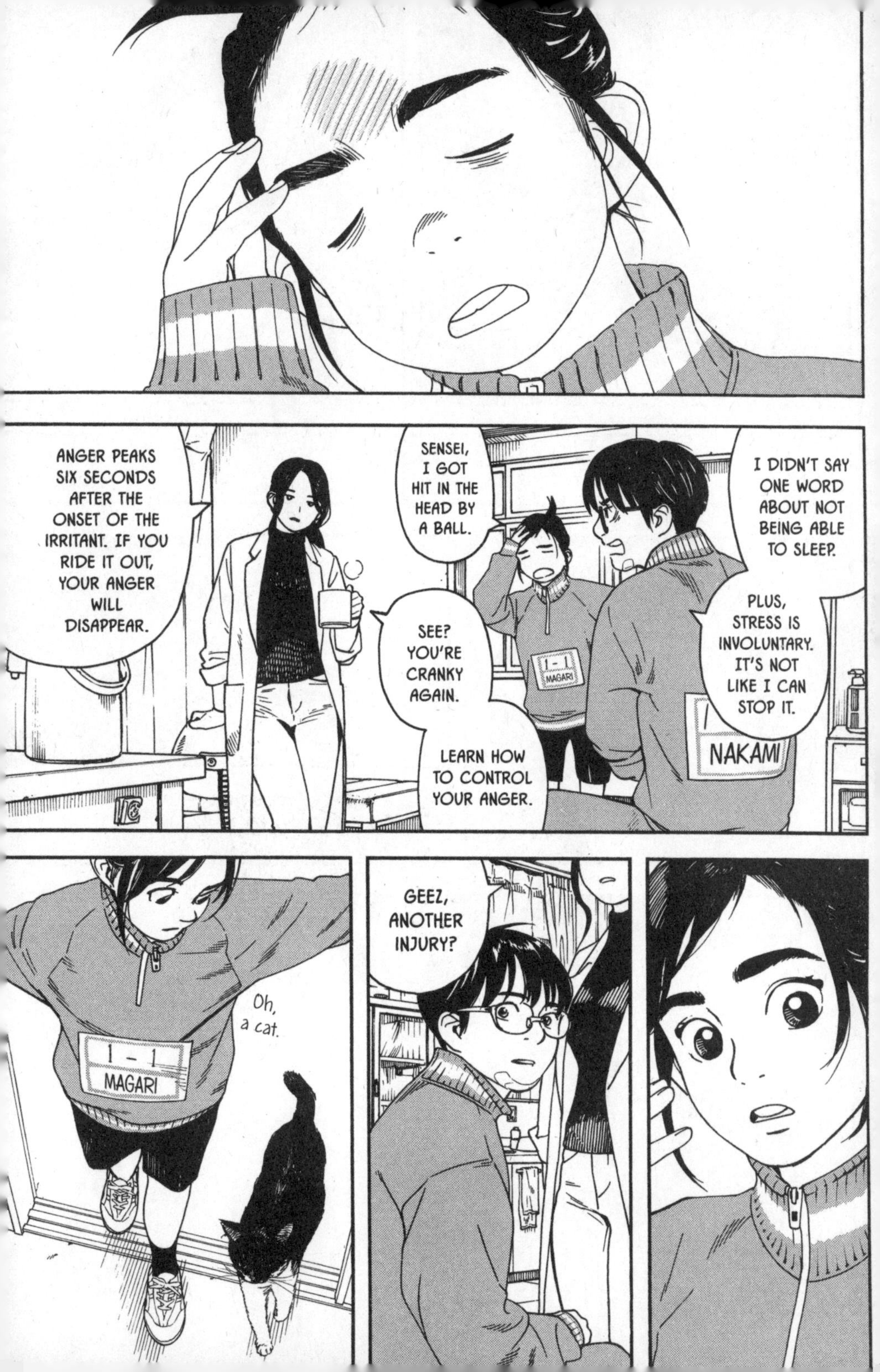

I DIDN'T SAY ONE WORD ABOUT NOT BEING ABLE TO SLEEP.
PLUS, STRESS IS INVOLUNTARY. IT'S NOT LIKE I CAN STOP IT.
NAKAMI
1 - 1 MAGARI
SEE? YOU'RE CRANKY AGAIN.
LEARN HOW TO CONTROL YOUR ANGER.
ANGER PEAKS SIX SECONDS AFTER THE ONSET OF THE IRRITANT. IF YOU RIDE IT OUT, YOUR ANGER WILL DISAPPEAR.
SENSEI, I GOT HIT IN THE HEAD BY A BALL.
GEEZ, ANOTHER INJURY?
Oh, a cat.
1 - 1 MAGARI

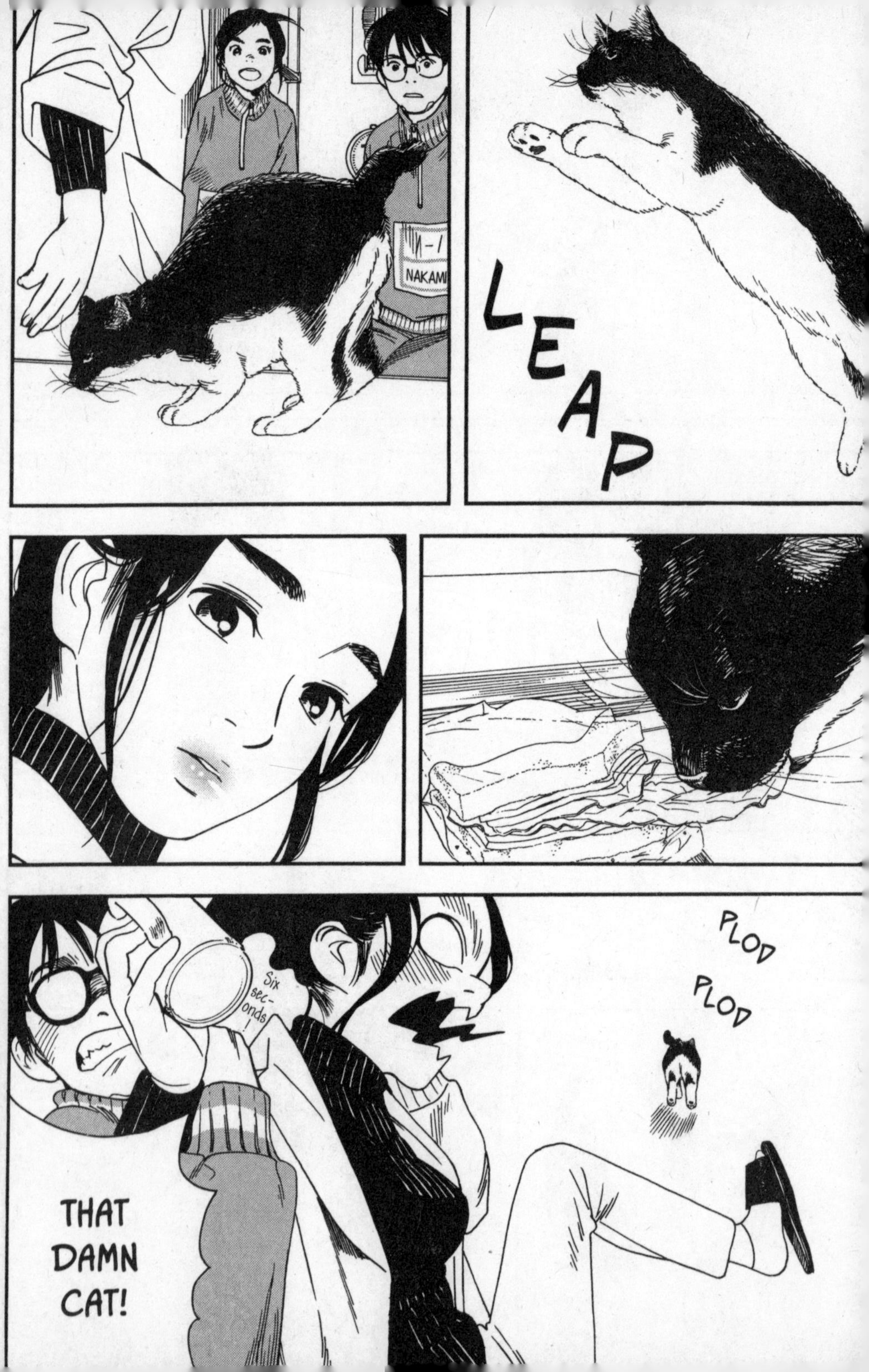
LEAP
NAKAMI
PLOD
PLOD
Six sec- onds!
THAT DAMN CAT!

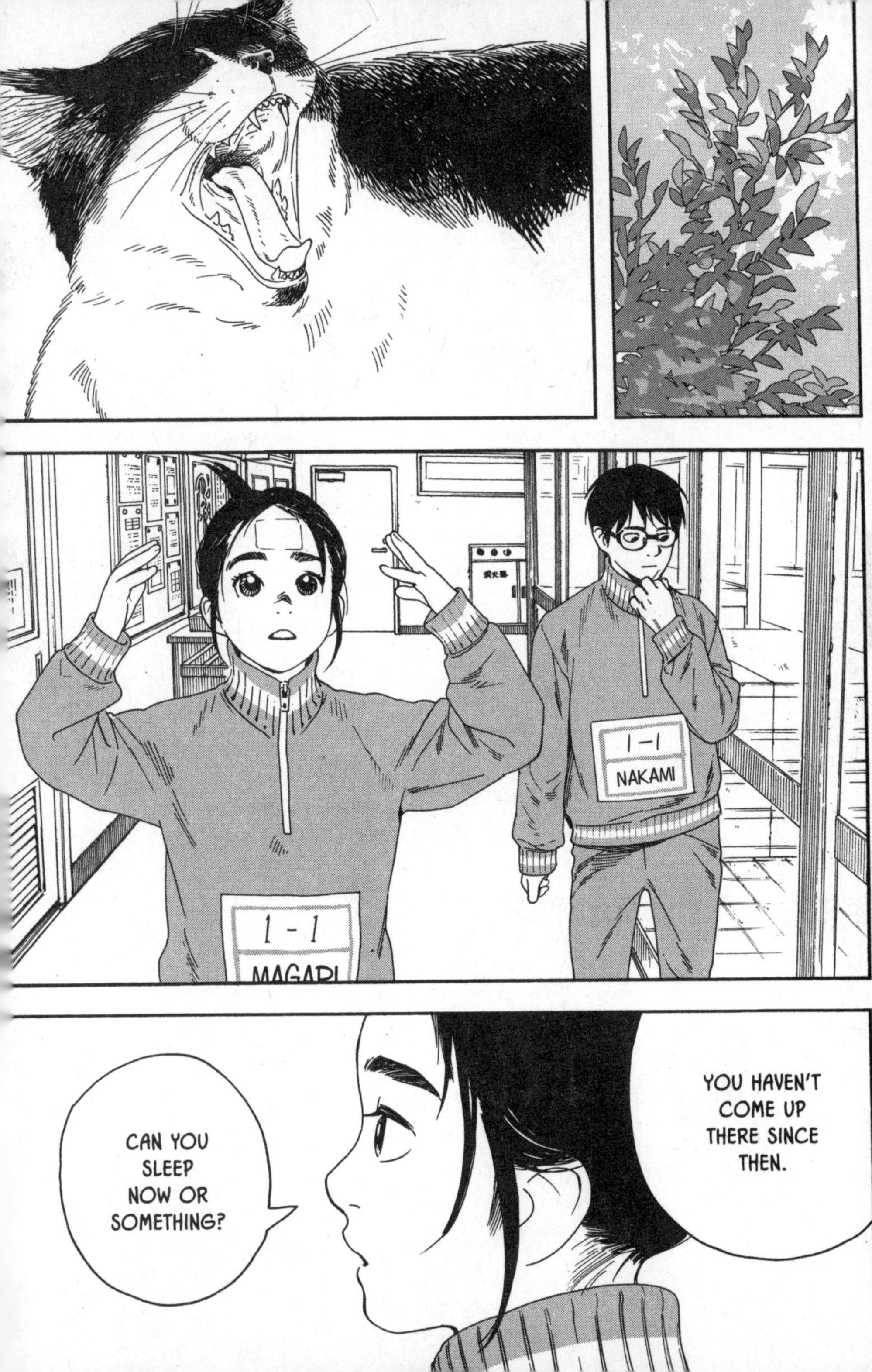
1-1
NAKAMI
YOU HAVEN'T COME UP THERE SINCE THEN.
CAN YOU SLEEP NOW OR SOMETHING?

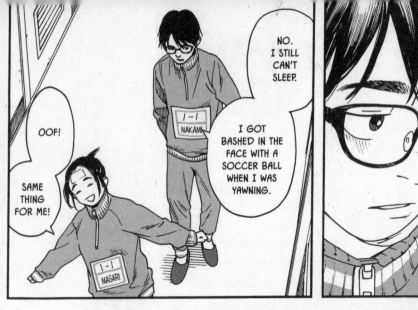

NO. I STILL CAN'T SLEEP.
1-1
NAKAMI
I GOT BASHED IN THE FACE WITH A SOCCER BALL WHEN I WAS YAWNING.
OOF!
SAME THING FOR ME!
1-1
MAGARI
WANNA COME UP TODAY?
THE OBSERVATORY IS A GOOD HIDEOUT.
...
BUT I FEEL...
...KINDA AWKWARD AROUND GIRLS.
HMM, I DUNNO.

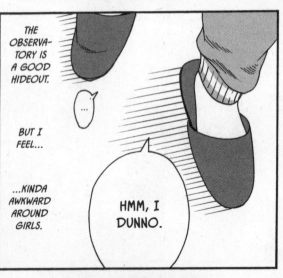

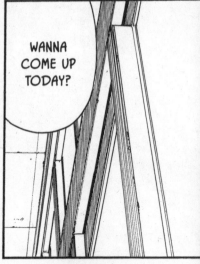

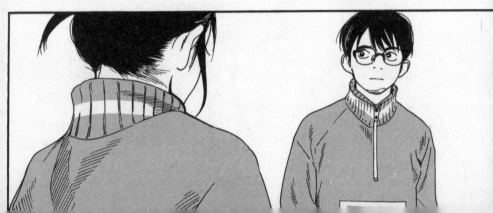

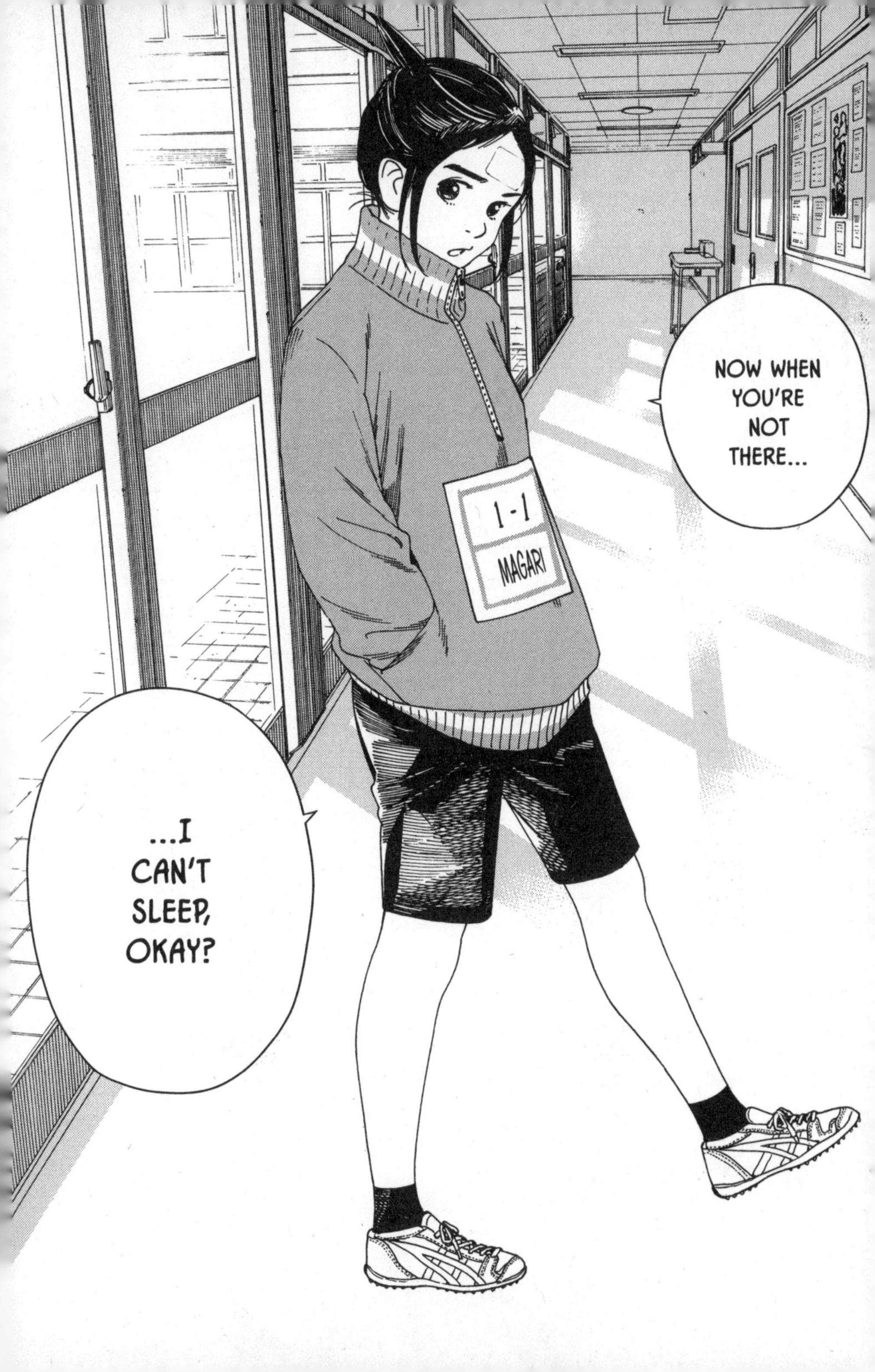
1-1
MAGARI
NOW WHEN YOU'RE NOT THERE...
...I CAN'T SLEEP, OKAY?

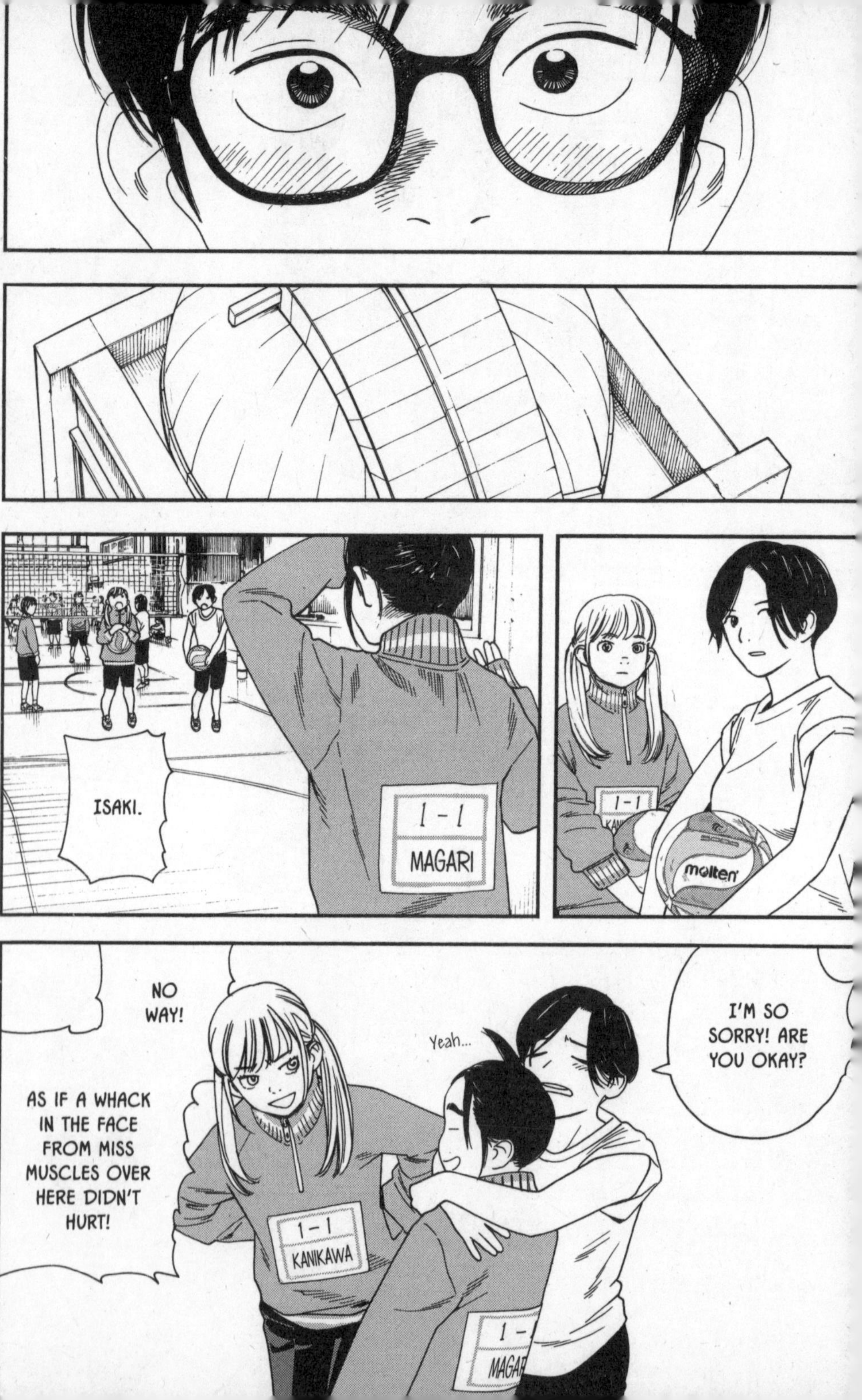
molten
ISAKI.
1-1
MAGARI
I'M SO SORRY! ARE YOU OKAY?
Yeah...
NO WAY!
AS IF A WHACK IN THE FACE FROM MISS MUSCLES OVER HERE DIDN'T HURT!
1-1
KANIKAWA

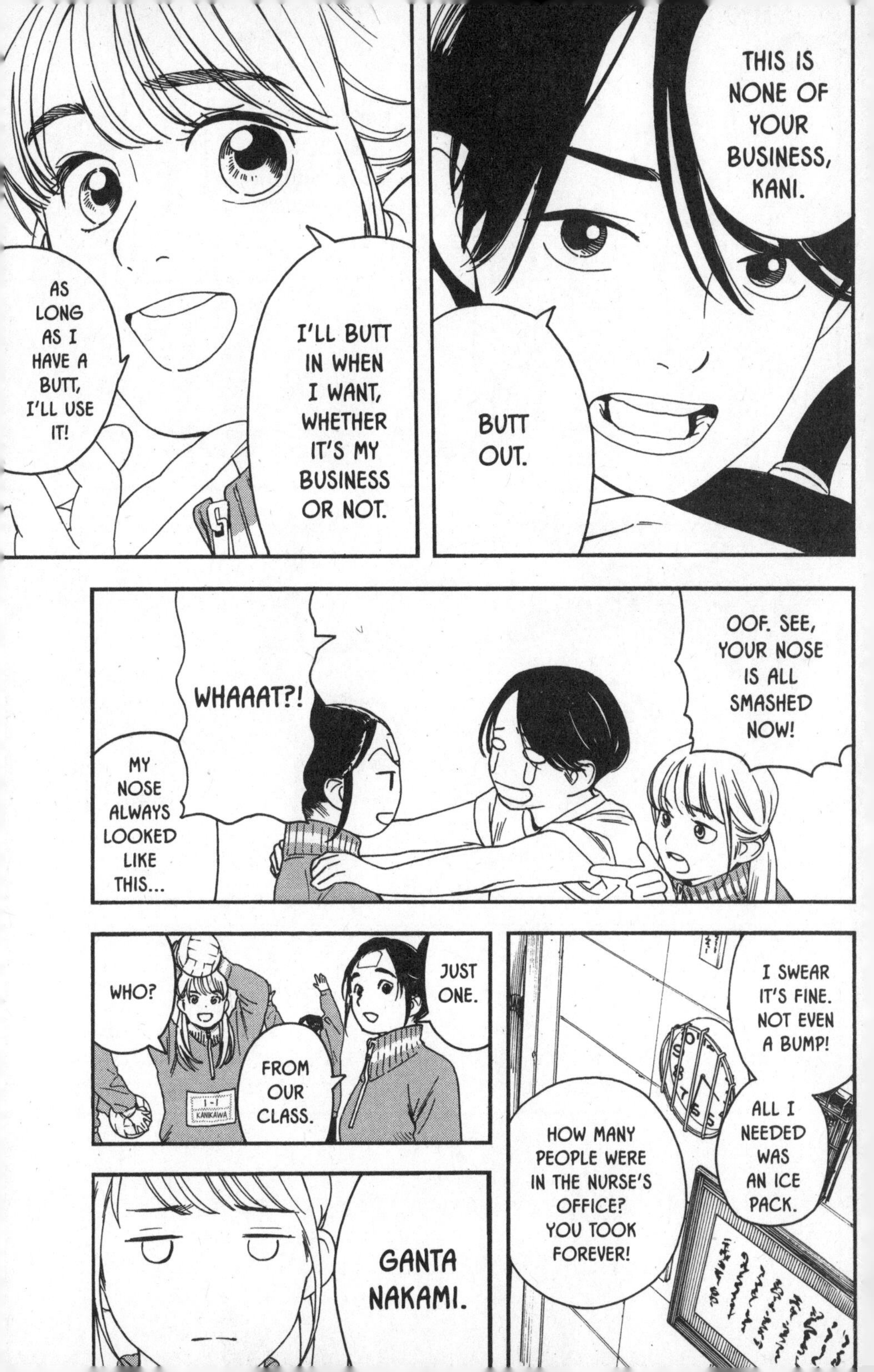
THIS IS NONE OF YOUR BUSINESS, KANI.
BUTT OUT.
I'LL BUTT IN WHEN I WANT, WHETHER IT'S MY BUSINESS OR NOT.
AS LONG AS I HAVE A BUTT, I'LL USE IT!
OOF. SEE, YOUR NOSE IS ALL SMASHED NOW!
WHAAAT?!
MY NOSE ALWAYS LOOKED LIKE THIS...
I SWEAR IT'S FINE. NOT EVEN A BUMP!
ALL I NEEDED WAS AN ICE PACK.
HOW MANY PEOPLE WERE IN THE NURSE'S OFFICE? YOU TOOK FOREVER!
JUST ONE.
WHO?
FROM OUR CLASS.
GANTA NAKAMI.

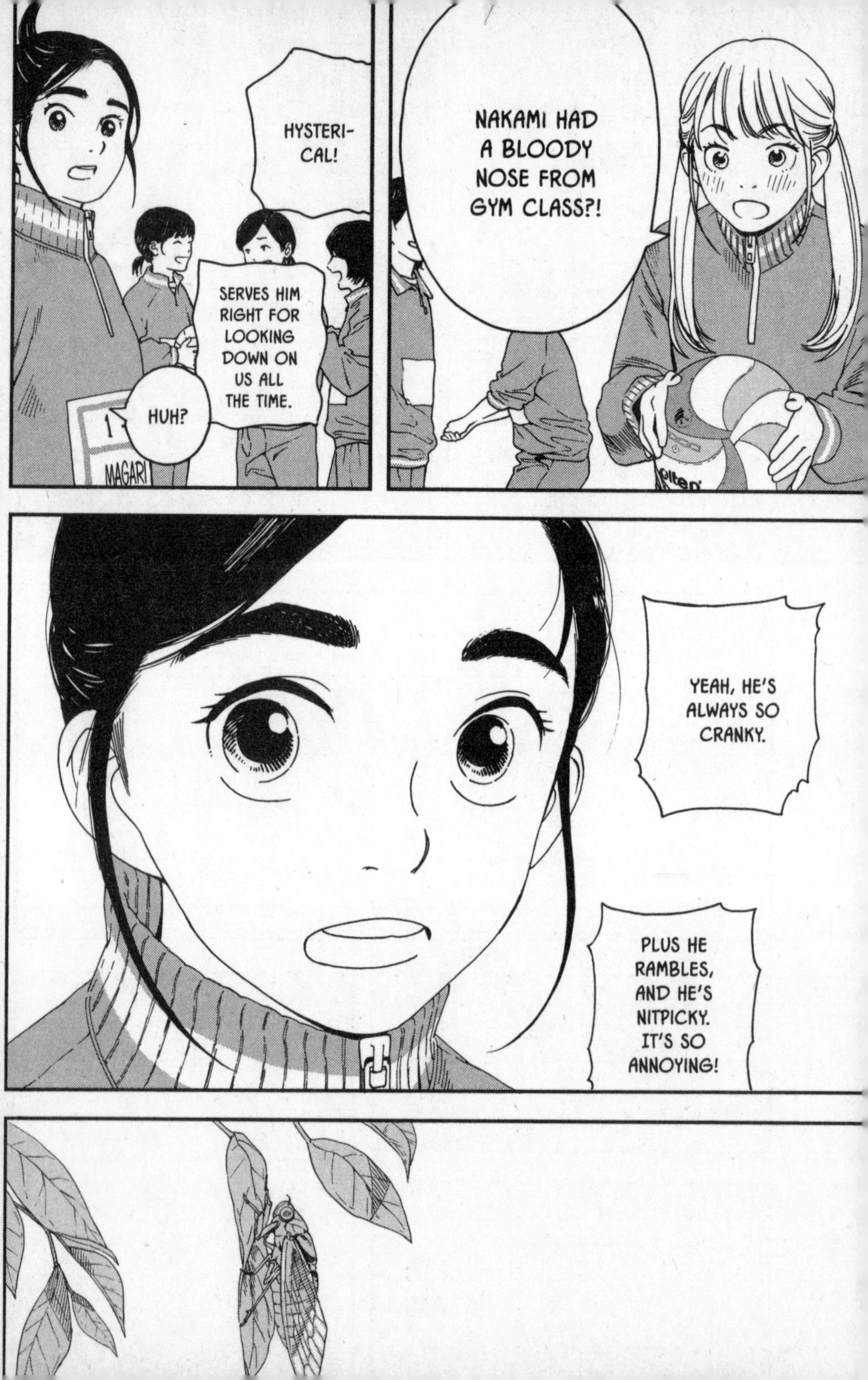
NAKAMI HAD A BLOODY NOSE FROM GYM CLASS?!
HYSTERI-CAL!
SERVES HIM RIGHT FOR LOOKING DOWN ON US ALL THE TIME.
HUH?
MAGARI
YEAH, HE'S ALWAYS SO CRANKY.
PLUS HE RAMBLES, AND HE'S NITPICKY. IT'S SO ANNOYING!

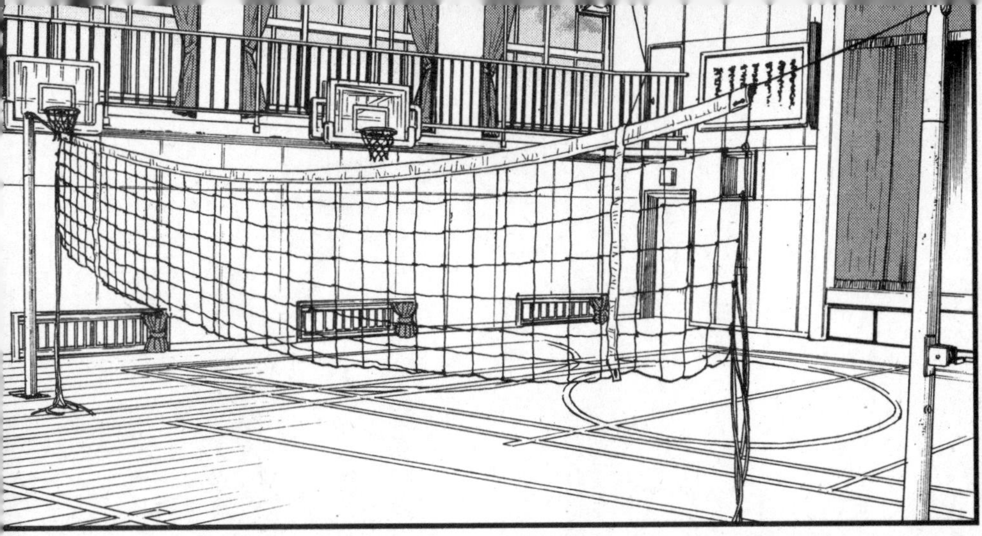
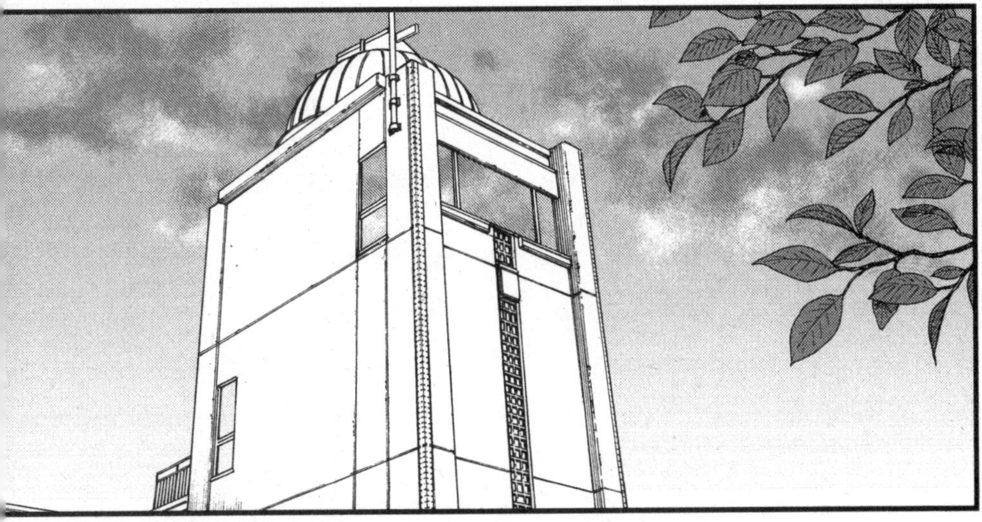
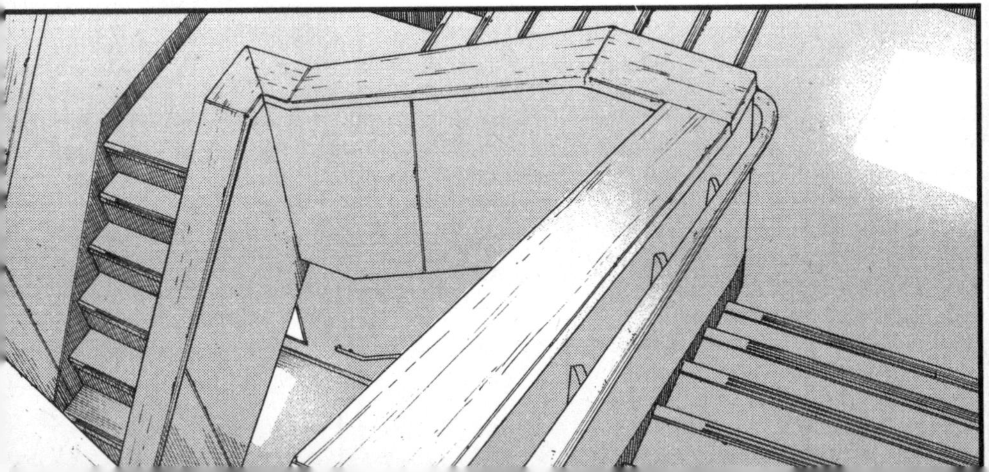

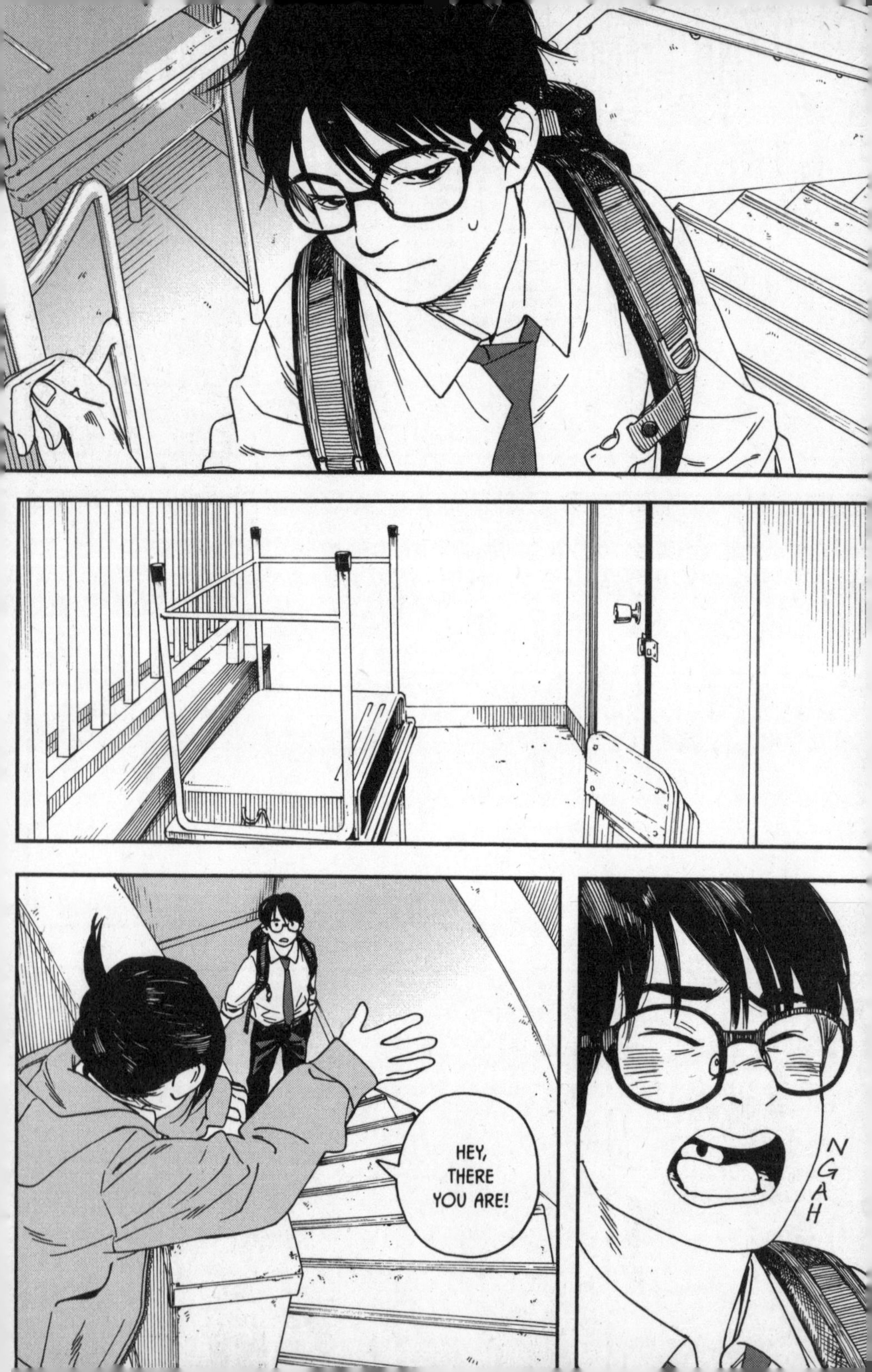
NGAH
HEY, THERE YOU ARE!

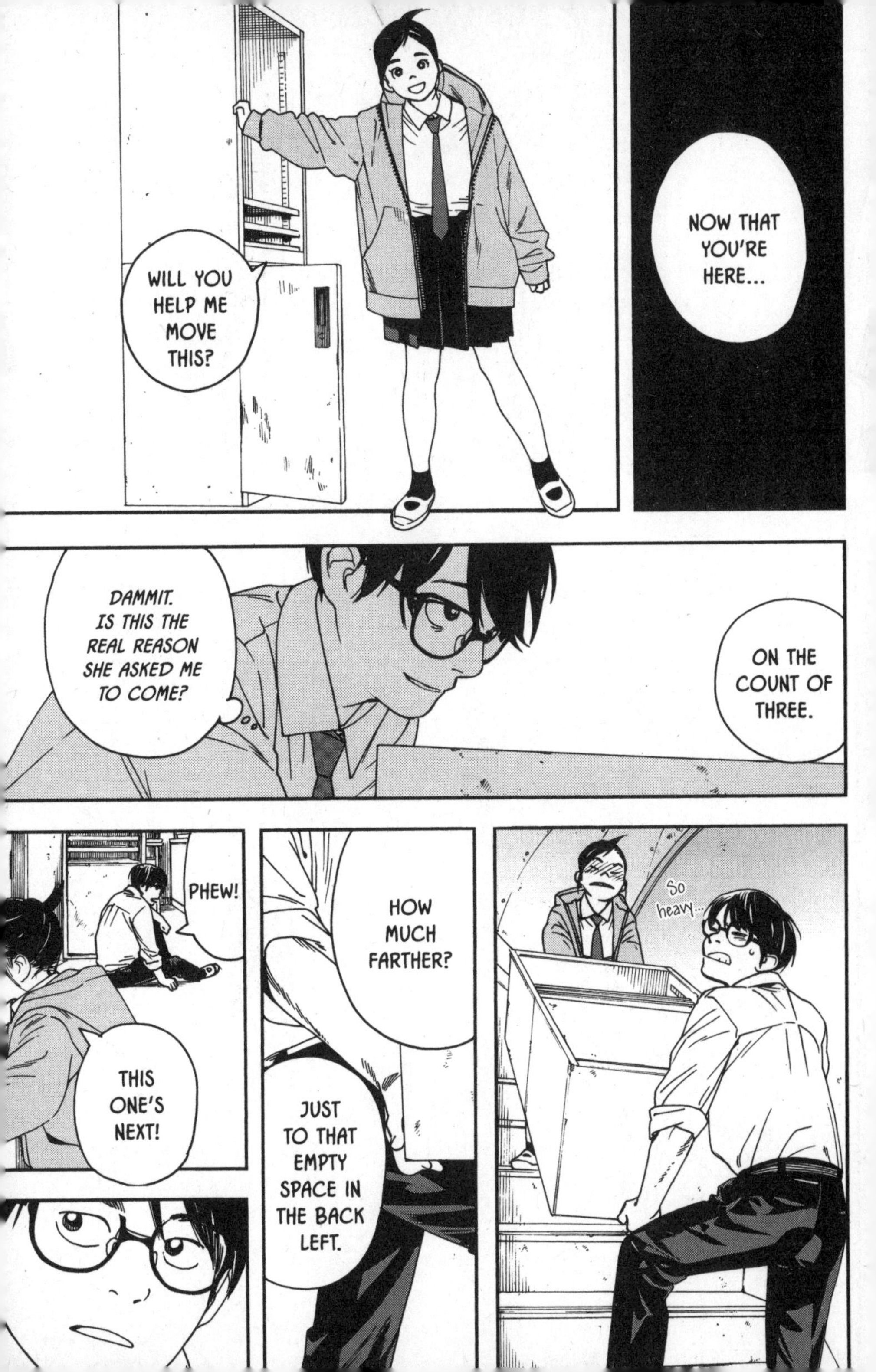
NOW THAT YOU'RE HERE...
WILL YOU HELP ME MOVE THIS?
ON THE COUNT OF THREE.
DAMMIT. IS THIS THE REAL REASON SHE ASKED ME TO COME?
So heavy...
HOW MUCH FARTHER?
JUST TO THAT EMPTY SPACE IN THE BACK LEFT.
PHEW!
THIS ONE'S NEXT!

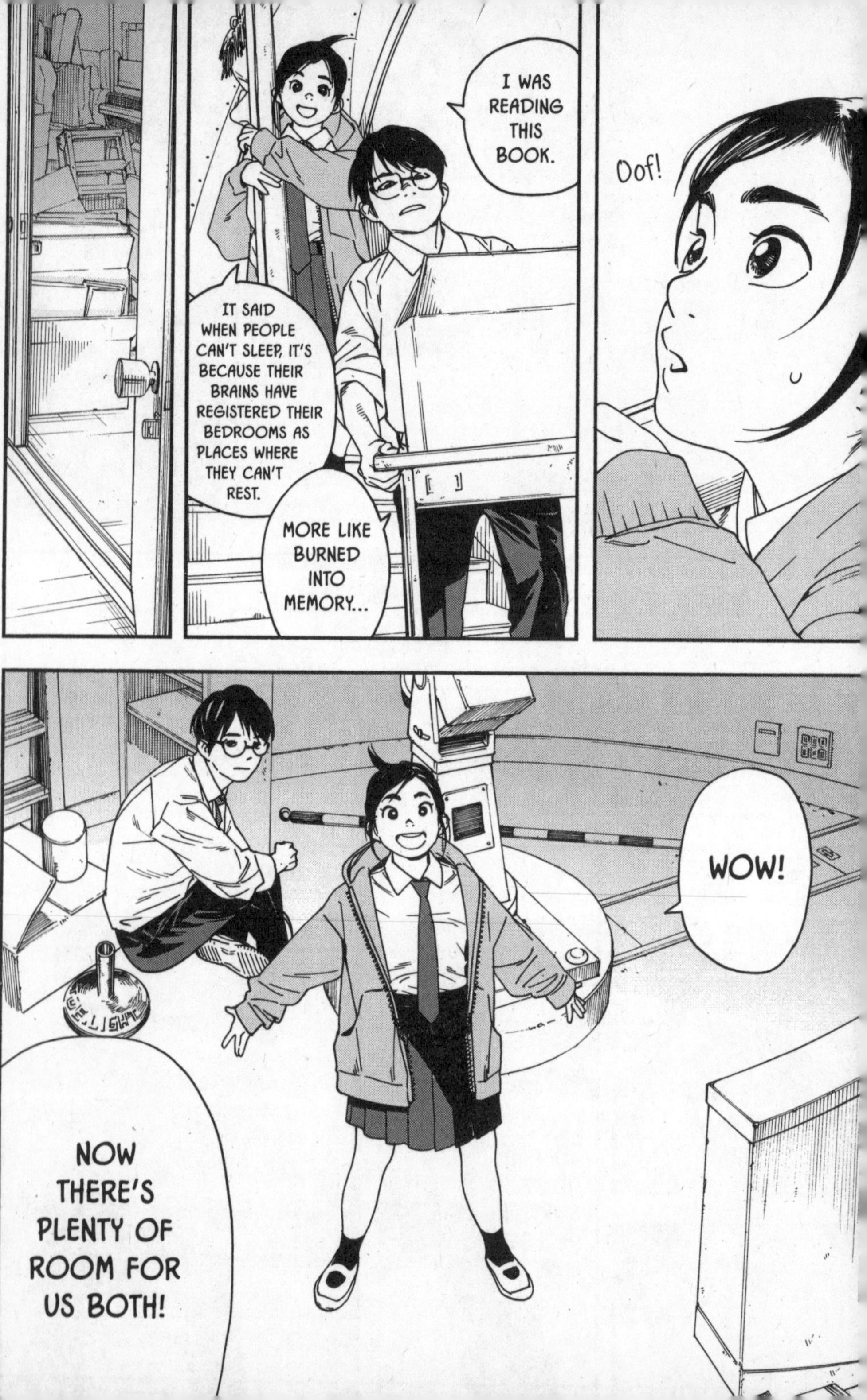
Oof!
I WAS READING THIS BOOK.
IT SAID WHEN PEOPLE CAN'T SLEEP, IT'S BECAUSE THEIR BRAINS HAVE REGISTERED THEIR BEDROOMS AS PLACES WHERE THEY CAN'T REST.
MORE LIKE BURNED INTO MEMORY...
WOW!
NOW THERE'S PLENTY OF ROOM FOR US BOTH!

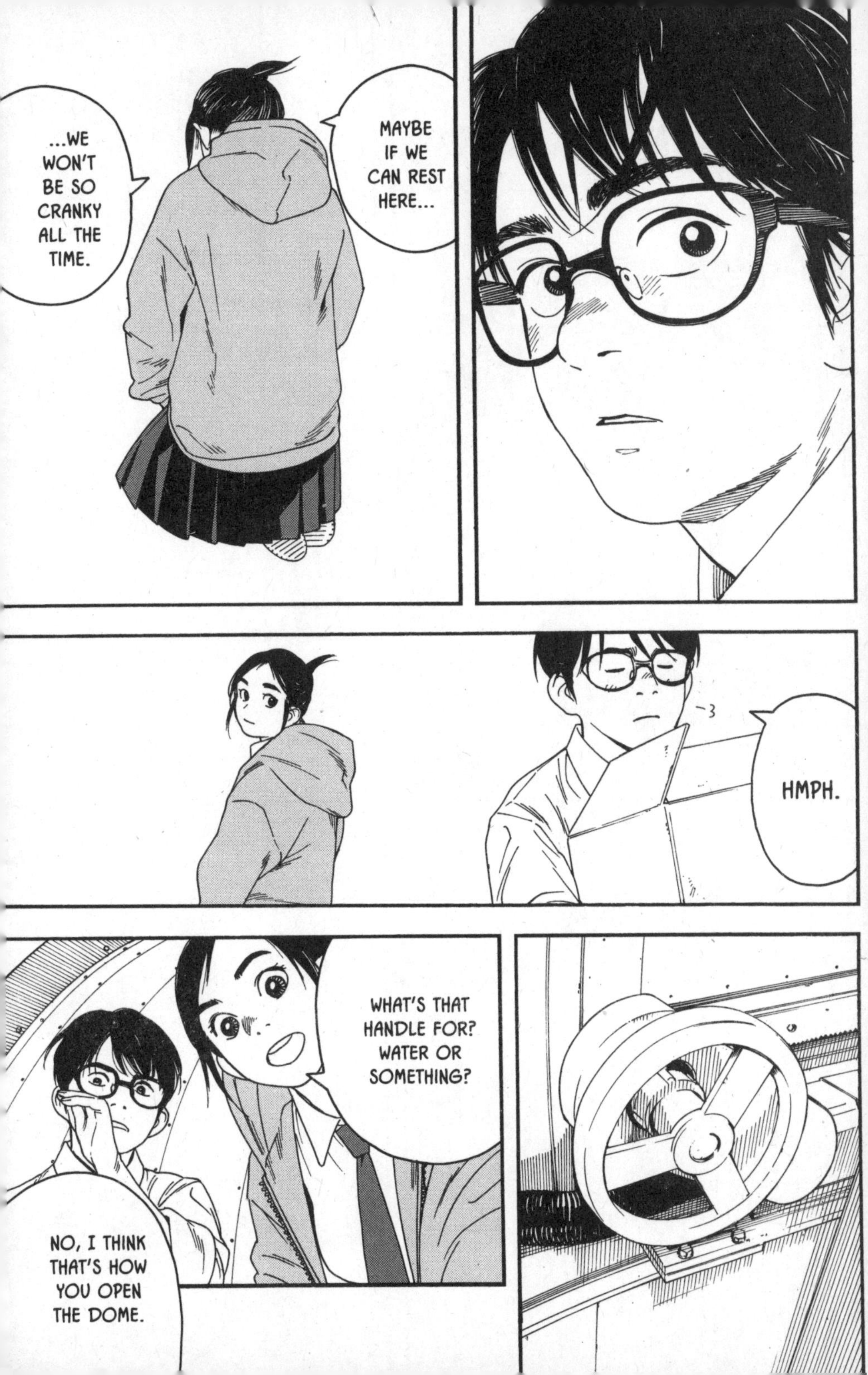
MAYBE IF WE CAN REST HERE...
...WE WON'T BE SO CRANKY ALL THE TIME.
HMPH.
WHAT'S THAT HANDLE FOR? WATER OR SOMETHING?
NO, I THINK THAT'S HOW YOU OPEN THE DOME.

HEY,
PUT THE
LADDER
UP!

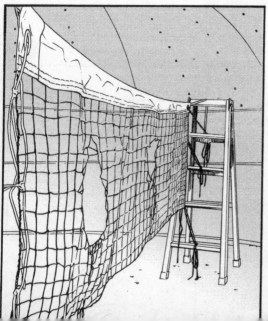

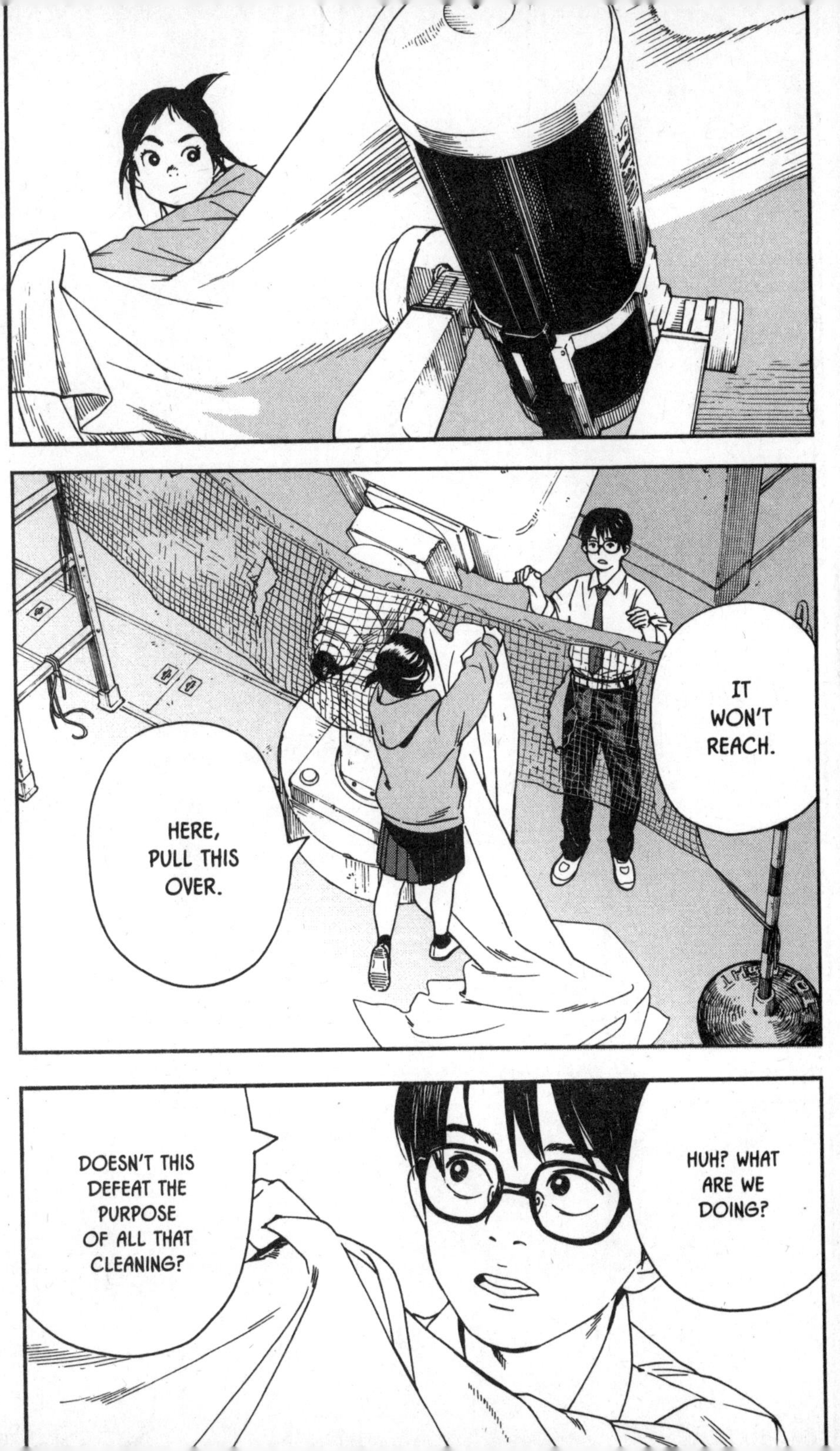
IT WON'T REACH.
HERE, PULL THIS OVER.
HUH? WHAT ARE WE DOING?
DOESN'T THIS DEFEAT THE PURPOSE OF ALL THAT CLEANING?

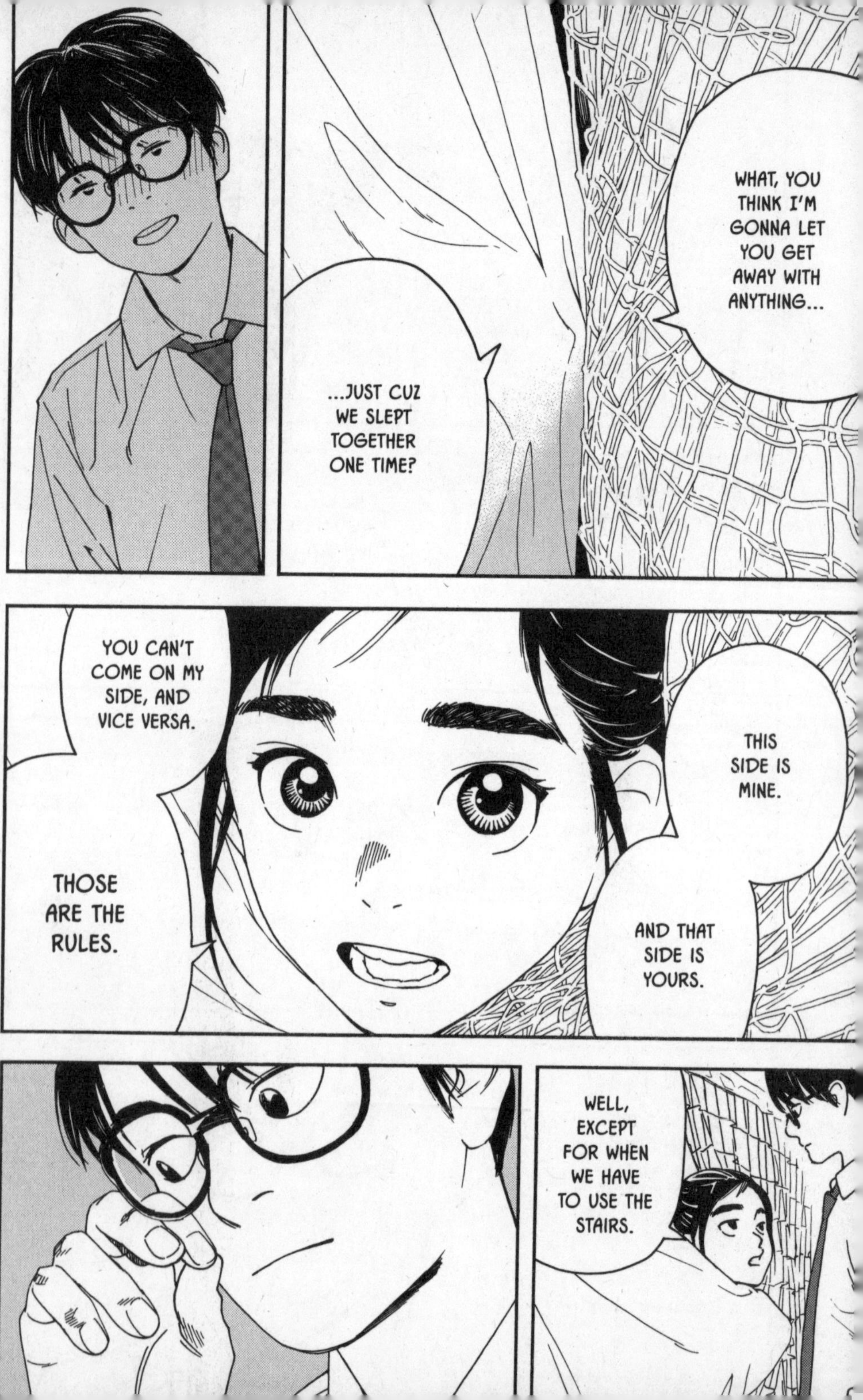
WHAT, YOU THINK I'M GONNA LET YOU GET AWAY WITH ANYTHING...
...JUST CUZ WE SLEPT TOGETHER ONE TIME?
THIS SIDE IS MINE.
AND THAT SIDE IS YOURS.
YOU CAN'T COME ON MY SIDE, AND VICE VERSA.
THOSE ARE THE RULES.
WELL, EXCEPT FOR WHEN WE HAVE TO USE THE STAIRS.

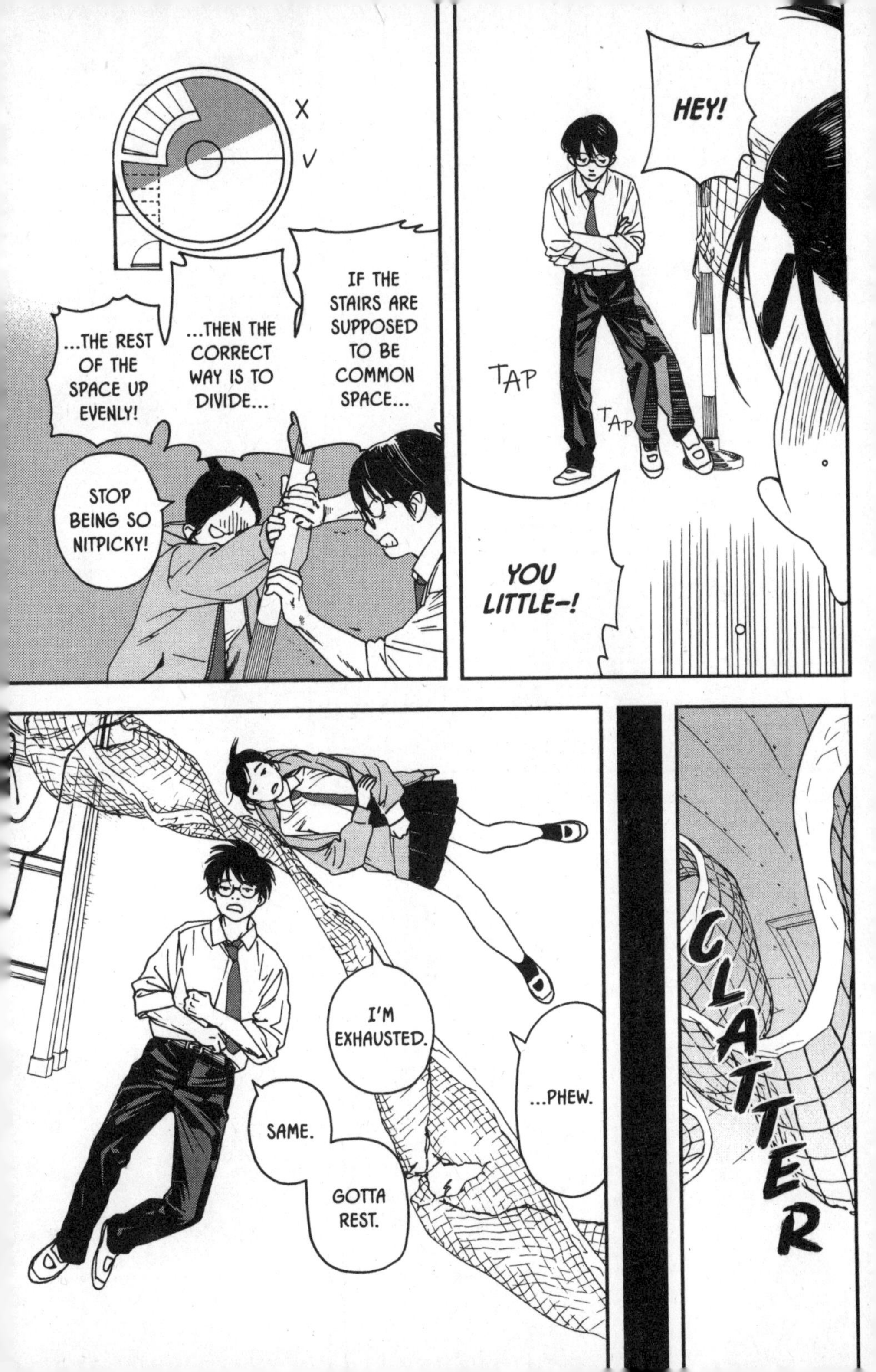
HEY!
TAP
TAP
YOU LITTLE-!
X
IF THE STAIRS ARE SUPPOSED TO BE COMMON SPACE...
...THEN THE CORRECT WAY IS TO DIVIDE...
...THE REST OF THE SPACE UP EVENLY!
STOP BEING SO NITPICKY!
CLATTER
...PHEW.
I'M EXHAUSTED.
SAME.
GOTTA REST.

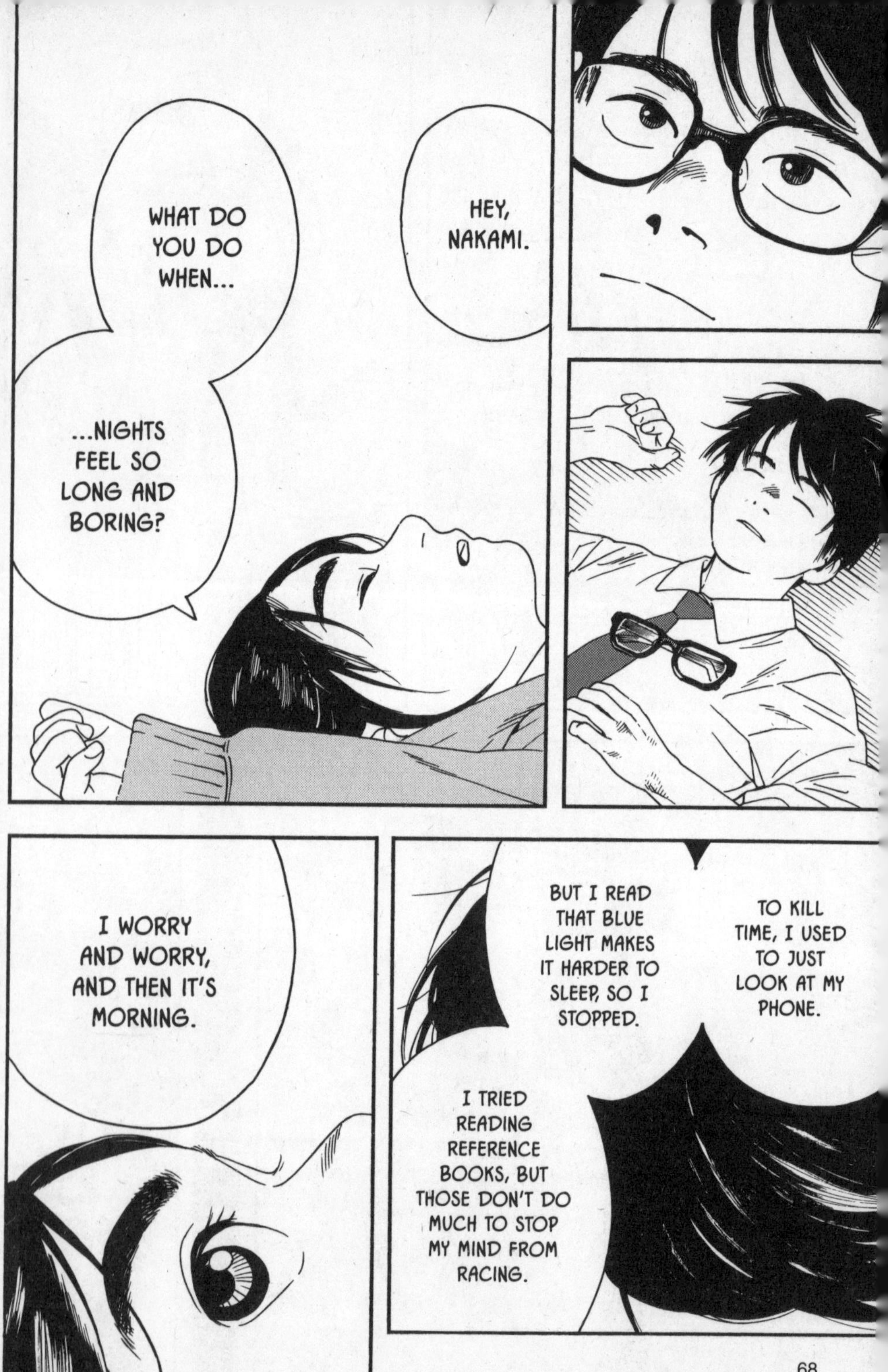
HEY, NAKAMI.
WHAT DO YOU DO WHEN...
...NIGHTS FEEL SO LONG AND BORING?
TO KILL TIME, I USED TO JUST LOOK AT MY PHONE.
BUT I READ THAT BLUE LIGHT MAKES IT HARDER TO SLEEP, SO I STOPPED.
I TRIED READING REFERENCE BOOKS, BUT THOSE DON'T DO MUCH TO STOP MY MIND FROM RACING.
I WORRY AND WORRY, AND THEN IT'S MORNING.

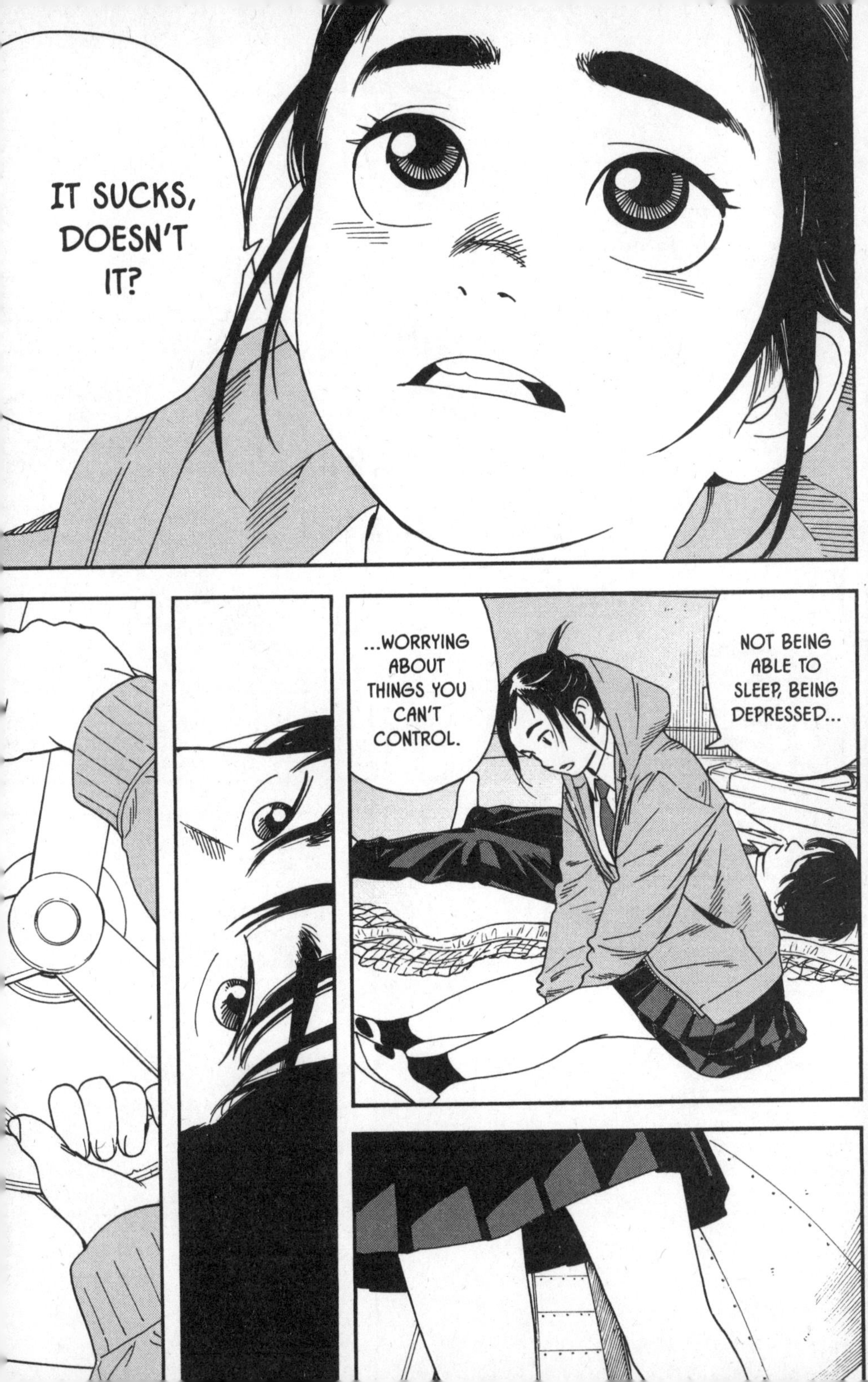
IT SUCKS, DOESN'T IT?
NOT BEING ABLE TO SLEEP, BEING DEPRESSED...
...WORRYING ABOUT THINGS YOU CAN'T CONTROL.

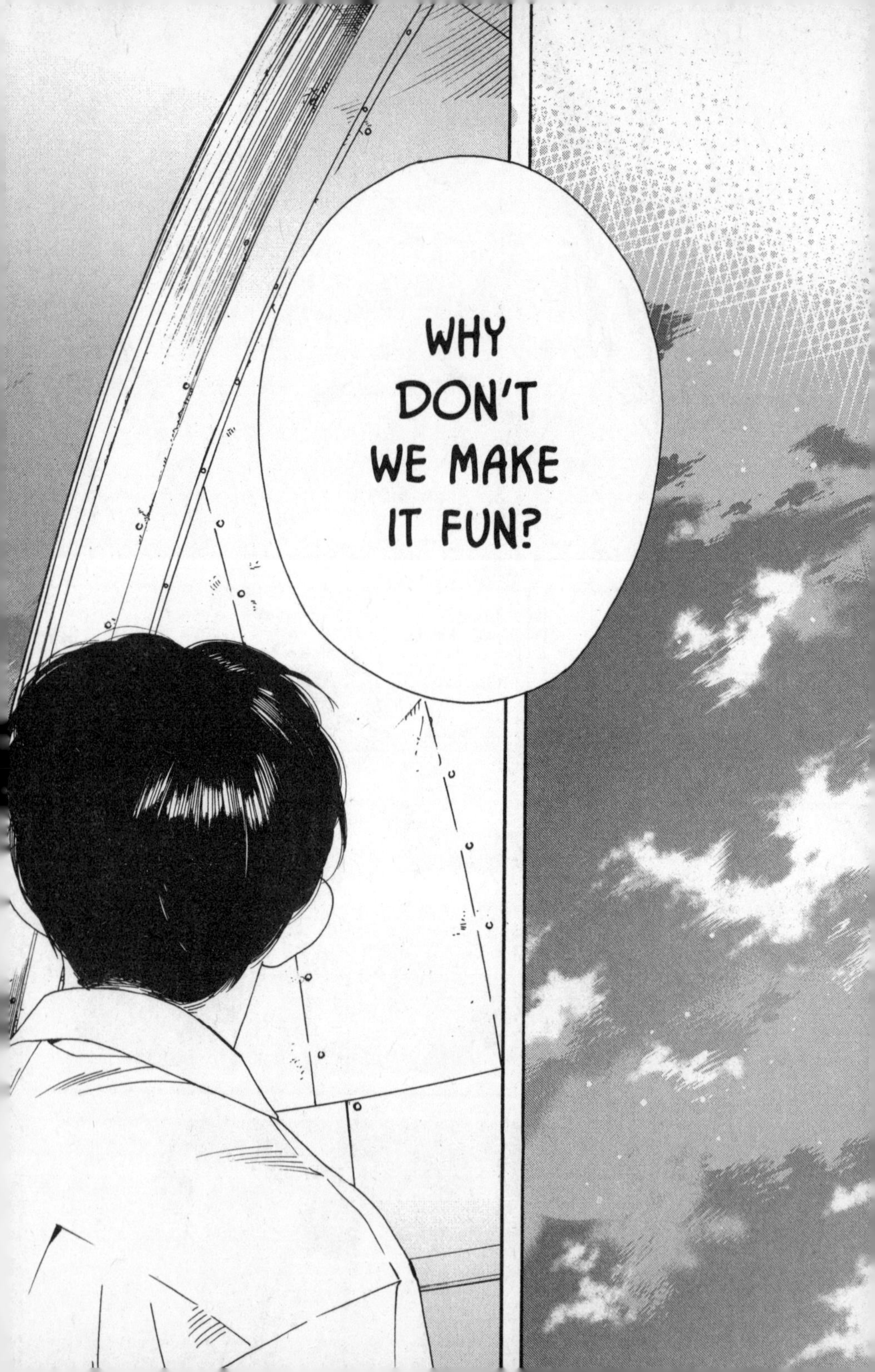
WHY DON'T WE MAKE IT FUN?

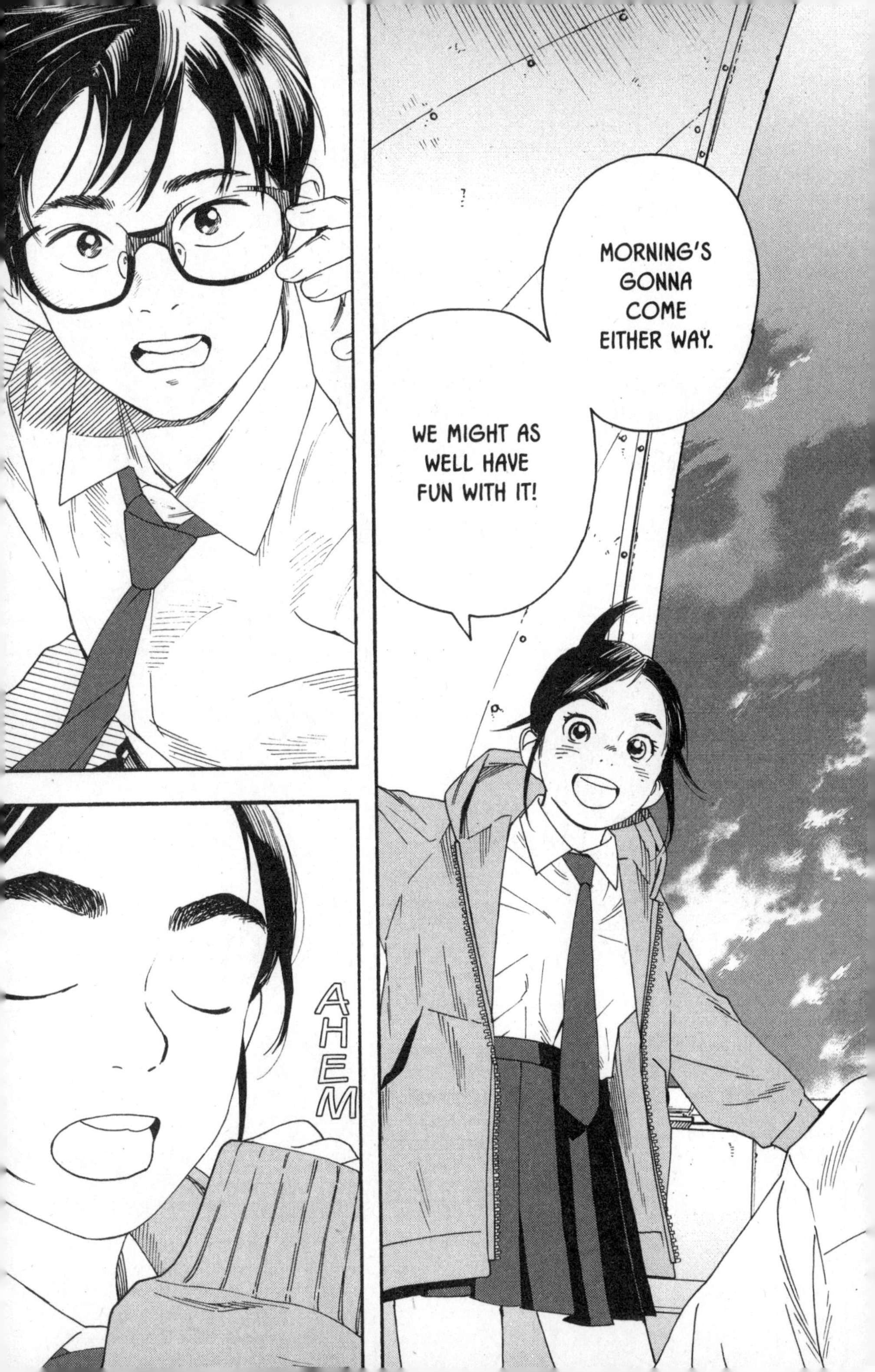
MORNING'S GONNA COME EITHER WAY.
WE MIGHT AS WELL HAVE FUN WITH IT!
AHEM

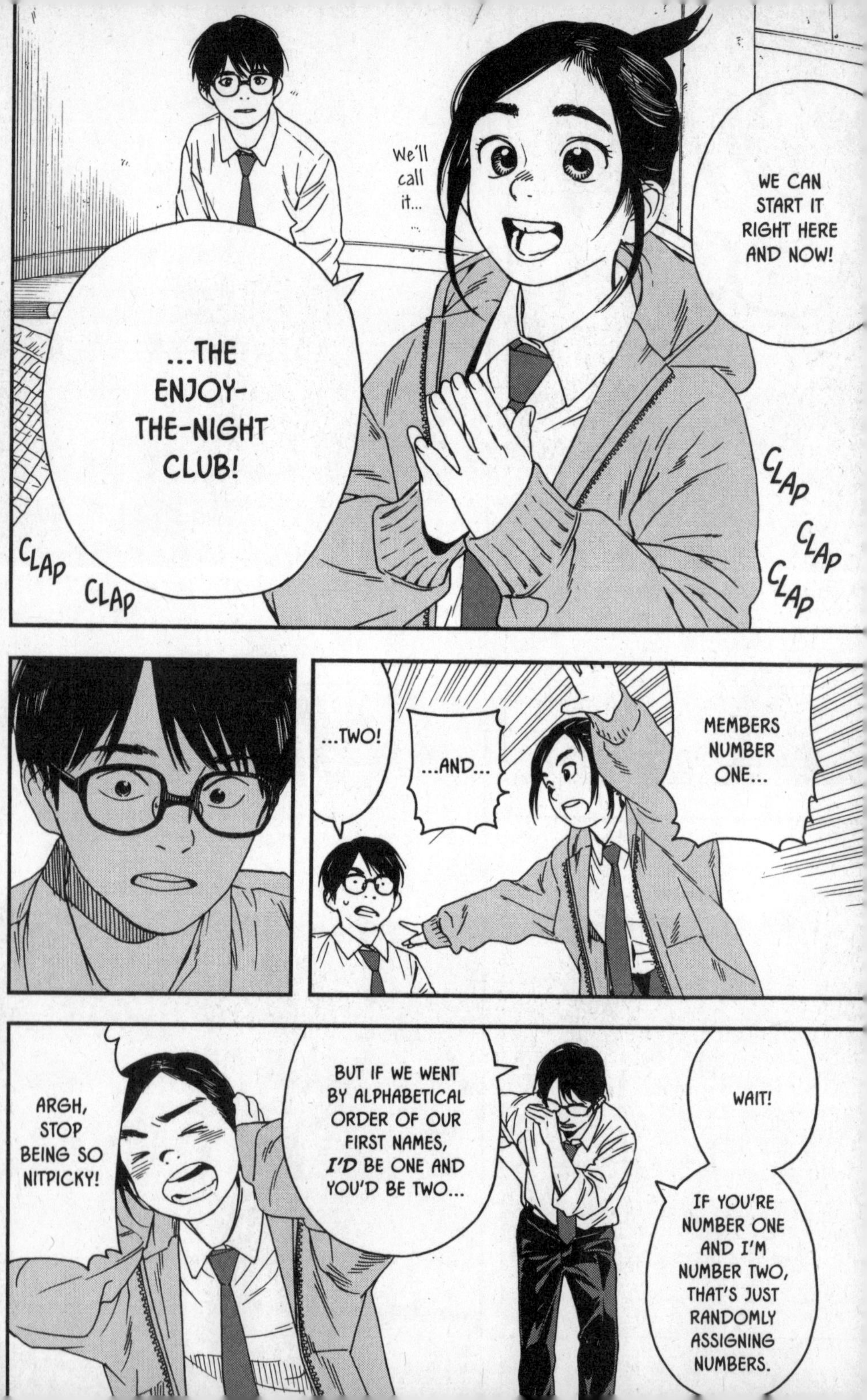
WE CAN START IT RIGHT HERE AND NOW!
We'll call it...
...THE ENJOY-THE-NIGHT CLUB!
CLAP CLAP CLAP
CLAP CLAP
MEMBERS NUMBER ONE...
...AND...
...TWO!
WAIT!
IF YOU'RE NUMBER ONE AND I'M NUMBER TWO, THAT'S JUST RANDOMLY ASSIGNING NUMBERS.
BUT IF WE WENT BY ALPHABETICAL ORDER OF OUR FIRST NAMES, *I'D* BE ONE AND YOU'D BE TWO...
ARGH, STOP BEING SO NITPICKY!

Chapter 3: Dawn Star

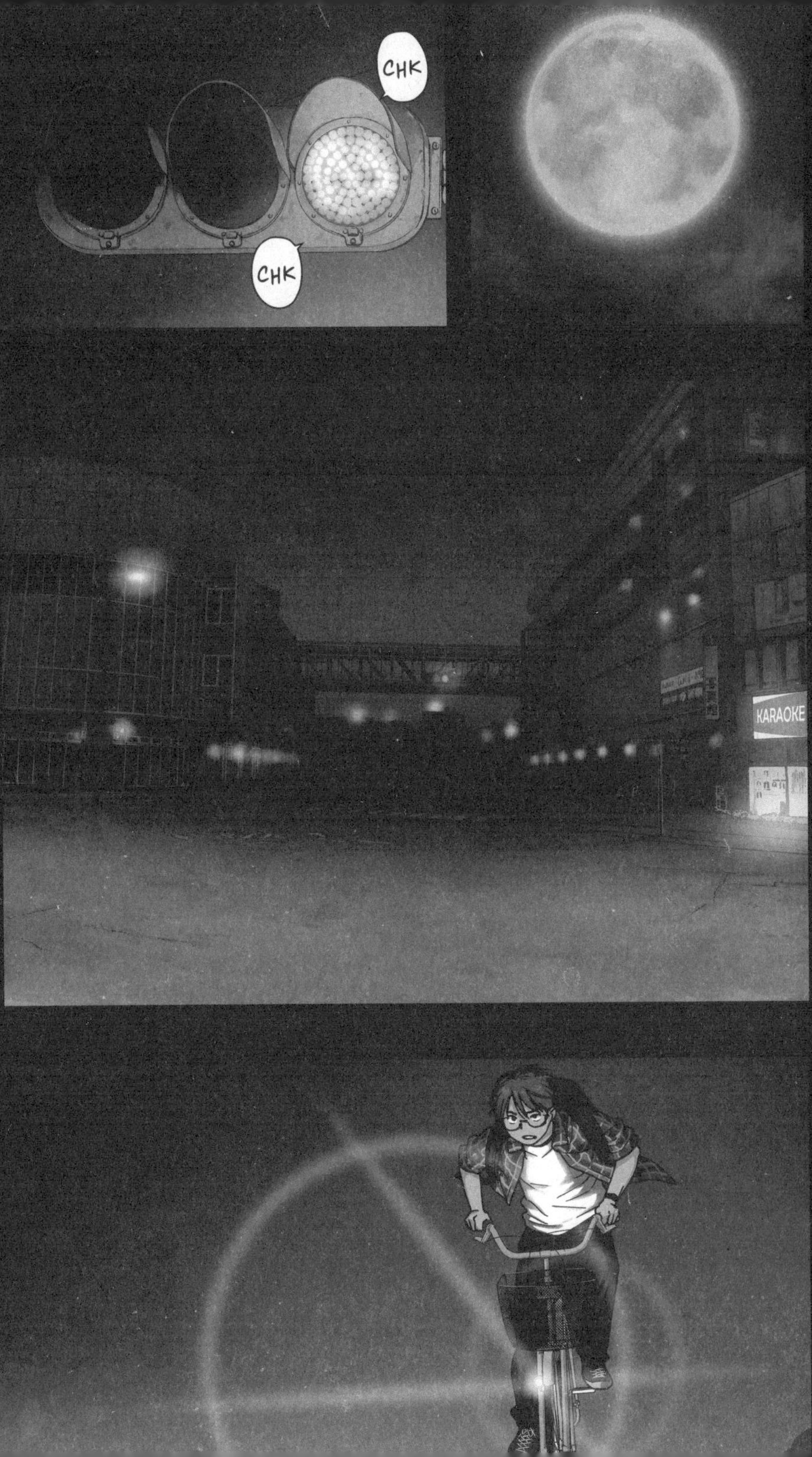
CHK
CHK
KARAOKE

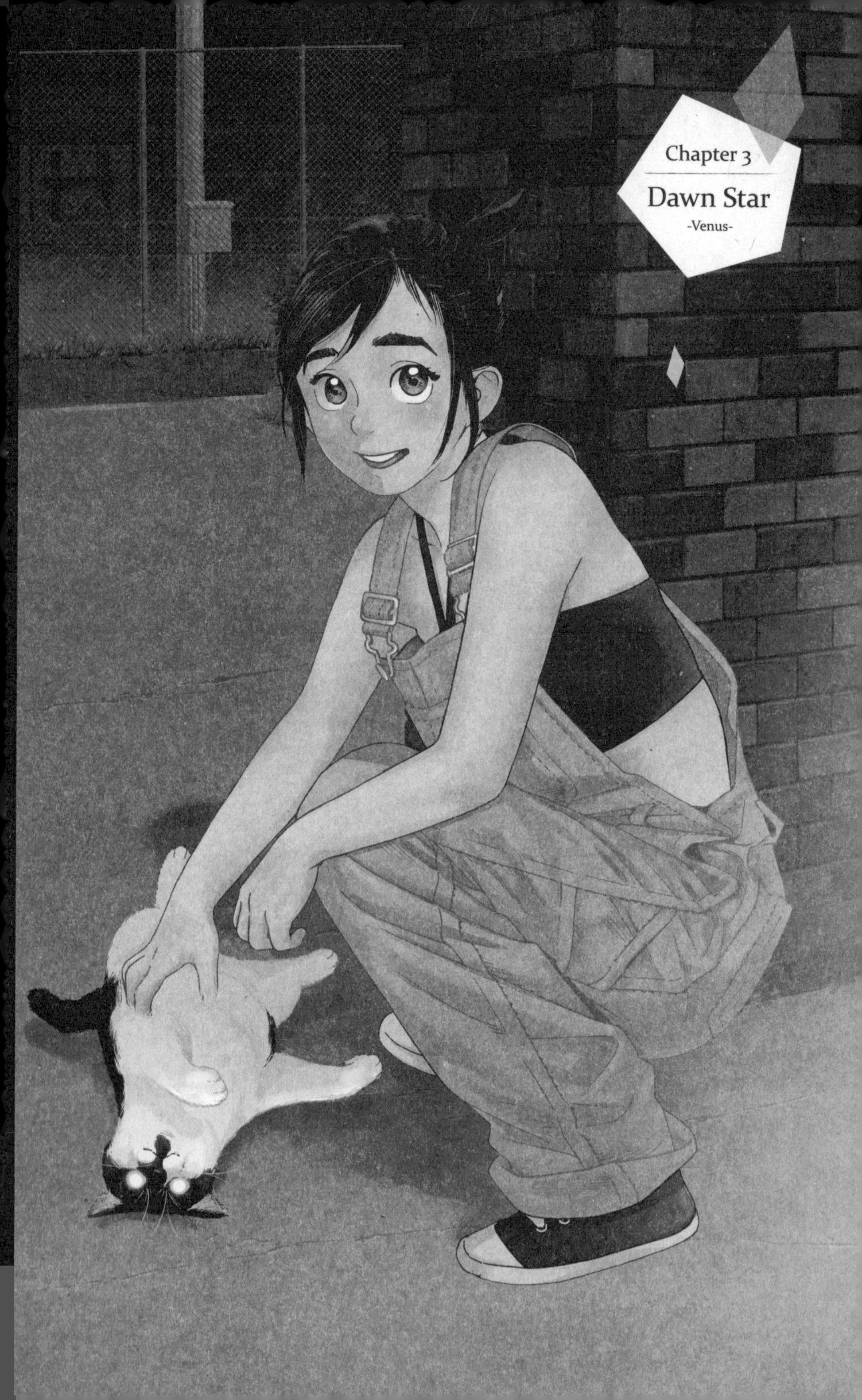
Chapter 3
Dawn Star
-Venus-

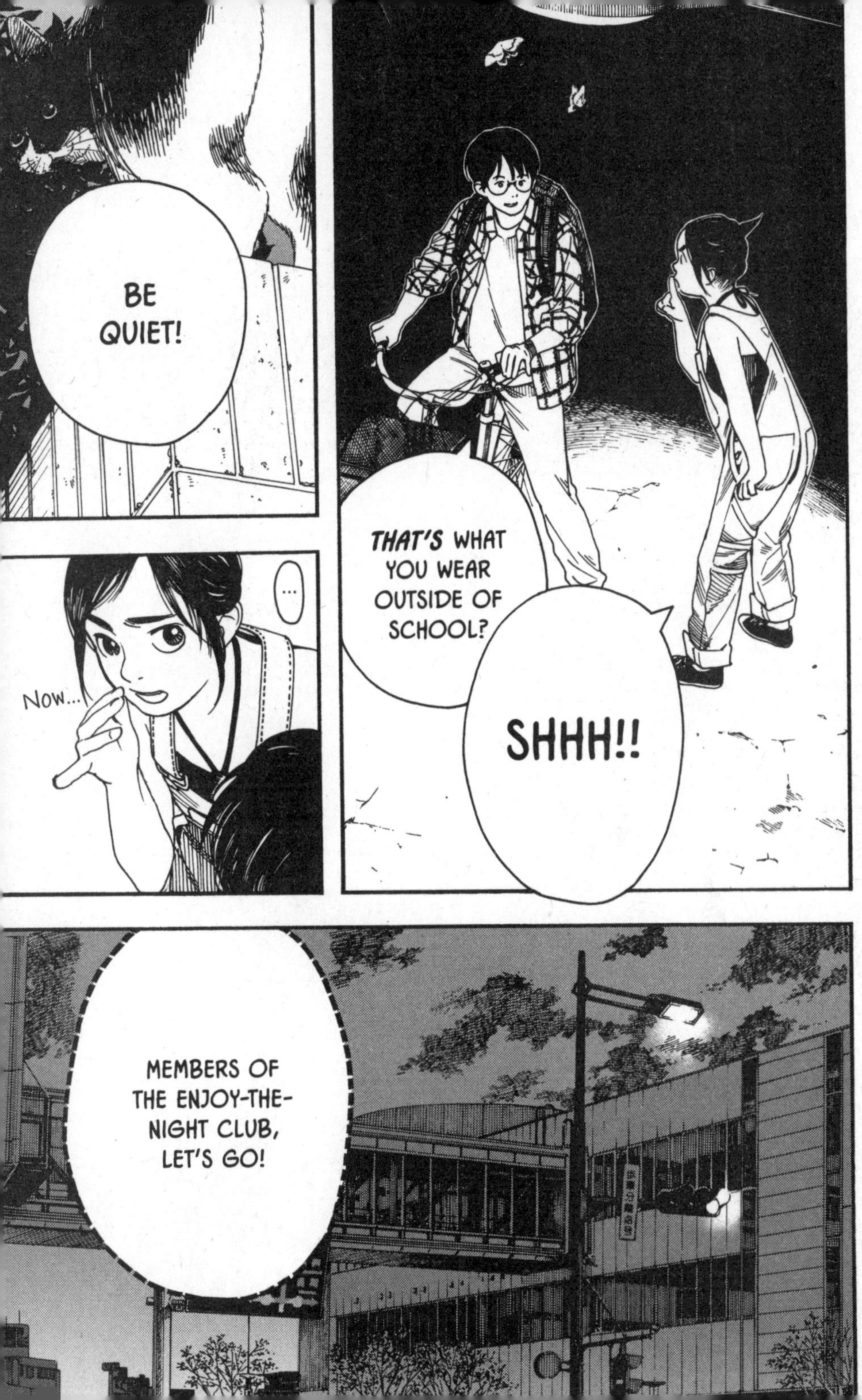
THAT'S WHAT YOU WEAR OUTSIDE OF SCHOOL?
SHHH!!
BE QUIET!
...
Now...
MEMBERS OF THE ENJOY-THE-NIGHT CLUB, LET'S GO!

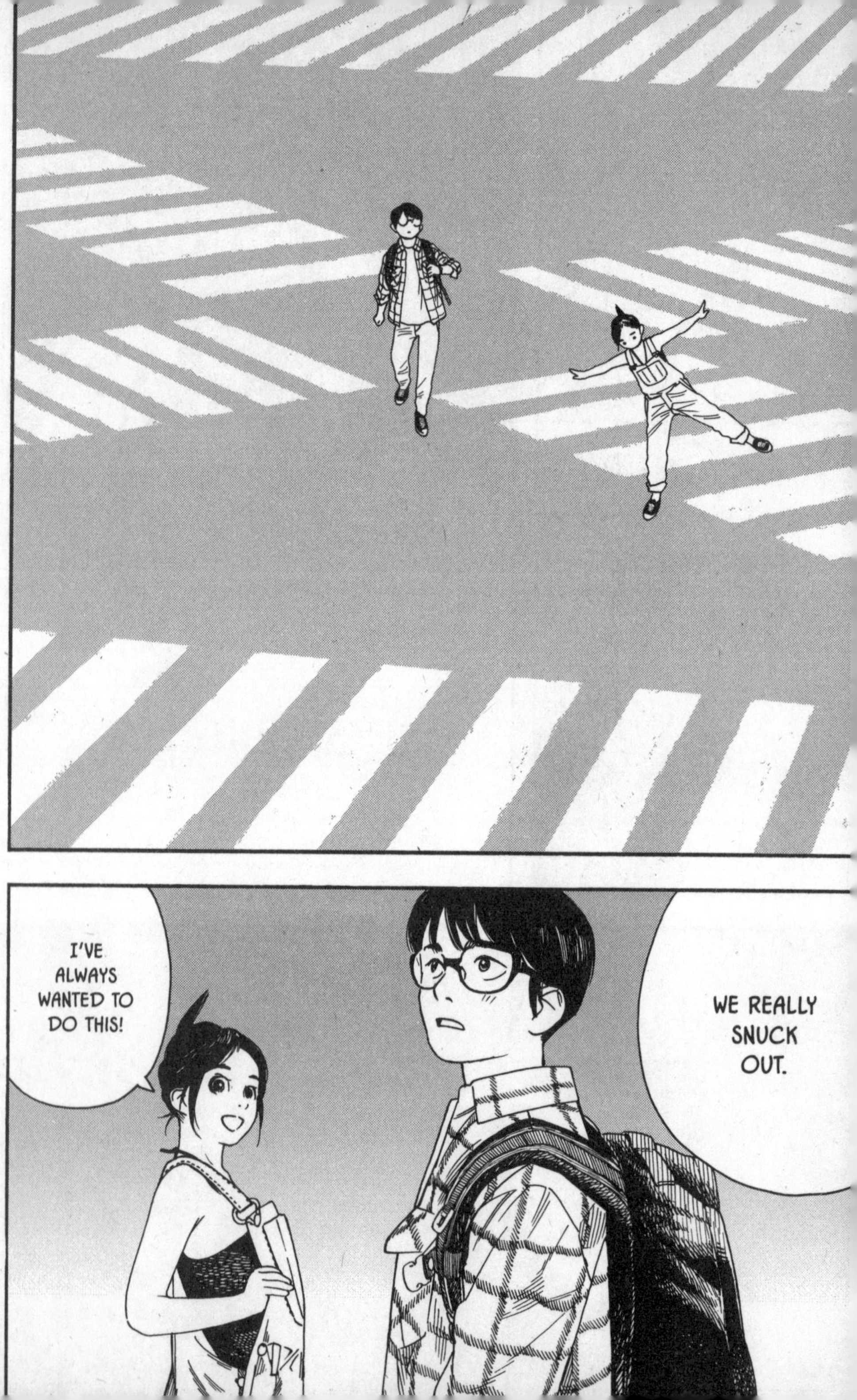
WE REALLY SNUCK OUT.
I'VE ALWAYS WANTED TO DO THIS!

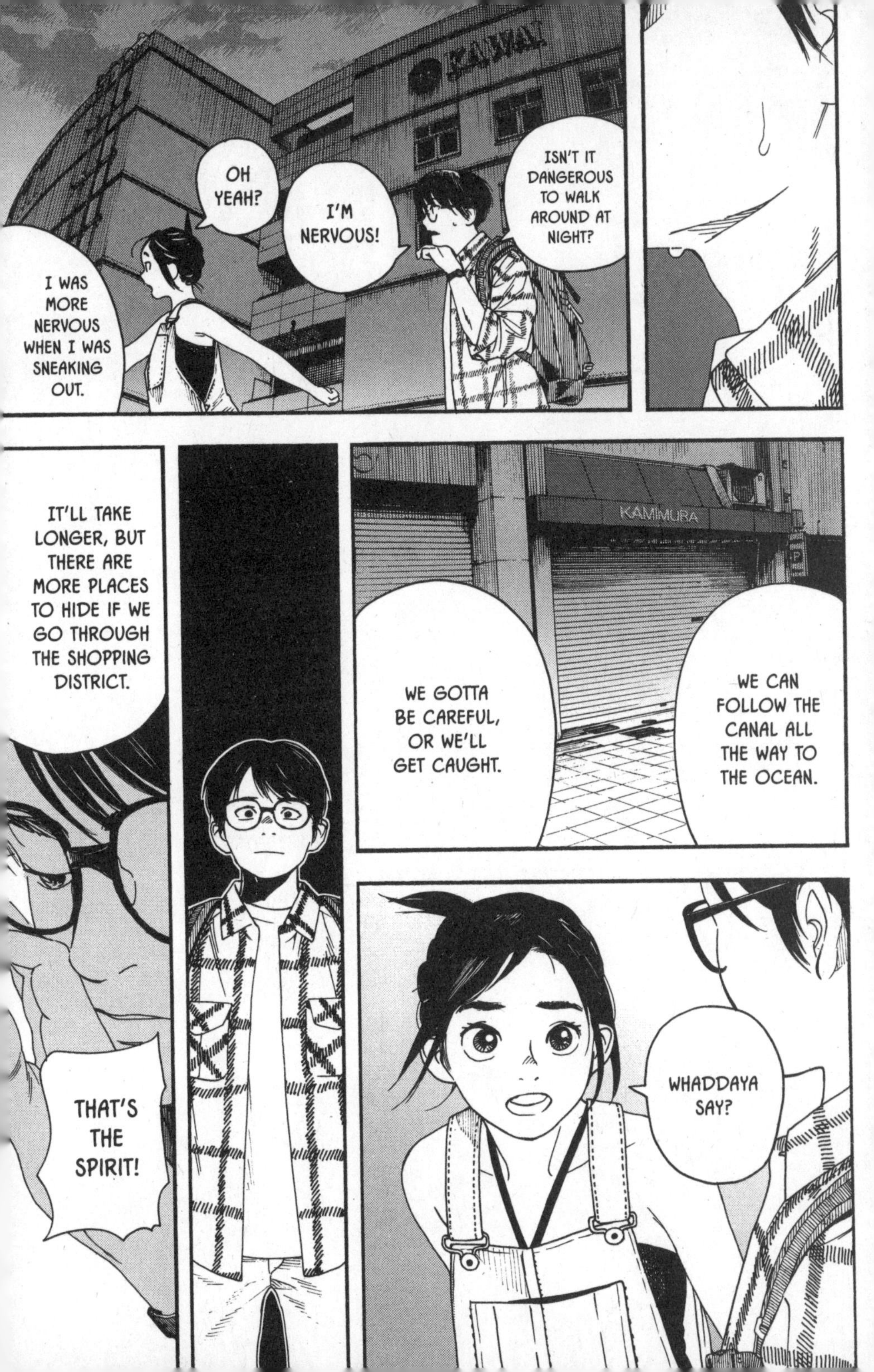
ISN'T IT DANGEROUS TO WALK AROUND AT NIGHT?
I'M NERVOUS!
OH YEAH?
I WAS MORE NERVOUS WHEN I WAS SNEAKING OUT.
KAMIMURA
WE CAN FOLLOW THE CANAL ALL THE WAY TO THE OCEAN.
WE GOTTA BE CAREFUL, OR WE'LL GET CAUGHT.
WHADDAYA SAY?
IT'LL TAKE LONGER, BUT THERE ARE MORE PLACES TO HIDE IF WE GO THROUGH THE SHOPPING DISTRICT.
THAT'S THE SPIRIT!

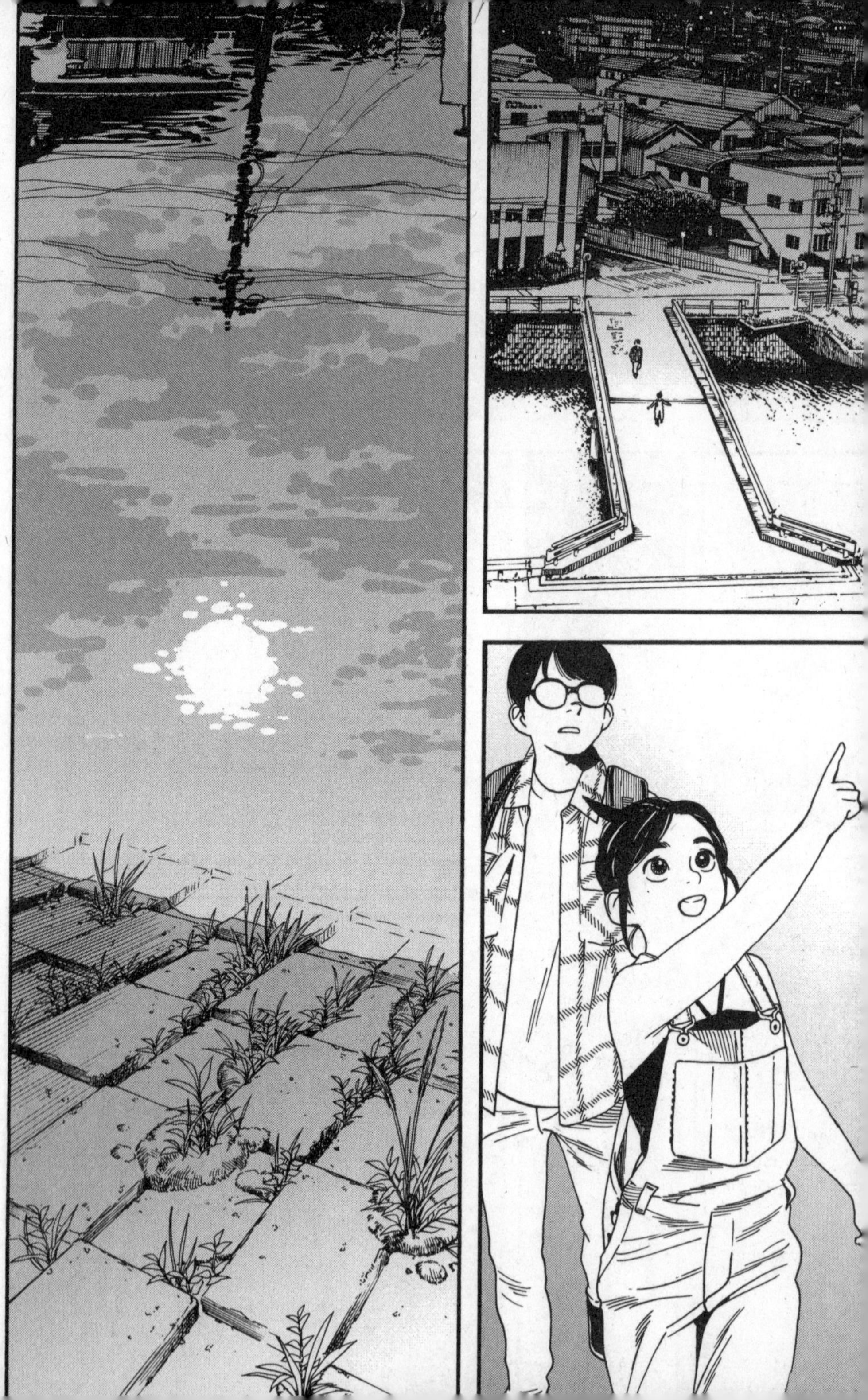

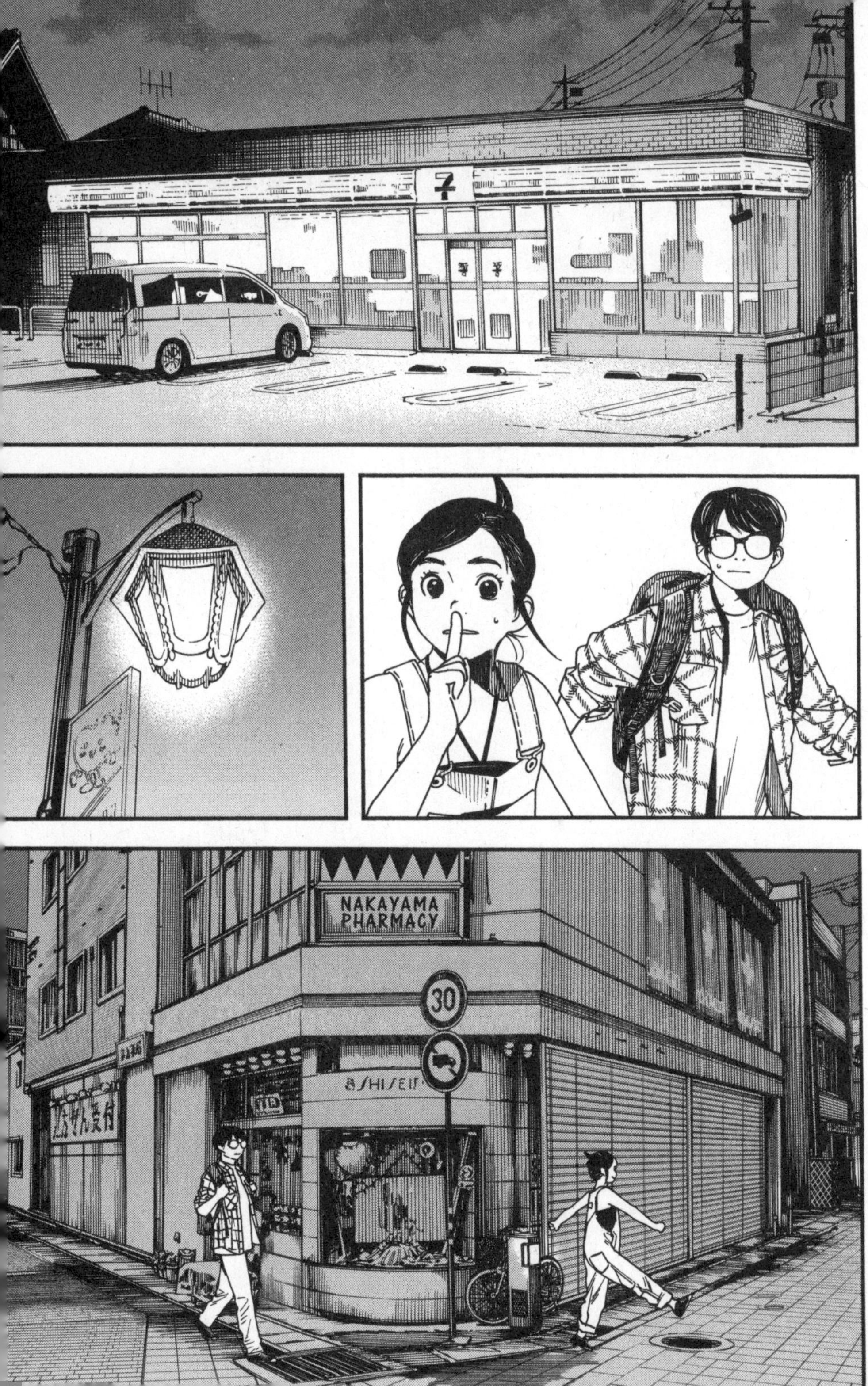
NAKAYAMA
PHARMACY
30

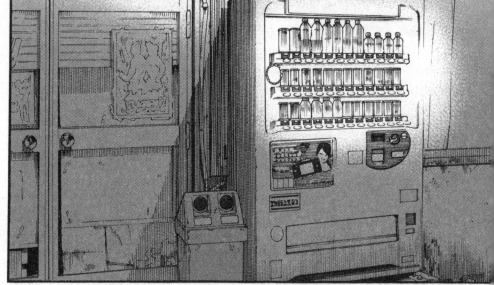

Hmm, what should I pick?

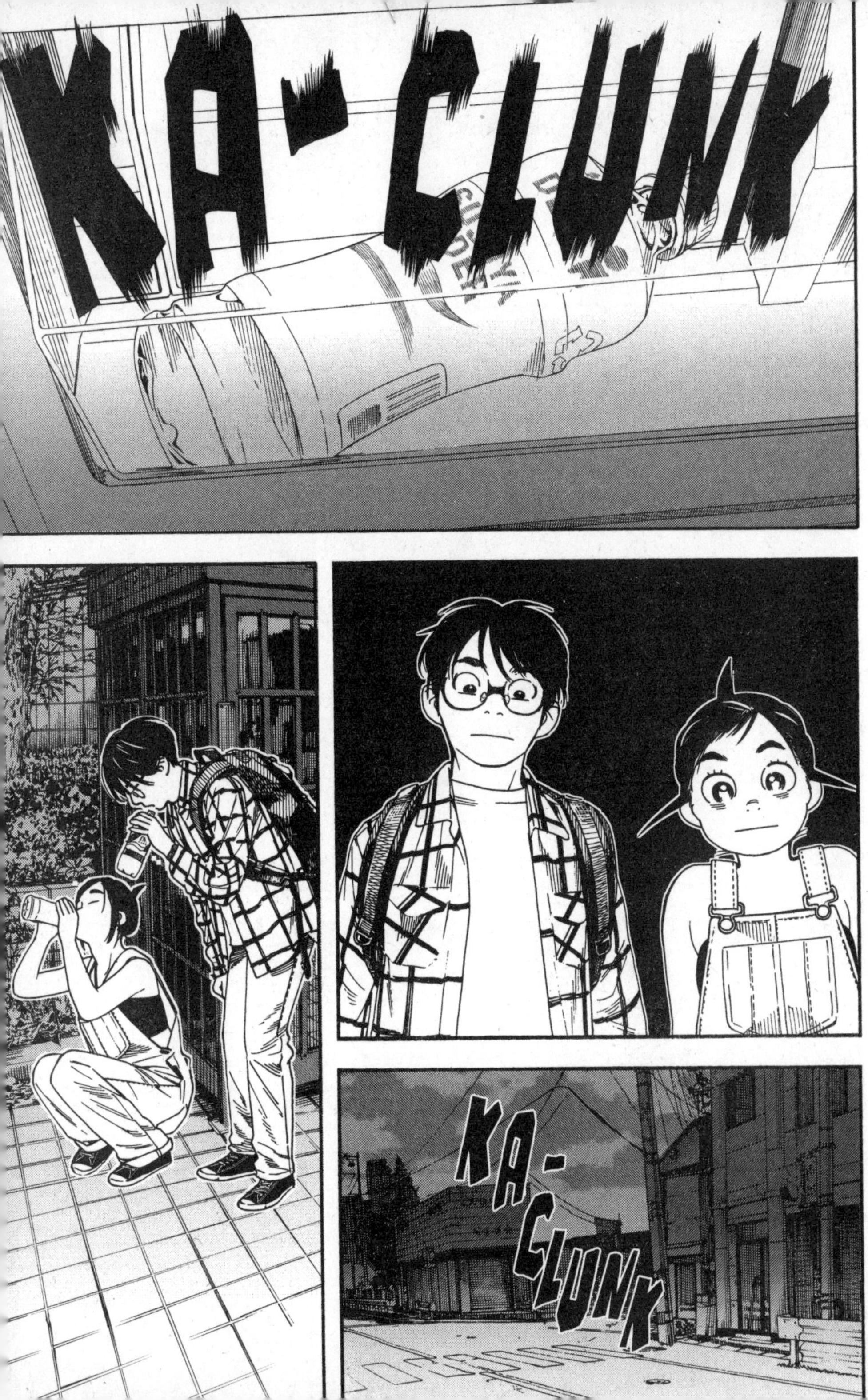
KA-CLUNK
KA-CLUNK

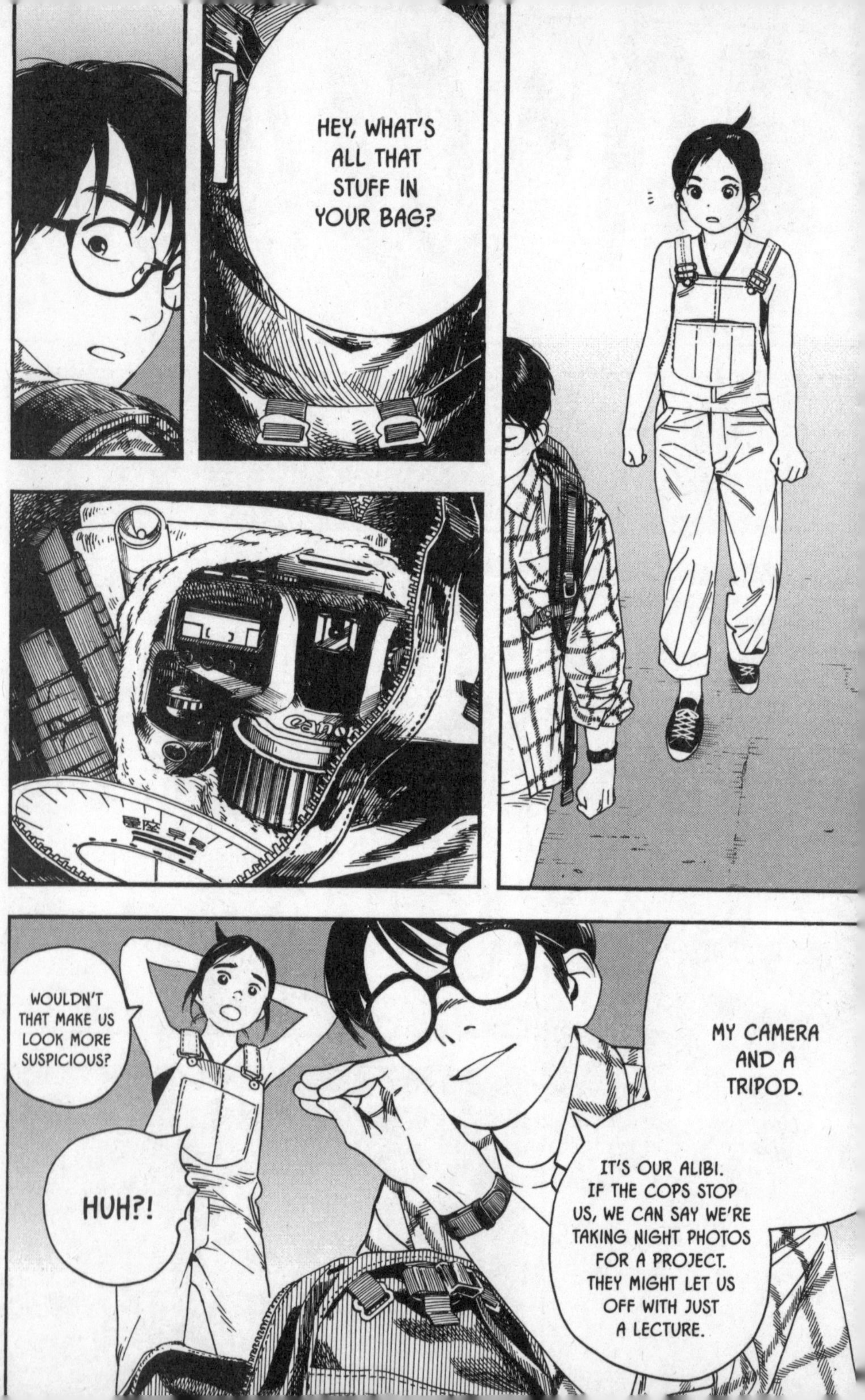
HEY, WHAT'S ALL THAT STUFF IN YOUR BAG?
MY CAMERA AND A TRIPOD.
HUH?!
IT'S OUR ALIBI. IF THE COPS STOP US, WE CAN SAY WE'RE TAKING NIGHT PHOTOS FOR A PROJECT. THEY MIGHT LET US OFF WITH JUST A LECTURE.
WOULDN'T THAT MAKE US LOOK MORE SUSPICIOUS?

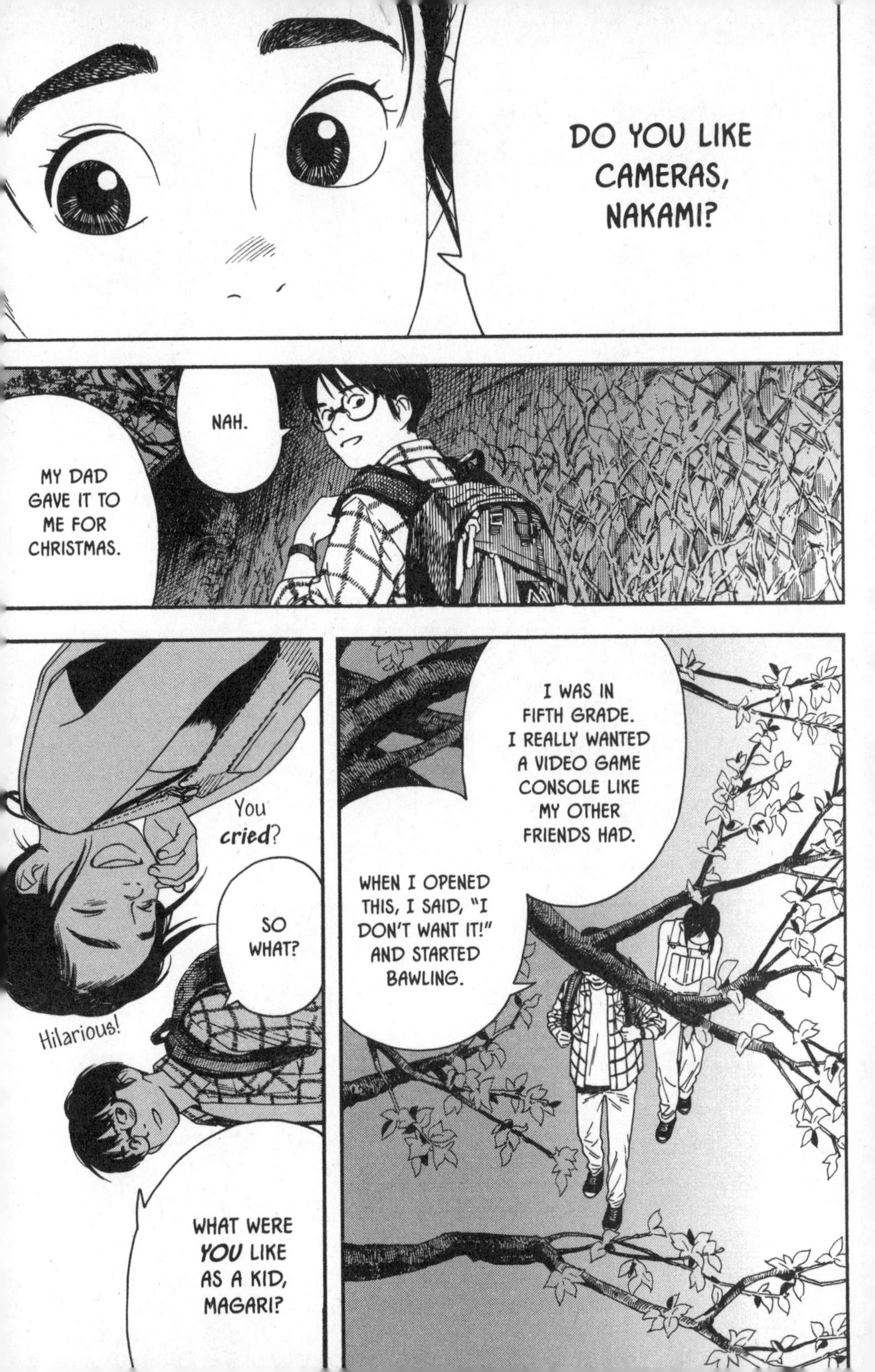
DO YOU LIKE CAMERAS, NAKAMI?
NAH.
MY DAD GAVE IT TO ME FOR CHRISTMAS.
I WAS IN FIFTH GRADE. I REALLY WANTED A VIDEO GAME CONSOLE LIKE MY OTHER FRIENDS HAD.
WHEN I OPENED THIS, I SAID, "I DON'T WANT IT!" AND STARTED BAWLING.
You *cried*?
SO WHAT?
Hilarious!
WHAT WERE *YOU* LIKE AS A KID, MAGARI?

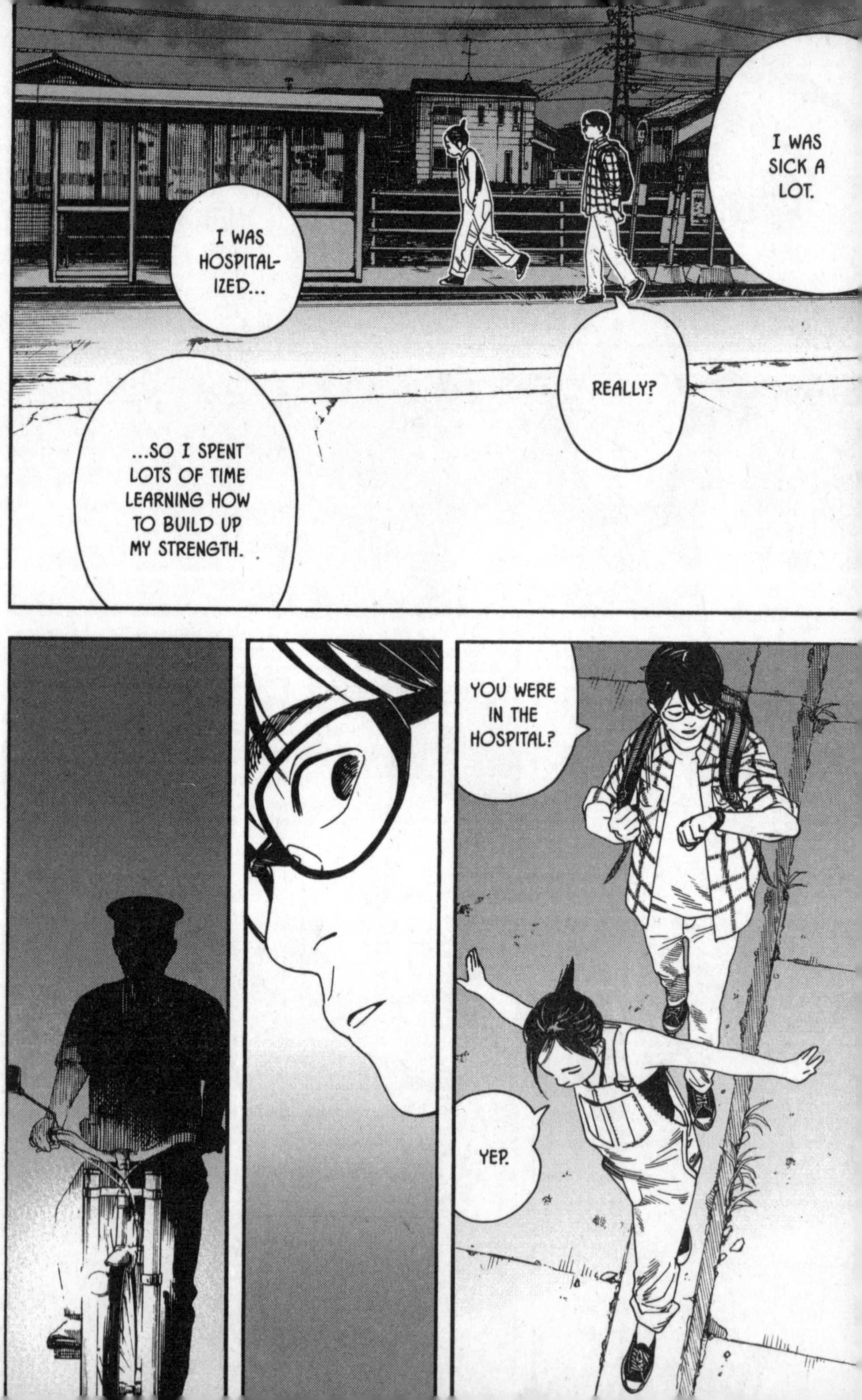
I WAS SICK A LOT.
REALLY?
I WAS HOSPITALIZED...
...SO I SPENT LOTS OF TIME LEARNING HOW TO BUILD UP MY STRENGTH.
YOU WERE IN THE HOSPITAL?
YEP.

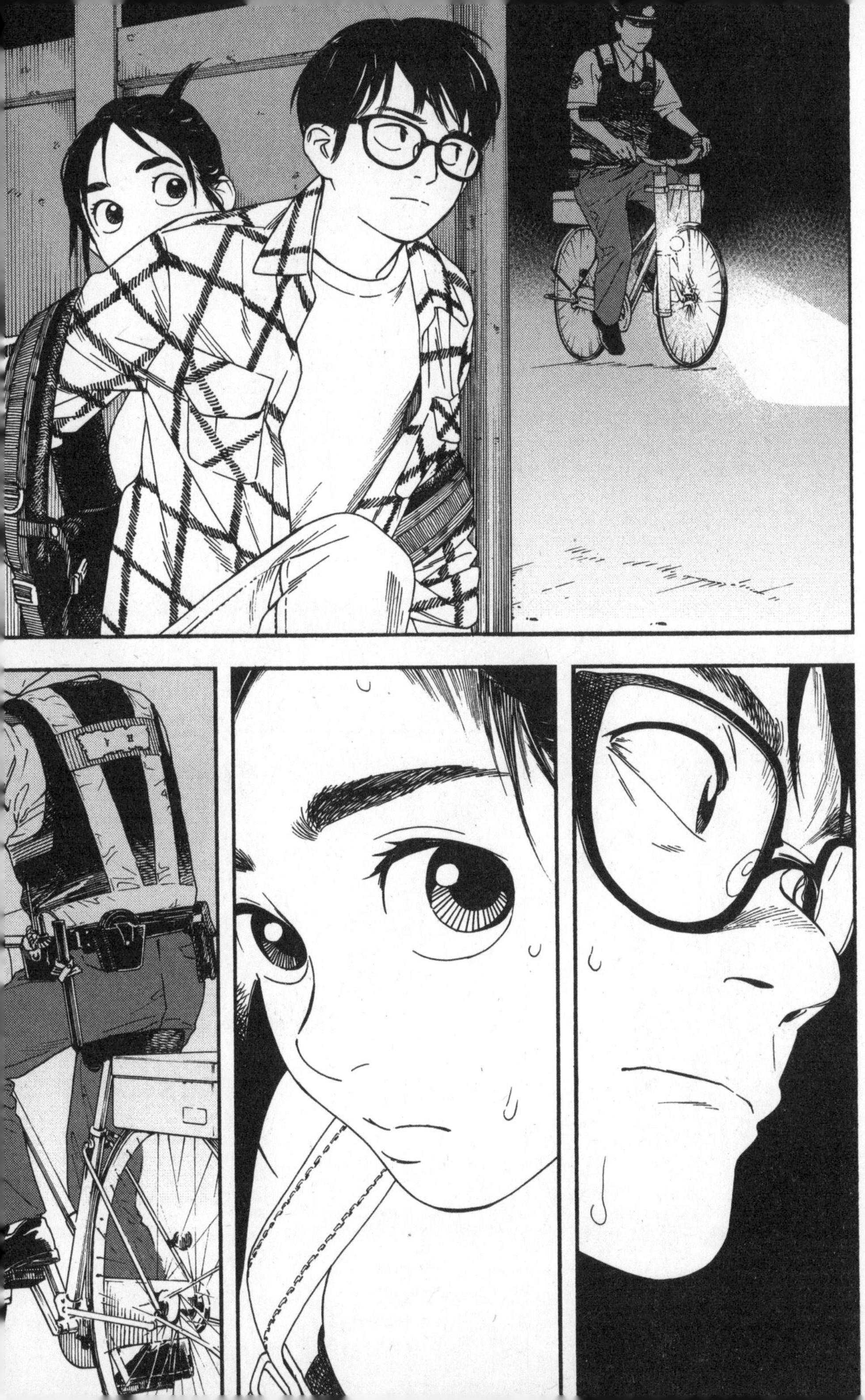

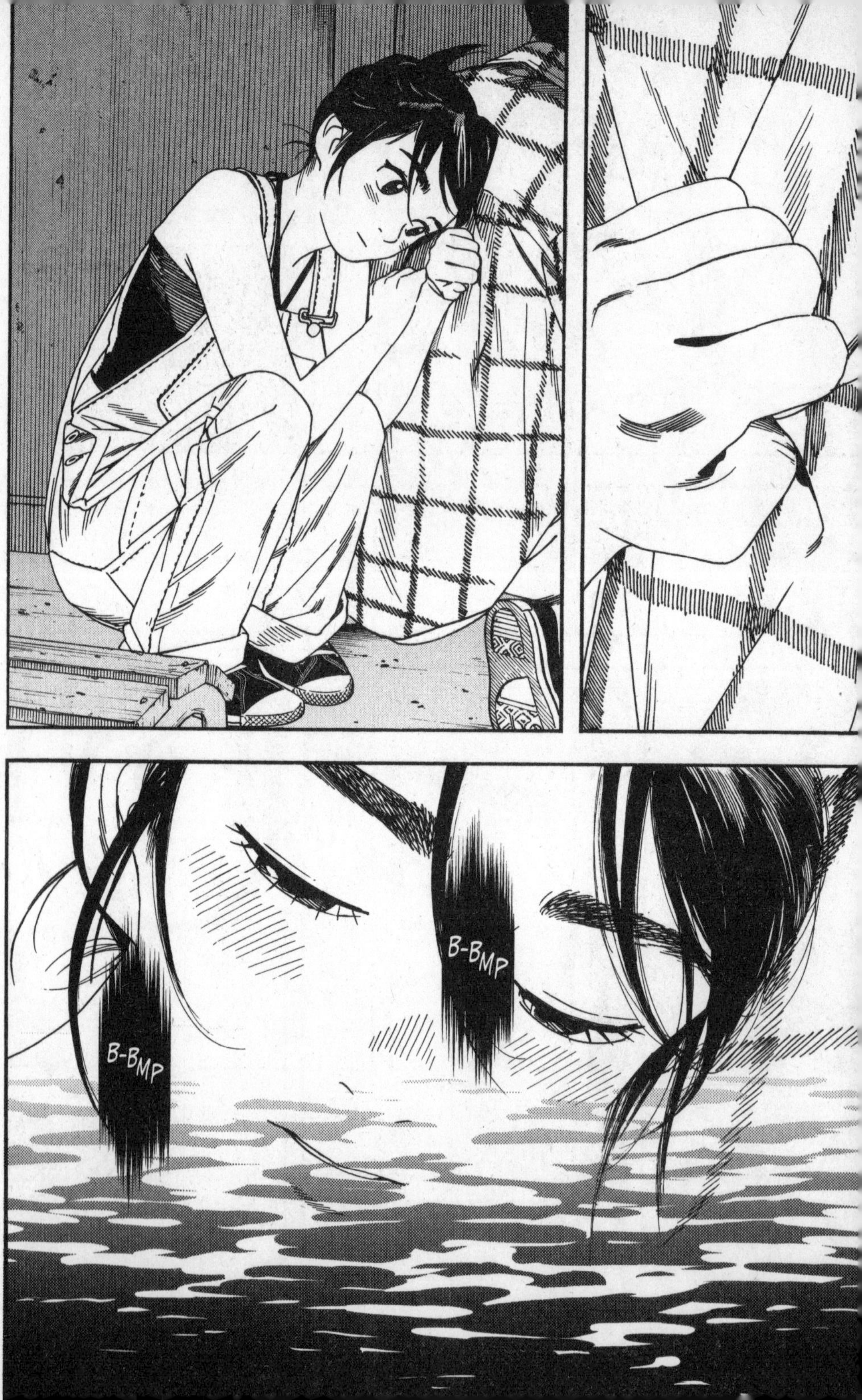
B-BMP
B-BMP

YOU OKAY?

MAGARI...

HE'S GONE.

MY HEART'S STILL POUNDING LIKE CRAZY...

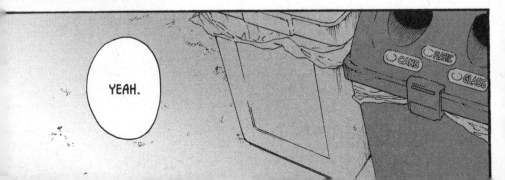

YEAH.

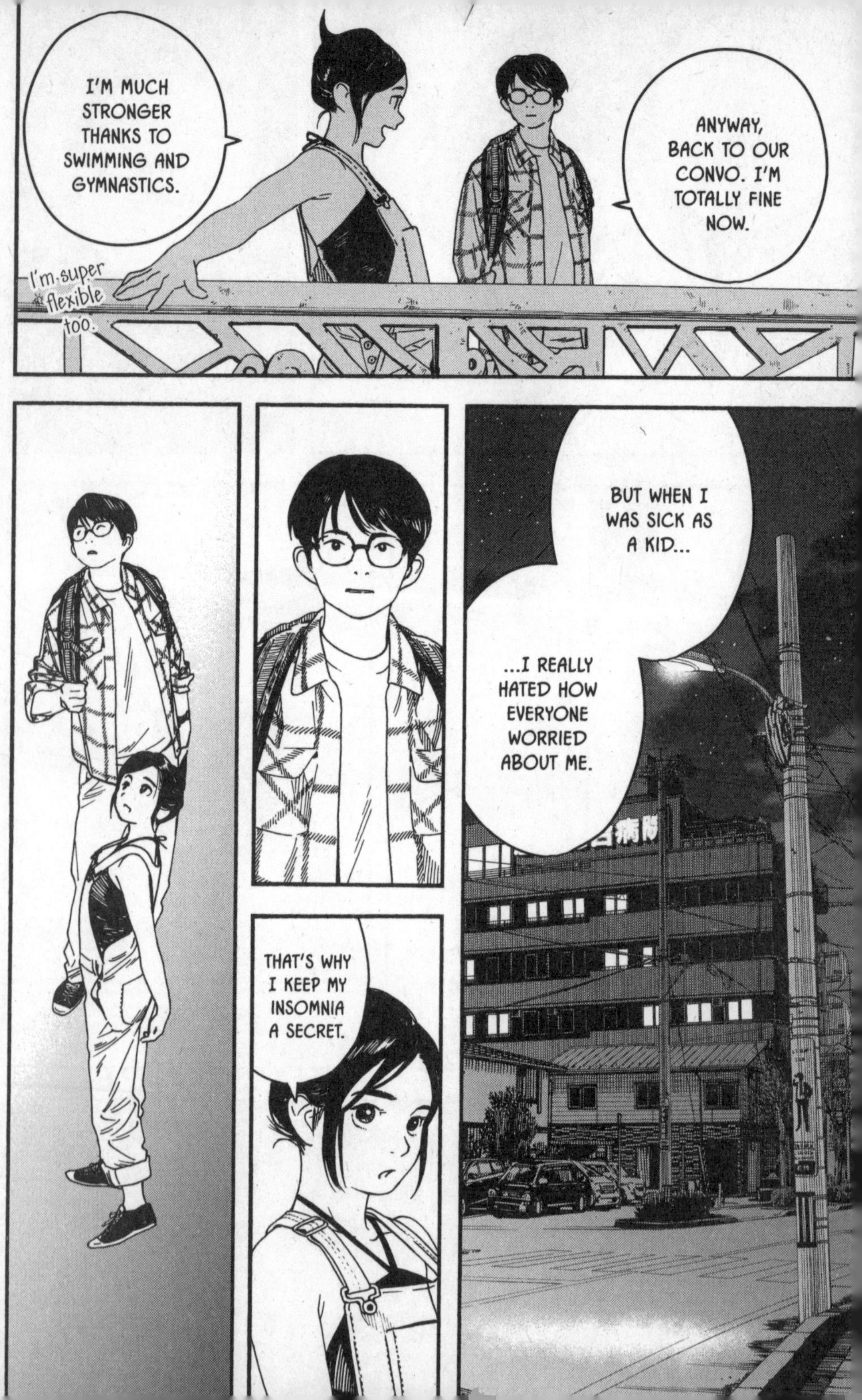
ANYWAY, BACK TO OUR CONVO. I'M TOTALLY FINE NOW.
I'M MUCH STRONGER THANKS TO SWIMMING AND GYMNASTICS.
I'm super flexible too.
BUT WHEN I WAS SICK AS A KID...
...I REALLY HATED HOW EVERYONE WORRIED ABOUT ME.
THAT'S WHY I KEEP MY INSOMNIA A SECRET.

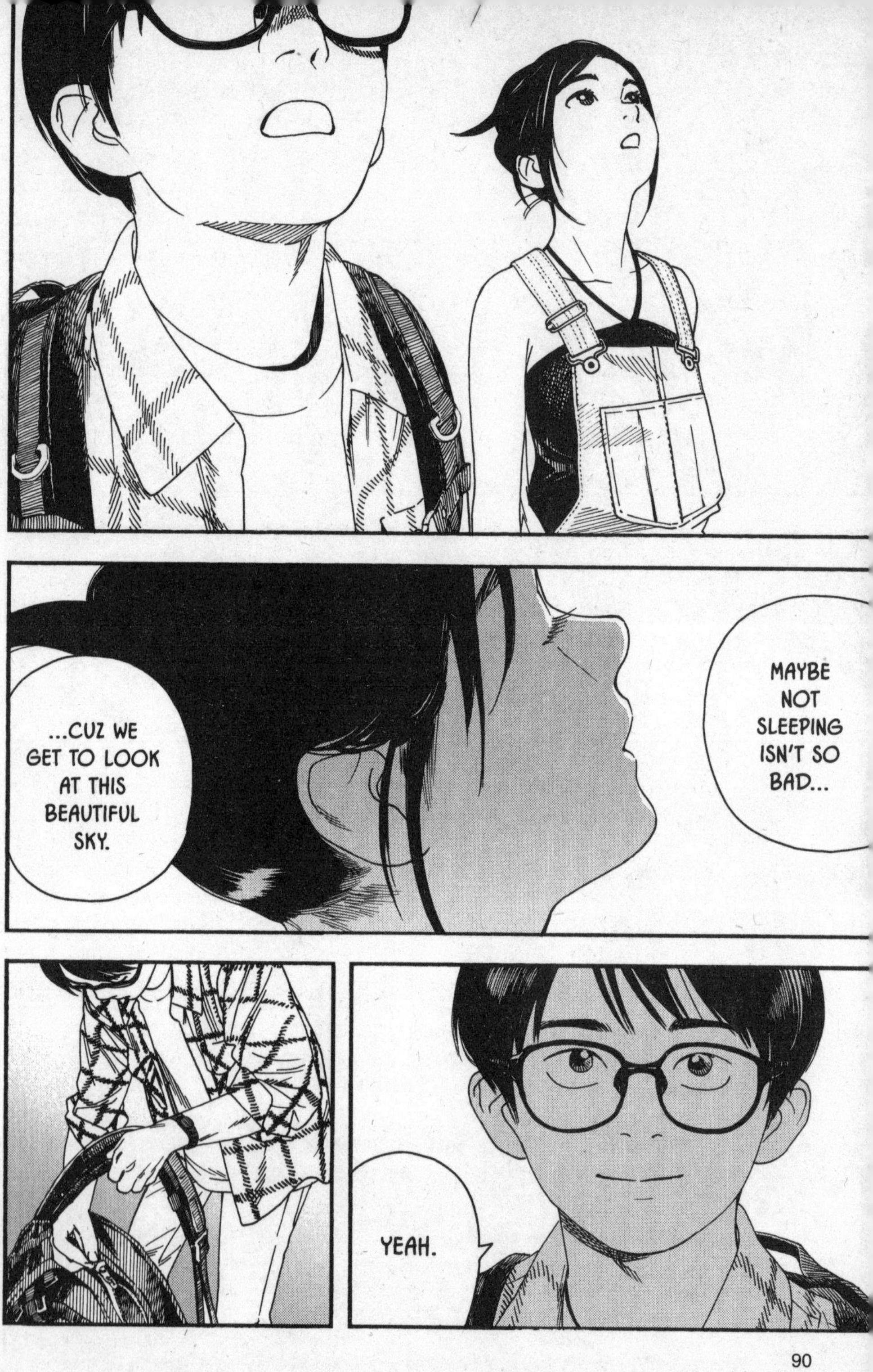
MAYBE NOT SLEEPING ISN'T SO BAD...
...CUZ WE GET TO LOOK AT THIS BEAUTIFUL SKY.
YEAH.

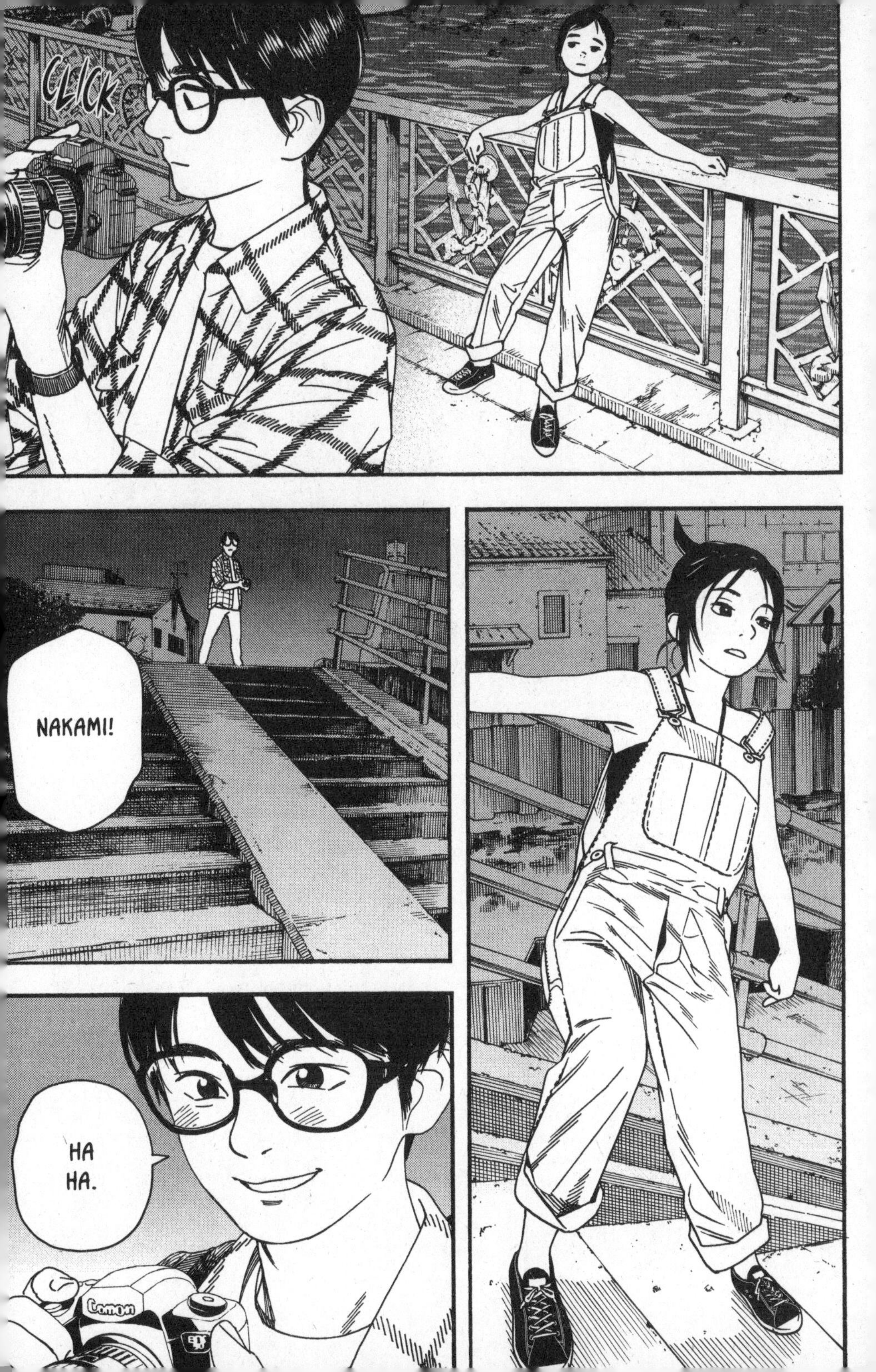
CLICK
NAKAMI!
HA HA.

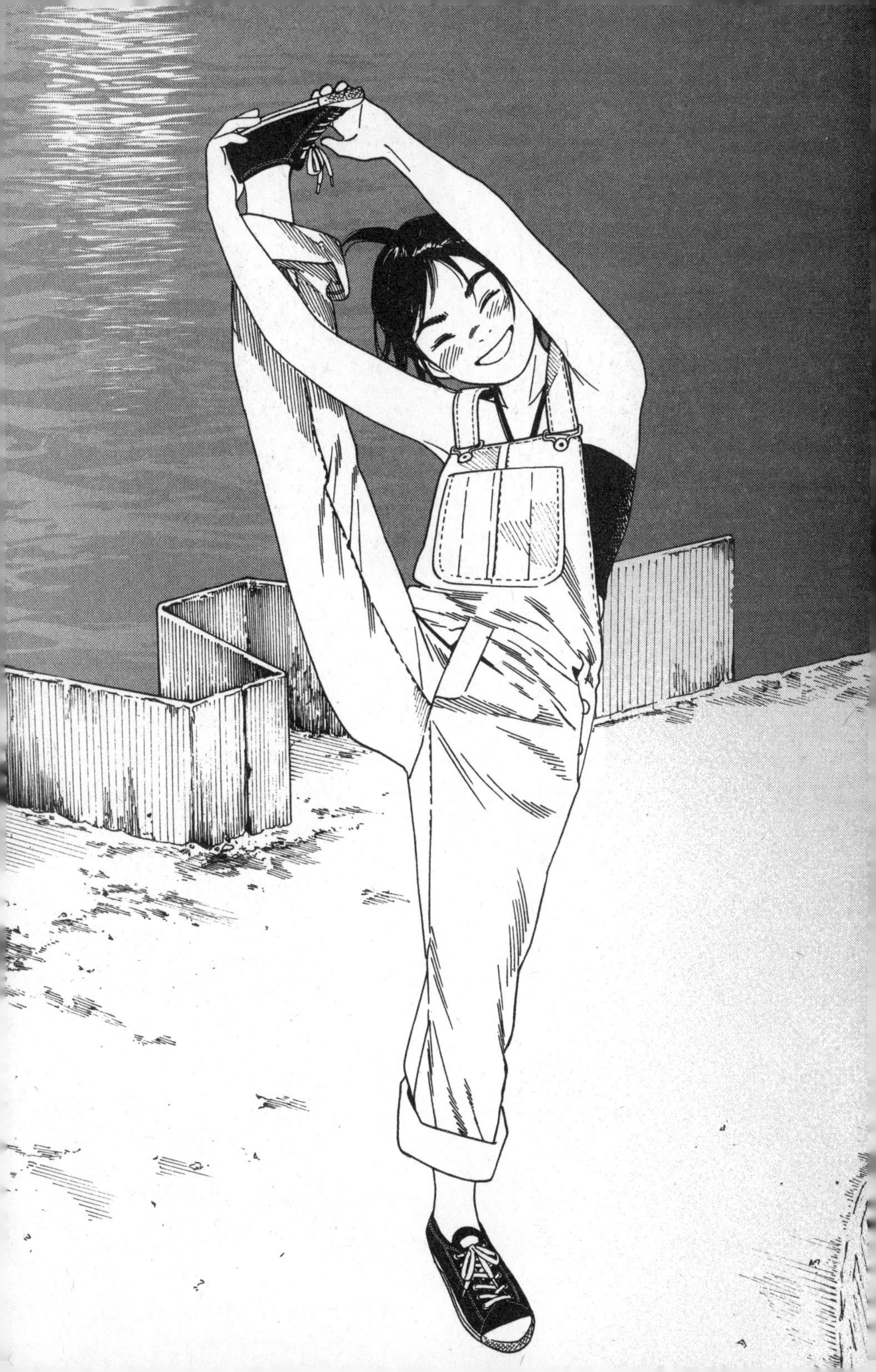

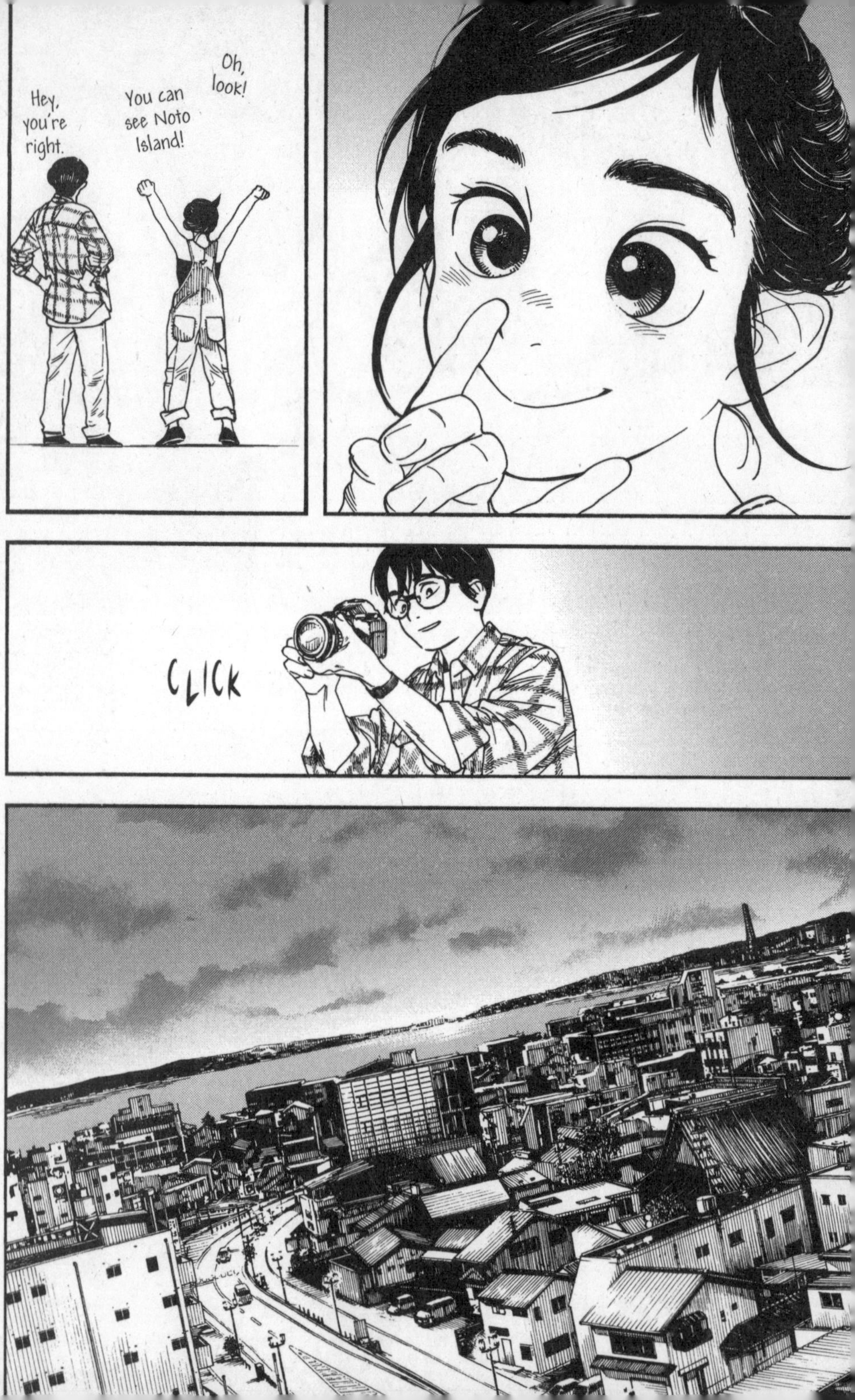
Oh, look!
You can see Noto Island!
Hey, you're right.
CLICK

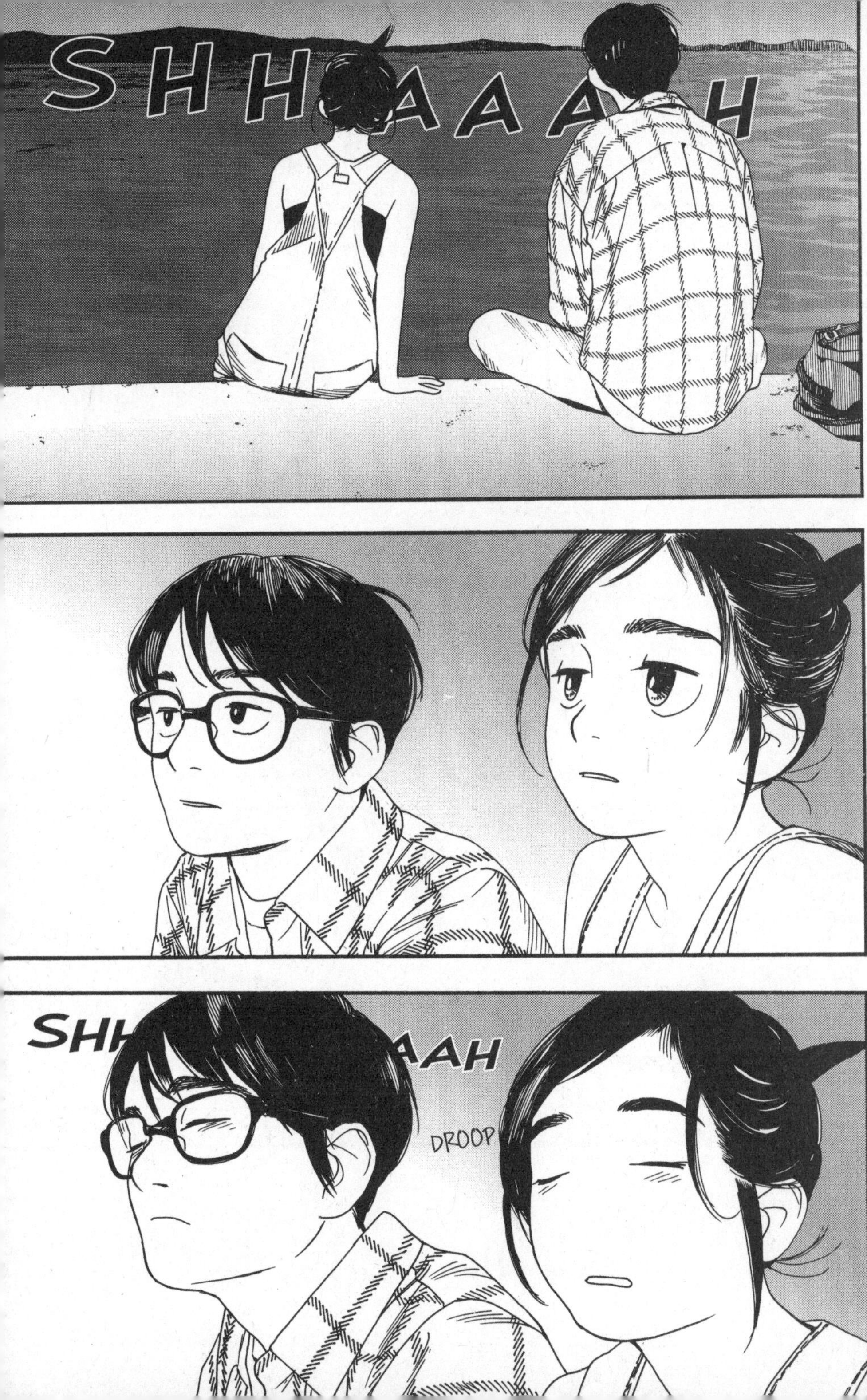
SHHAAAAH
SHHAAH
DROOP

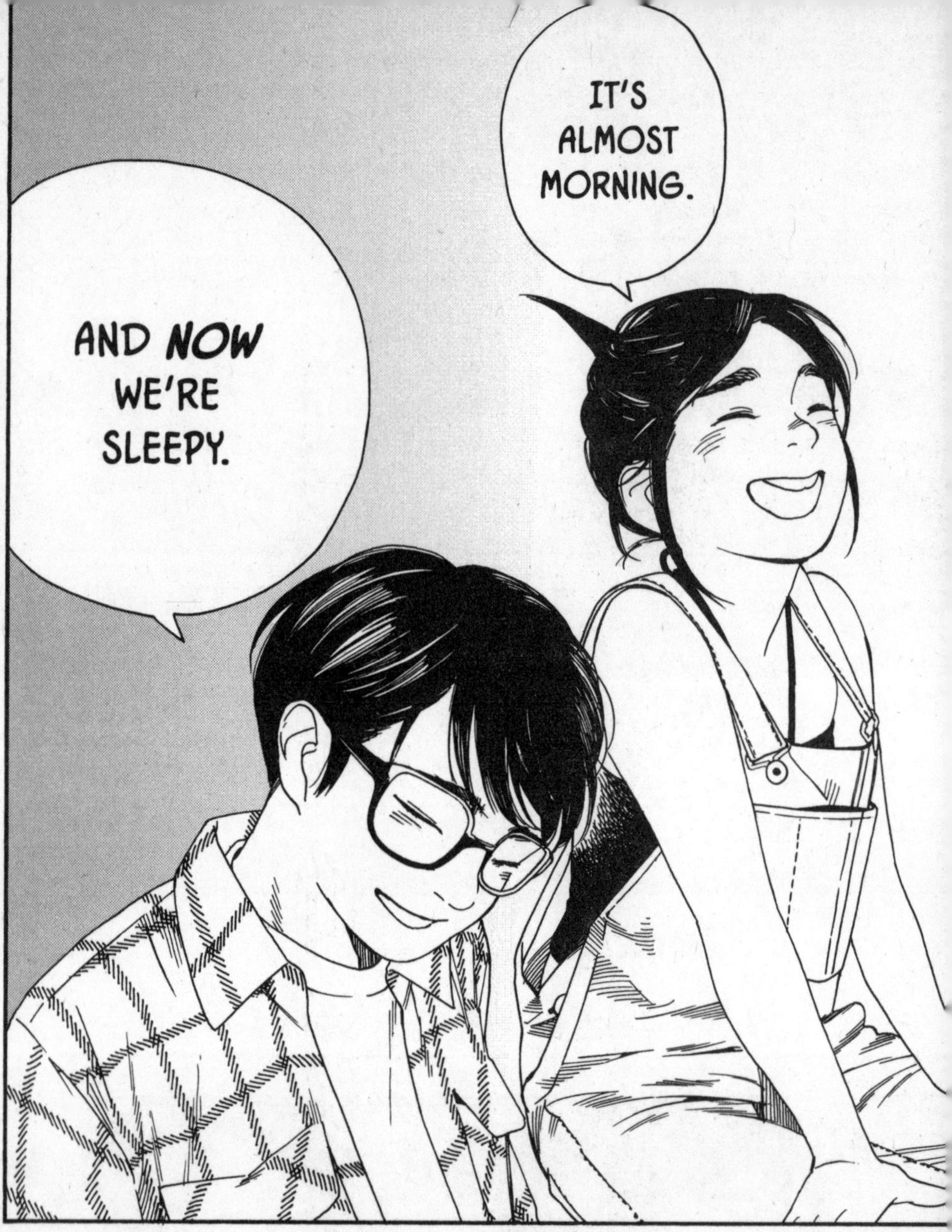
IT'S ALMOST MORNING.
AND *NOW* WE'RE SLEEPY.

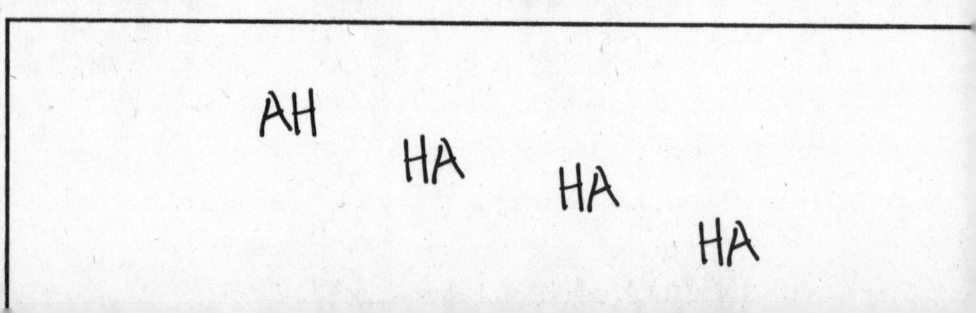
AH HA HA HA

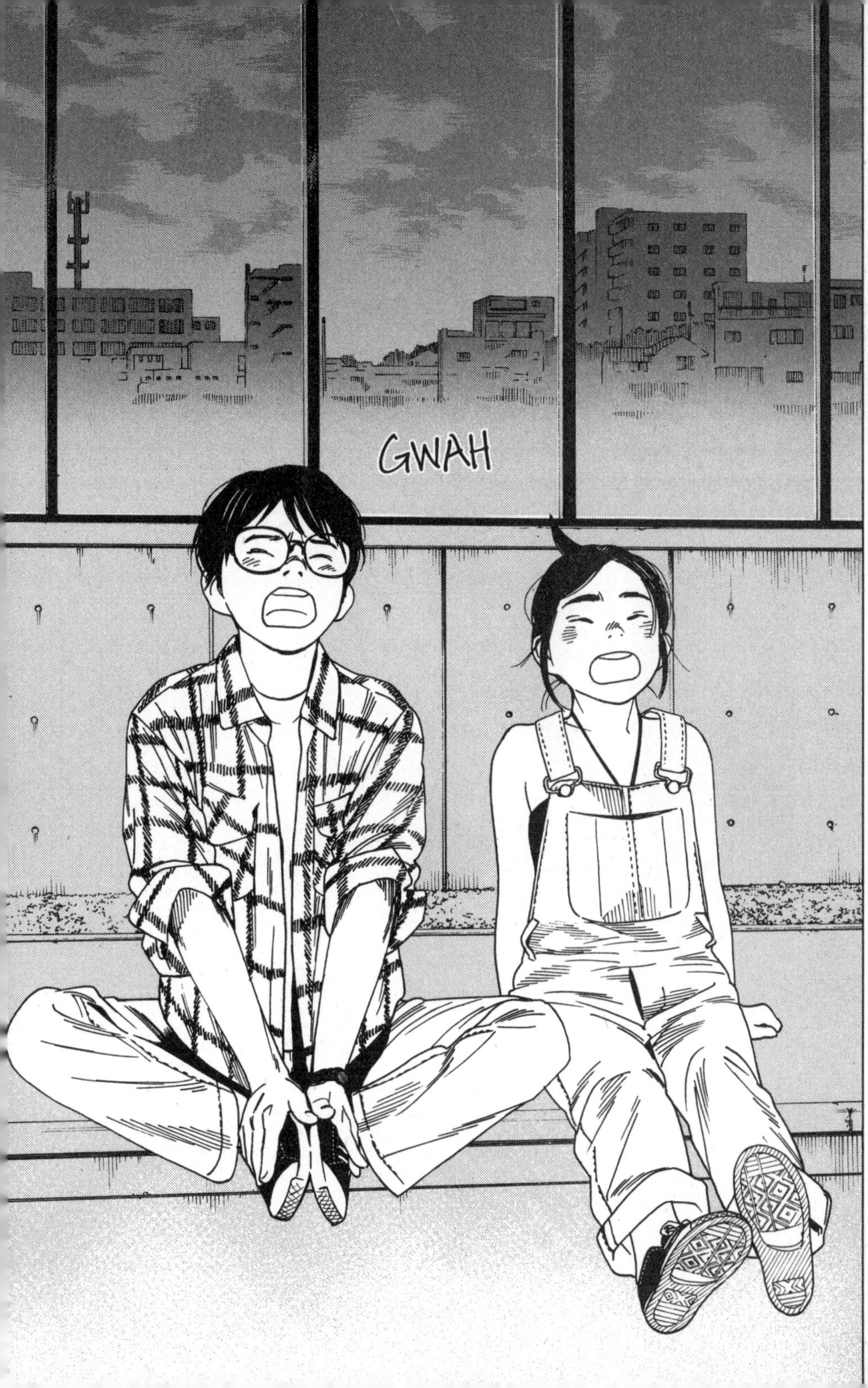
GWAH

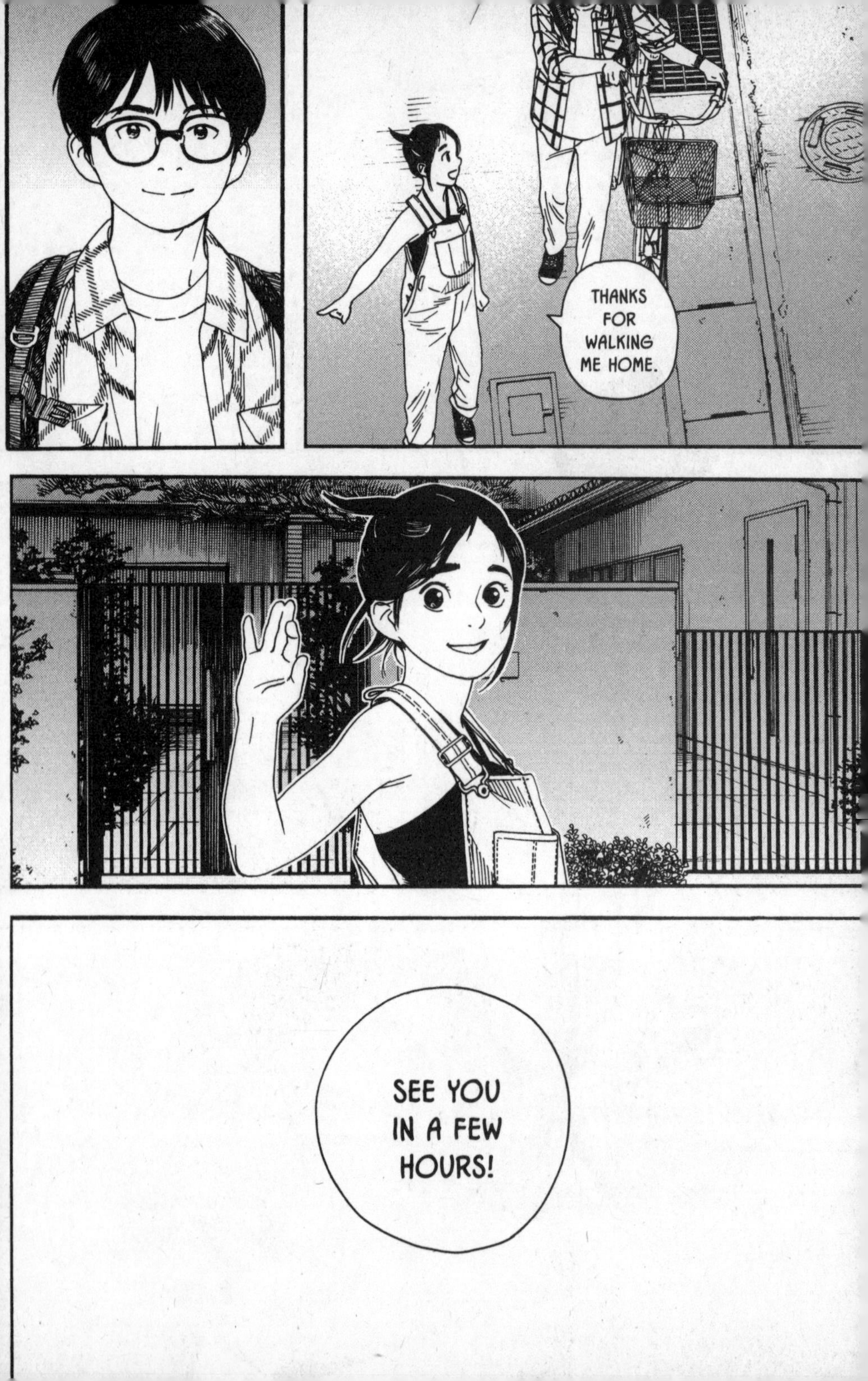
THANKS FOR WALKING ME HOME.
SEE YOU IN A FEW HOURS!

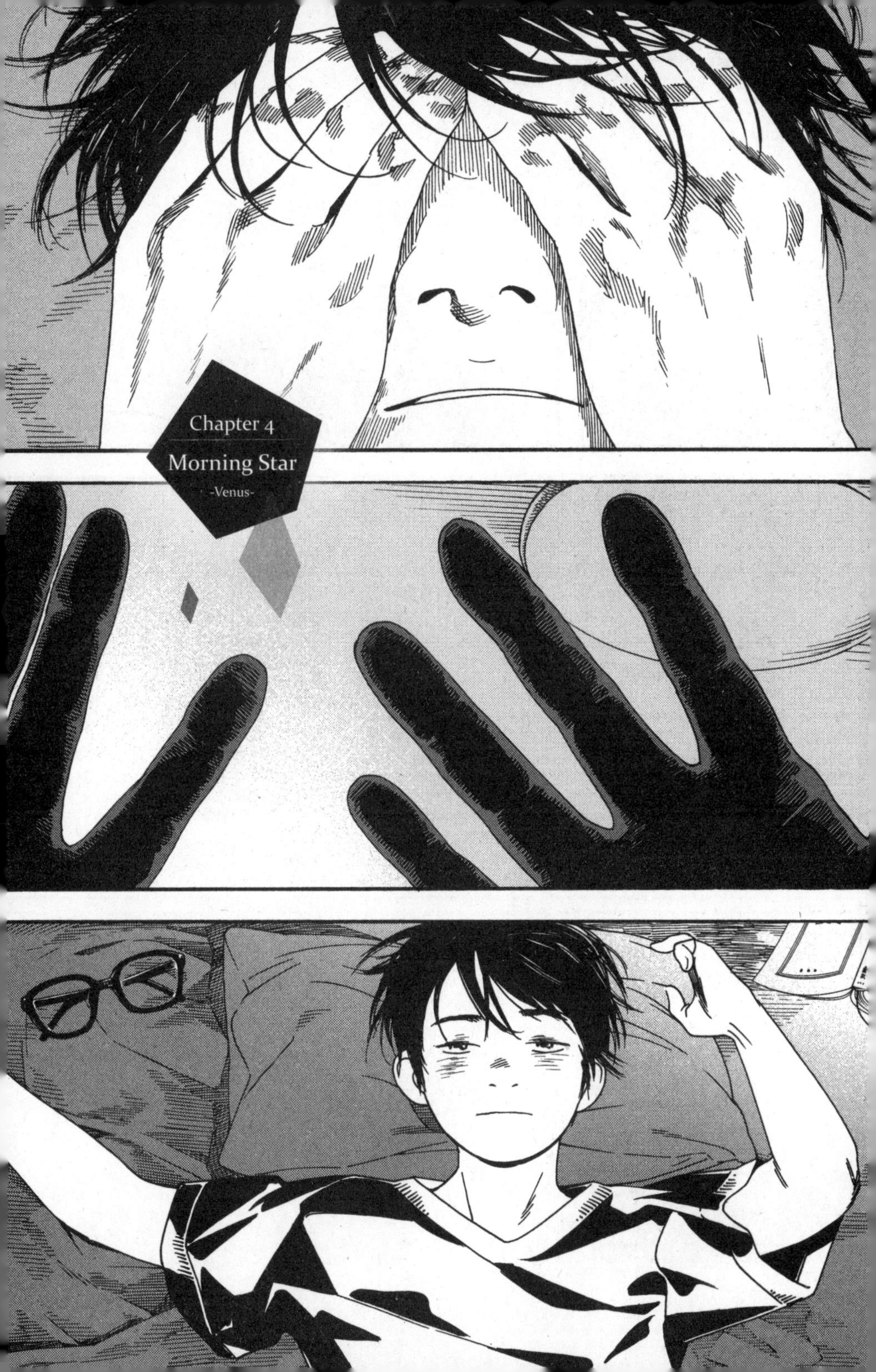

Chapter 4
Morning Star
-Venus-

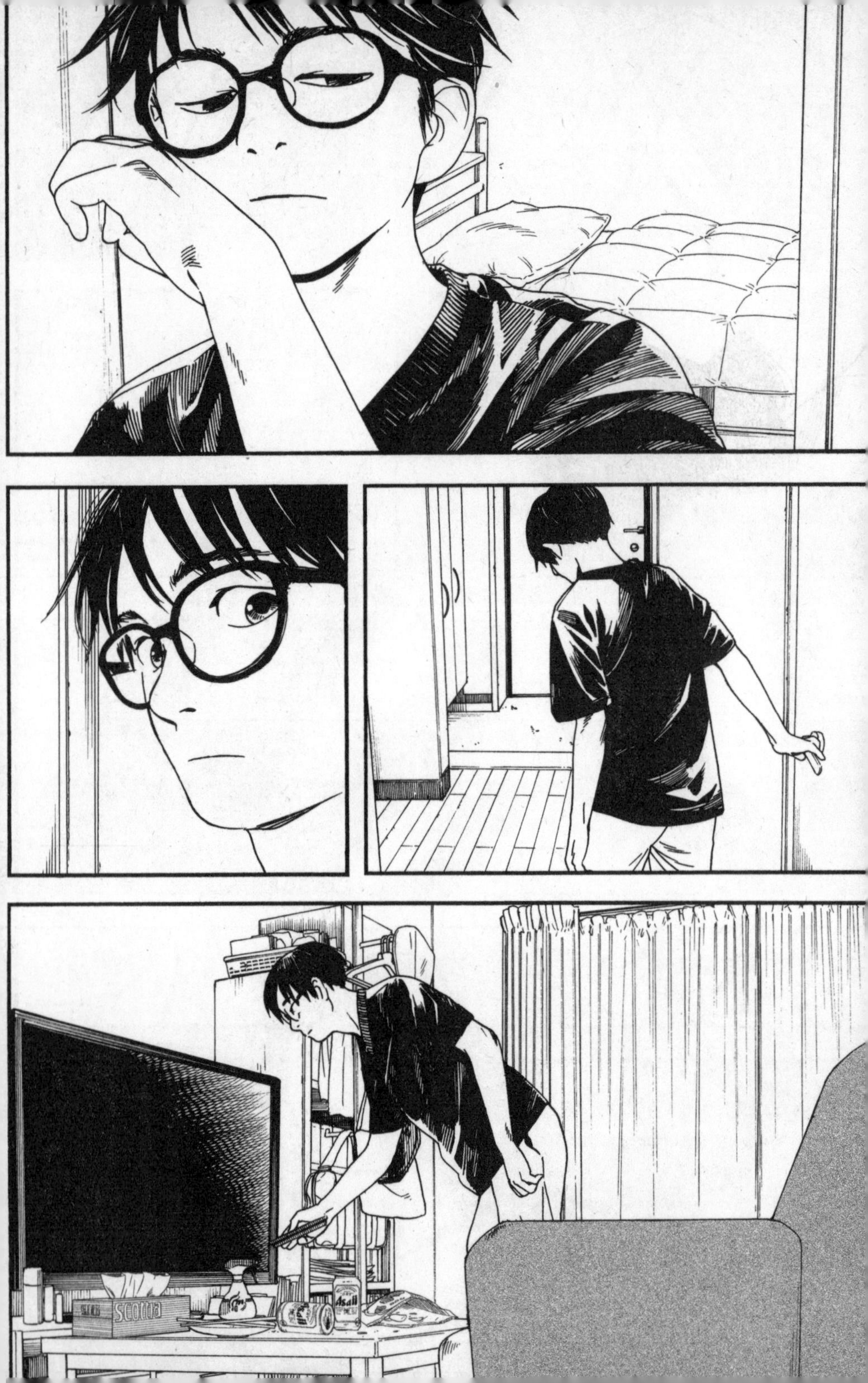

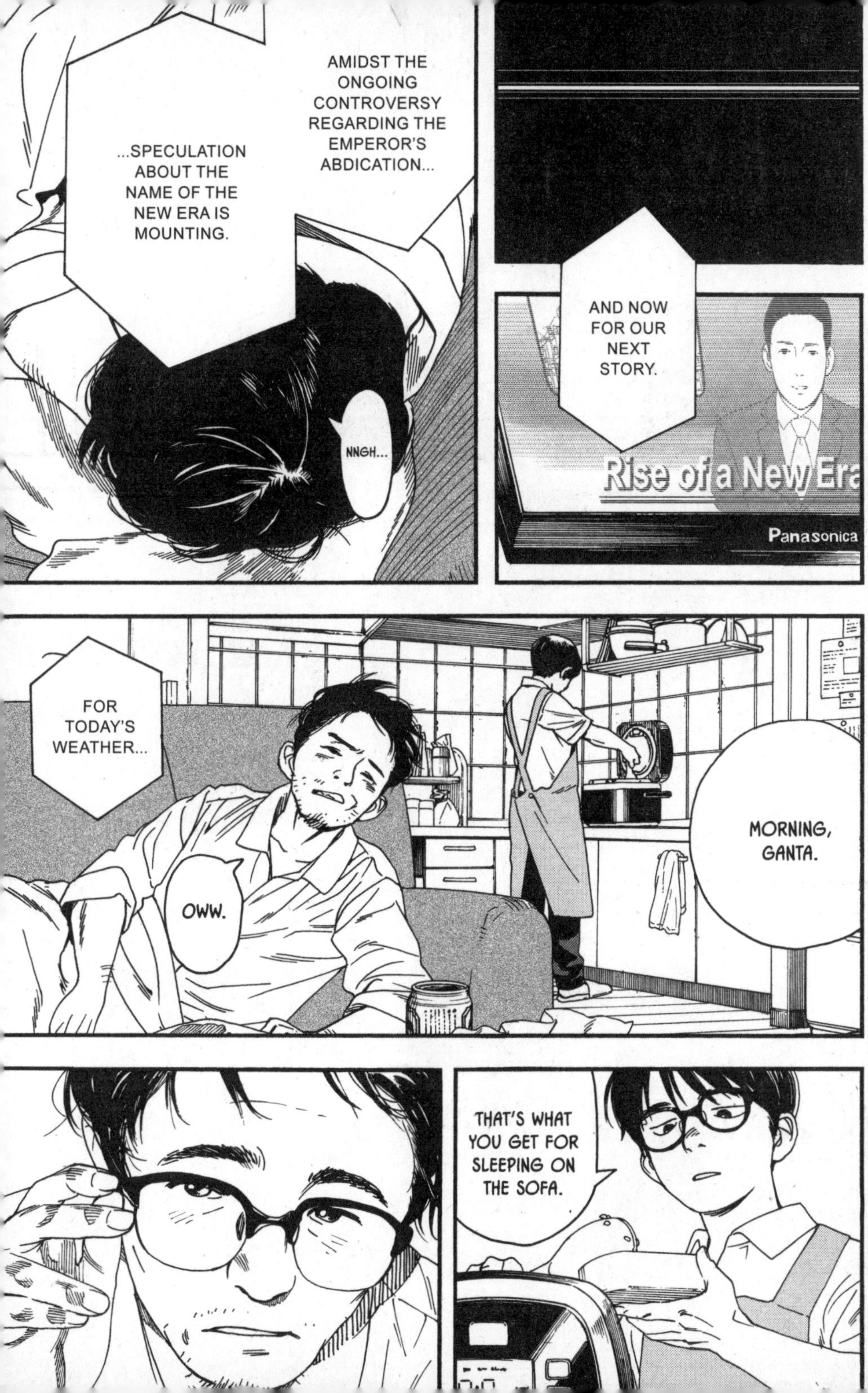
AND NOW FOR OUR NEXT STORY.
Rise of a New Era
Panasonica
AMIDST THE ONGOING CONTROVERSY REGARDING THE EMPEROR'S ABDICATION...
...SPECULATION ABOUT THE NAME OF THE NEW ERA IS MOUNTING.
NNGH...
MORNING, GANTA.
FOR TODAY'S WEATHER...
OWW.
THAT'S WHAT YOU GET FOR SLEEPING ON THE SOFA.

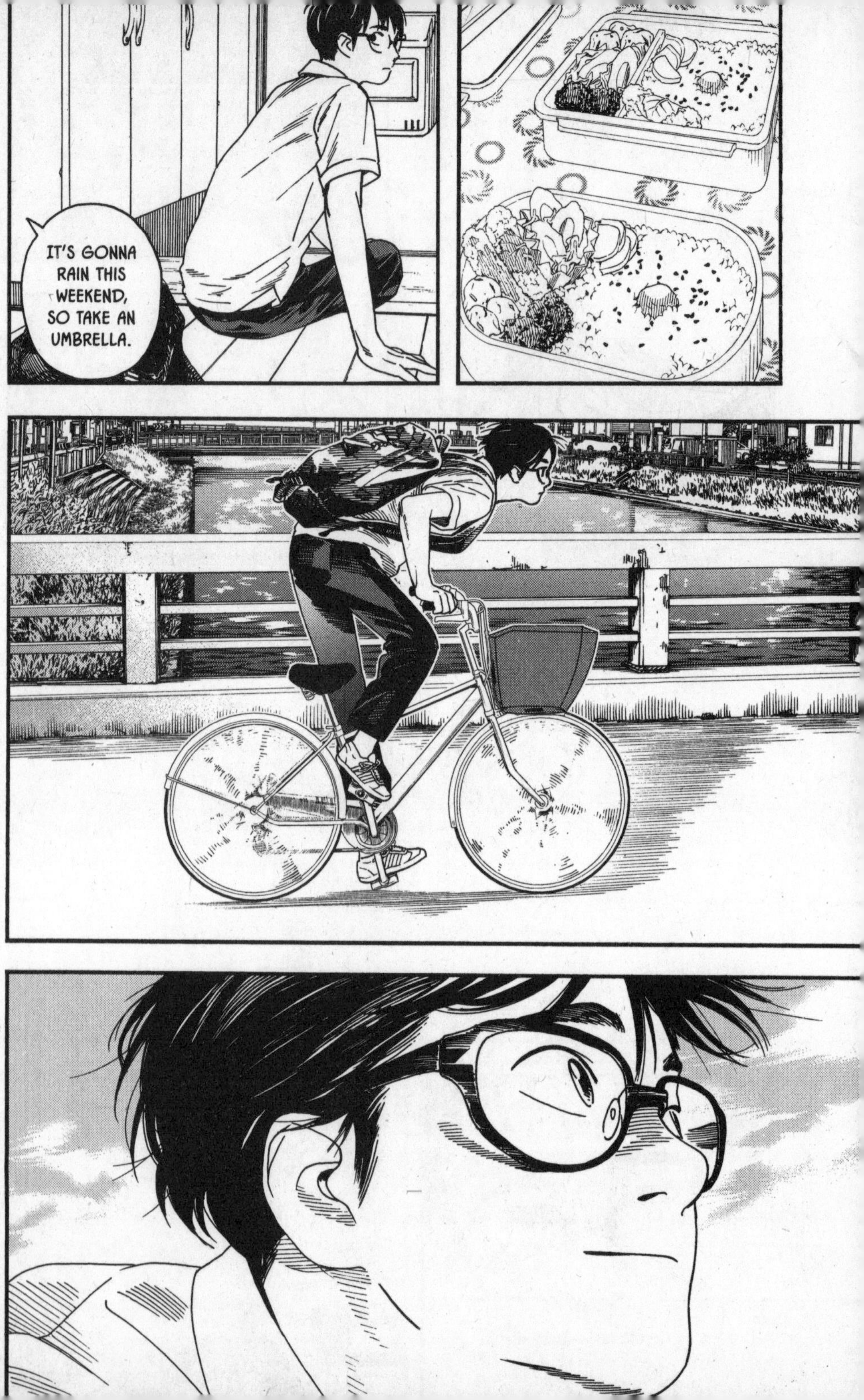
IT'S GONNA RAIN THIS WEEKEND, SO TAKE AN UMBRELLA.

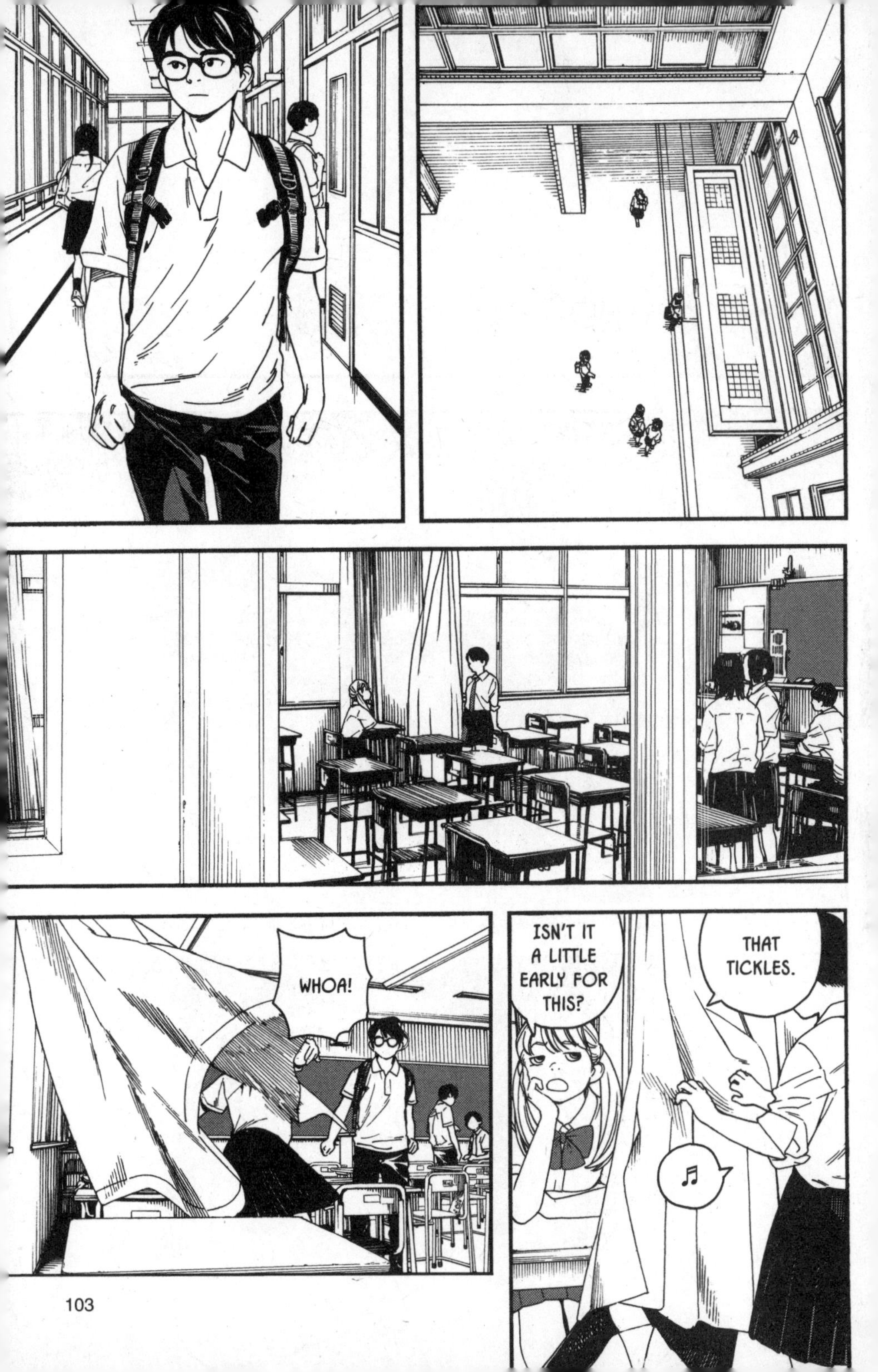
THAT TICKLES.
ISN'T IT A LITTLE EARLY FOR THIS?
♪
WHOA!

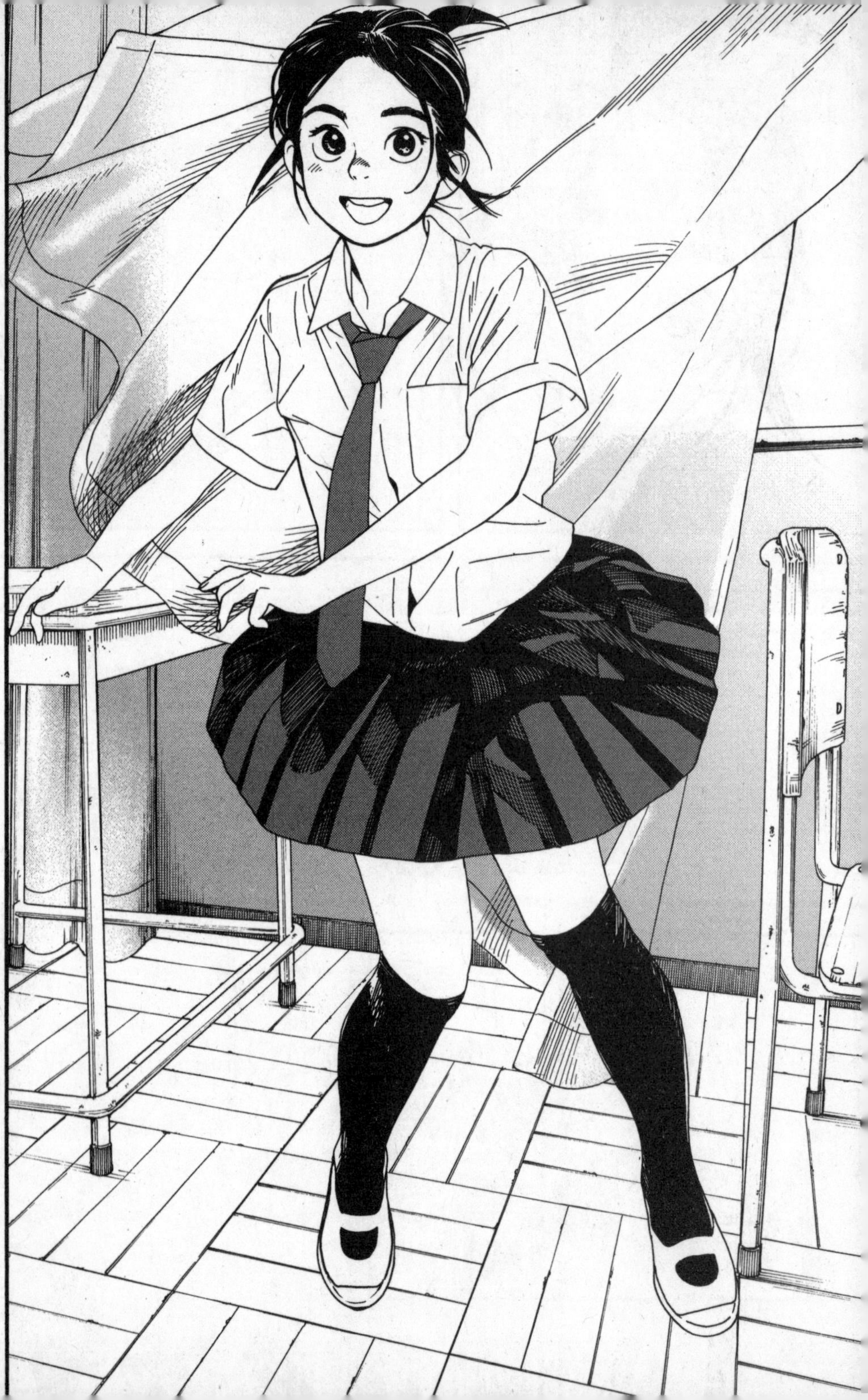

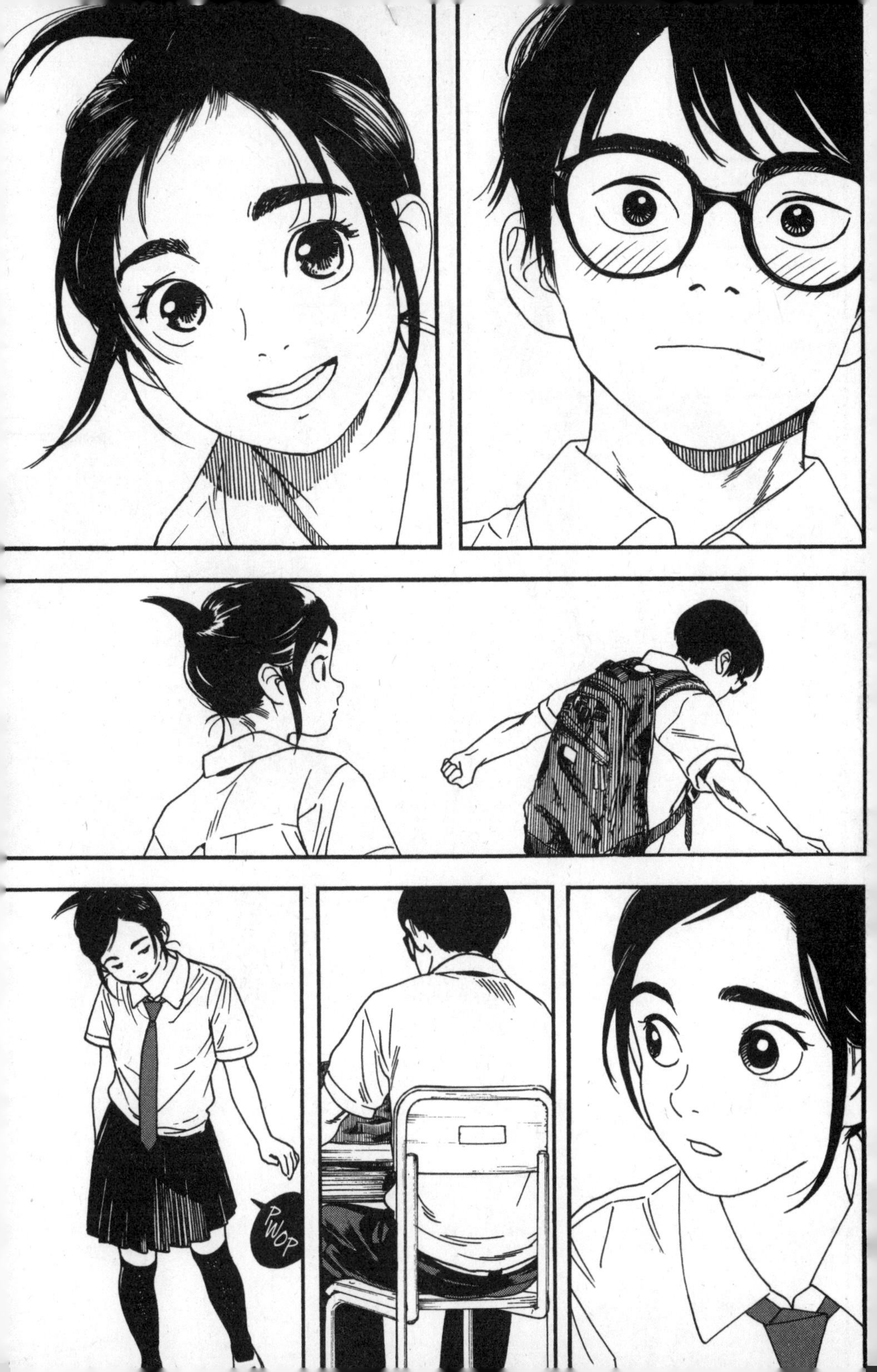
PWOP

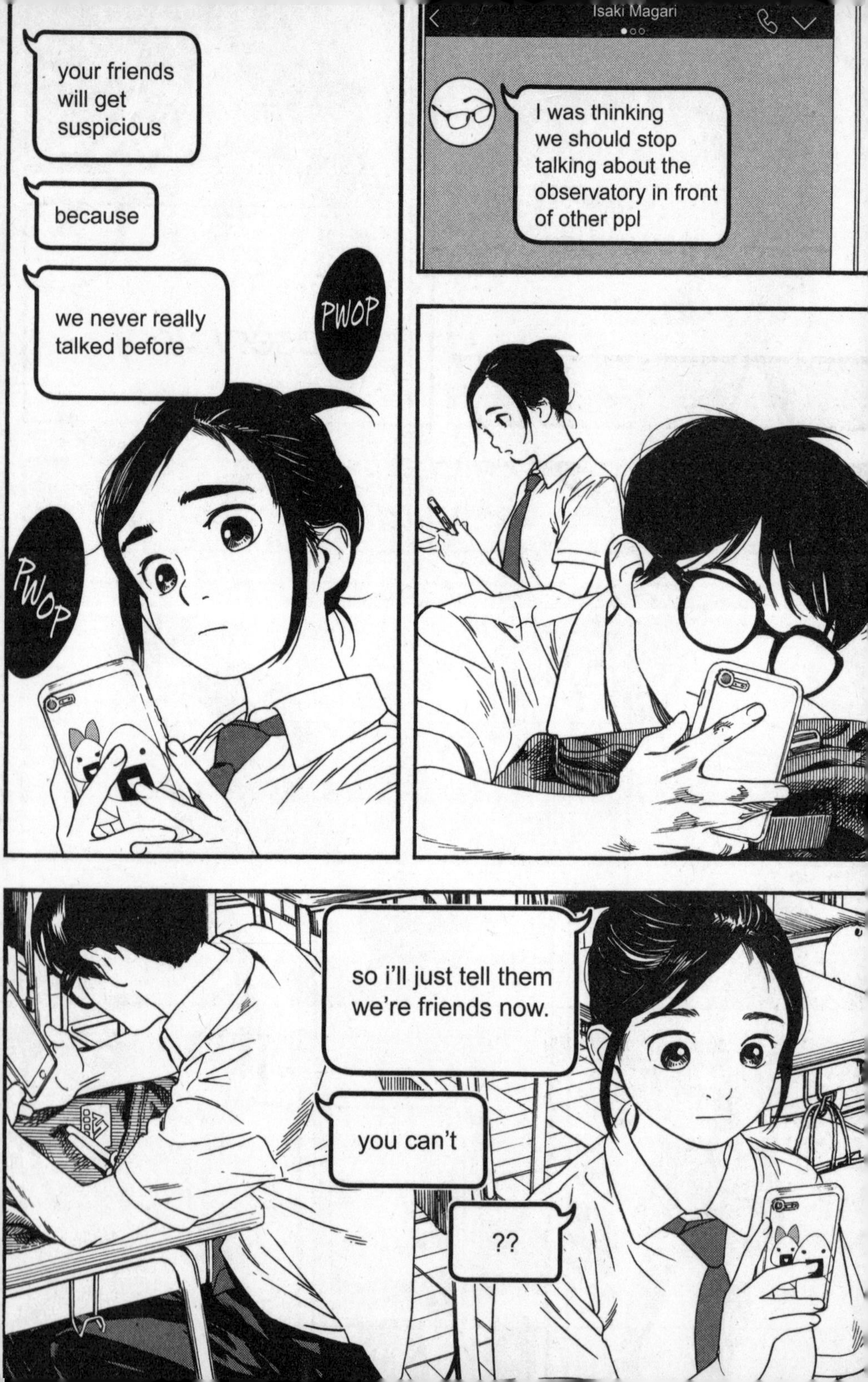
Isaki Magari
I was thinking we should stop talking about the observatory in front of other ppl
your friends will get suspicious
because
we never really talked before
PWOP
PWOP
so i'll just tell them we're friends now.
you can't
??

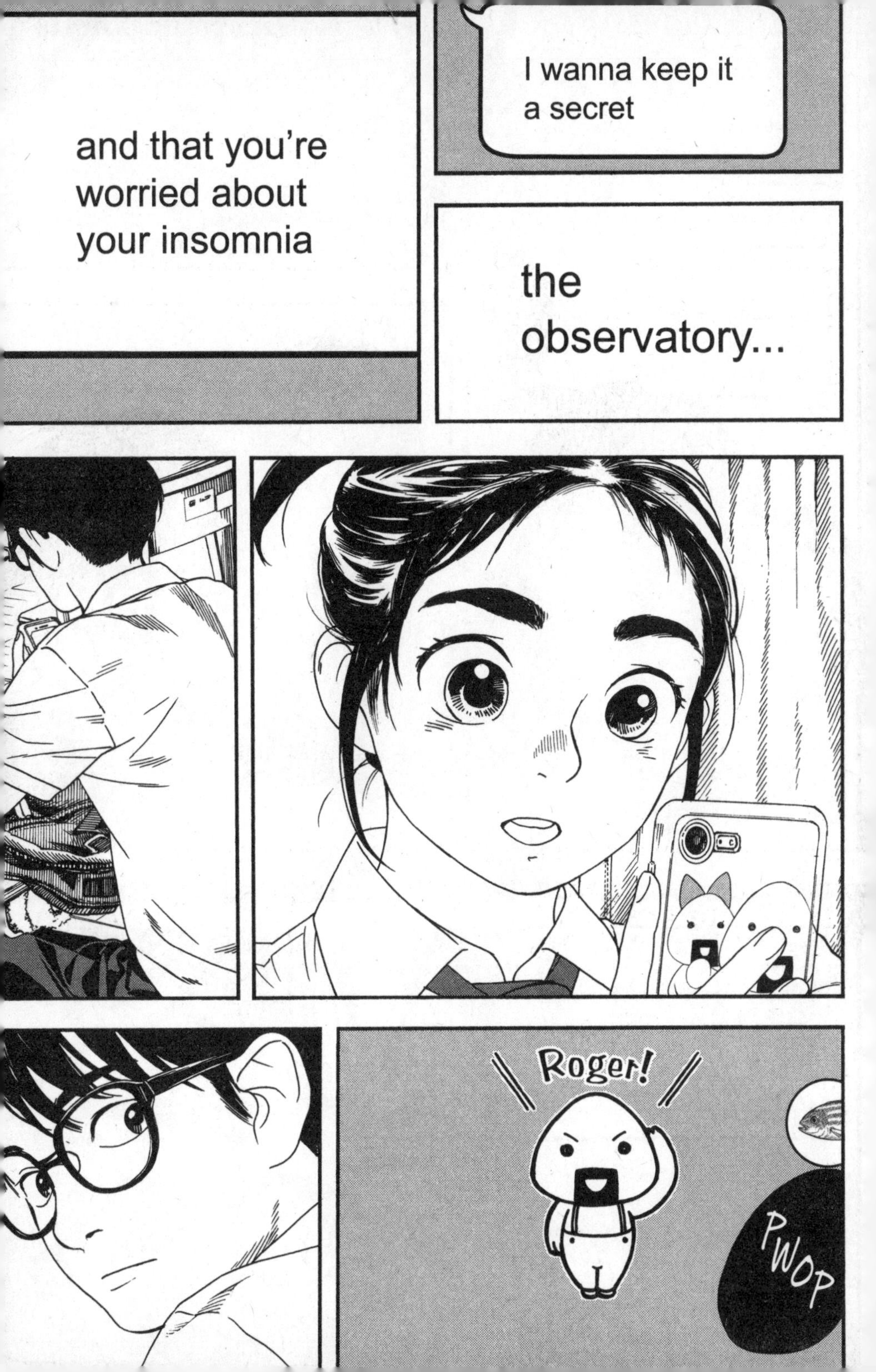
I wanna keep it a secret
the observatory...
and that you're worried about your insomnia
Roger!
PWOP

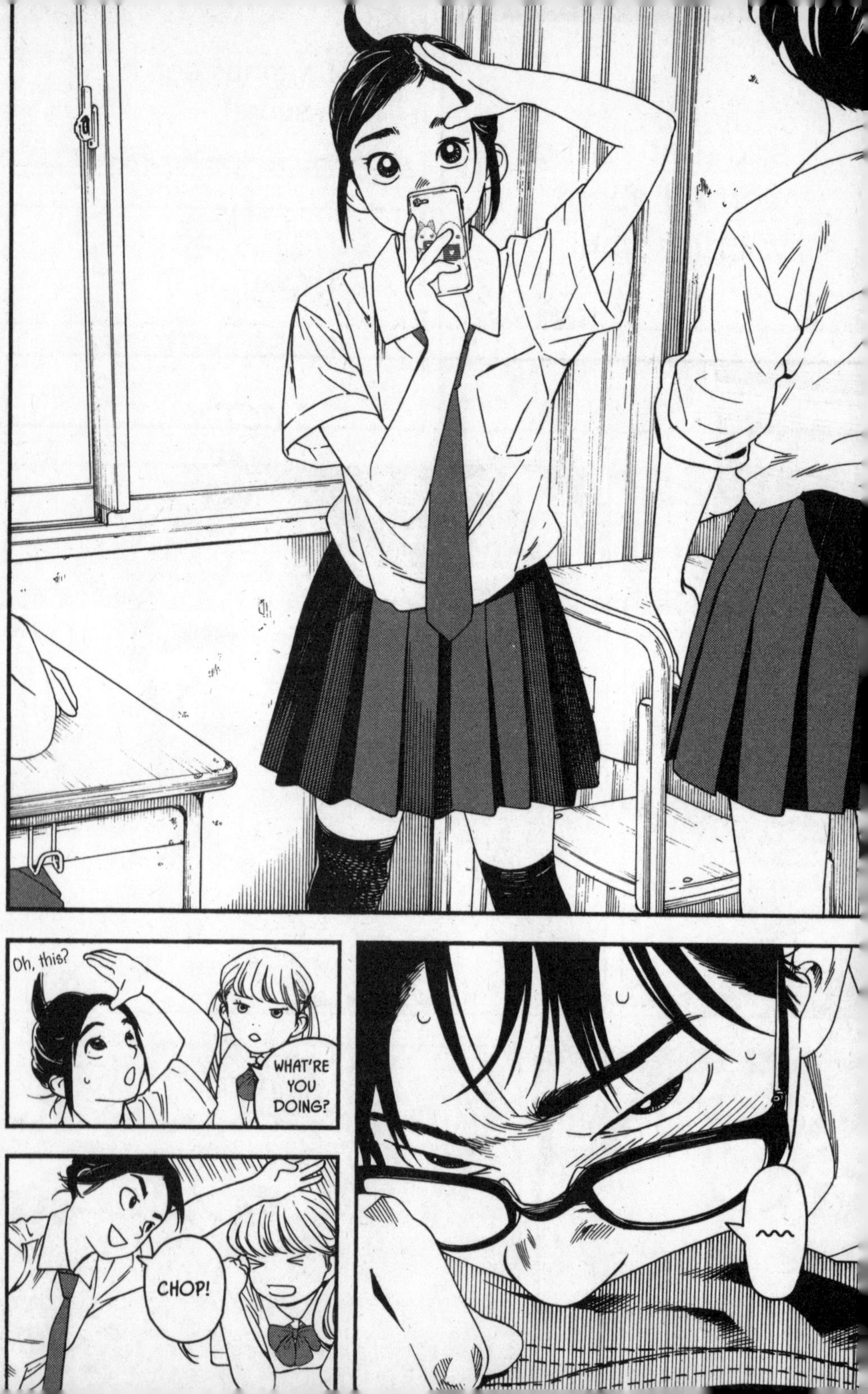
WHAT'RE YOU DOING?
Oh, this?
CHOP!

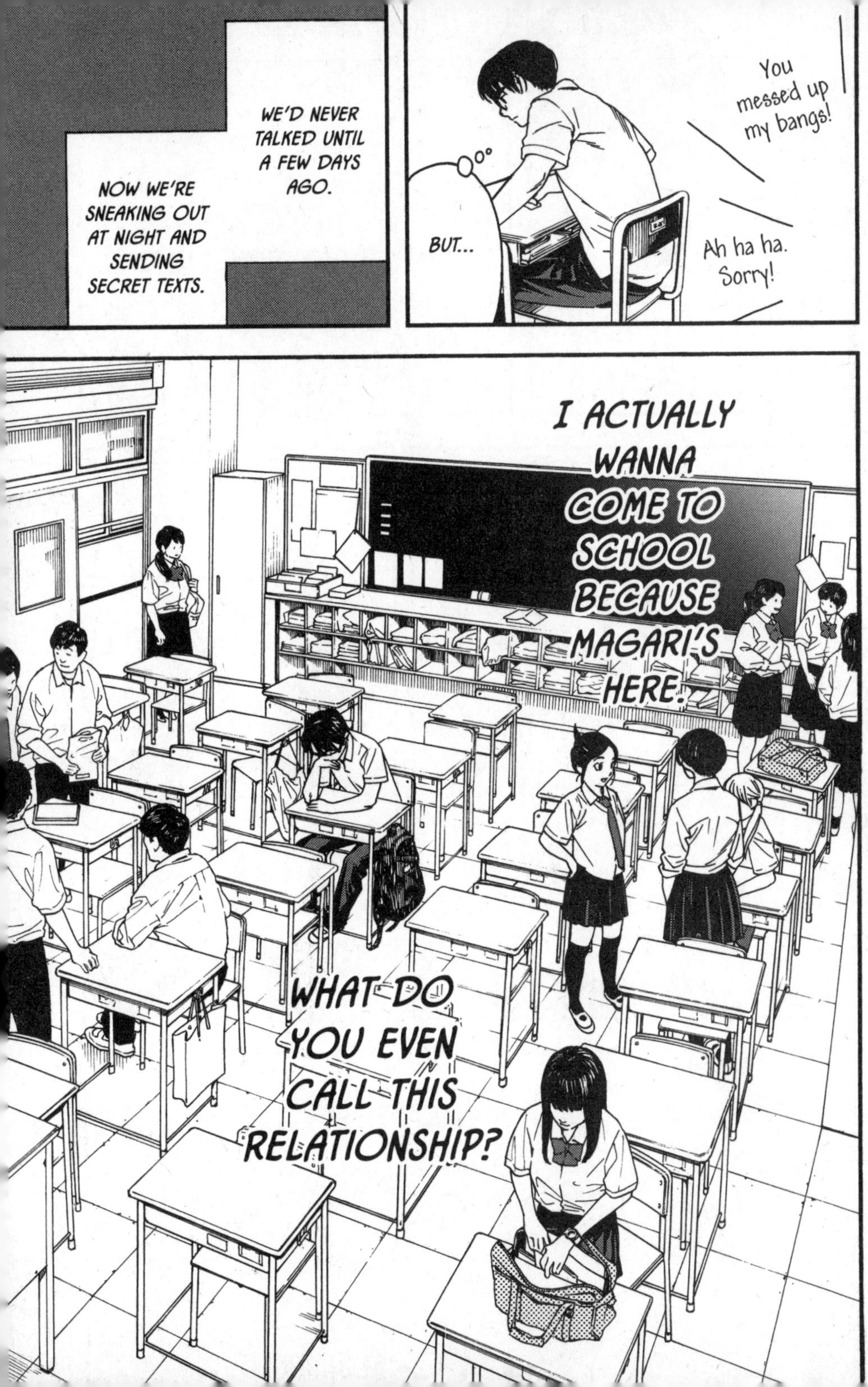
You messed up my bangs!
Ah ha ha. Sorry!
BUT...
WE'D NEVER TALKED UNTIL A FEW DAYS AGO.
NOW WE'RE SNEAKING OUT AT NIGHT AND SENDING SECRET TEXTS.
I ACTUALLY WANNA COME TO SCHOOL BECAUSE MAGARI'S HERE.
WHAT DO YOU EVEN CALL THIS RELATIONSHIP?

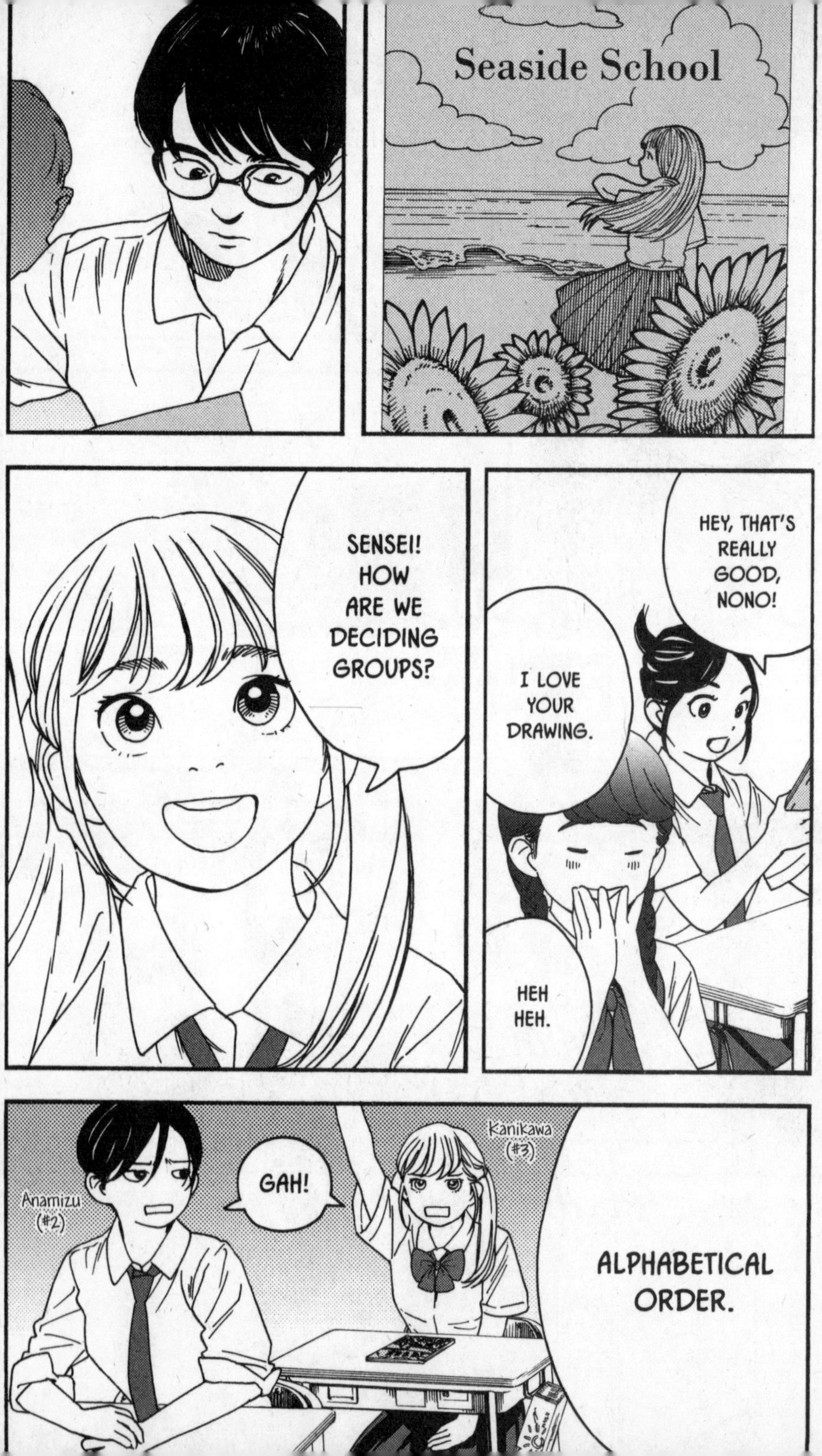
Seaside School
HEY, THAT'S REALLY GOOD, NONO!
I LOVE YOUR DRAWING.
HEH HEH.
SENSEI! HOW ARE WE DECIDING GROUPS?
ALPHABETICAL ORDER.
Kanikawa (#3)
GAH!
Anamizu (#2)

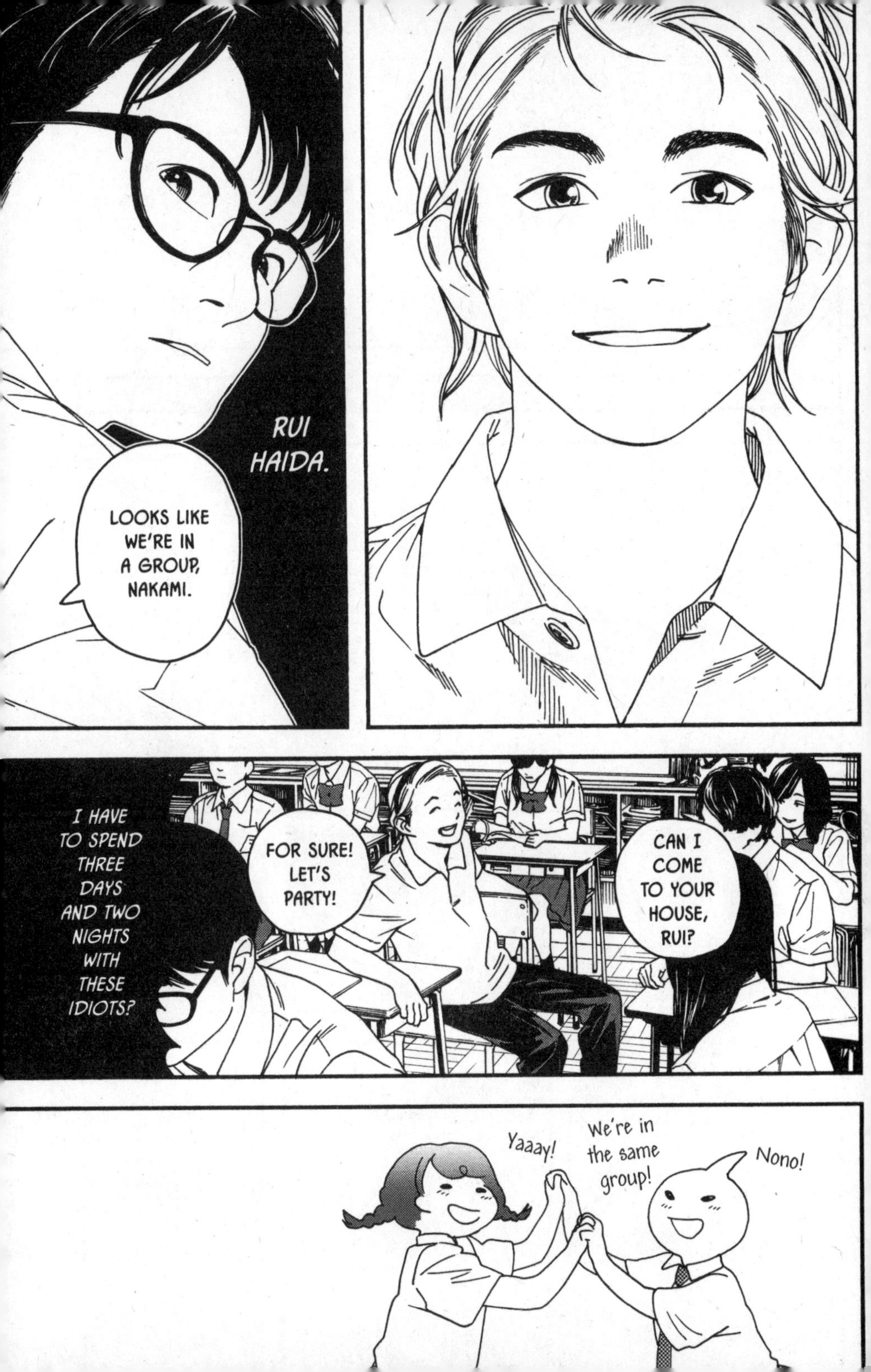
RUI HAIDA.
LOOKS LIKE WE'RE IN A GROUP, NAKAMI.
CAN I COME TO YOUR HOUSE, RUI?
FOR SURE! LET'S PARTY!
I HAVE TO SPEND THREE DAYS AND TWO NIGHTS WITH THESE IDIOTS?
Nono!
We're in the same group!
Yaaay!

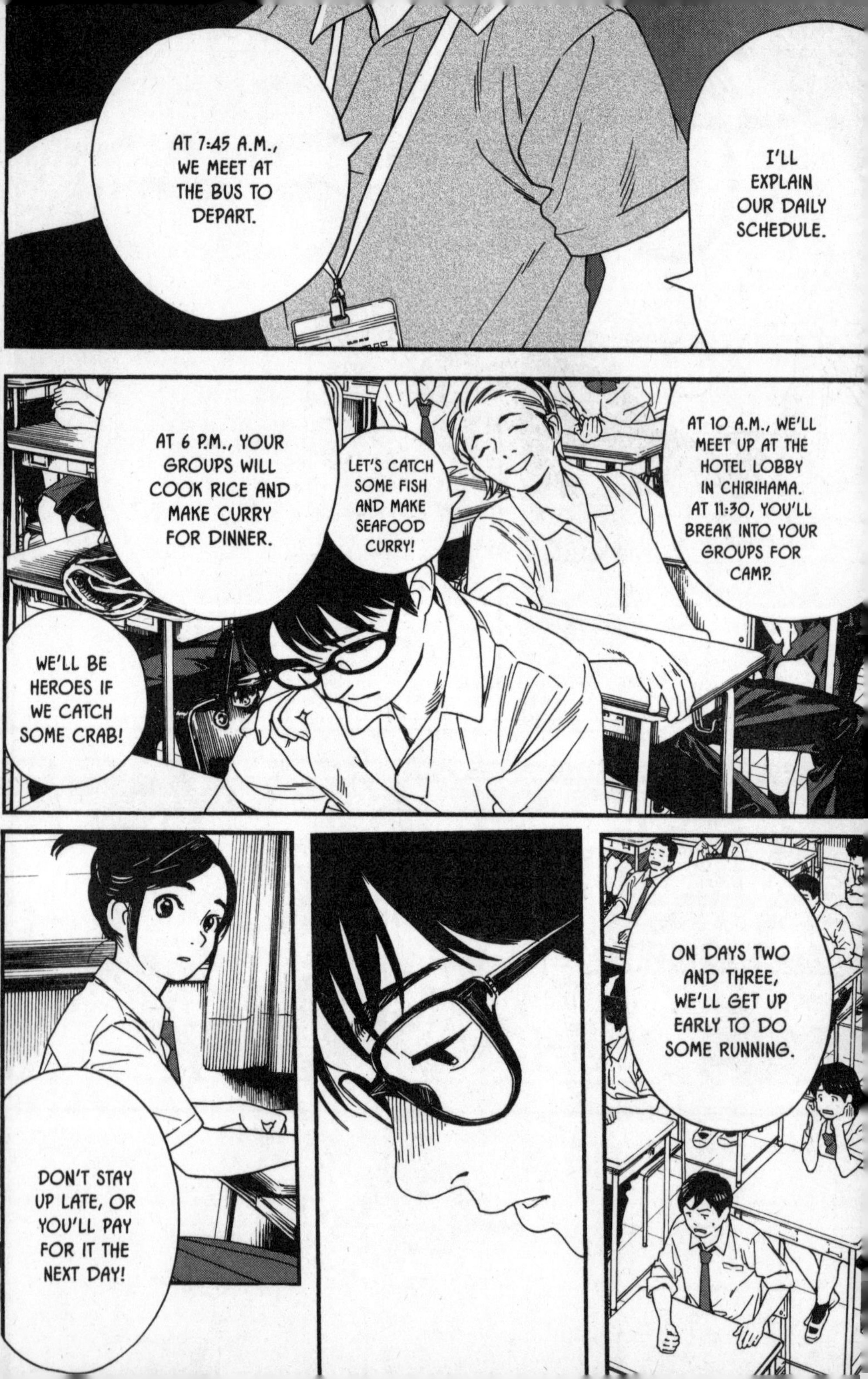
I'LL EXPLAIN OUR DAILY SCHEDULE.
AT 7:45 A.M., WE MEET AT THE BUS TO DEPART.
AT 10 A.M., WE'LL MEET UP AT THE HOTEL LOBBY IN CHIRIHAMA. AT 11:30, YOU'LL BREAK INTO YOUR GROUPS FOR CAMP.
AT 6 P.M., YOUR GROUPS WILL COOK RICE AND MAKE CURRY FOR DINNER.
LET'S CATCH SOME FISH AND MAKE SEAFOOD CURRY!
WE'LL BE HEROES IF WE CATCH SOME CRAB!
ON DAYS TWO AND THREE, WE'LL GET UP EARLY TO DO SOME RUNNING.
DON'T STAY UP LATE, OR YOU'LL PAY FOR IT THE NEXT DAY!

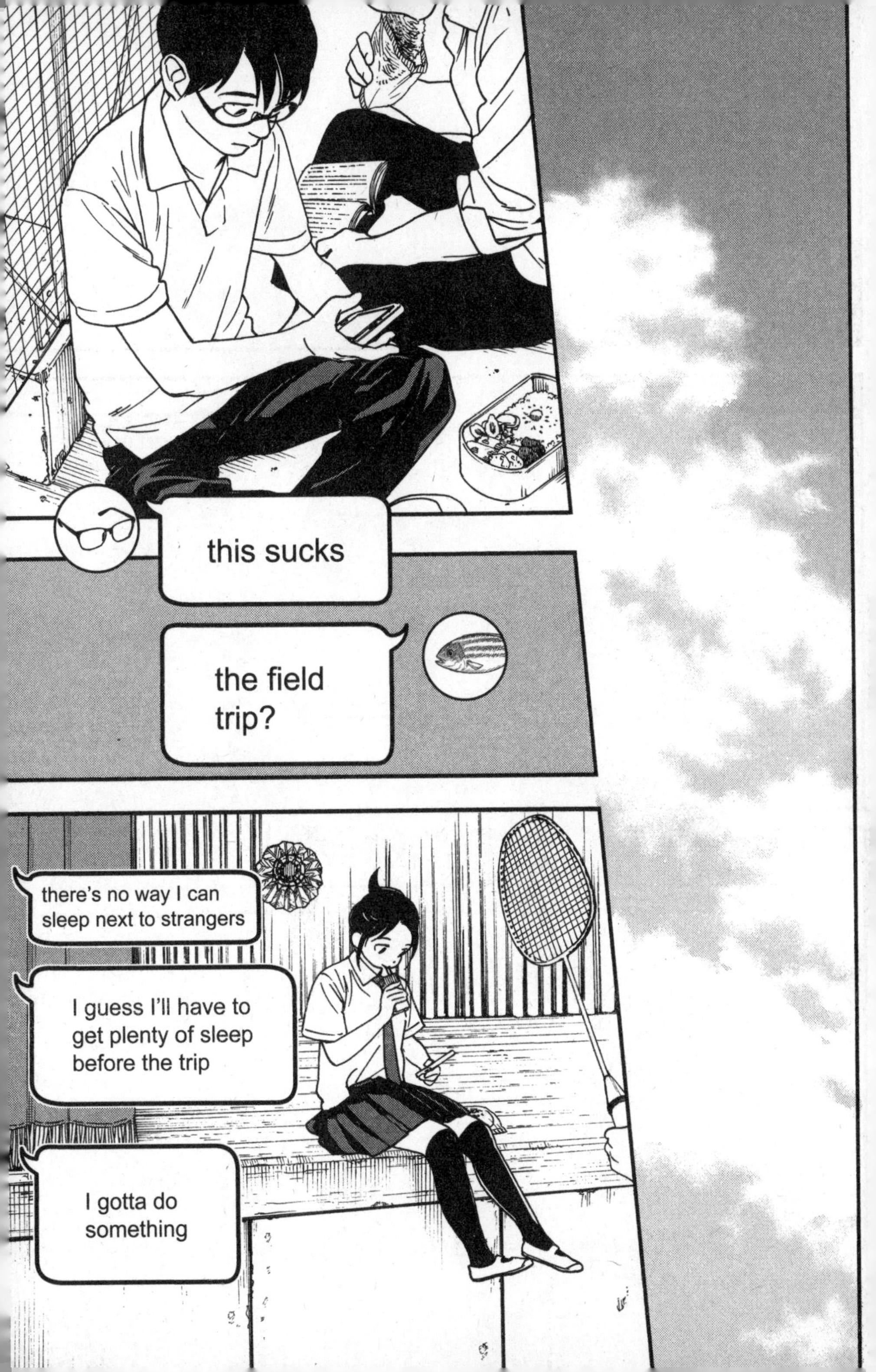
this sucks
the field trip?
there's no way I can sleep next to strangers
I guess I'll have to get plenty of sleep before the trip
I gotta do something

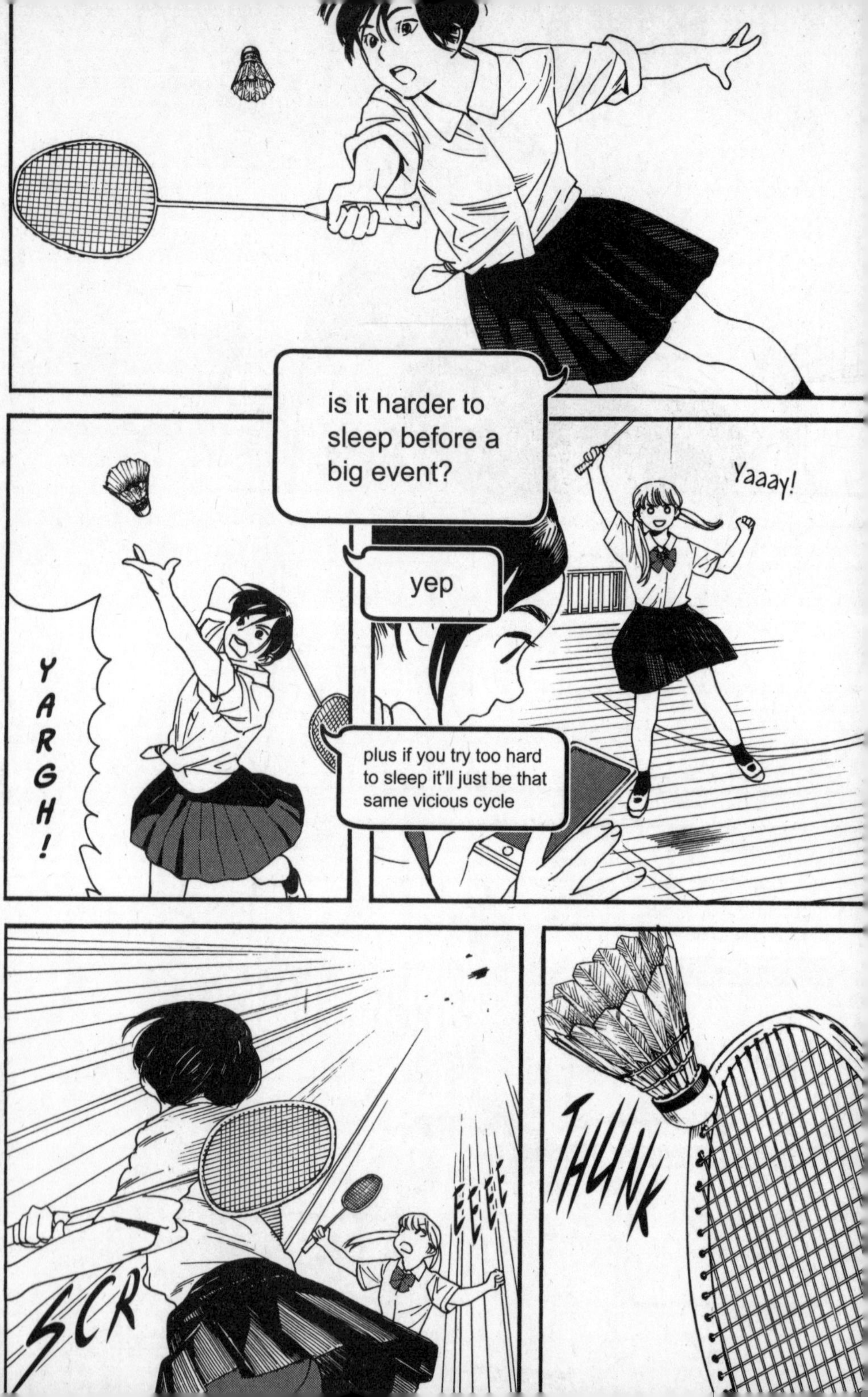
Yaaay!
is it harder to sleep before a big event?
yep
plus if you try too hard to sleep it'll just be that same vicious cycle
YARGH!
THUNK
EEEE
SCR

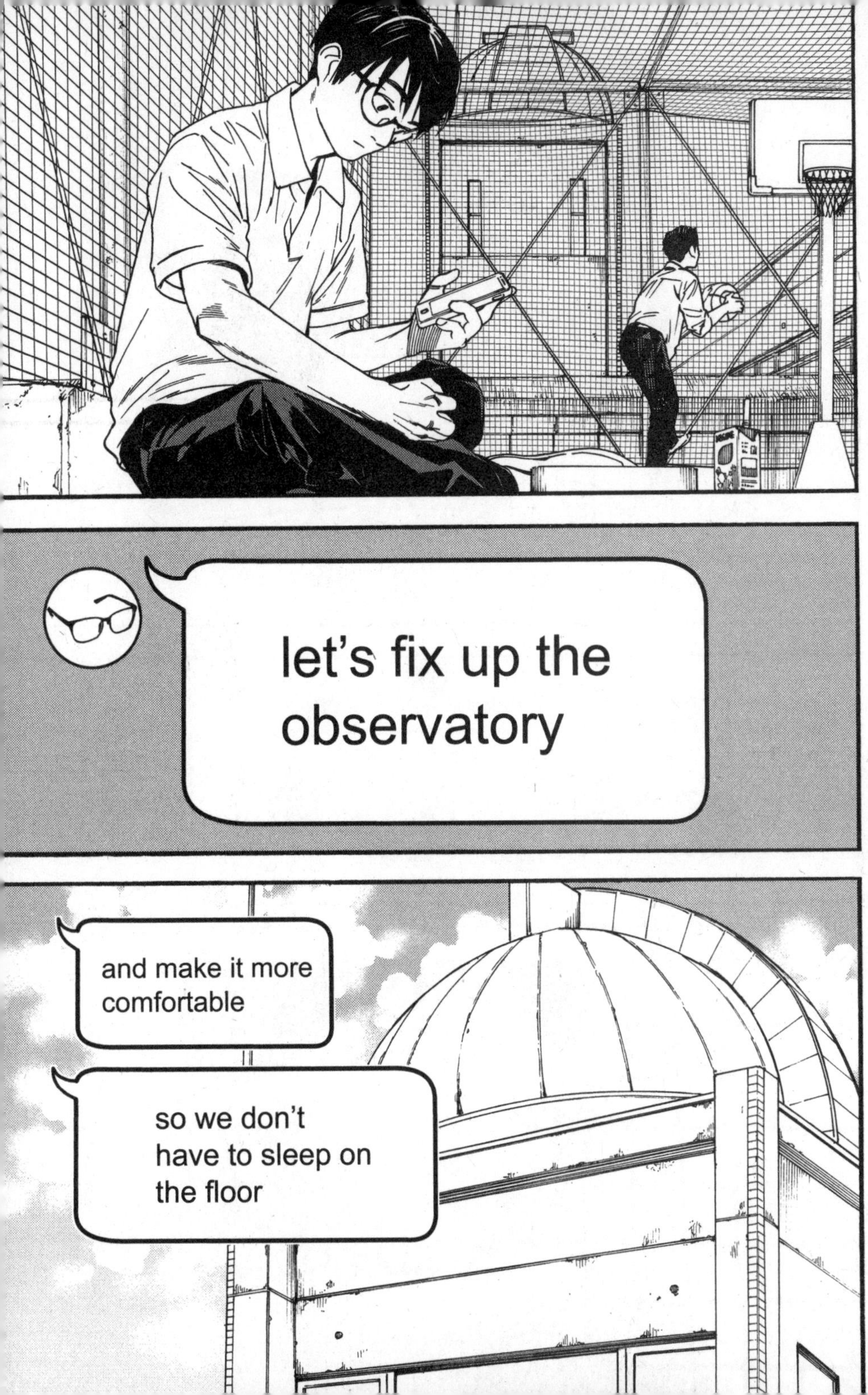
let's fix up the observatory
and make it more comfortable
so we don't have to sleep on the floor

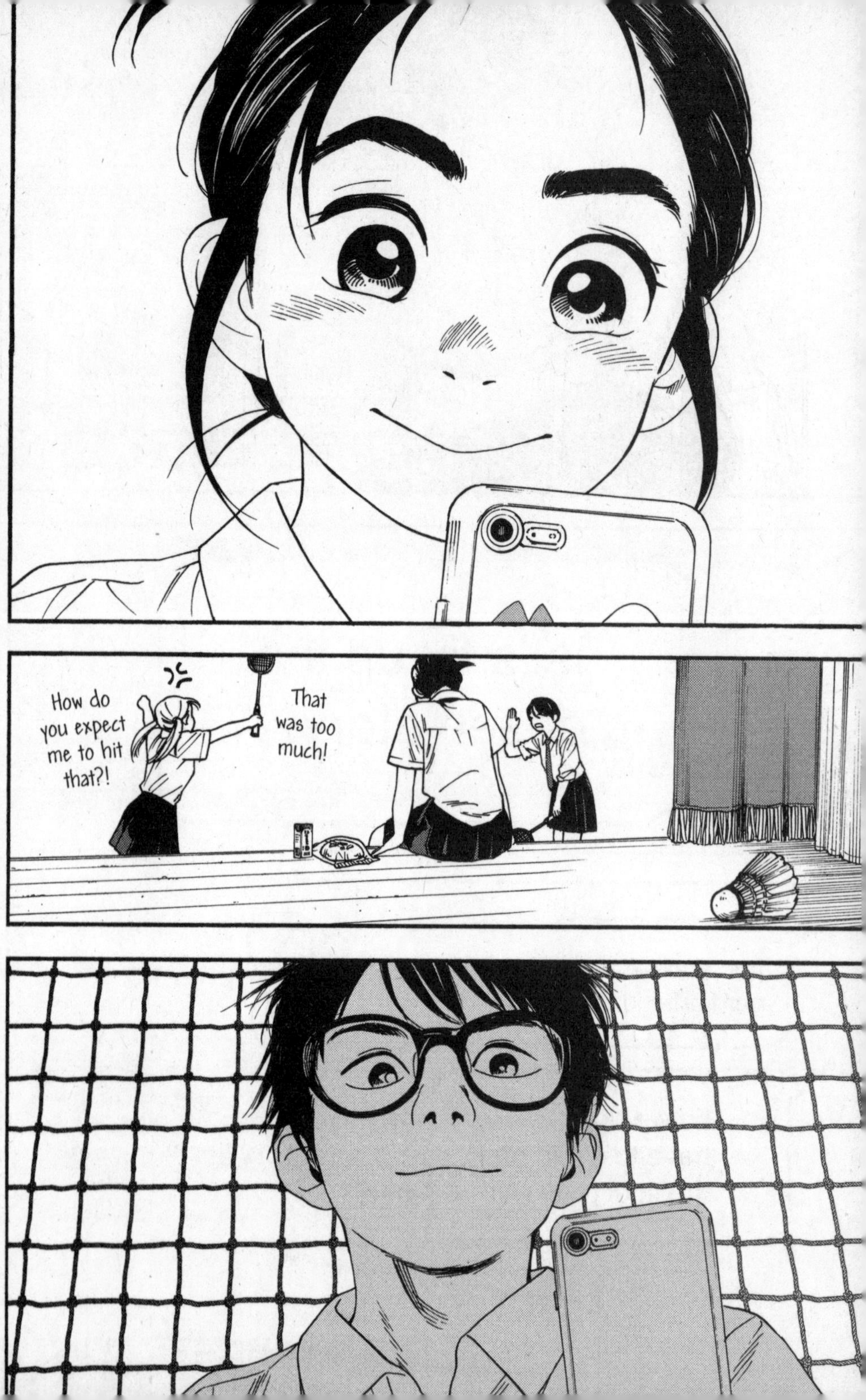
That was too much!
How do you expect me to hit that?!

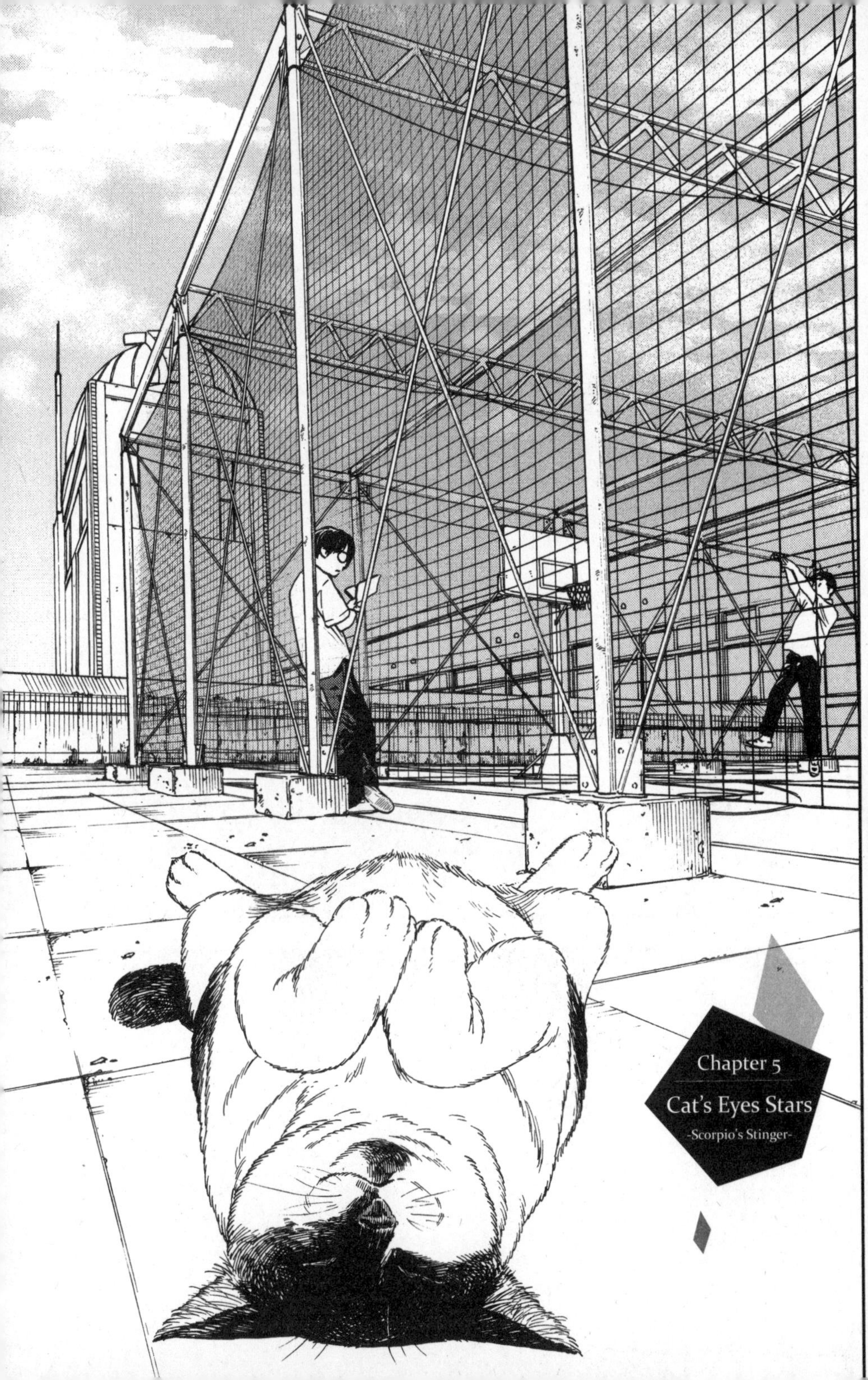
Chapter 5
Cat's Eyes Stars
-Scorpio's Stinger-

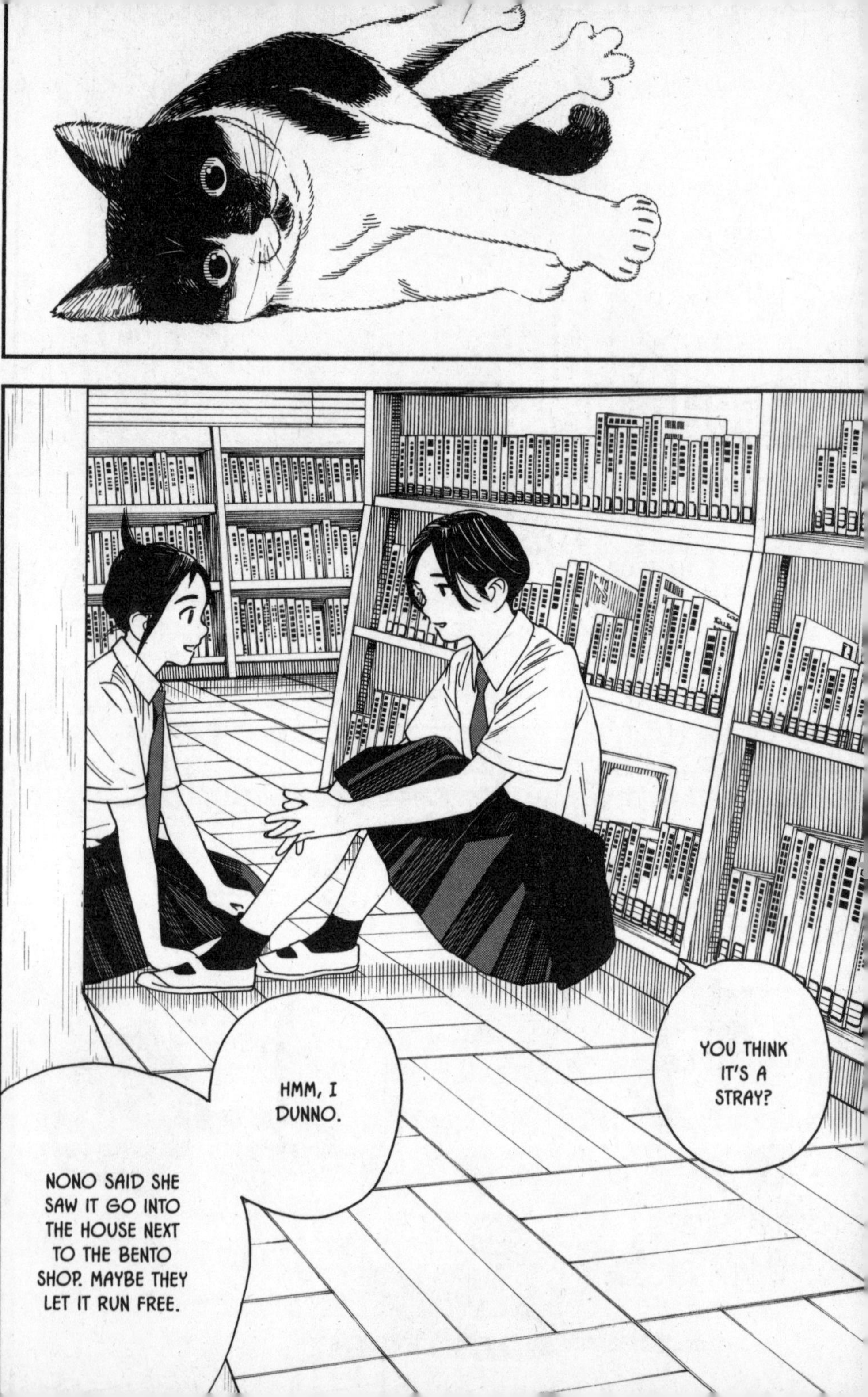
YOU THINK IT'S A STRAY?
HMM, I DUNNO.
NONO SAID SHE SAW IT GO INTO THE HOUSE NEXT TO THE BENTO SHOP. MAYBE THEY LET IT RUN FREE.

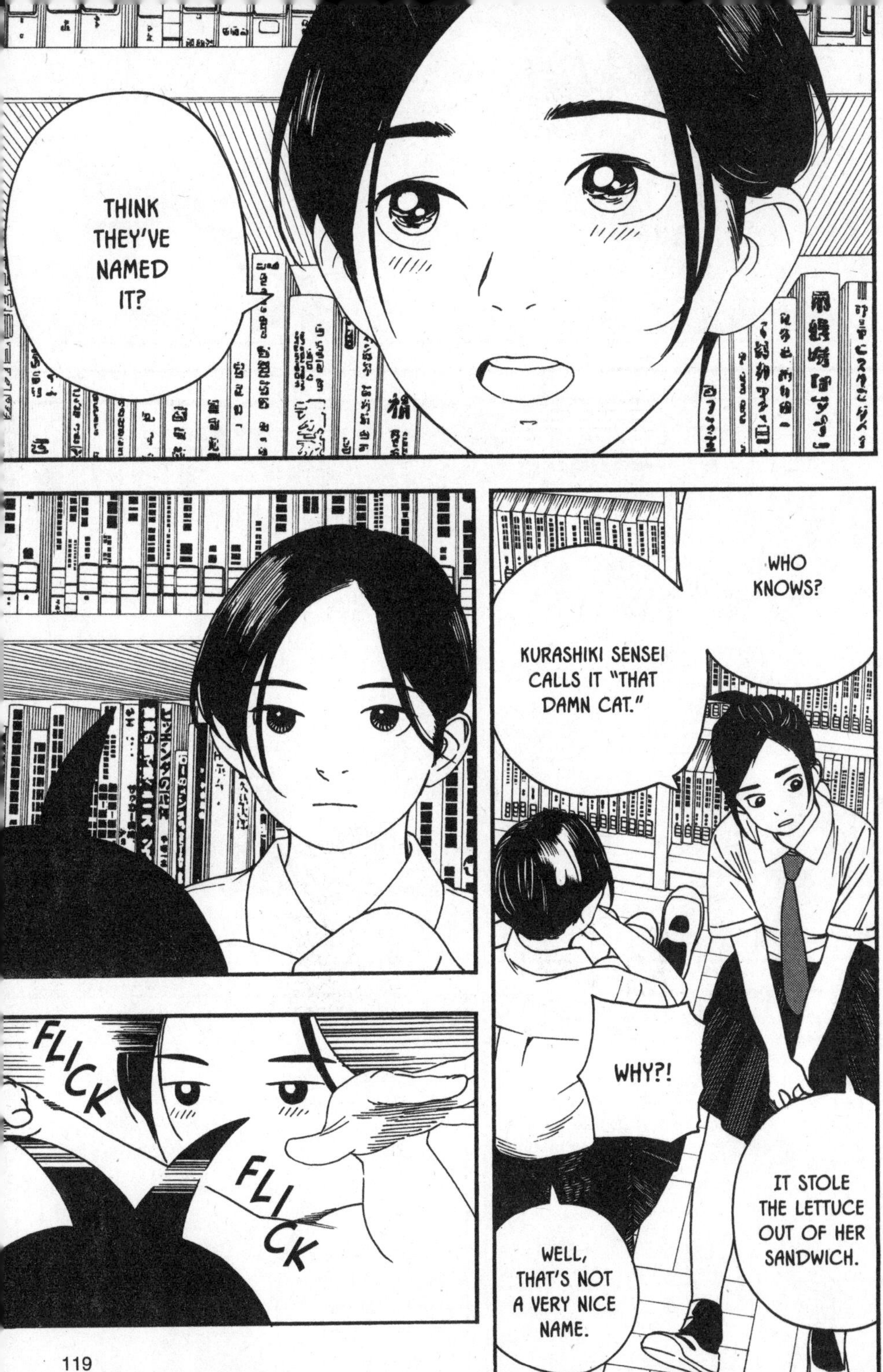
THINK THEY'VE NAMED IT?
WHO KNOWS?
KURASHIKI SENSEI CALLS IT "THAT DAMN CAT."
WHY?!
IT STOLE THE LETTUCE OUT OF HER SANDWICH.
WELL, THAT'S NOT A VERY NICE NAME.
FLICK
FLICK

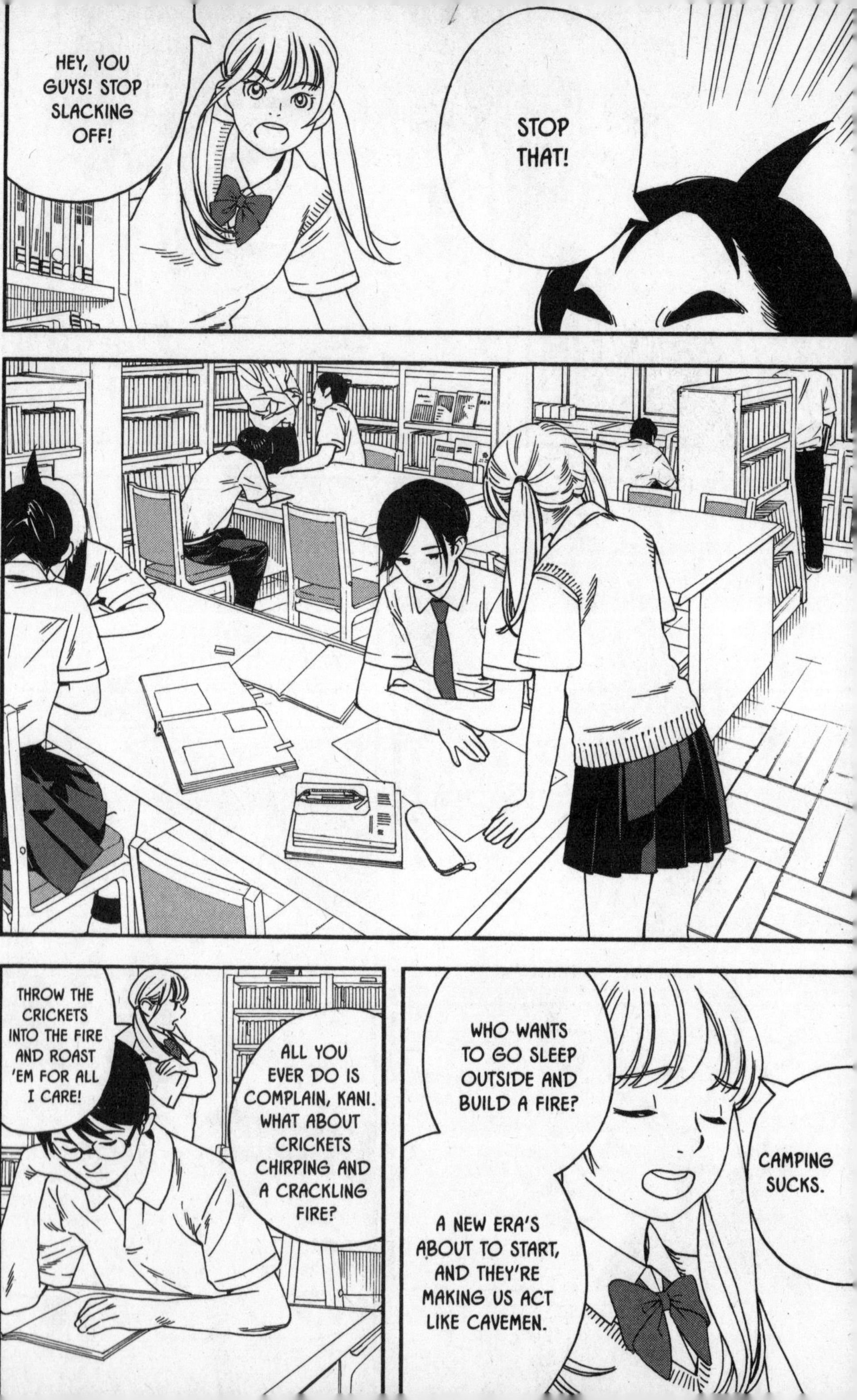
STOP THAT!
HEY, YOU GUYS! STOP SLACKING OFF!
CAMPING SUCKS.
WHO WANTS TO GO SLEEP OUTSIDE AND BUILD A FIRE?
A NEW ERA'S ABOUT TO START, AND THEY'RE MAKING US ACT LIKE CAVEMEN.
ALL YOU EVER DO IS COMPLAIN, KANI. WHAT ABOUT CRICKETS CHIRPING AND A CRACKLING FIRE?
THROW THE CRICKETS INTO THE FIRE AND ROAST 'EM FOR ALL I CARE!

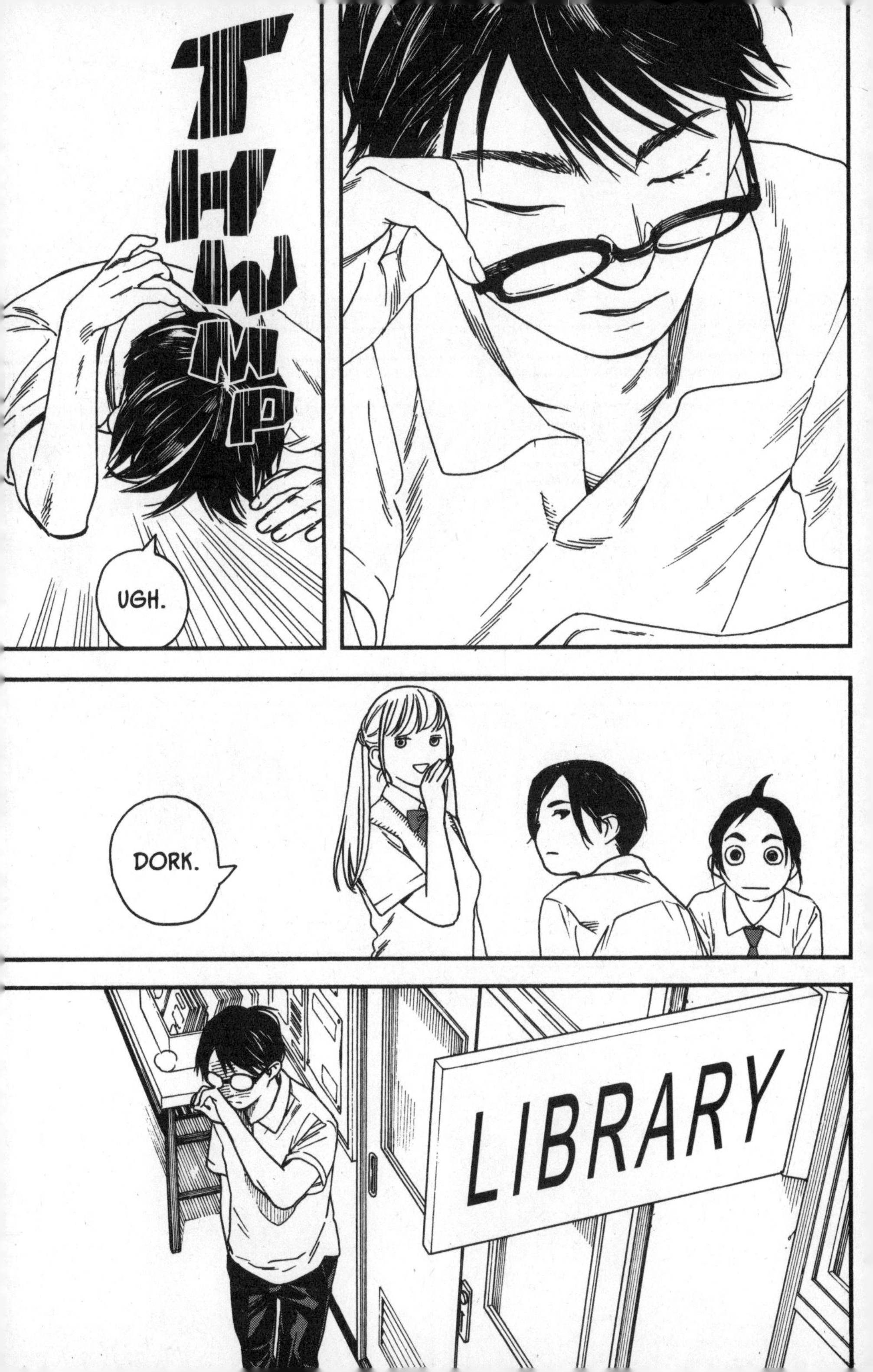
THWMP
UGH.
DORK.
LIBRARY

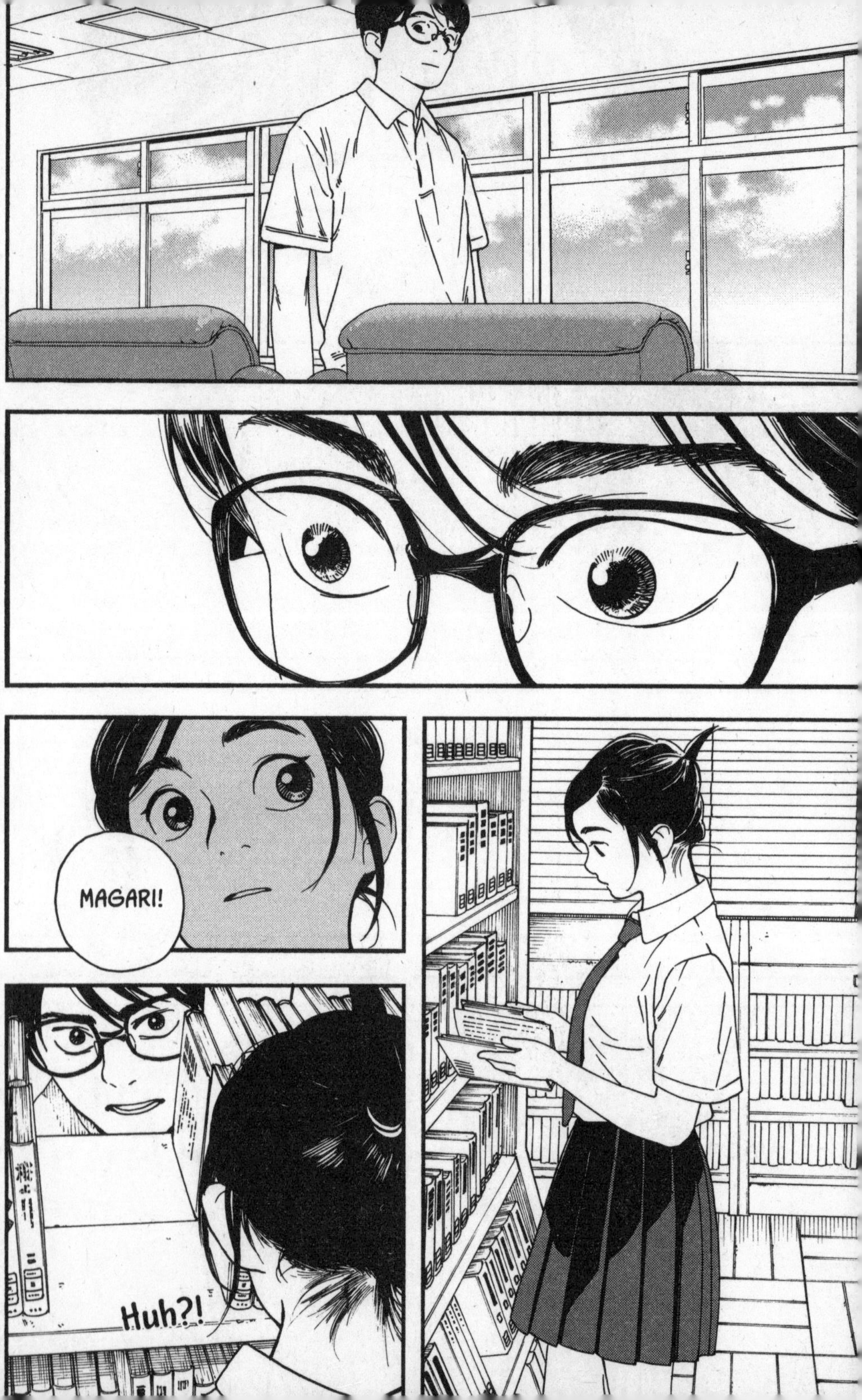
MAGARI!
Huh?!

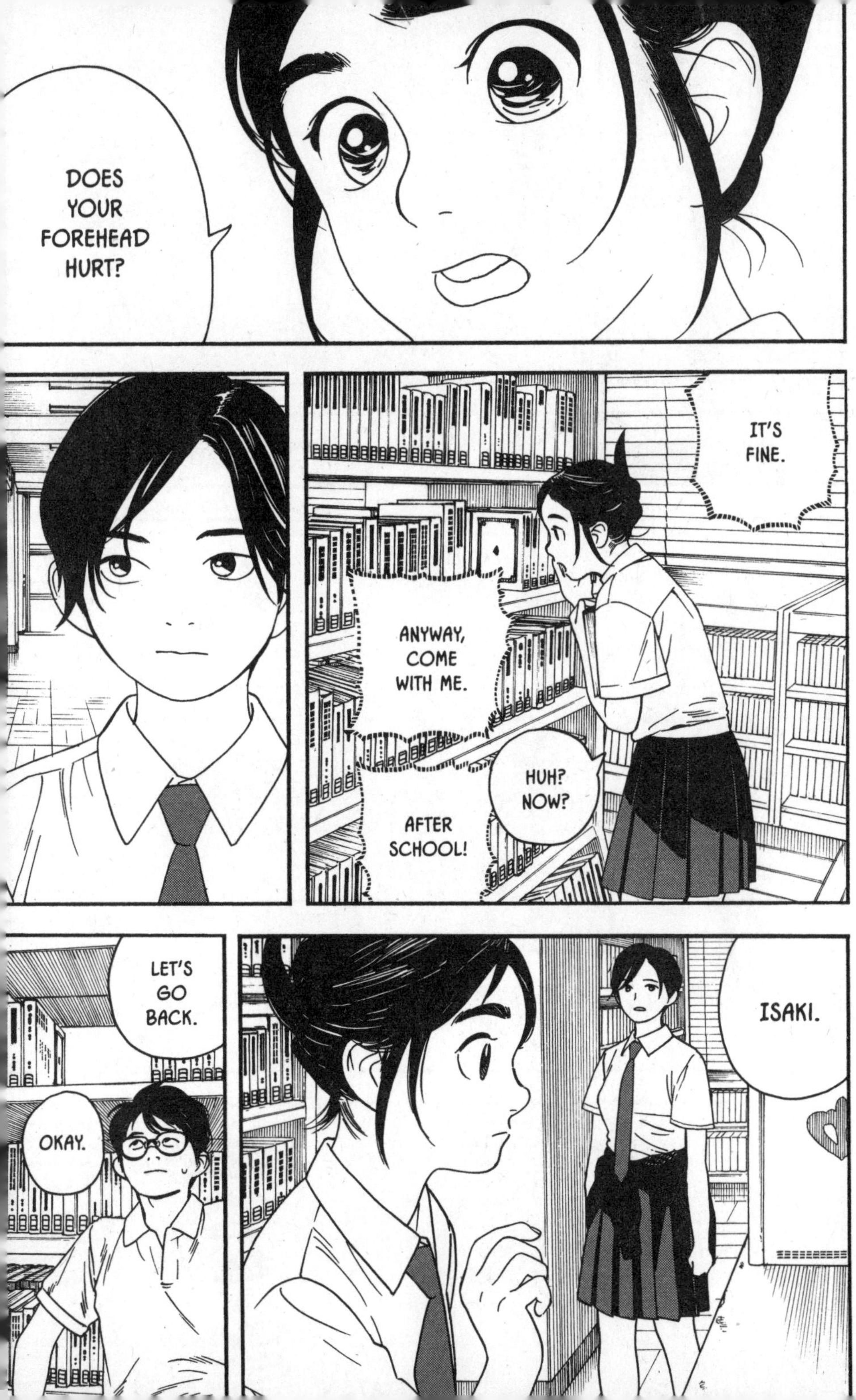
DOES YOUR FOREHEAD HURT?
IT'S FINE.
ANYWAY, COME WITH ME.
HUH? NOW?
AFTER SCHOOL!
ISAKI.
LET'S GO BACK.
OKAY.

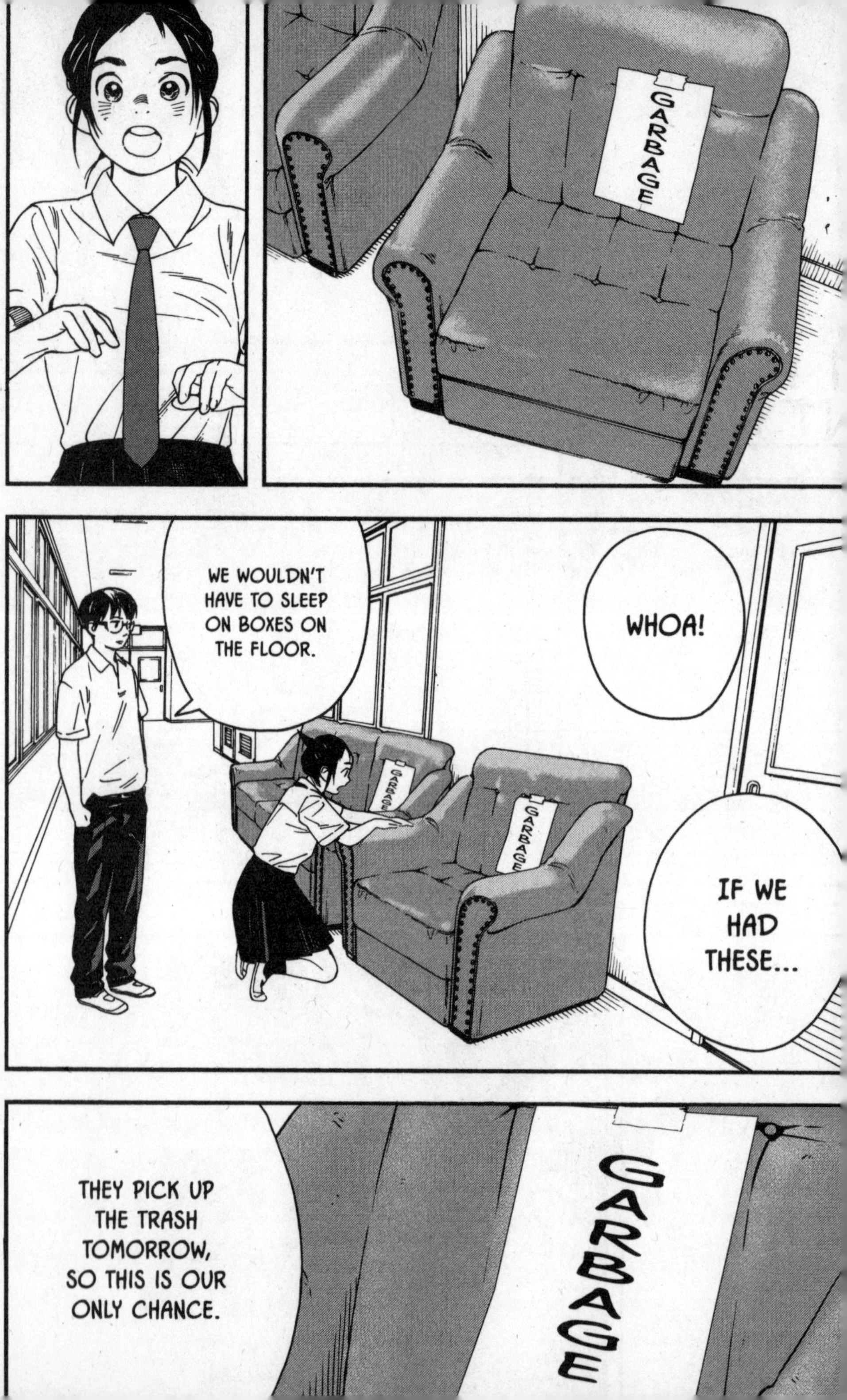
GARBAGE
WHOA!
IF WE HAD THESE...
WE WOULDN'T HAVE TO SLEEP ON BOXES ON THE FLOOR.
GARBAGE
GARBAGE
GARBAGE
THEY PICK UP THE TRASH TOMORROW, SO THIS IS OUR ONLY CHANCE.

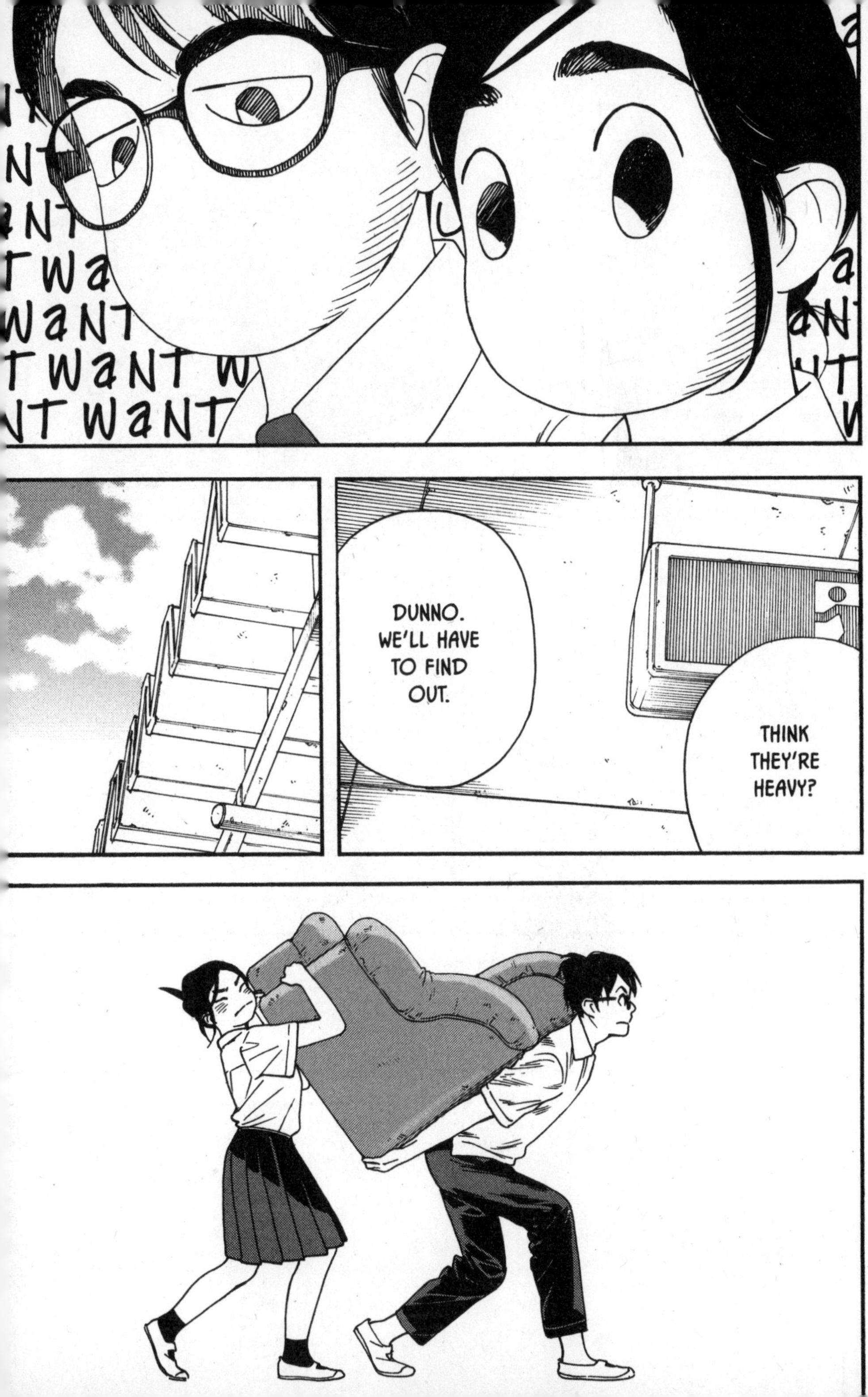
WANT WANT WANT
THINK THEY'RE HEAVY?
DUNNO. WE'LL HAVE TO FIND OUT.

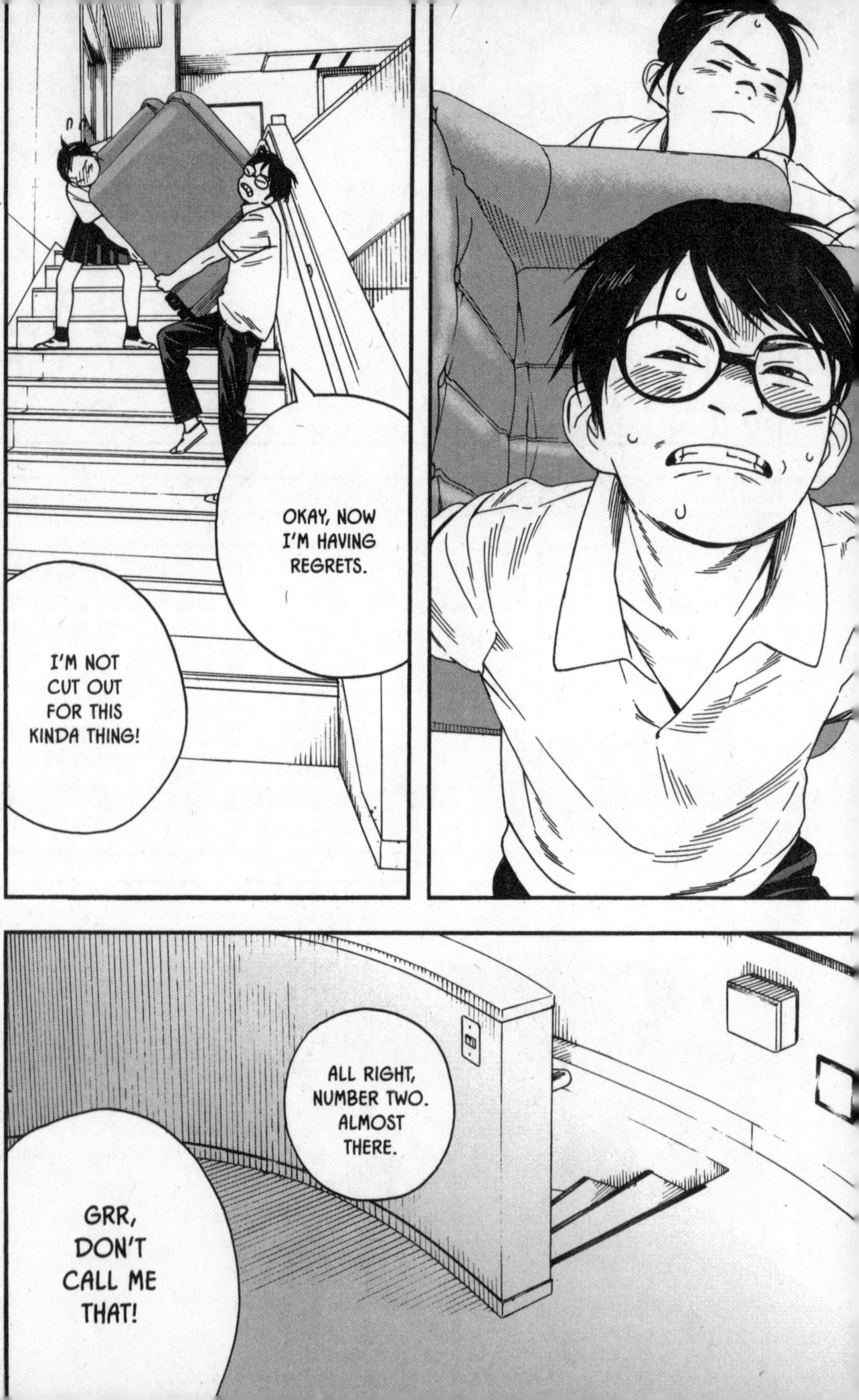
OKAY, NOW I'M HAVING REGRETS.
I'M NOT CUT OUT FOR THIS KINDA THING!
ALL RIGHT, NUMBER TWO. ALMOST THERE.
GRR, DON'T CALL ME THAT!

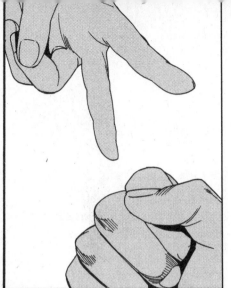

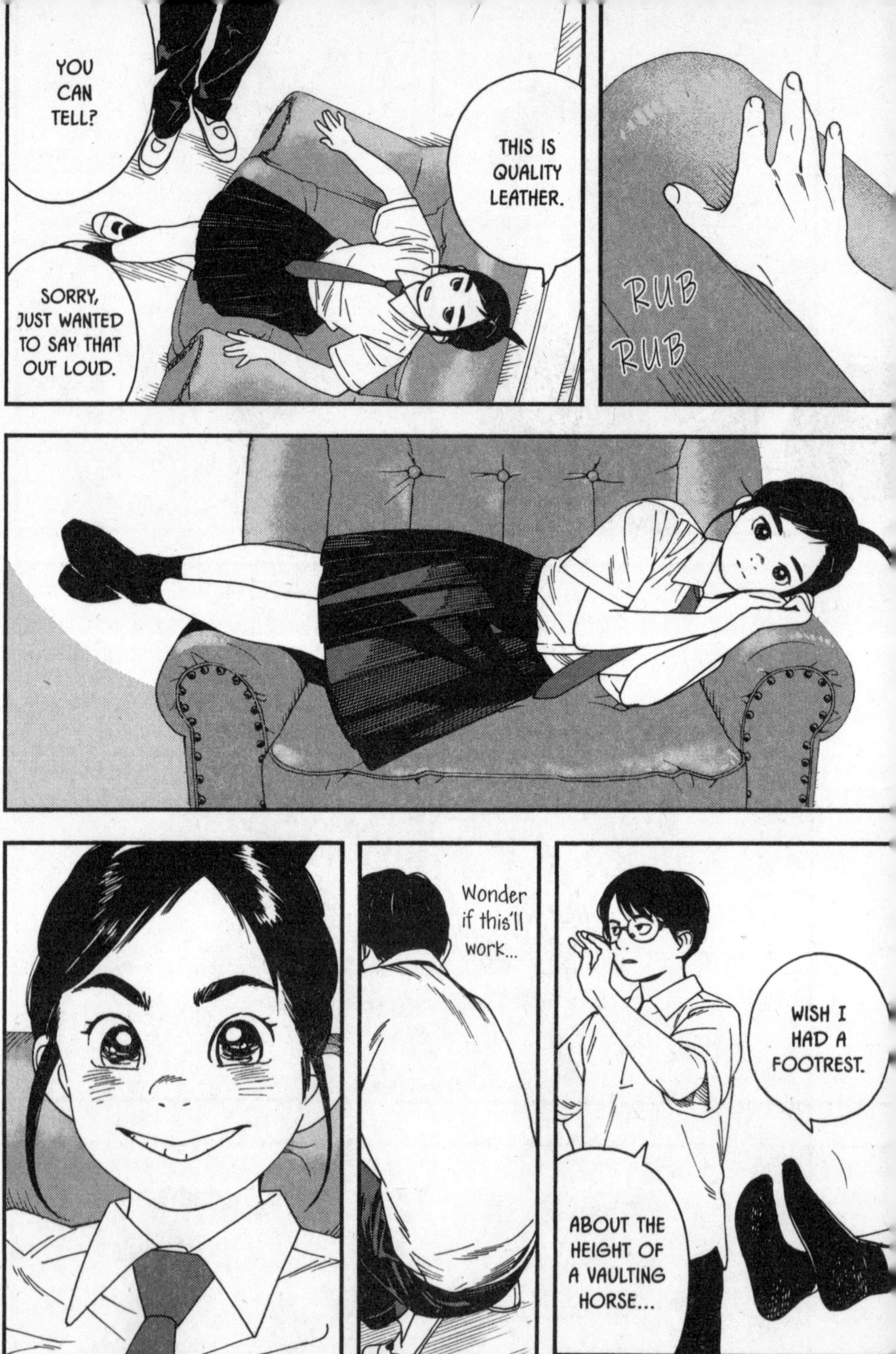
RUB
RUB
THIS IS QUALITY LEATHER.
YOU CAN TELL?
SORRY, JUST WANTED TO SAY THAT OUT LOUD.
WISH I HAD A FOOTREST.
ABOUT THE HEIGHT OF A VAULTING HORSE...
Wonder if this'll work...

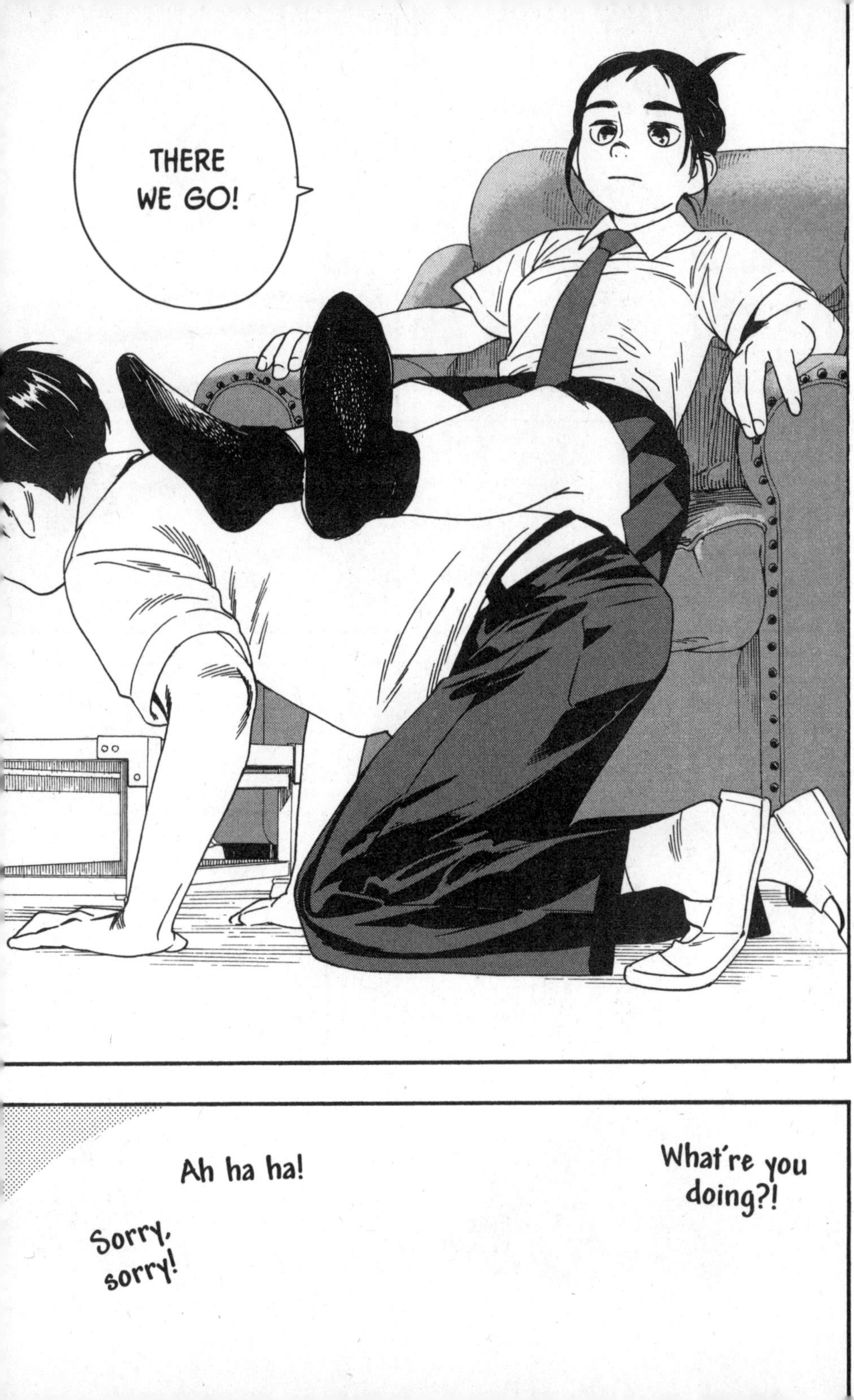
THERE WE GO!
What're you doing?!
Ah ha ha!
Sorry, sorry!

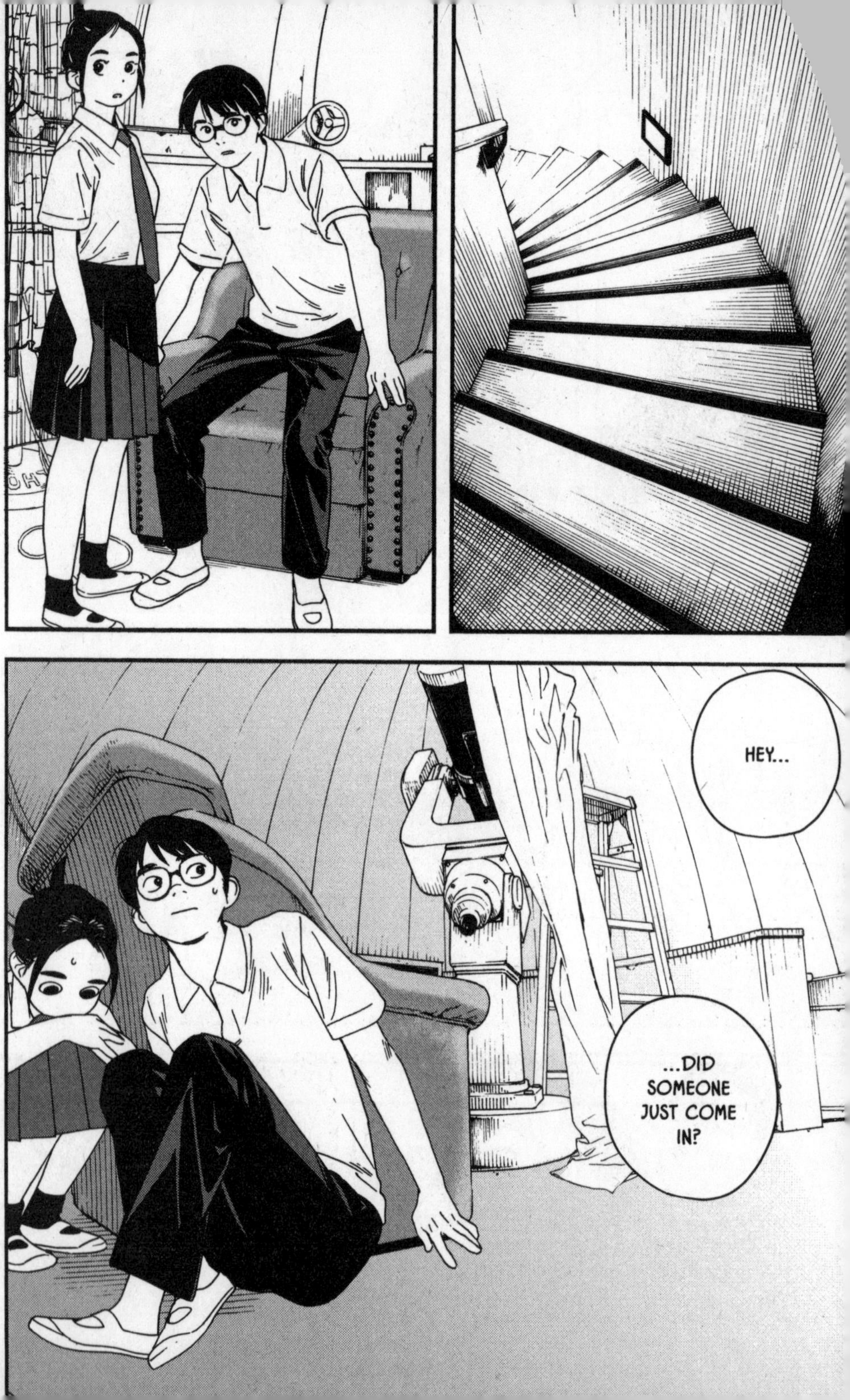
HEY...
...DID SOMEONE JUST COME IN?

Mew.

ALREADY ASLEEP.

!

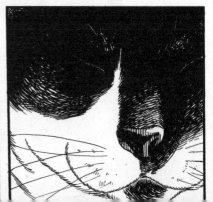

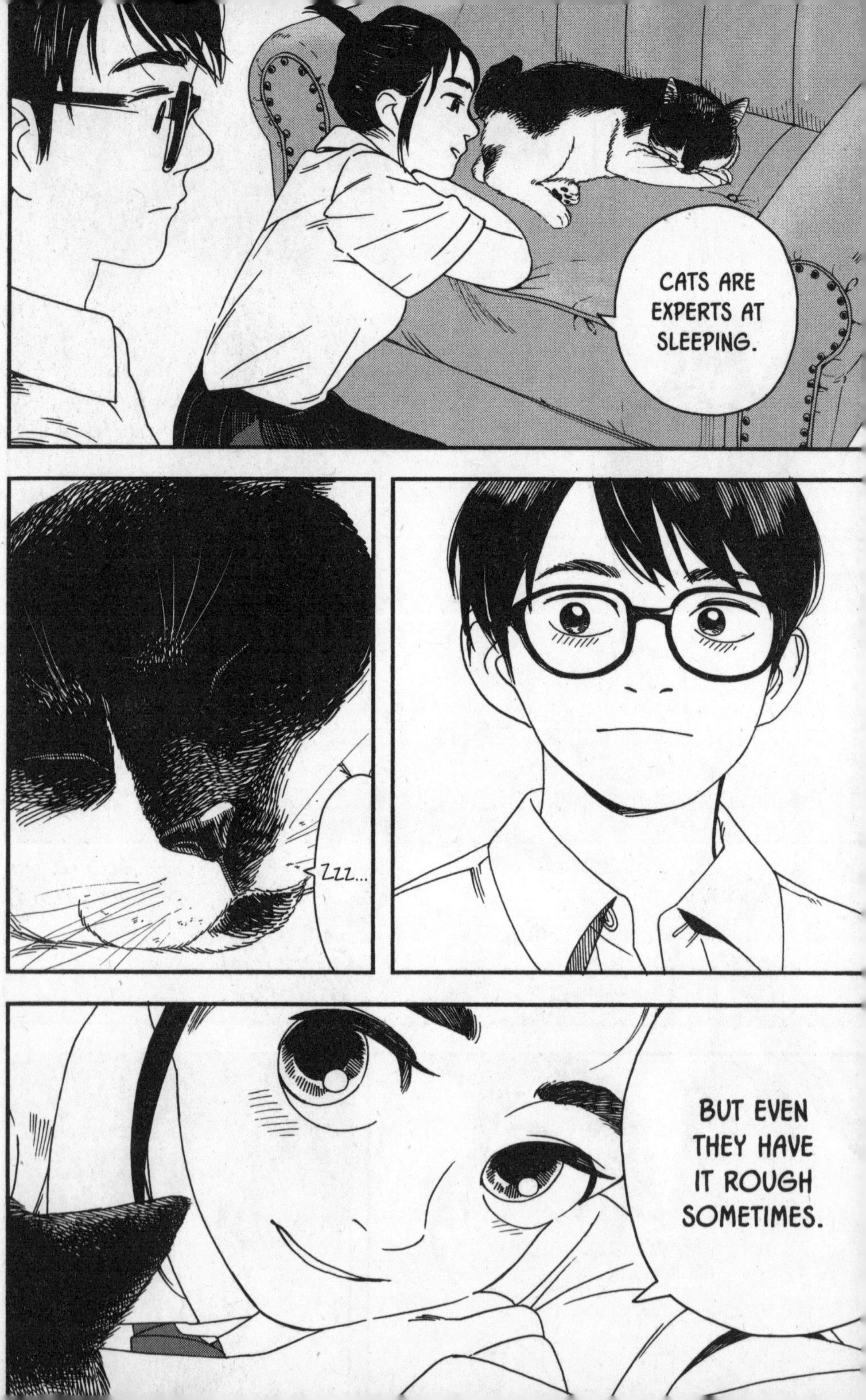
CATS ARE EXPERTS AT SLEEPING.
Zzz...
BUT EVEN THEY HAVE IT ROUGH SOMETIMES.

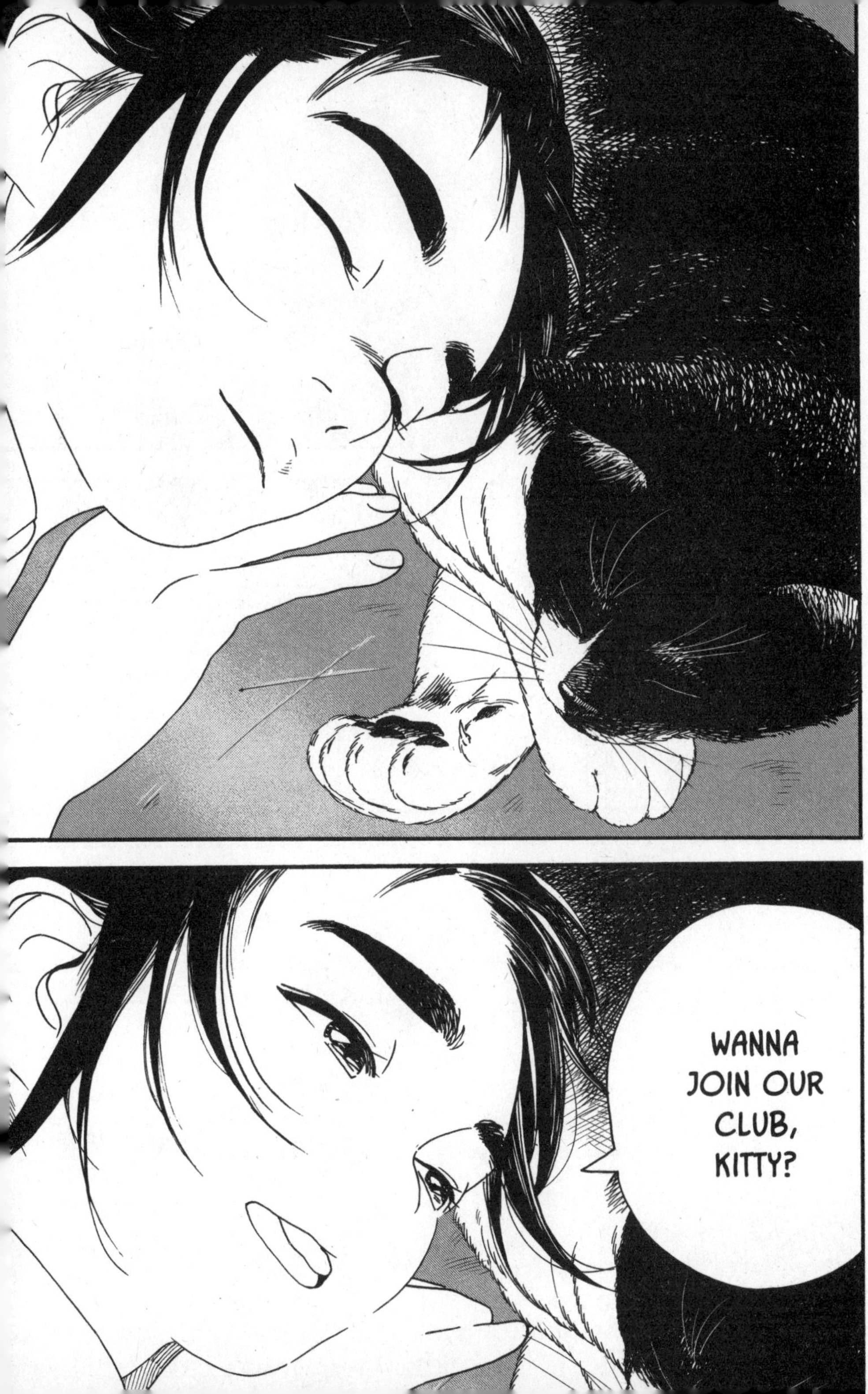
WANNA JOIN OUR CLUB, KITTY?

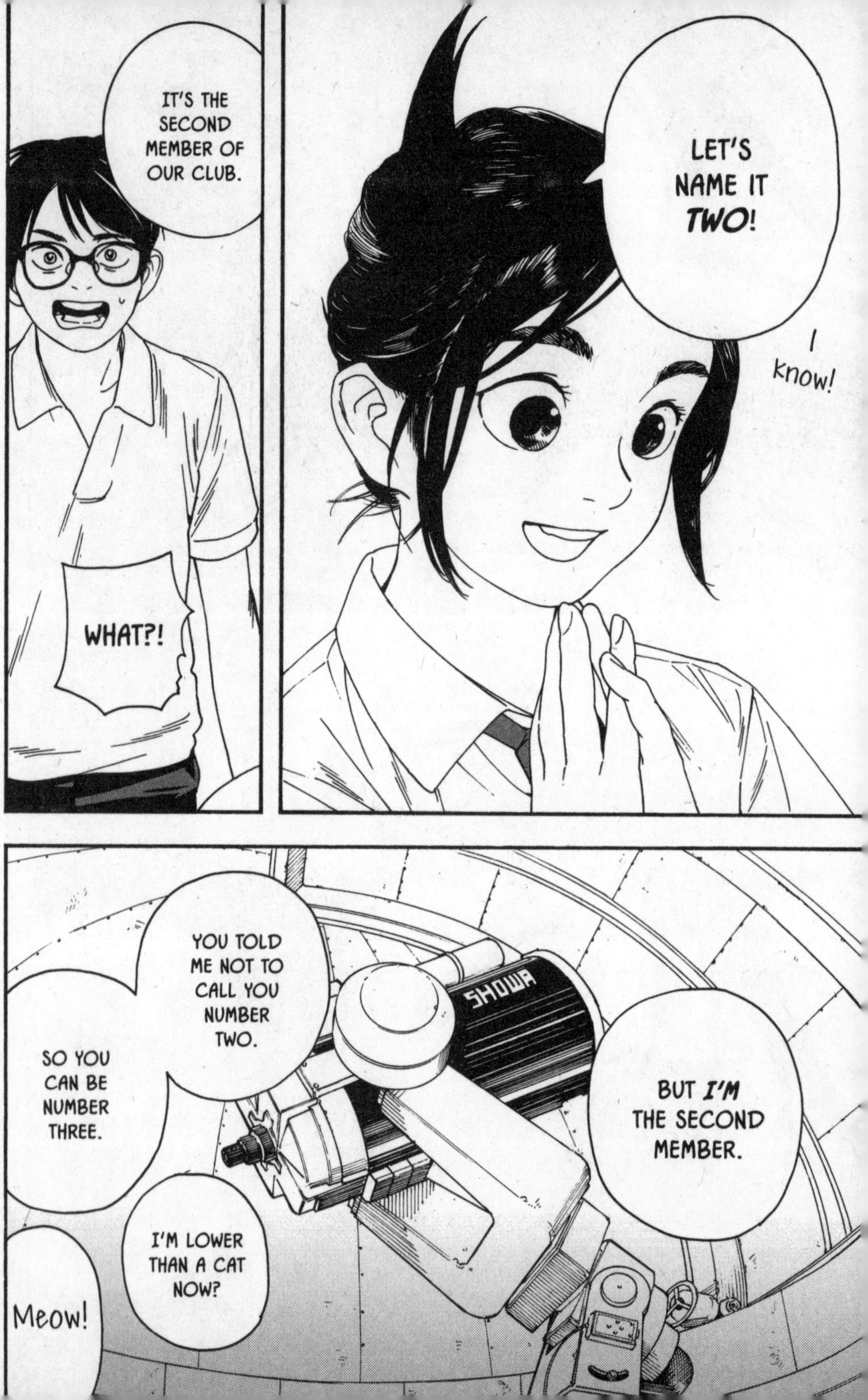
I know!
LET'S NAME IT *TWO*!
IT'S THE SECOND MEMBER OF OUR CLUB.
WHAT?!
SHOWA
BUT *I'M* THE SECOND MEMBER.
YOU TOLD ME NOT TO CALL YOU NUMBER TWO.
SO YOU CAN BE NUMBER THREE.
I'M LOWER THAN A CAT NOW?
Meow!

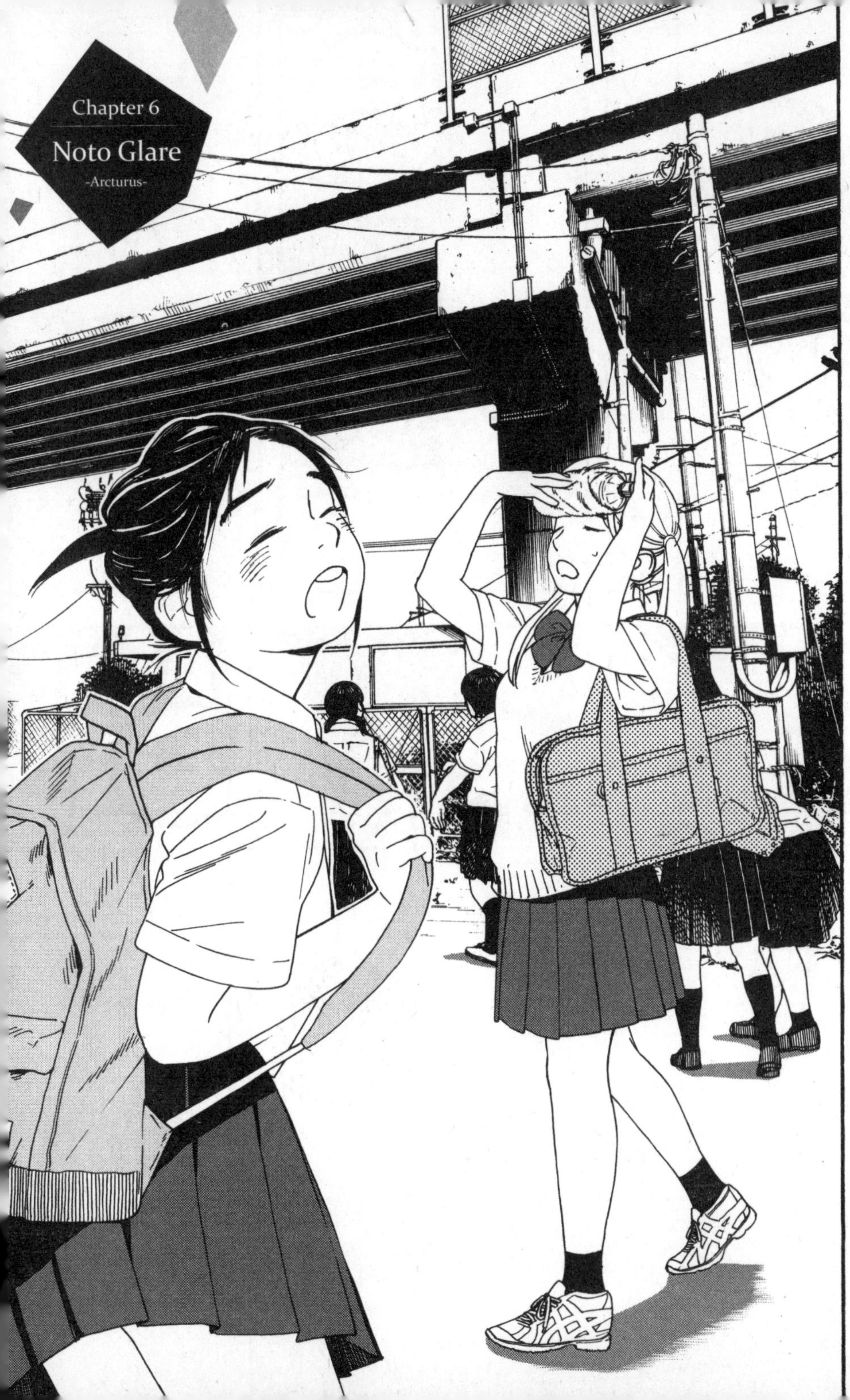
Chapter 6
Noto Glare
-Arcturus-

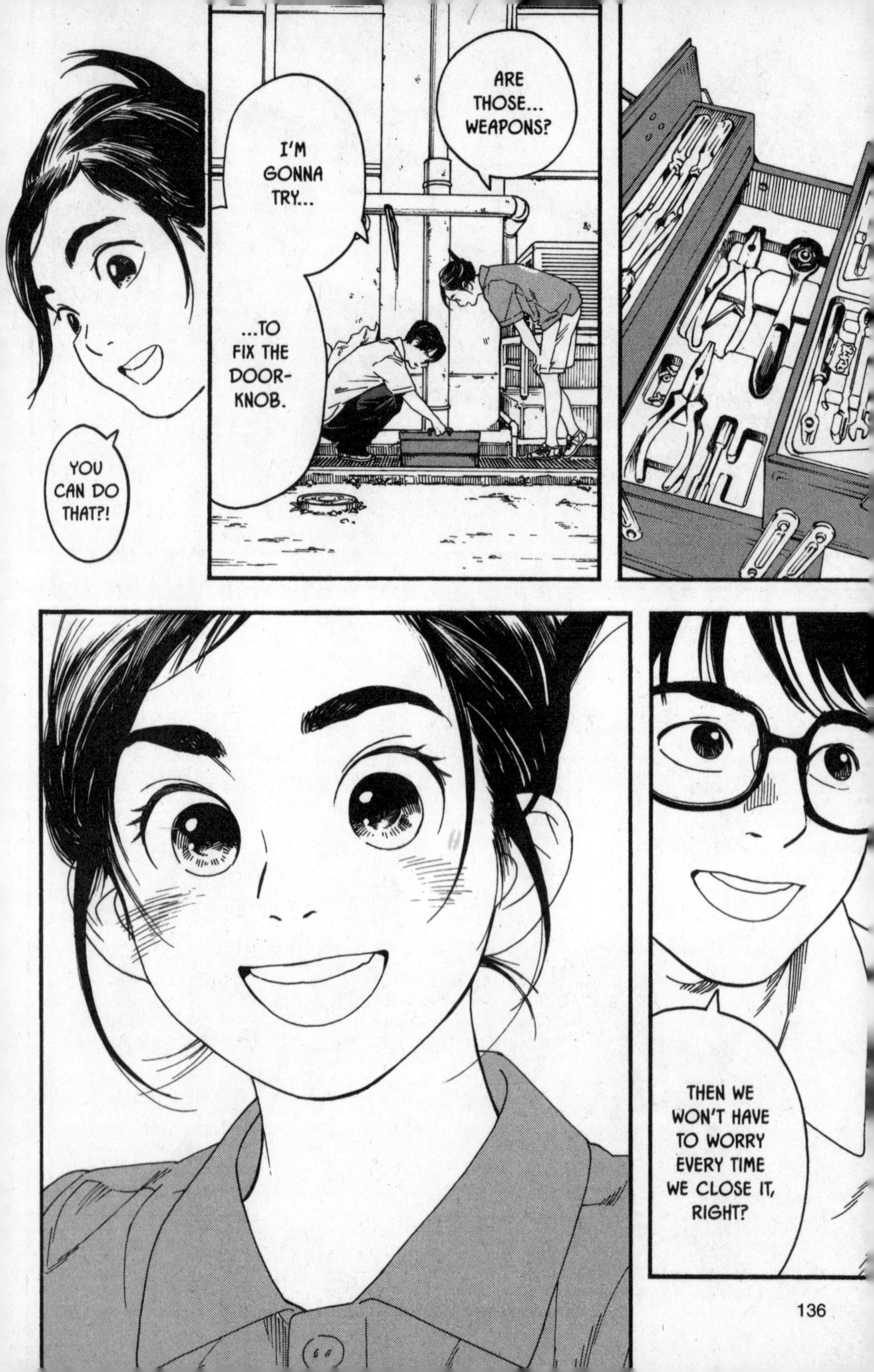
ARE THOSE... WEAPONS?
I'M GONNA TRY...
...TO FIX THE DOOR-KNOB.
YOU CAN DO THAT?!
THEN WE WON'T HAVE TO WORRY EVERY TIME WE CLOSE IT, RIGHT?

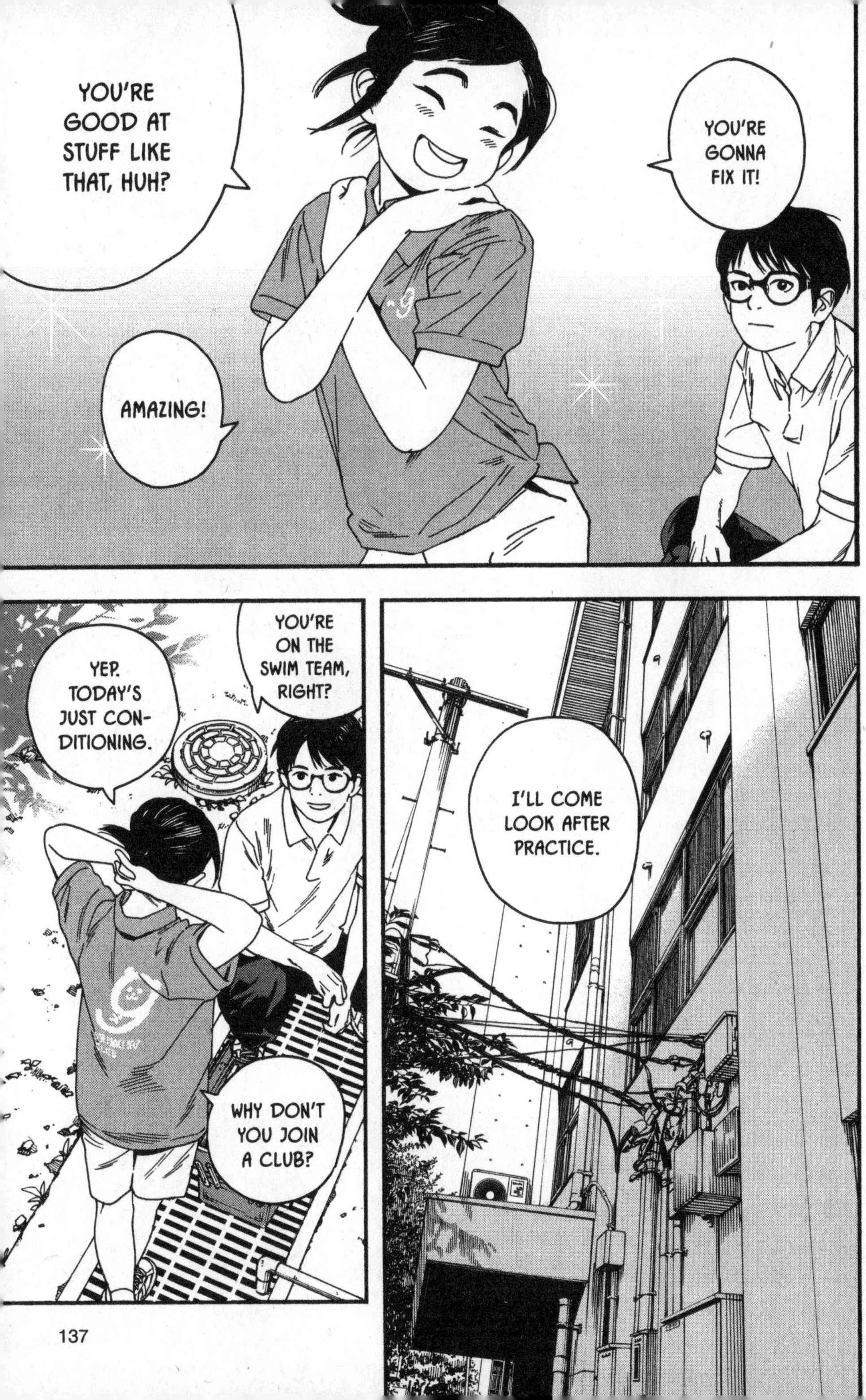
YOU'RE GONNA FIX IT!
YOU'RE GOOD AT STUFF LIKE THAT, HUH?
AMAZING!
I'LL COME LOOK AFTER PRACTICE.
YOU'RE ON THE SWIM TEAM, RIGHT?
YEP. TODAY'S JUST CON-DITIONING.
WHY DON'T YOU JOIN A CLUB?

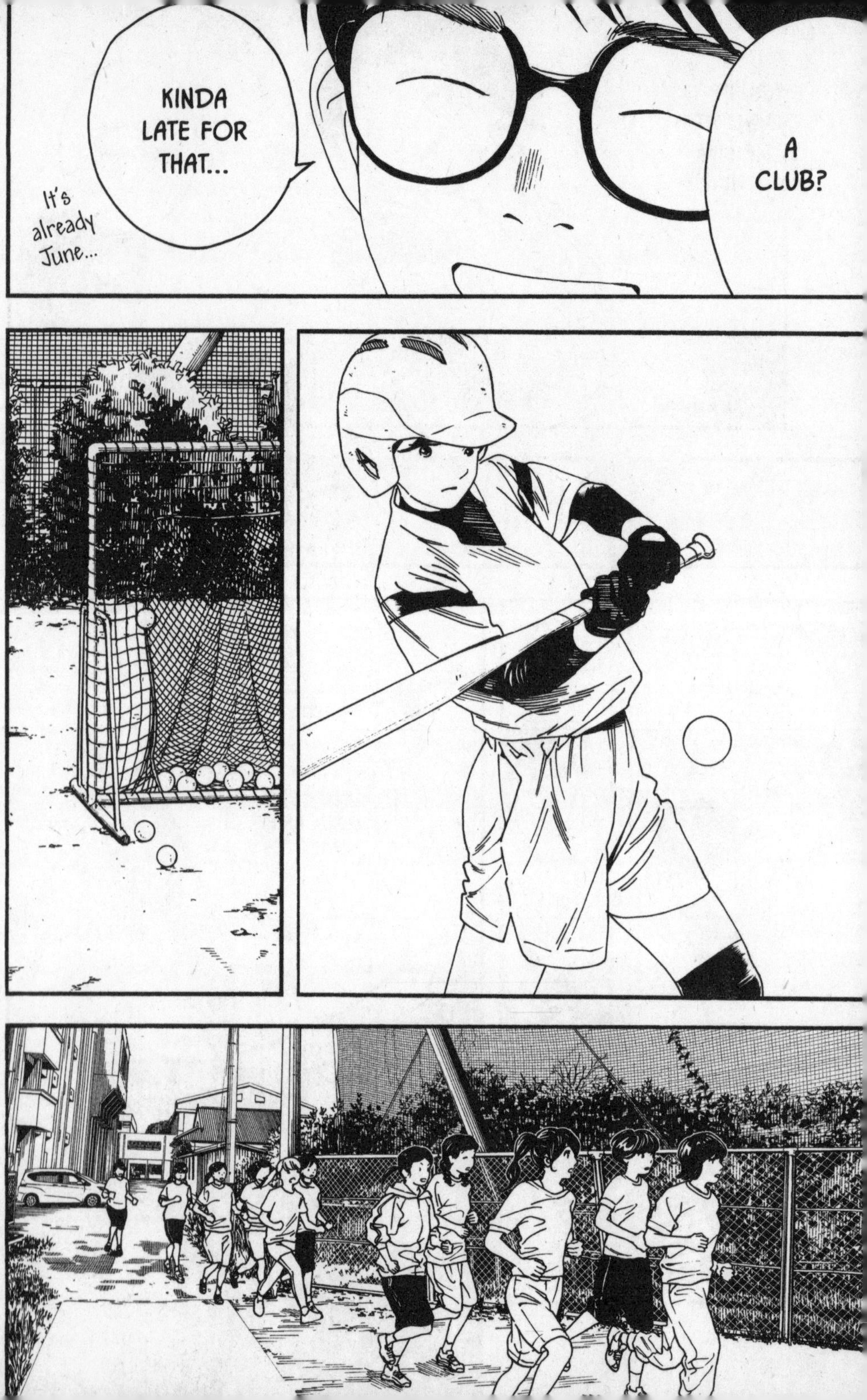
A CLUB?
KINDA LATE FOR THAT...
It's already June...

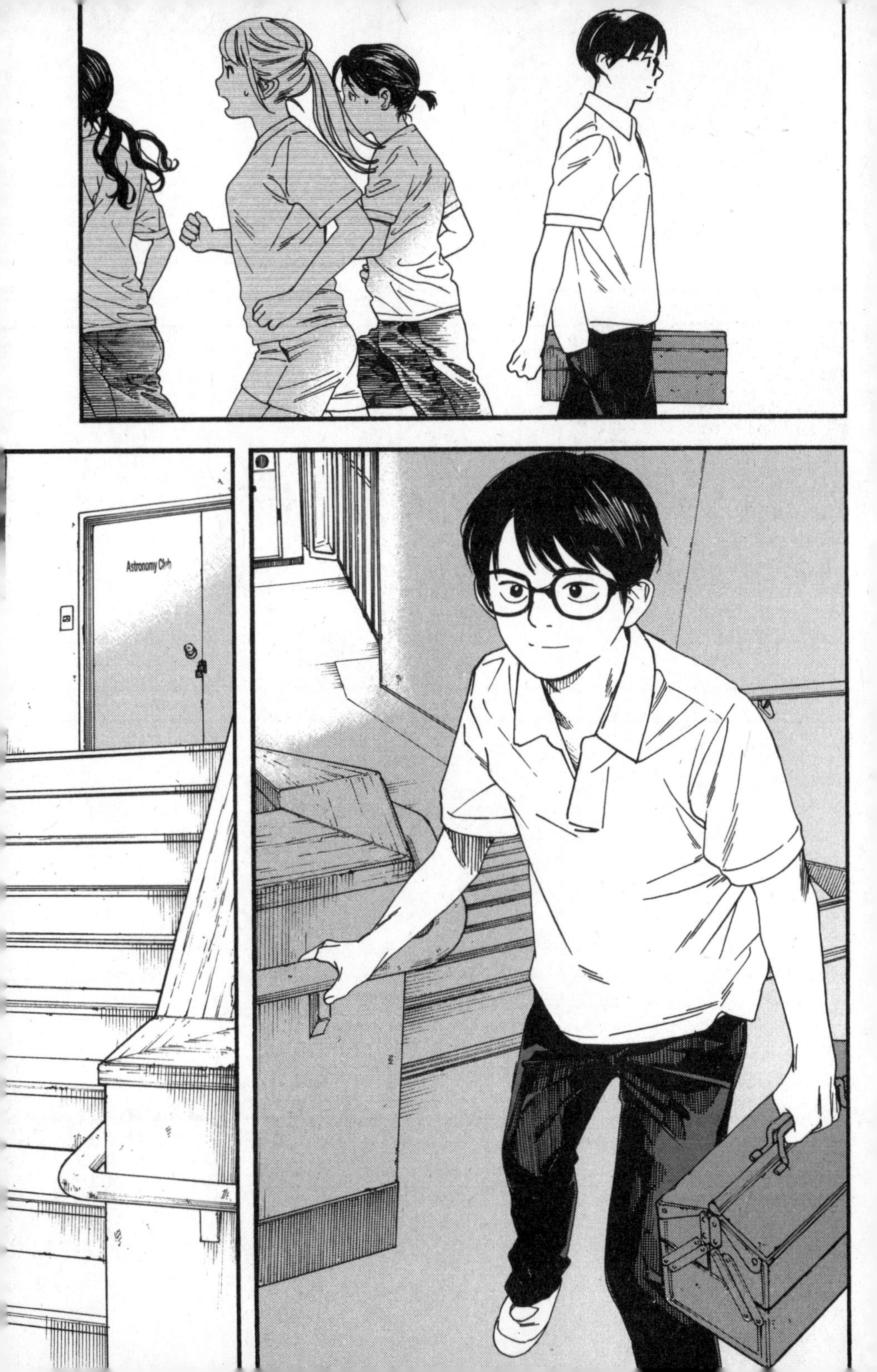
Astronomy Club

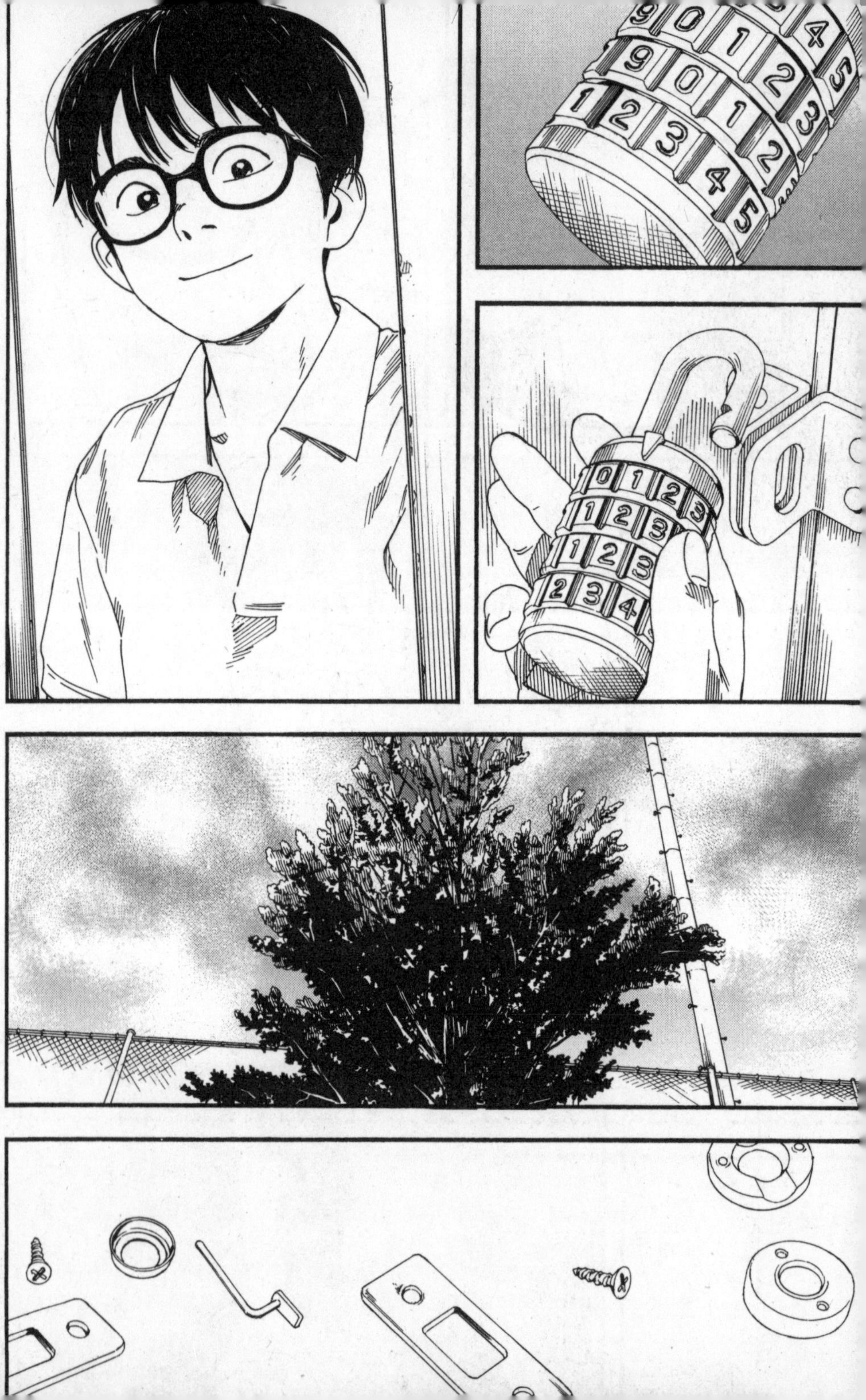

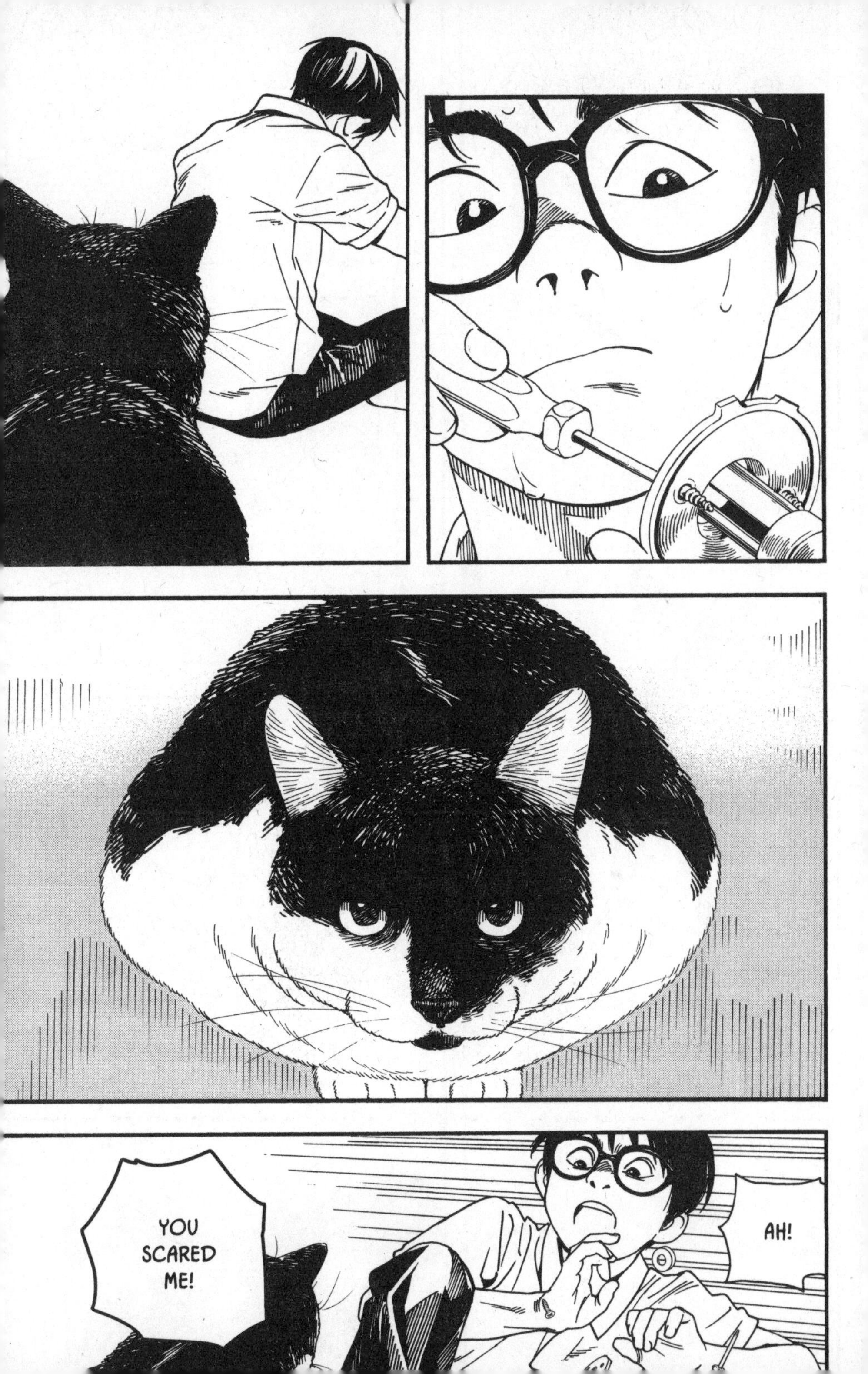
AH!
YOU SCARED ME!

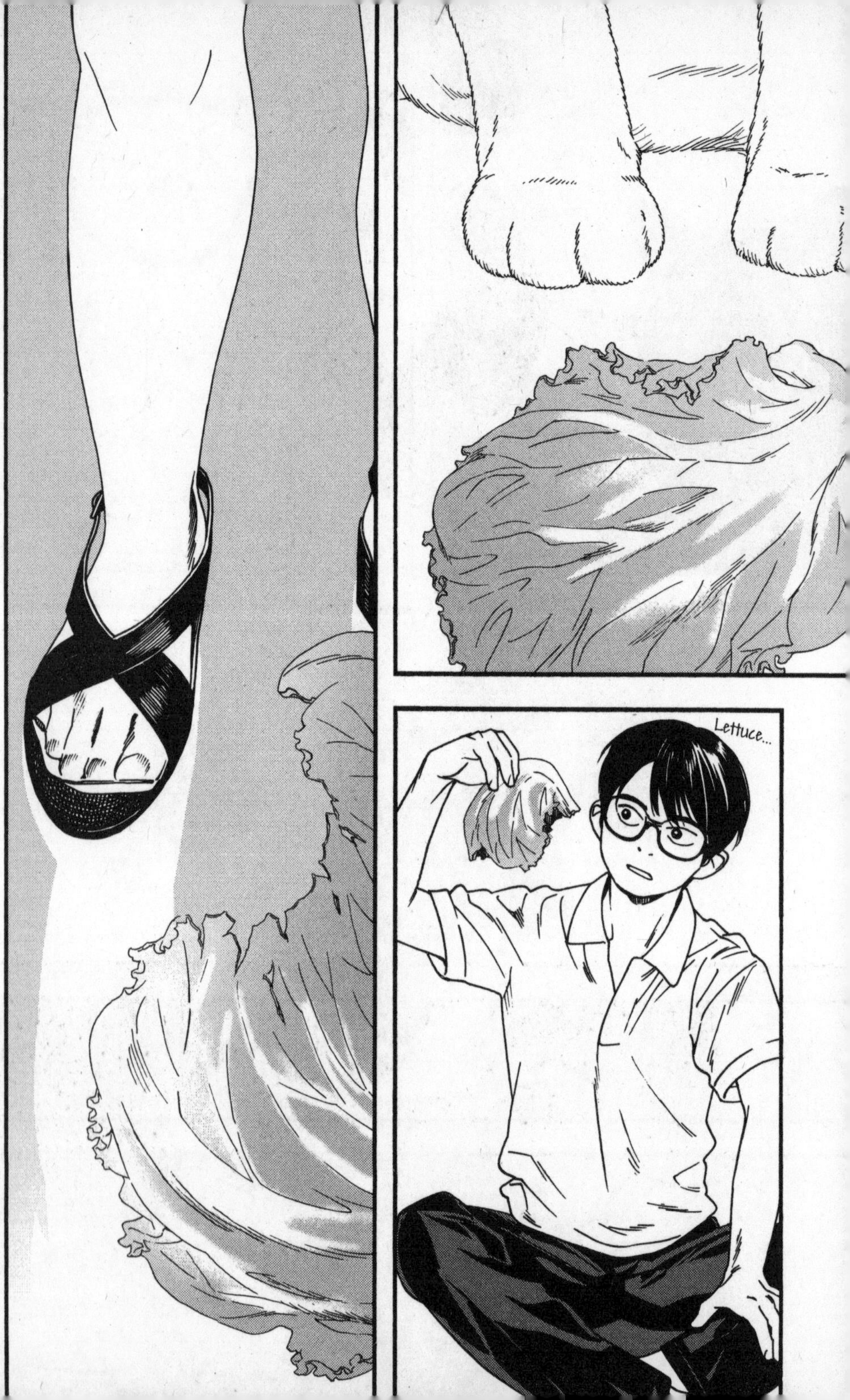
Lettuce...

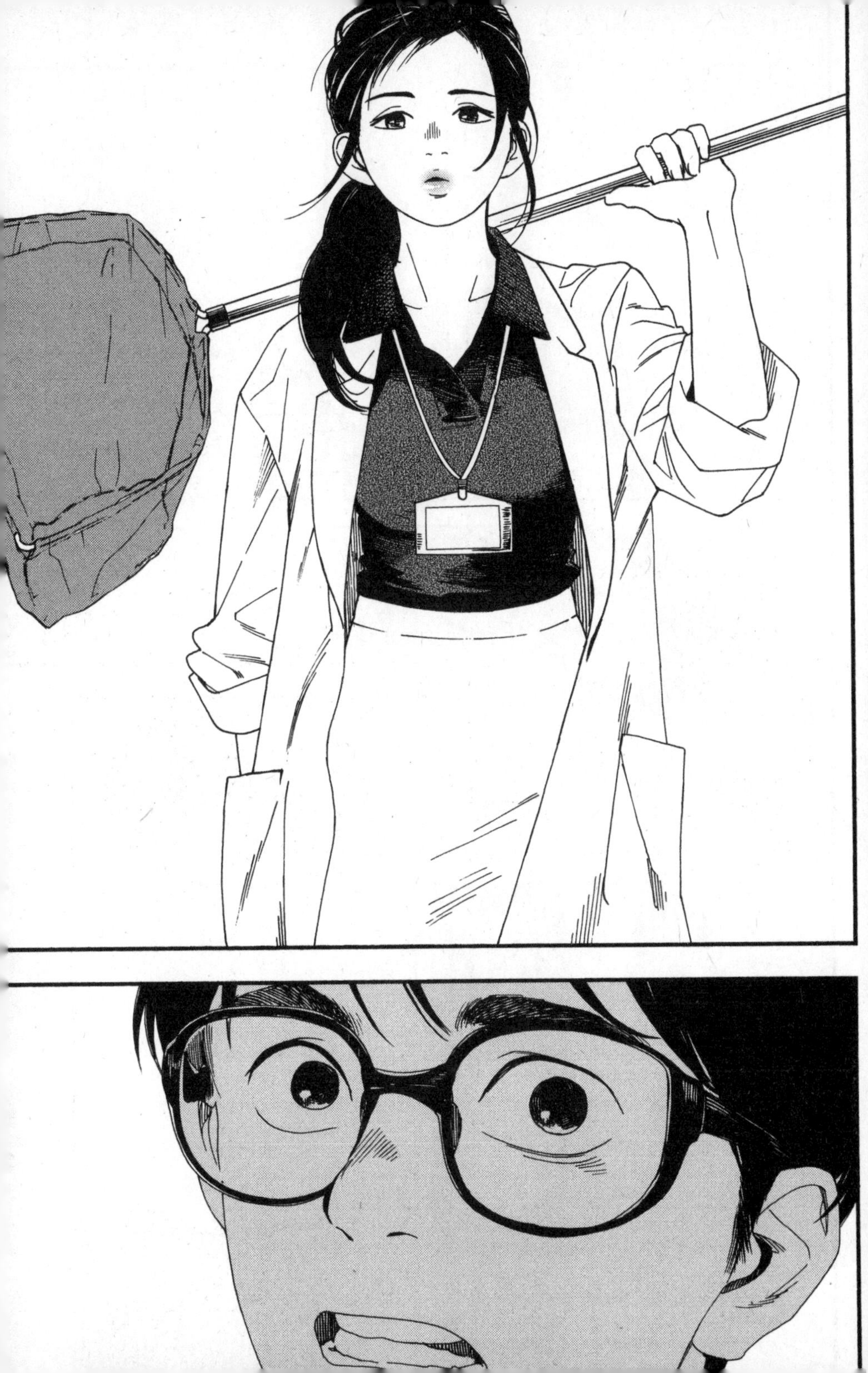

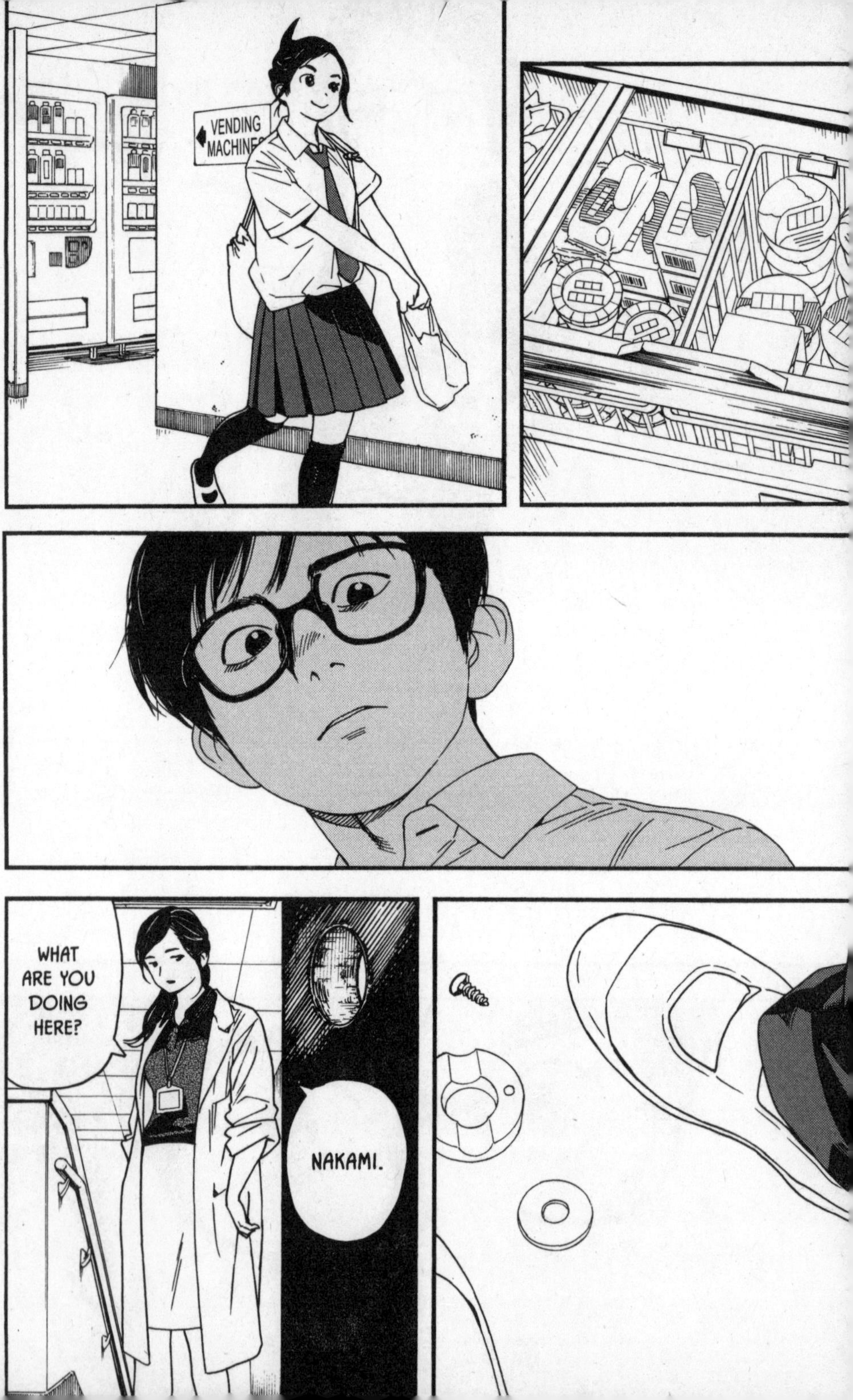
VENDING MACHINE
NAKAMI.
WHAT ARE YOU DOING HERE?

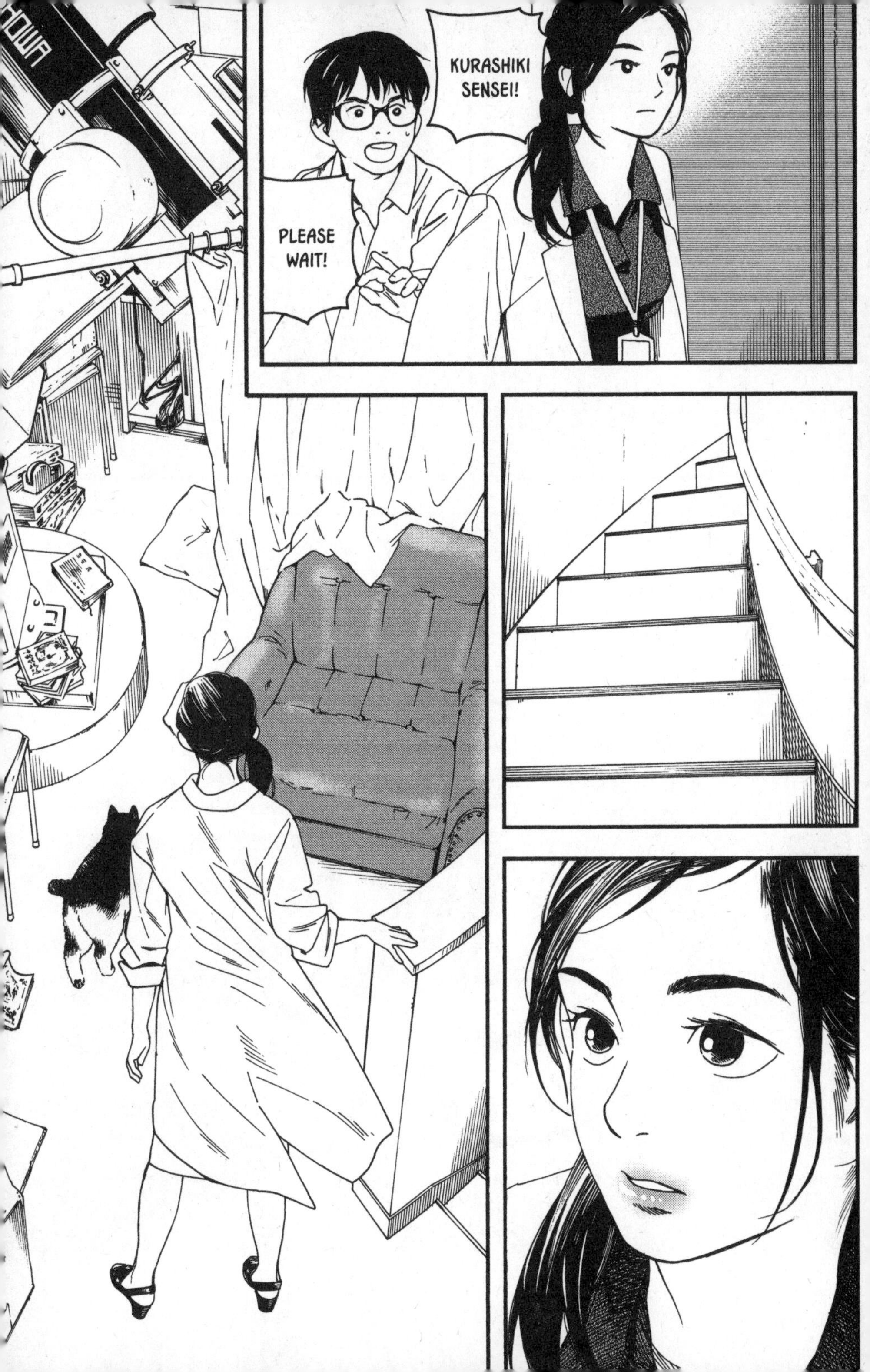
KURASHIKI SENSEI!
PLEASE WAIT!

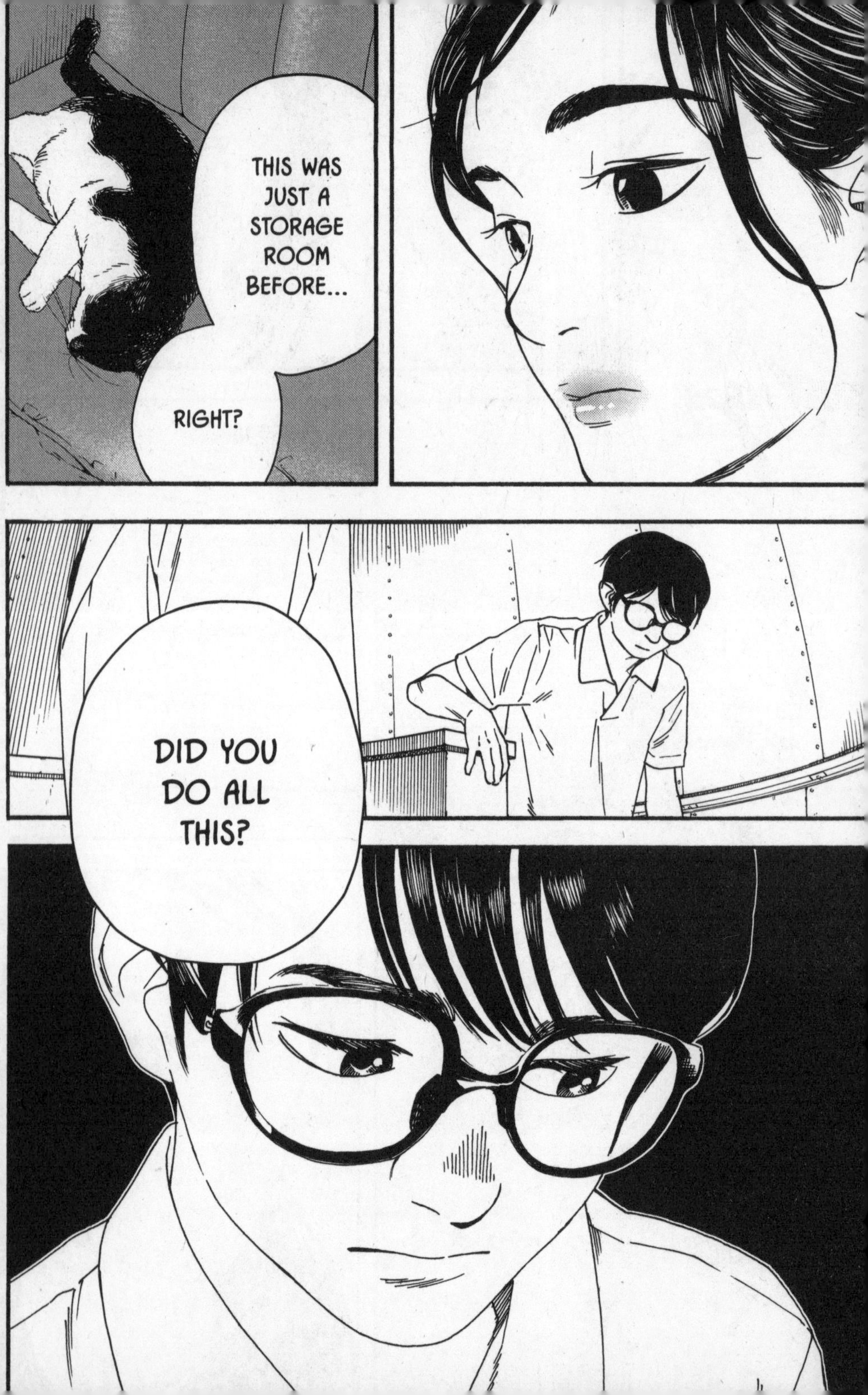
THIS WAS JUST A STORAGE ROOM BEFORE...
RIGHT?
DID YOU DO ALL THIS?

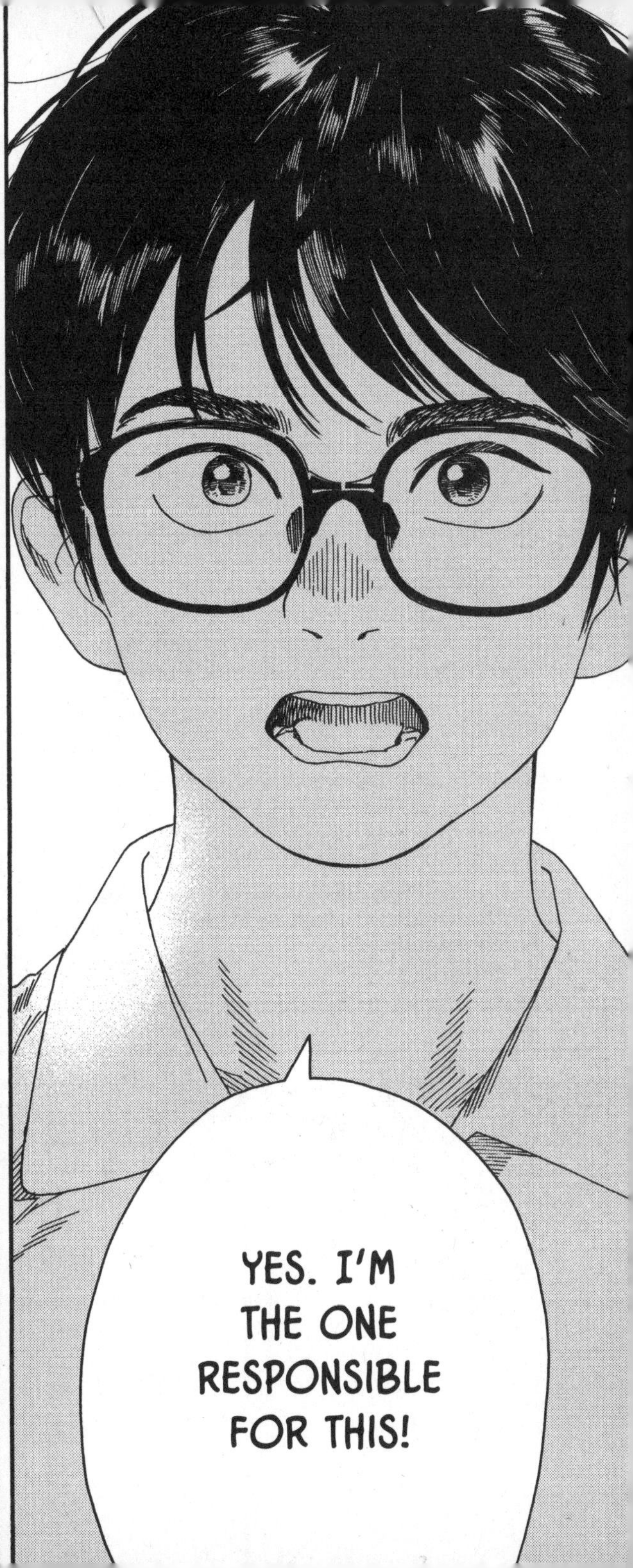
YES. I'M THE ONE RESPONSIBLE FOR THIS!
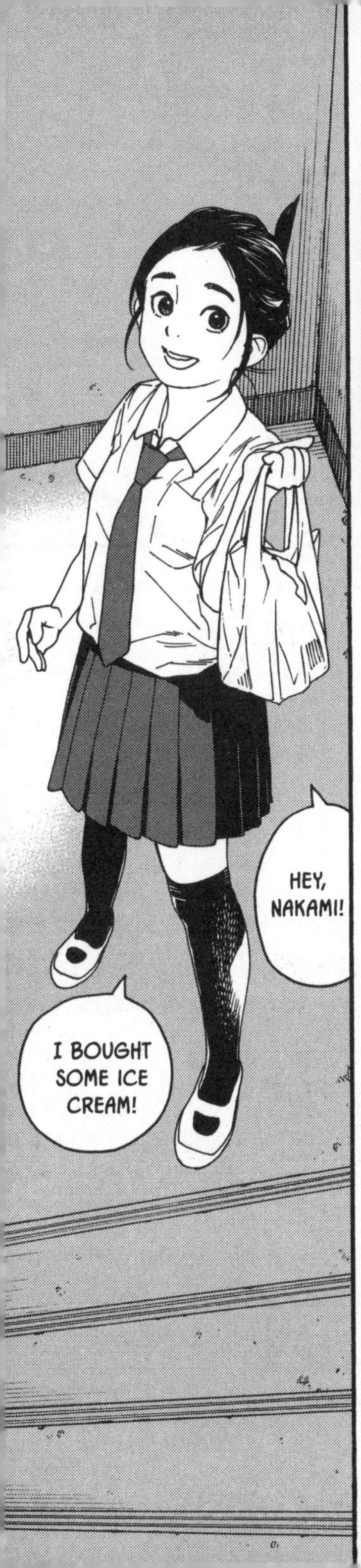
HEY, NAKAMI!
I BOUGHT SOME ICE CREAM!

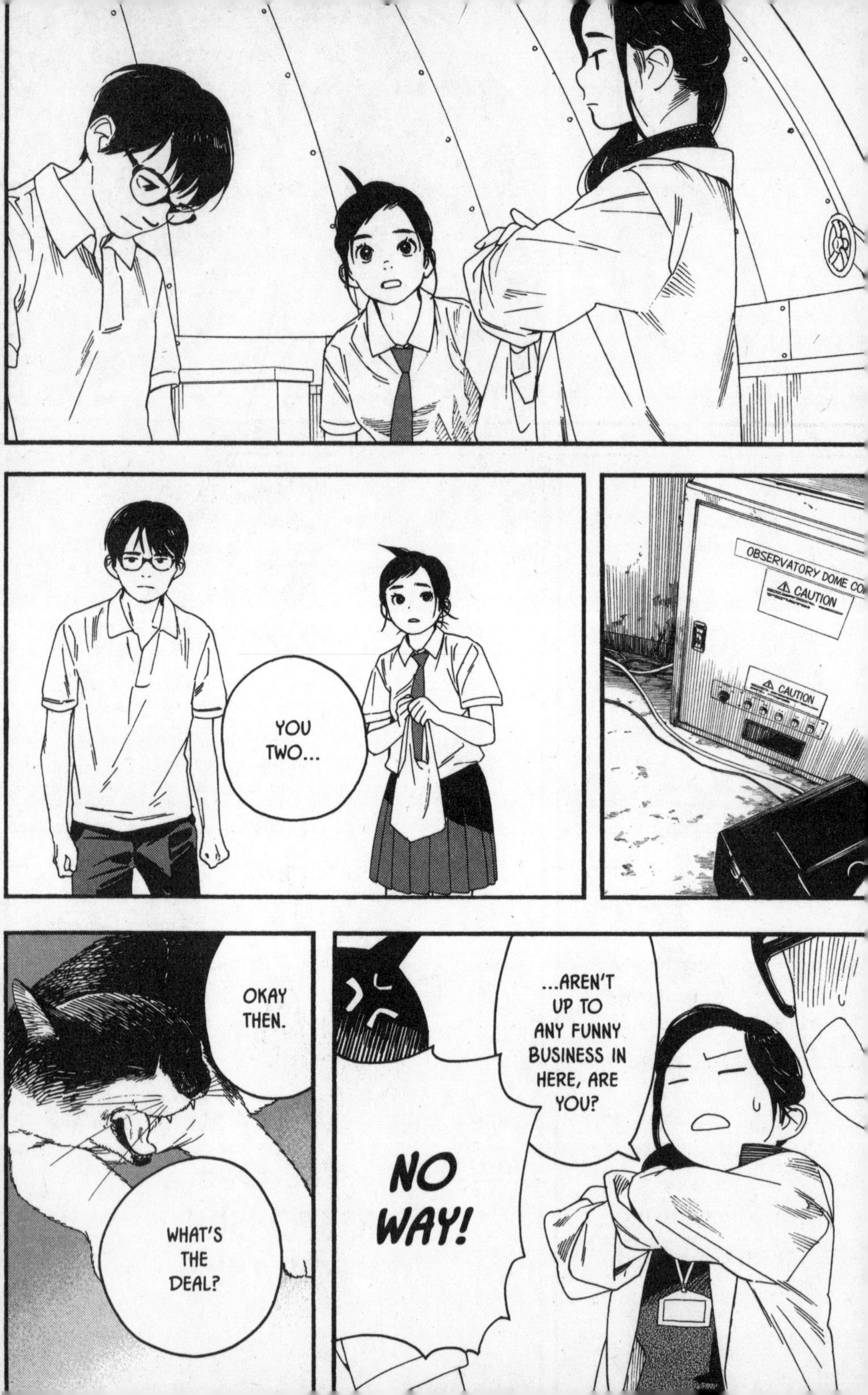
OBSERVATORY DOME CO
CAUTION
CAUTION
YOU TWO...
...AREN'T UP TO ANY FUNNY BUSINESS IN HERE, ARE YOU?
NO WAY!
OKAY THEN.
WHAT'S THE DEAL?

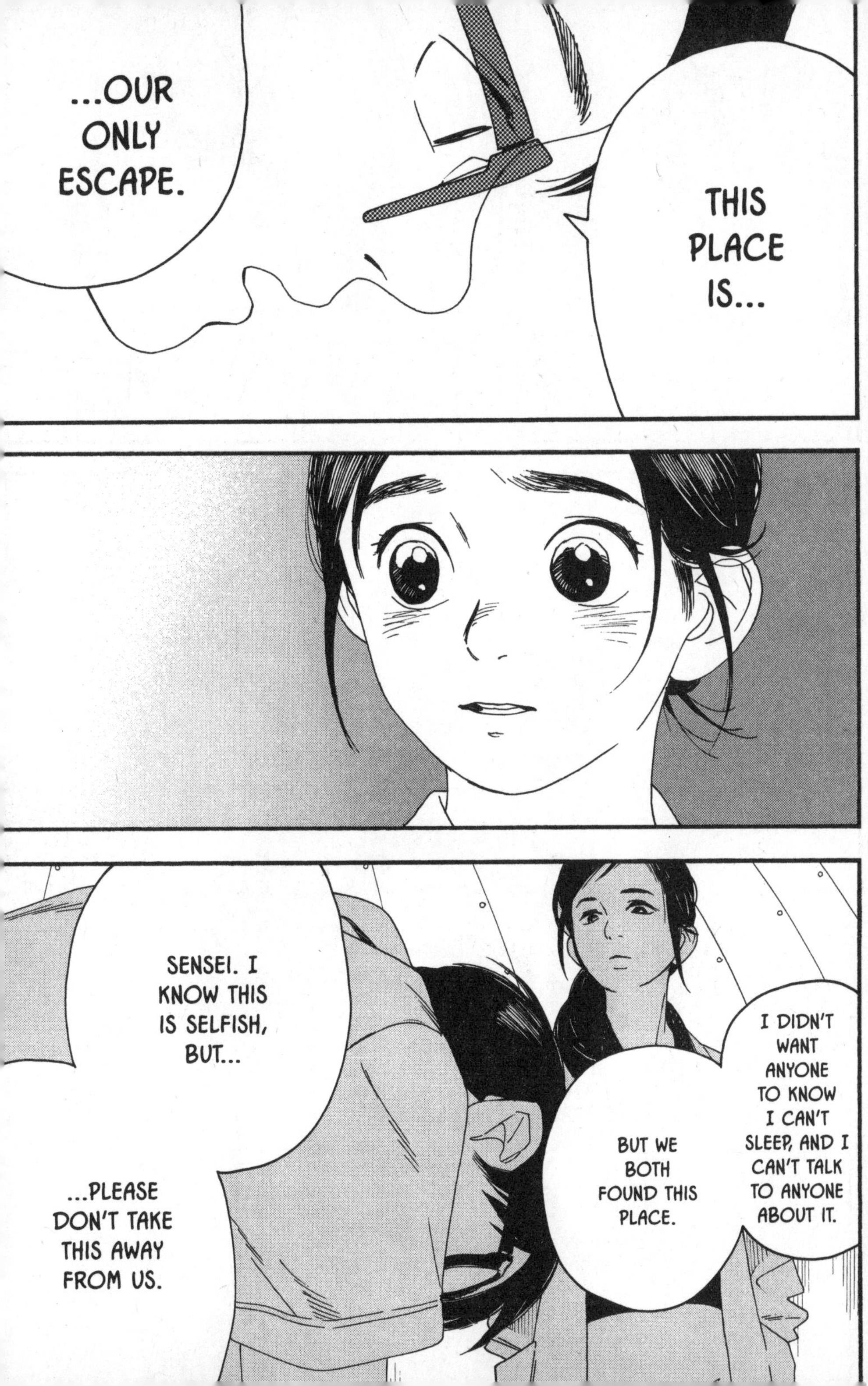
THIS PLACE IS...
...OUR ONLY ESCAPE.
I DIDN'T WANT ANYONE TO KNOW I CAN'T SLEEP, AND I CAN'T TALK TO ANYONE ABOUT IT.
BUT WE BOTH FOUND THIS PLACE.
SENSEI. I KNOW THIS IS SELFISH, BUT...
...PLEASE DON'T TAKE THIS AWAY FROM US.

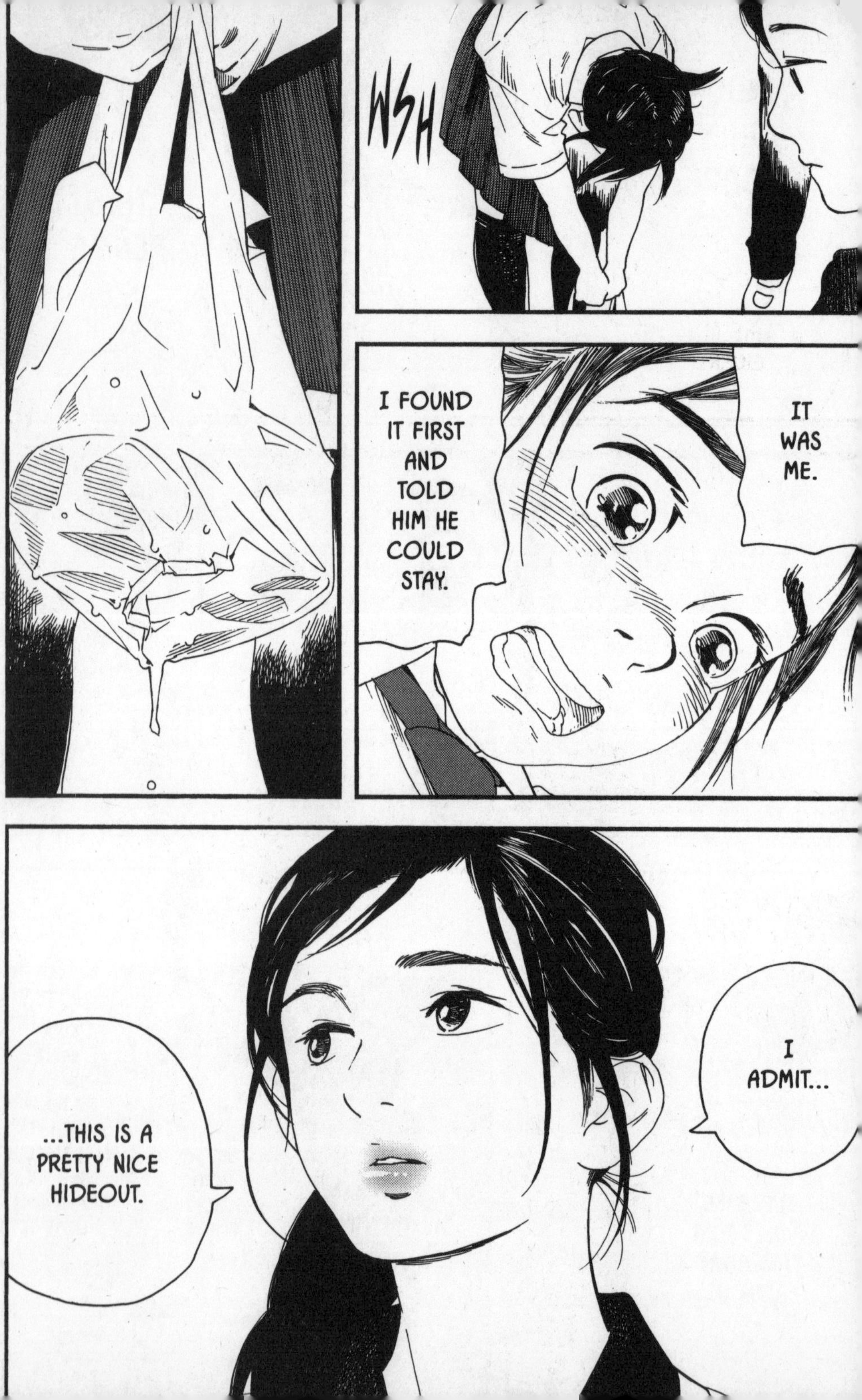
WSH
IT WAS ME.
I FOUND IT FIRST AND TOLD HIM HE COULD STAY.
I ADMIT...
...THIS IS A PRETTY NICE HIDEOUT.

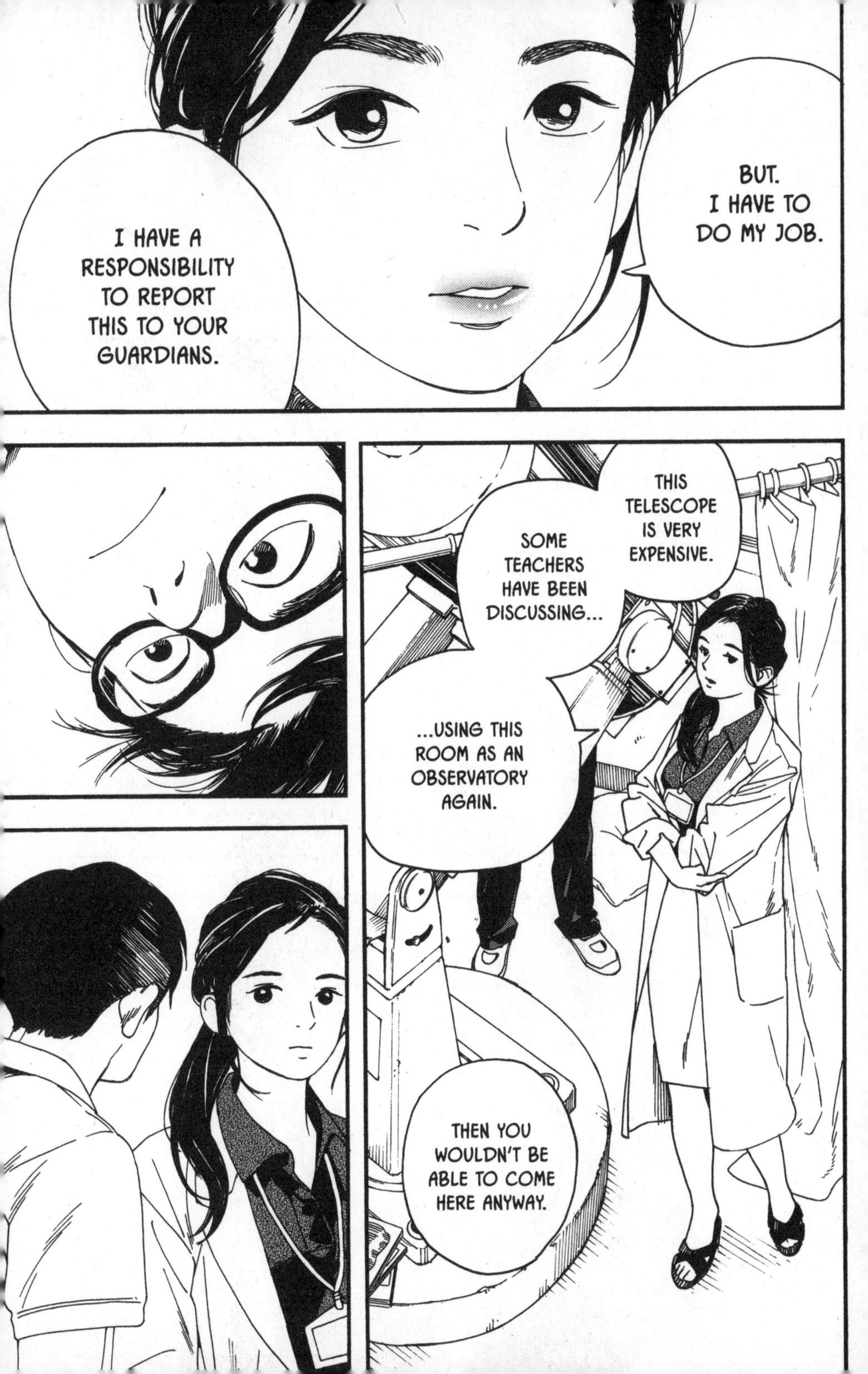
BUT. I HAVE TO DO MY JOB.
I HAVE A RESPONSIBILITY TO REPORT THIS TO YOUR GUARDIANS.
THIS TELESCOPE IS VERY EXPENSIVE.
SOME TEACHERS HAVE BEEN DISCUSSING...
...USING THIS ROOM AS AN OBSERVATORY AGAIN.
THEN YOU WOULDN'T BE ABLE TO COME HERE ANYWAY.

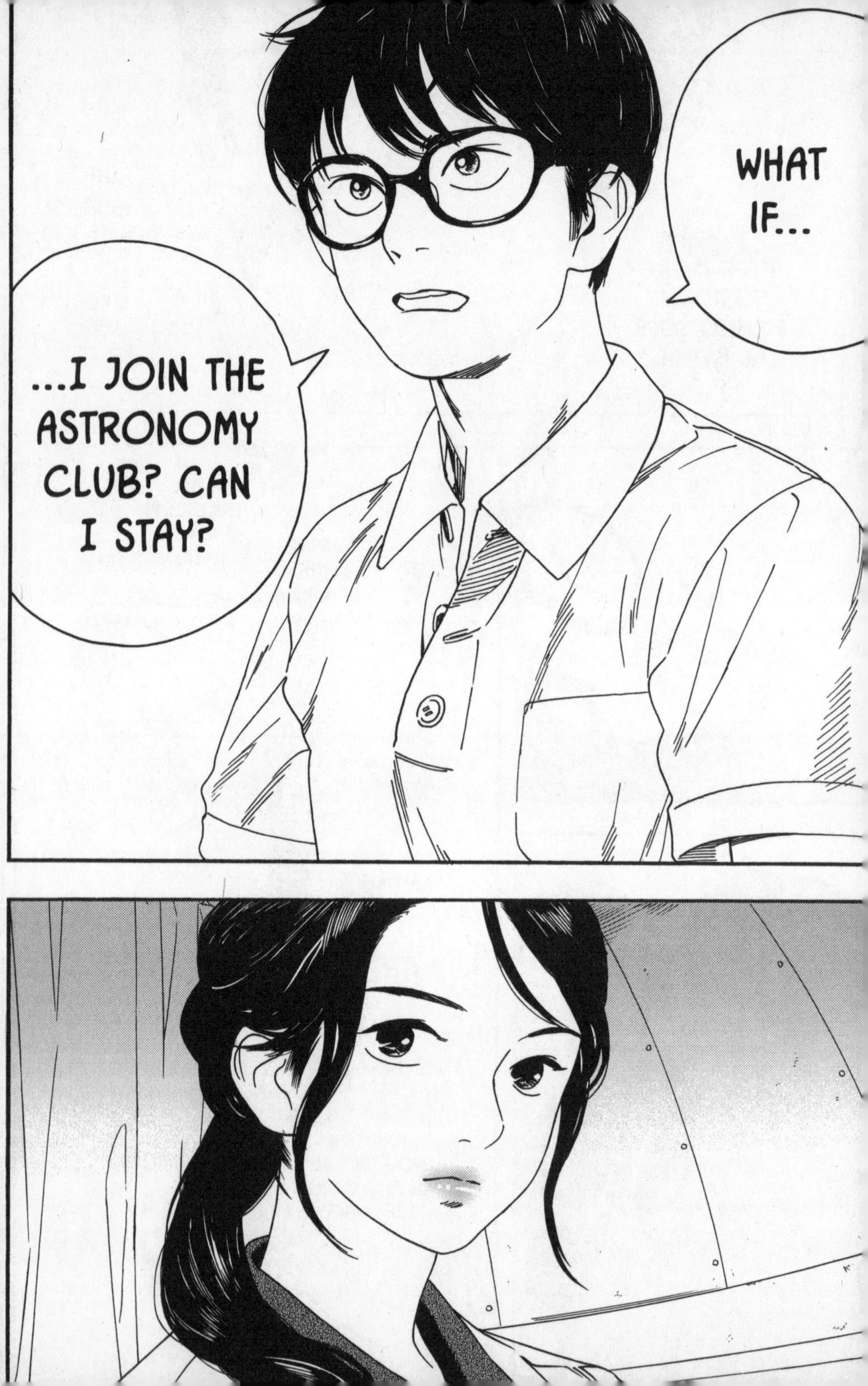
WHAT IF...
...I JOIN THE ASTRONOMY CLUB? CAN I STAY?

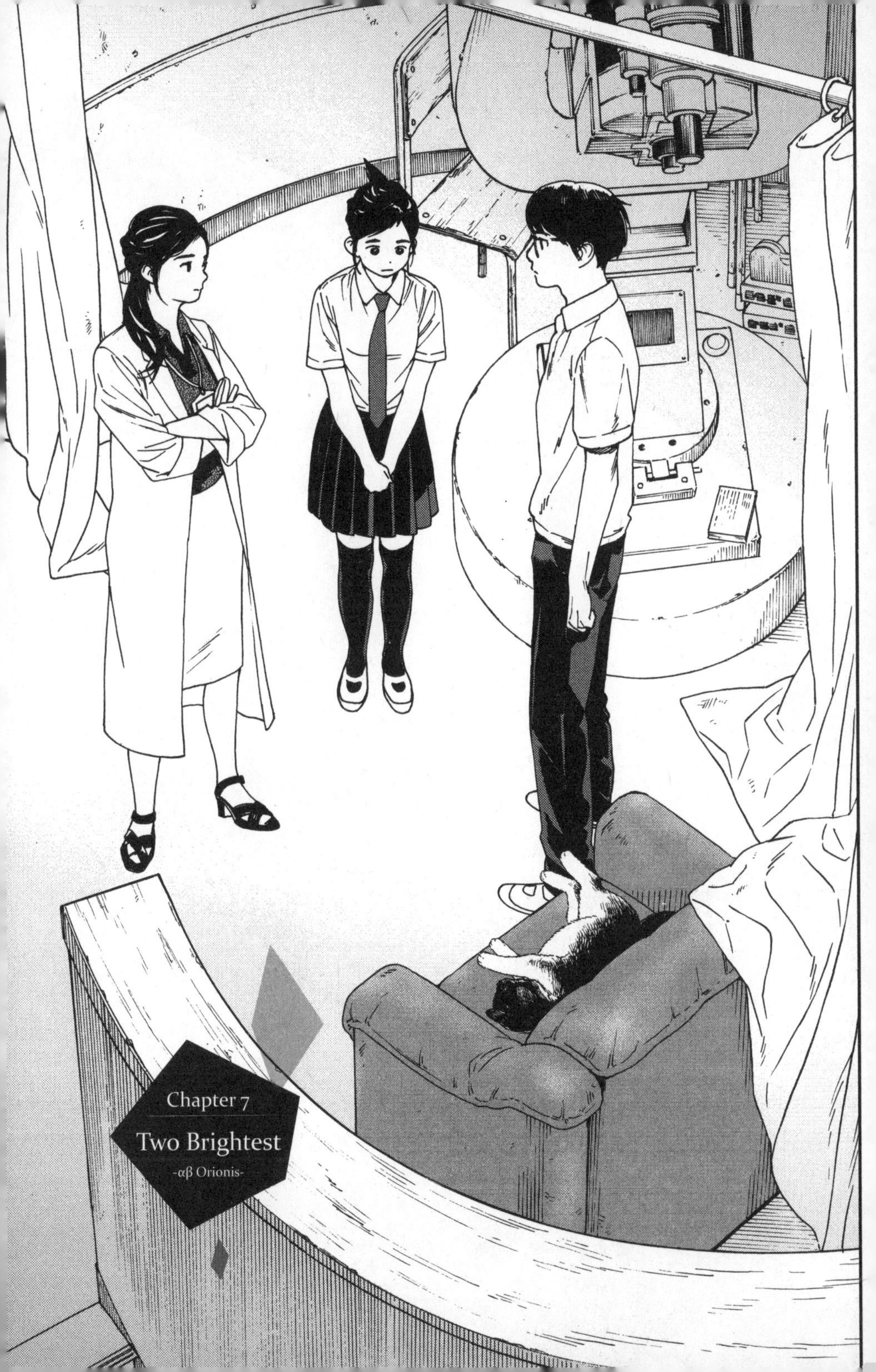
Chapter 7
Two Brightest
-αβ Orionis-

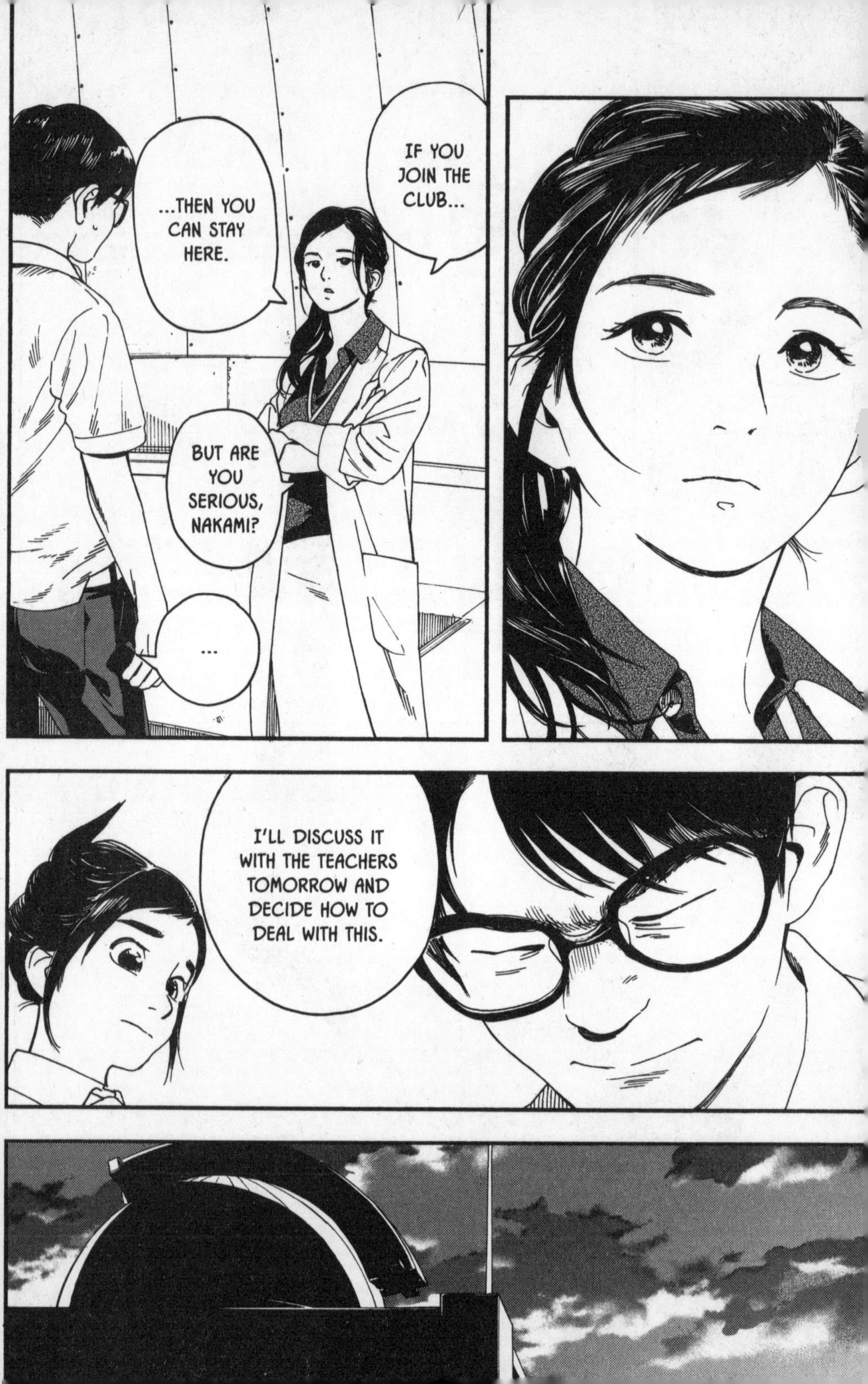
IF YOU JOIN THE CLUB...
...THEN YOU CAN STAY HERE.
BUT ARE YOU SERIOUS, NAKAMI?
...
I'LL DISCUSS IT WITH THE TEACHERS TOMORROW AND DECIDE HOW TO DEAL WITH THIS.

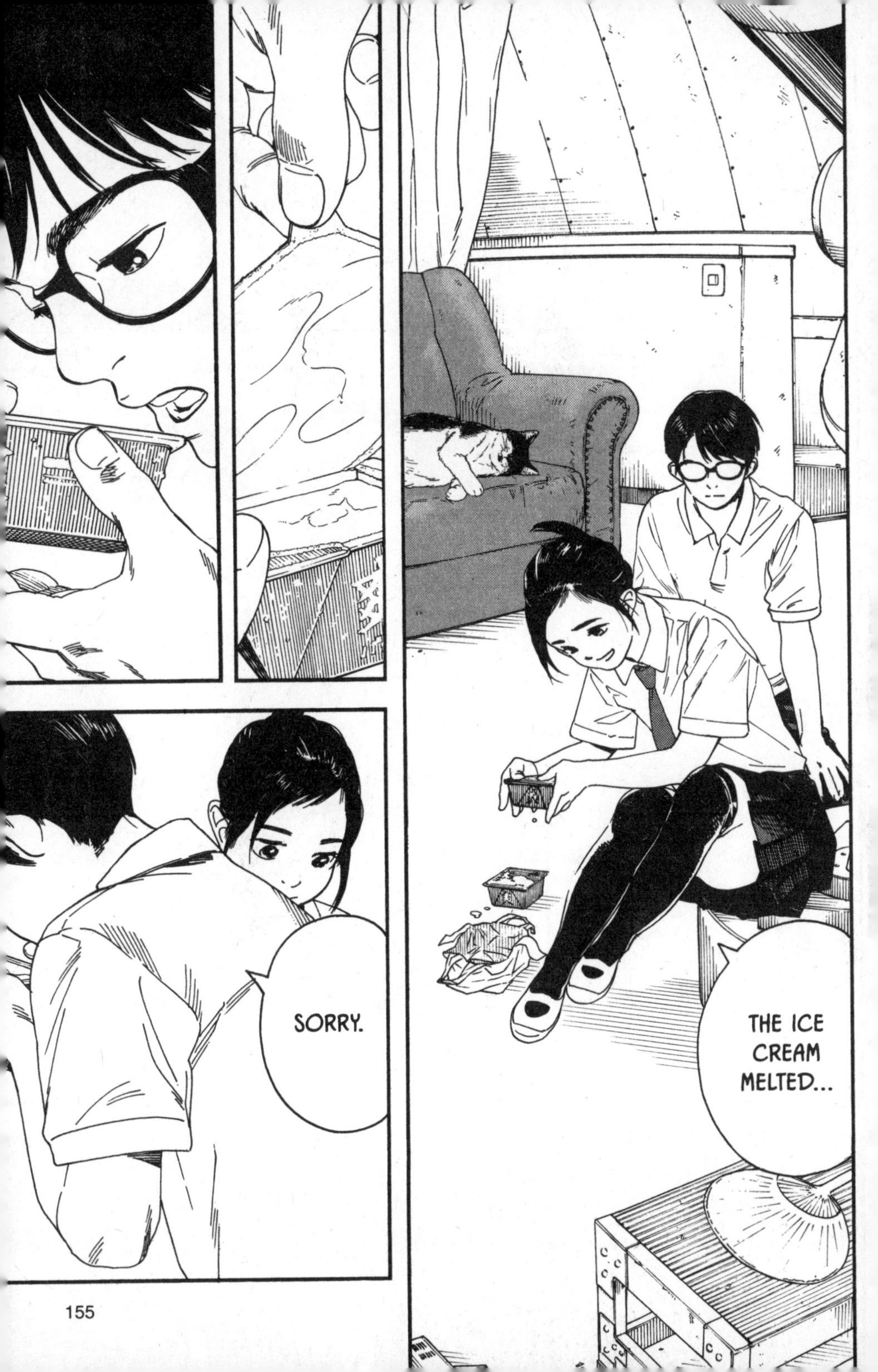
THE ICE CREAM MELTED...
SORRY.

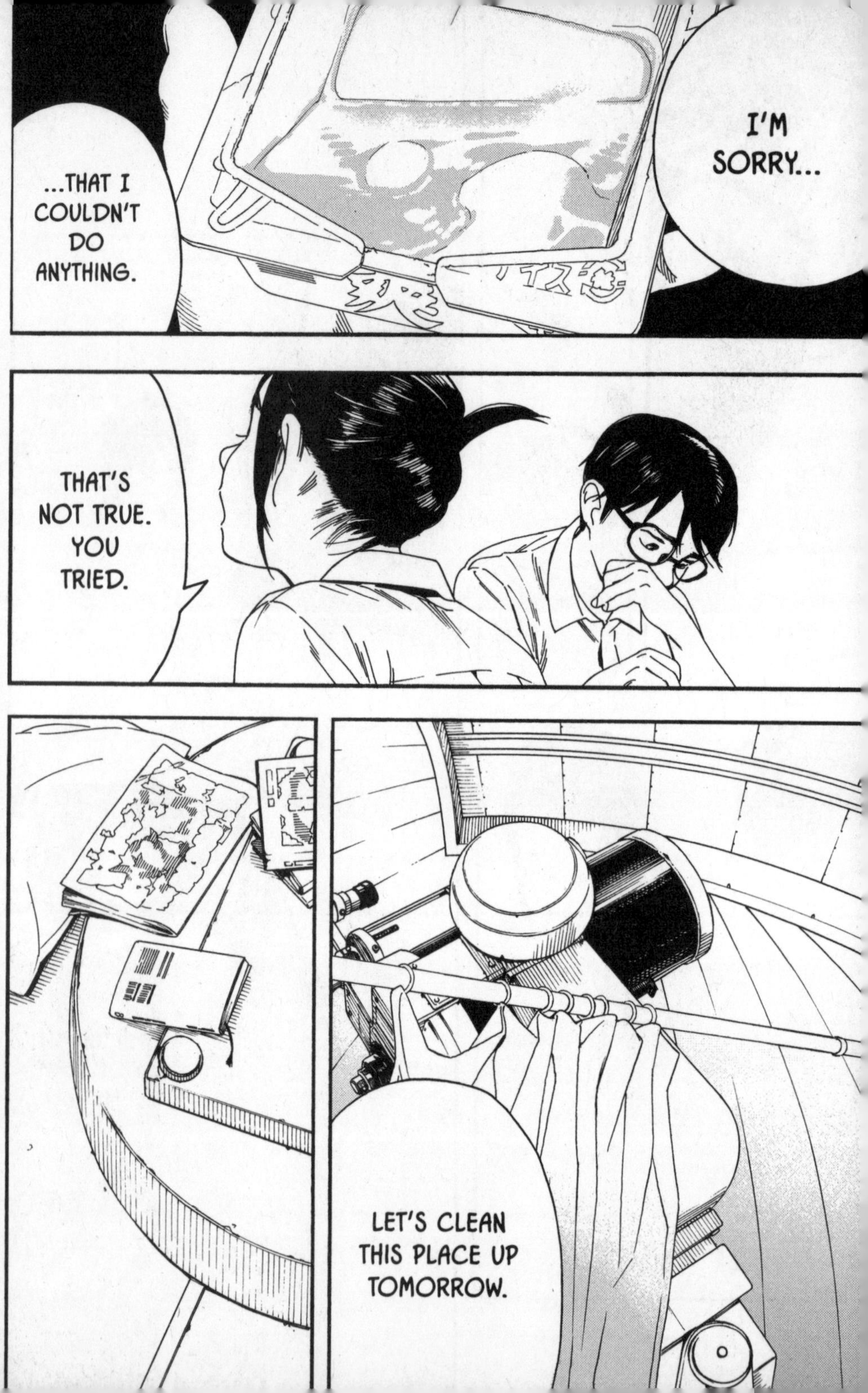
I'M SORRY...
...THAT I COULDN'T DO ANYTHING.
THAT'S NOT TRUE. YOU TRIED.
LET'S CLEAN THIS PLACE UP TOMORROW.

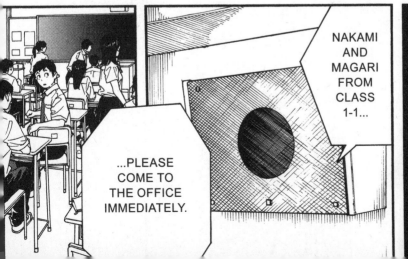

NAKAMI AND MAGARI FROM CLASS 1-1...

...PLEASE COME TO THE OFFICE IMMEDIATELY.

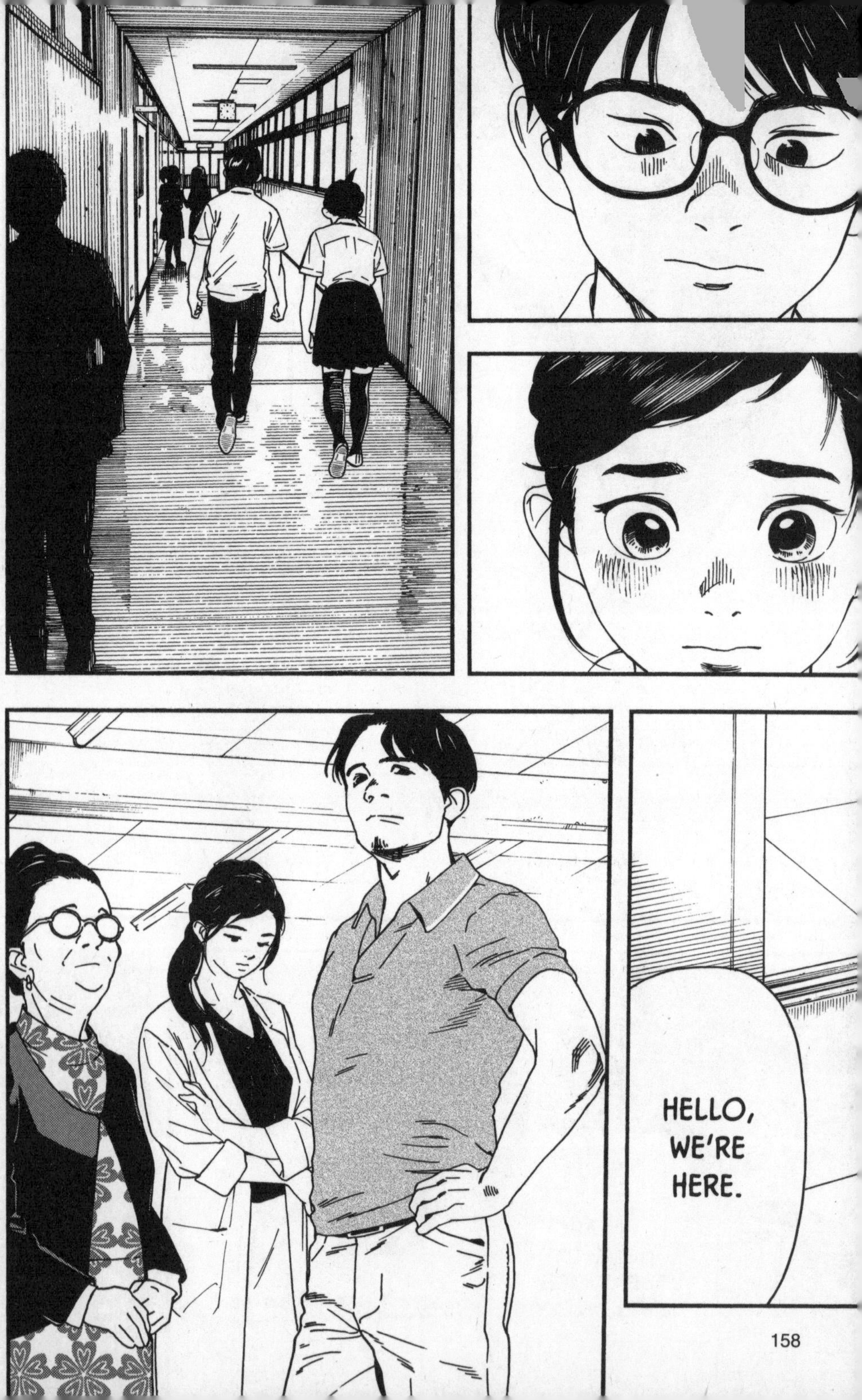
HELLO, WE'RE HERE.

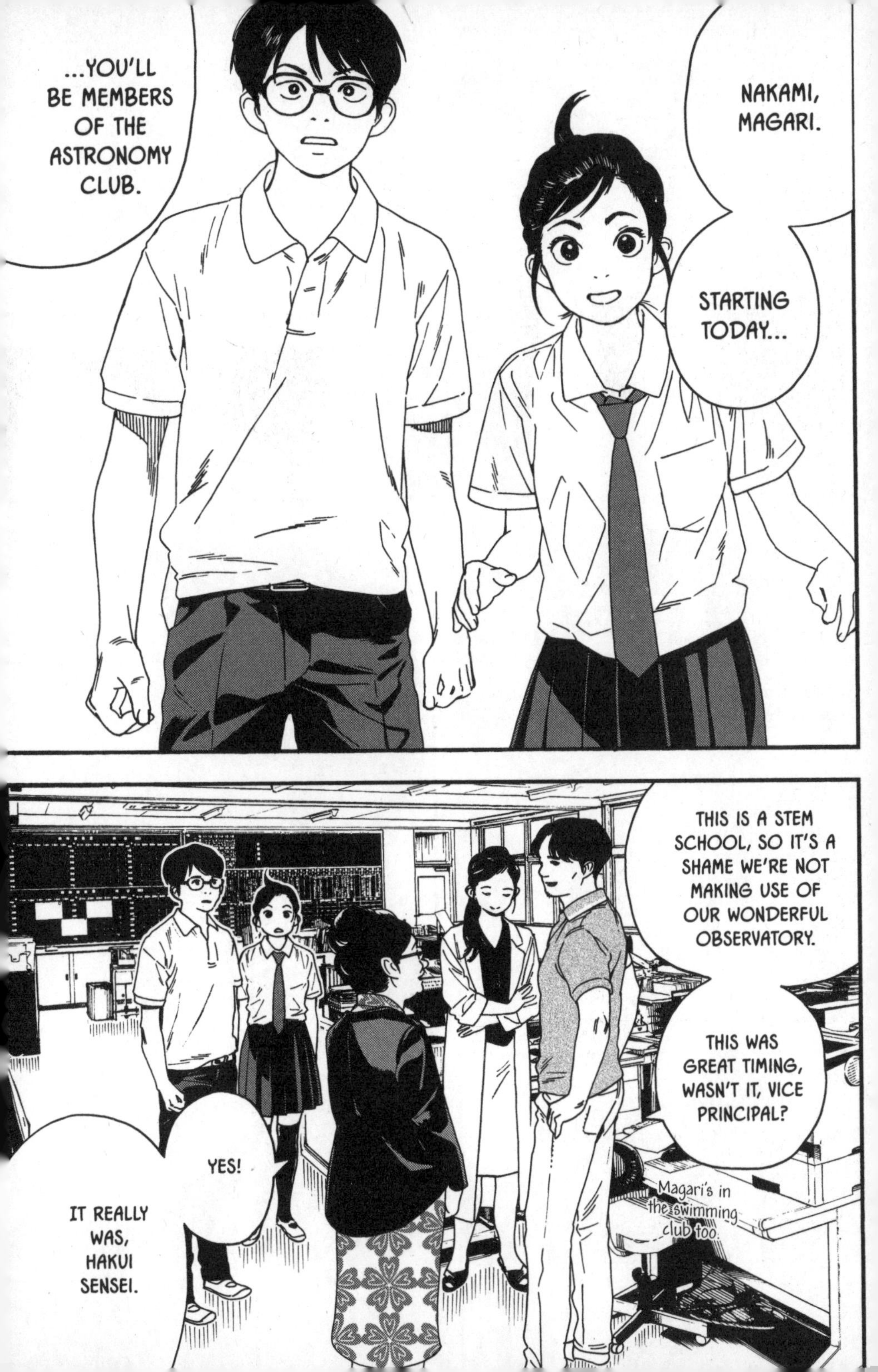
NAKAMI, MAGARI.
STARTING TODAY...
...YOU'LL BE MEMBERS OF THE ASTRONOMY CLUB.
THIS IS A STEM SCHOOL, SO IT'S A SHAME WE'RE NOT MAKING USE OF OUR WONDERFUL OBSERVATORY.
THIS WAS GREAT TIMING, WASN'T IT, VICE PRINCIPAL?
Magari's in the swimming club too.
YES!
IT REALLY WAS, HAKUI SENSEI.

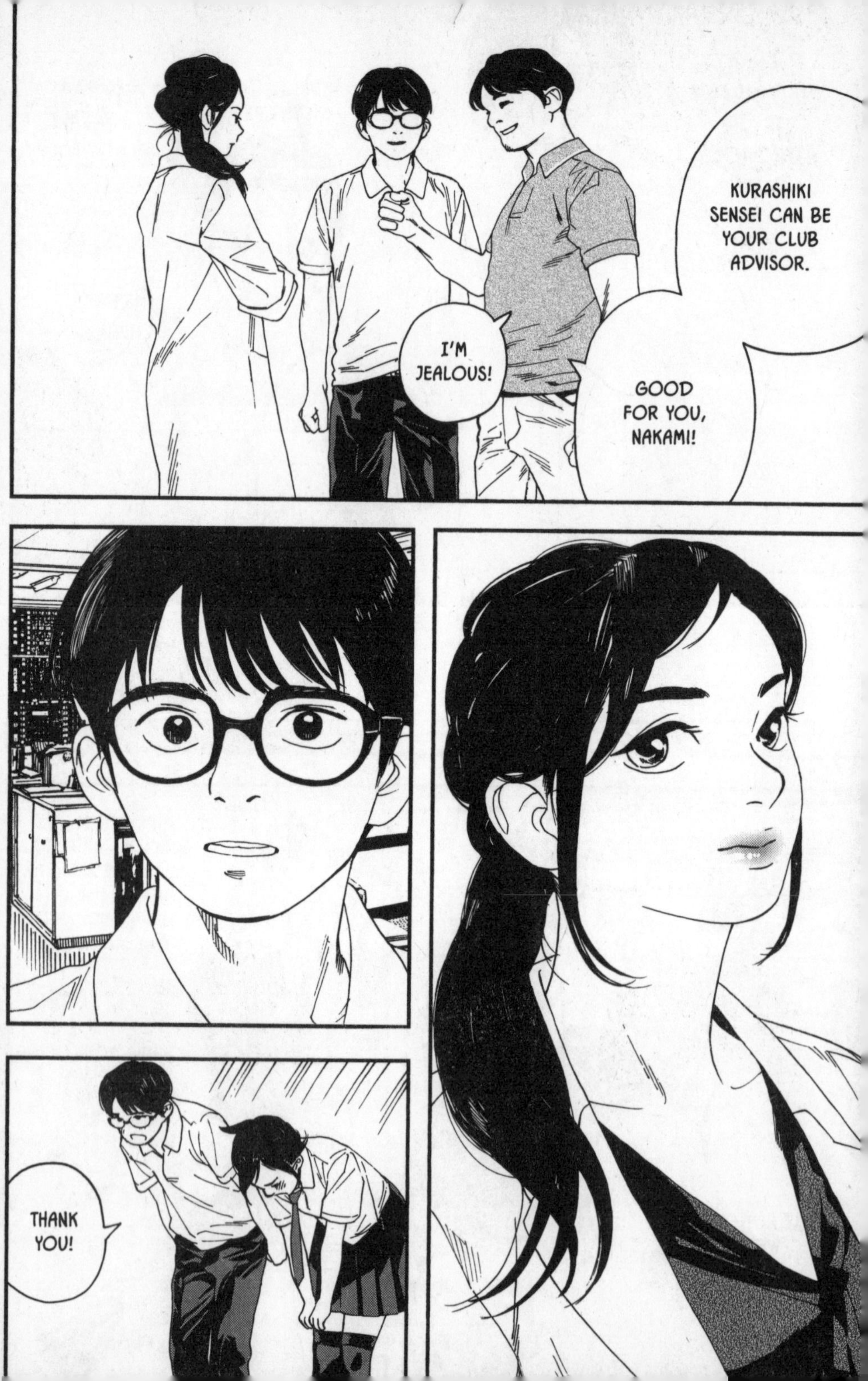
KURASHIKI SENSEI CAN BE YOUR CLUB ADVISOR.
GOOD FOR YOU, NAKAMI!
I'M JEALOUS!
THANK YOU!

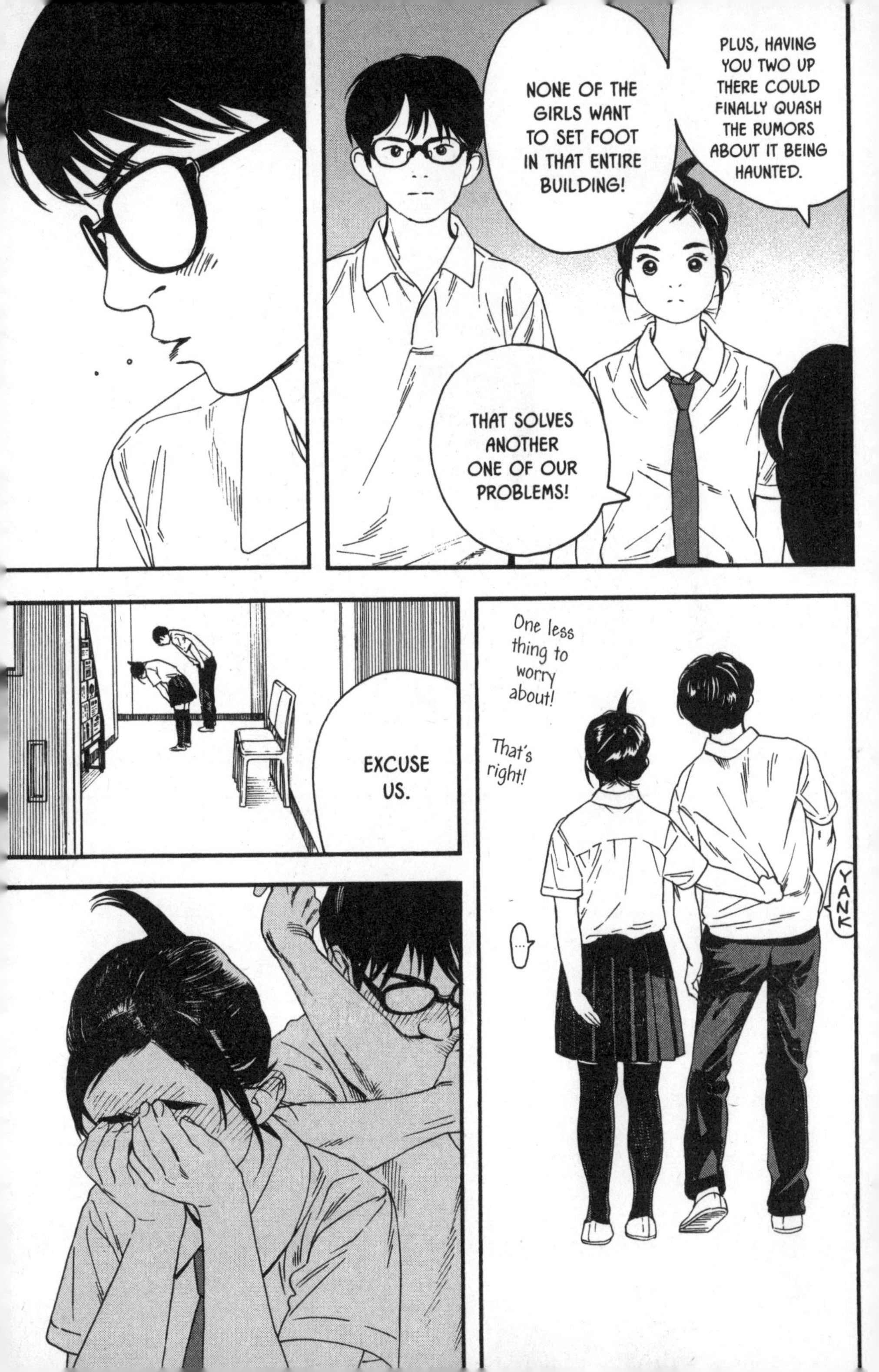
PLUS, HAVING YOU TWO UP THERE COULD FINALLY QUASH THE RUMORS ABOUT IT BEING HAUNTED.
NONE OF THE GIRLS WANT TO SET FOOT IN THAT ENTIRE BUILDING!
THAT SOLVES ANOTHER ONE OF OUR PROBLEMS!
One less thing to worry about!
That's right!
YANK
...
EXCUSE US.

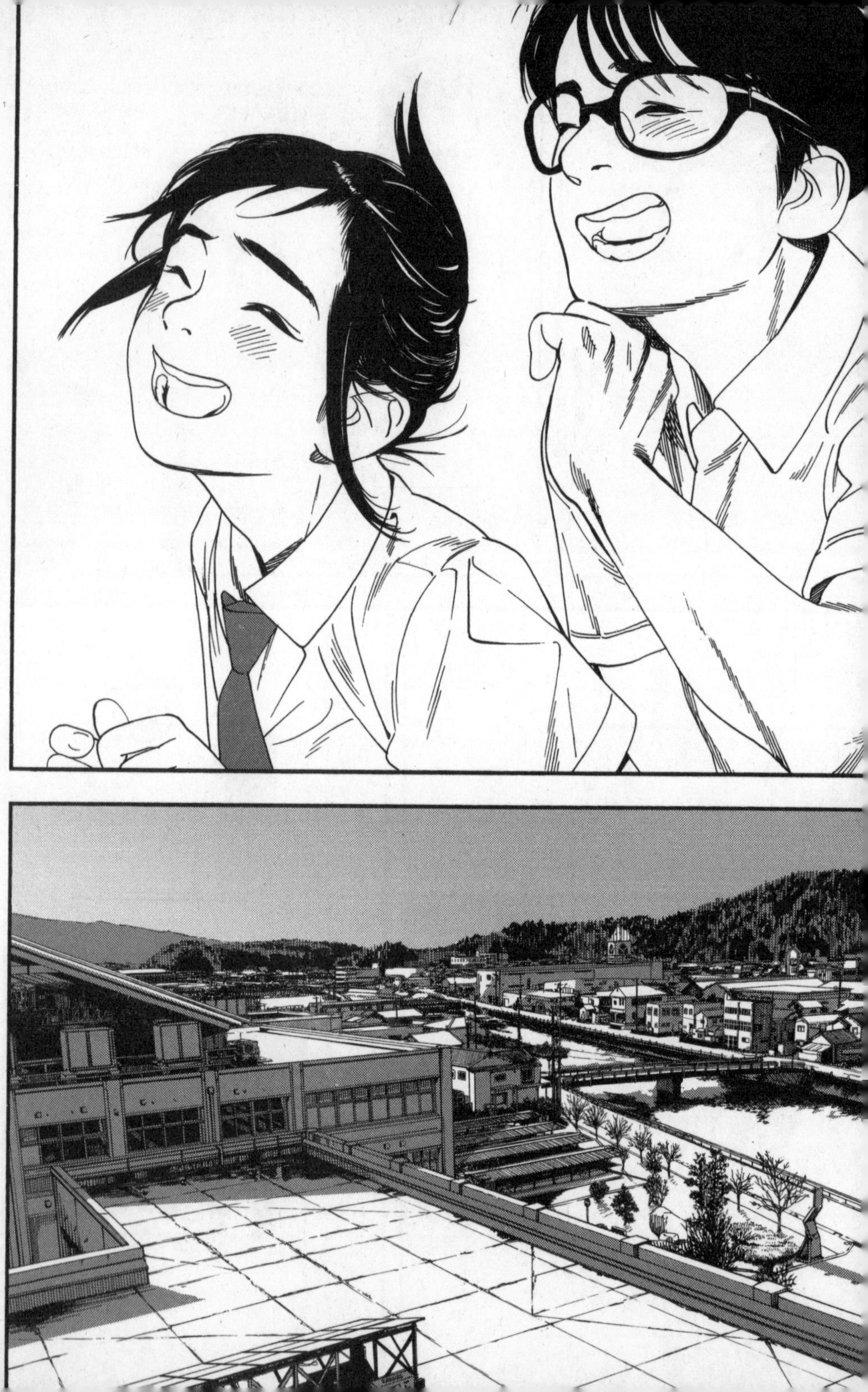

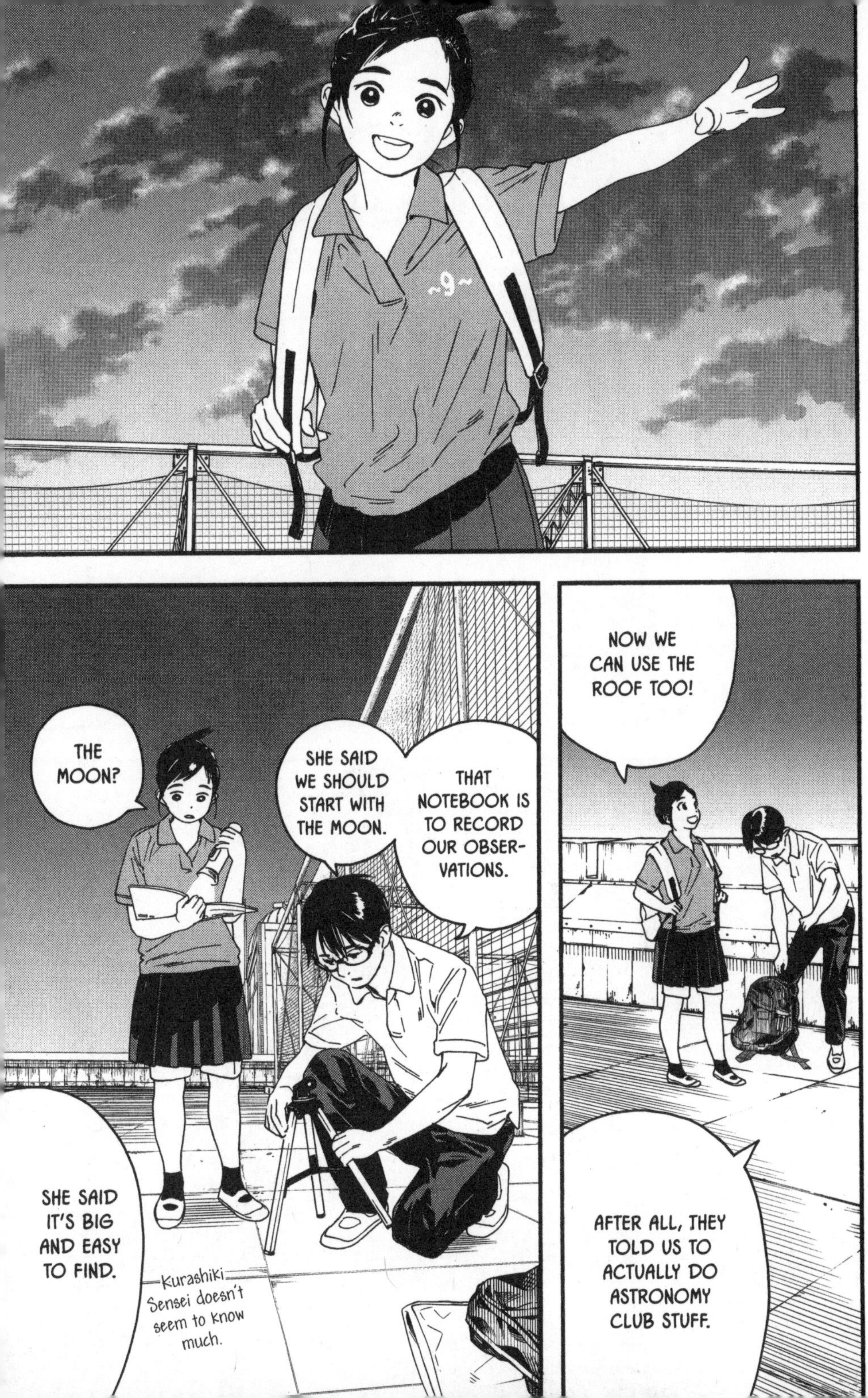
NOW WE CAN USE THE ROOF TOO!
AFTER ALL, THEY TOLD US TO ACTUALLY DO ASTRONOMY CLUB STUFF.
THAT NOTEBOOK IS TO RECORD OUR OBSER-VATIONS.
SHE SAID WE SHOULD START WITH THE MOON.
THE MOON?
SHE SAID IT'S BIG AND EASY TO FIND.
Kurashiki Sensei doesn't seem to know much.

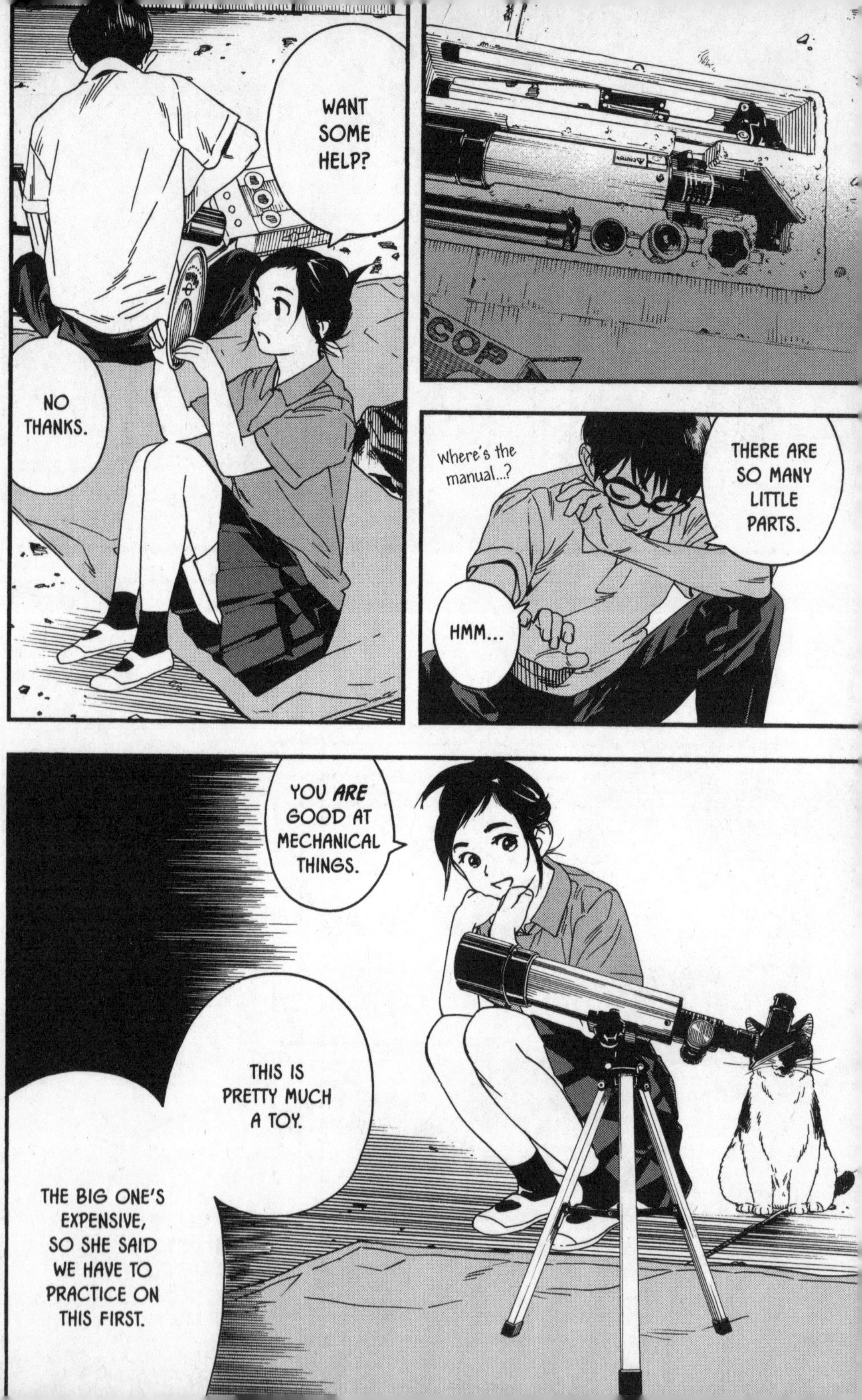
THERE ARE SO MANY LITTLE PARTS.
Where's the manual...?
HMM...
WANT SOME HELP?
NO THANKS.
YOU *ARE* GOOD AT MECHANICAL THINGS.
THIS IS PRETTY MUCH A TOY.
THE BIG ONE'S EXPENSIVE, SO SHE SAID WE HAVE TO PRACTICE ON THIS FIRST.

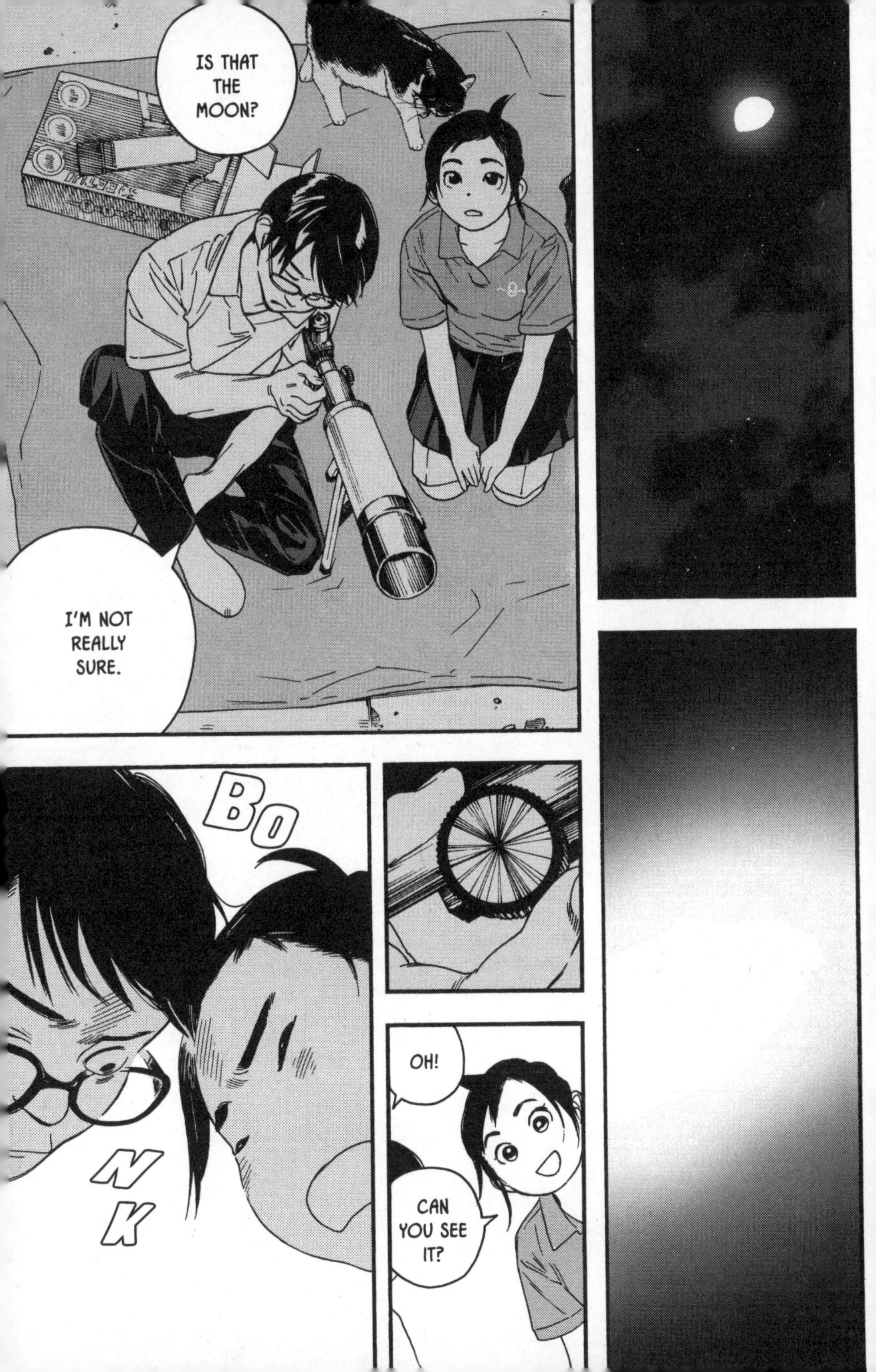
IS THAT THE MOON?
I'M NOT REALLY SURE.
OH!
CAN YOU SEE IT?
BO
NK

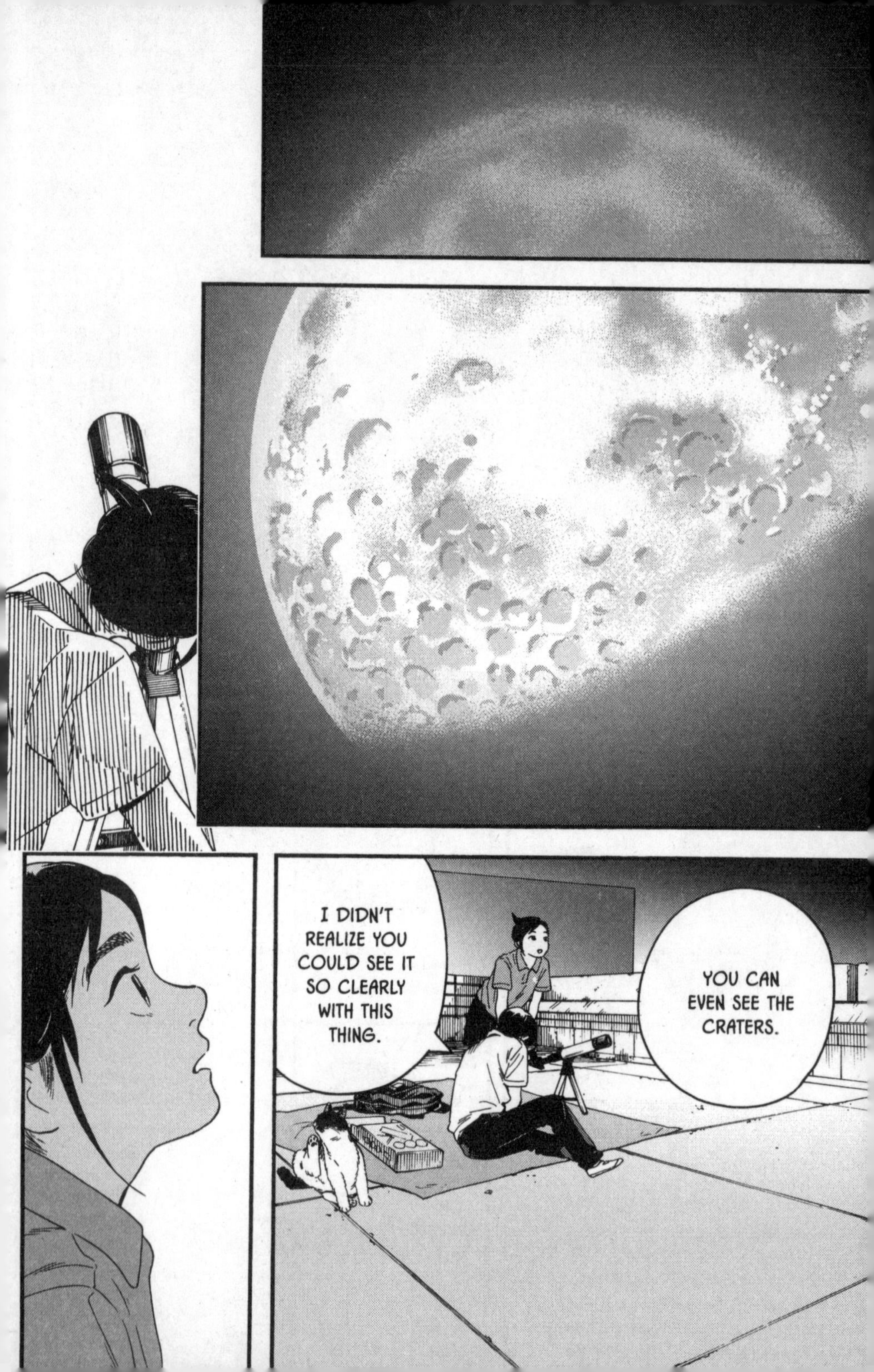
YOU CAN EVEN SEE THE CRATERS.
I DIDN'T REALIZE YOU COULD SEE IT SO CLEARLY WITH THIS THING.

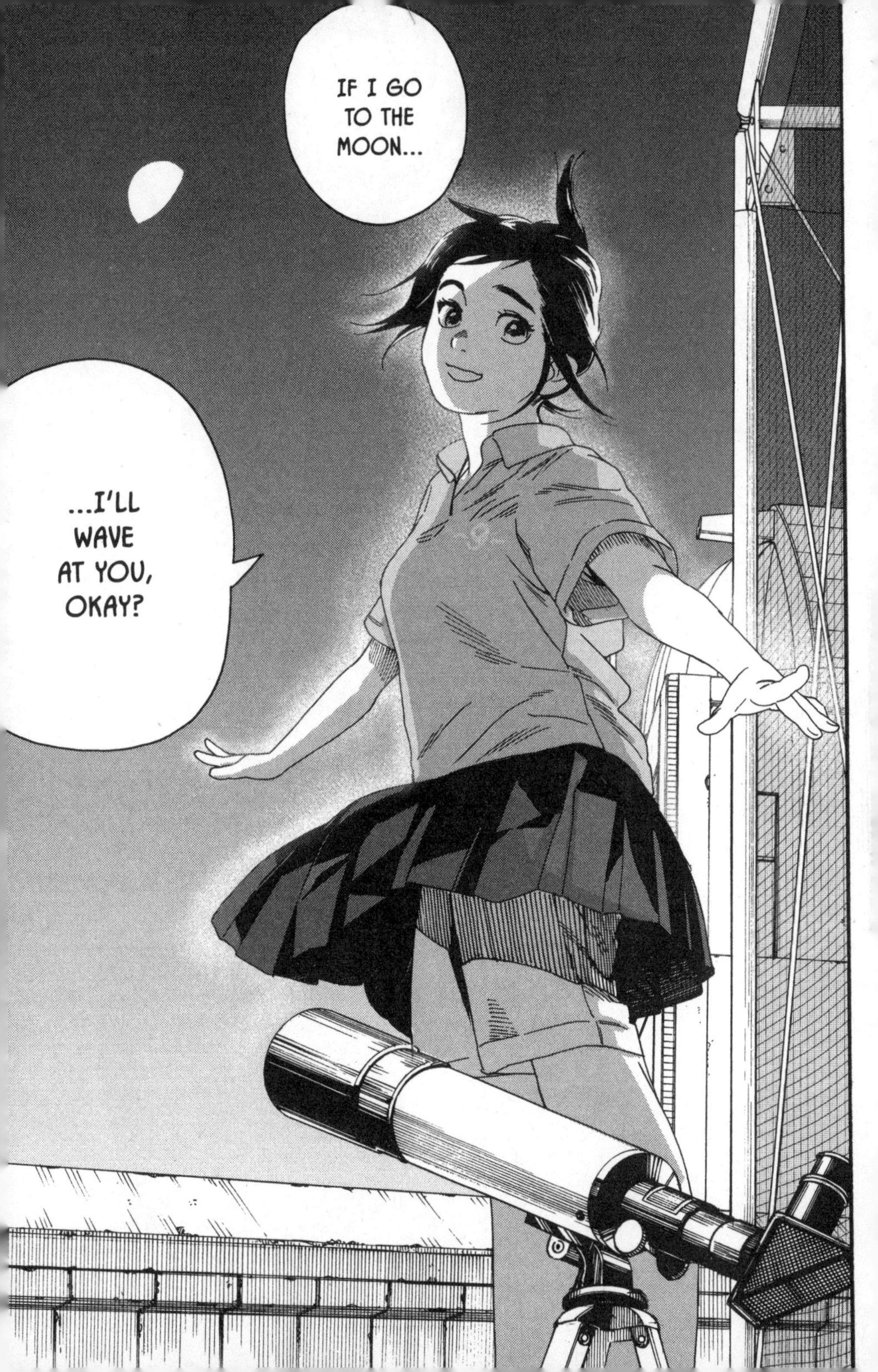
IF I GO TO THE MOON...
...I'LL WAVE AT YOU, OKAY?

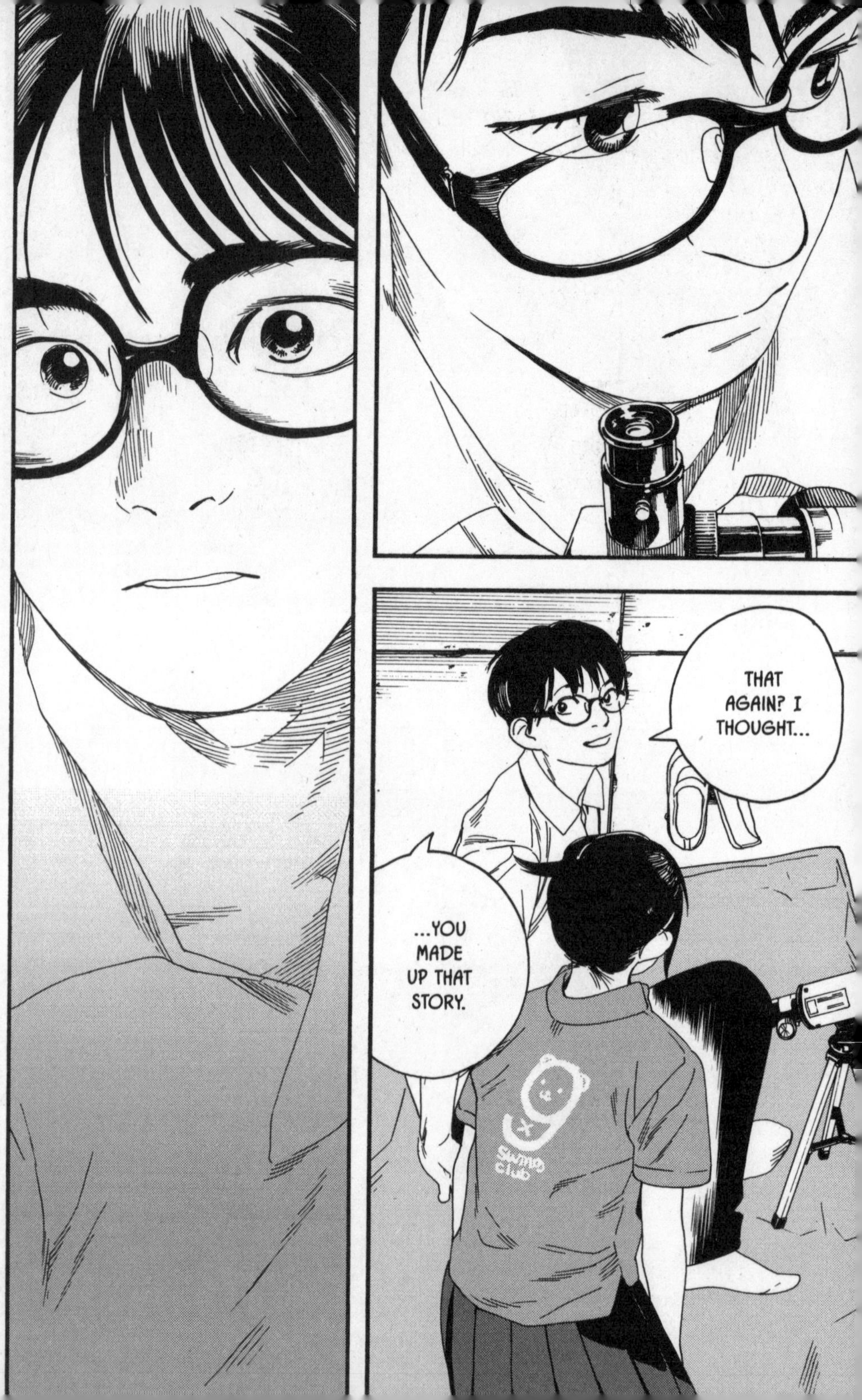
THAT AGAIN? I THOUGHT...
...YOU MADE UP THAT STORY.
Swing club

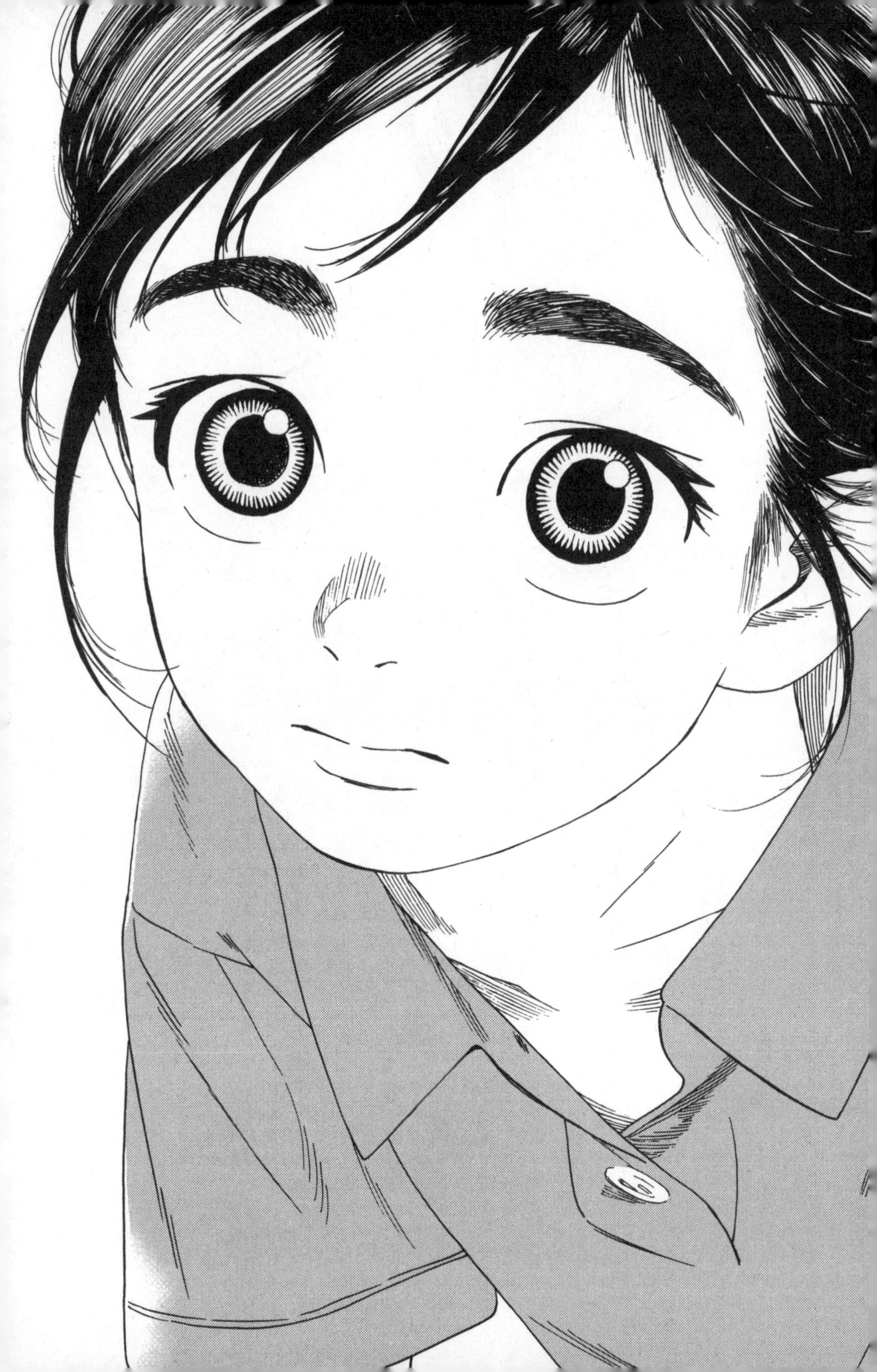

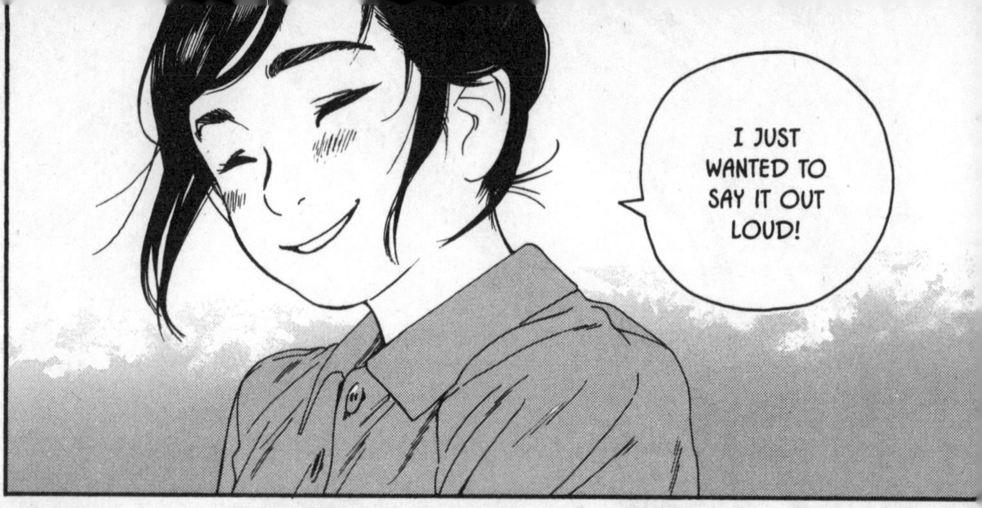
I JUST WANTED TO SAY IT OUT LOUD!
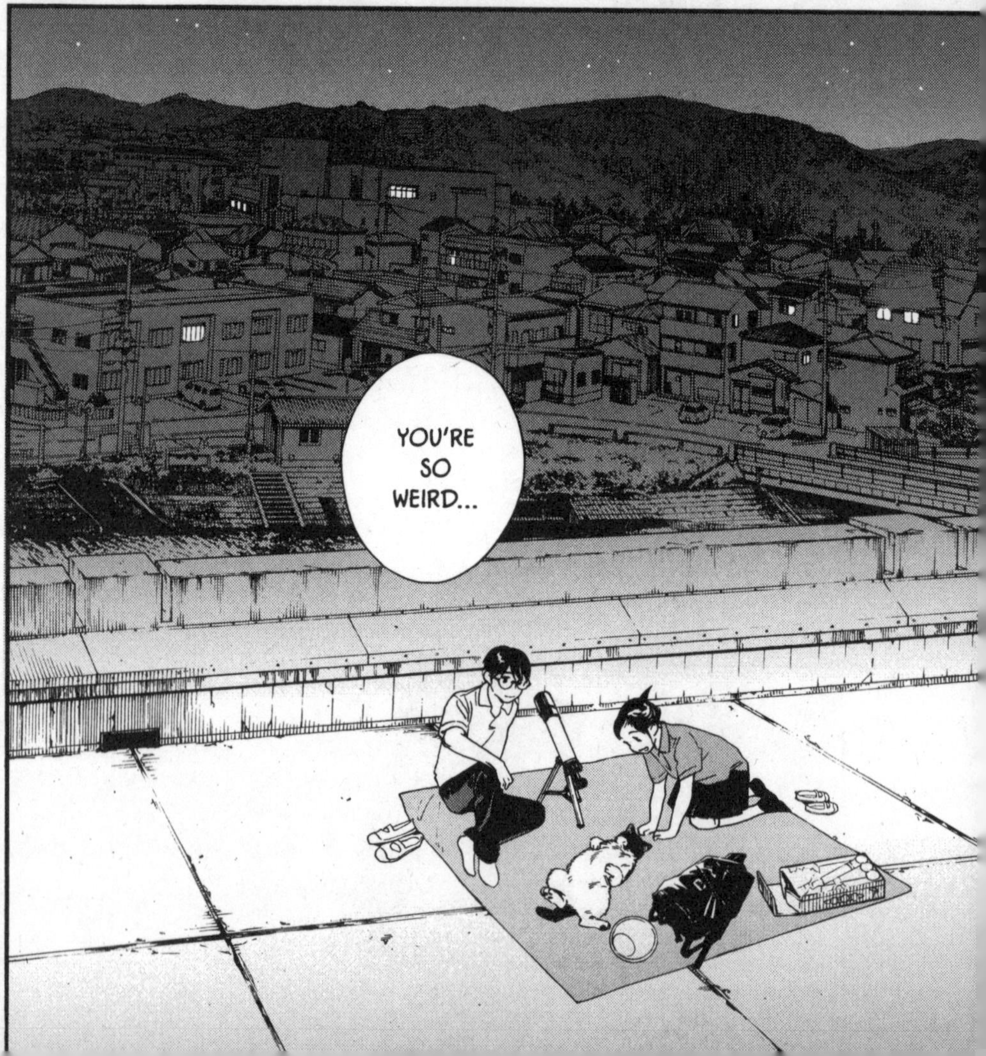
YOU'RE SO WEIRD...

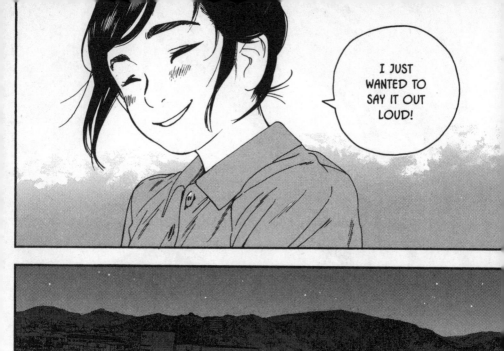

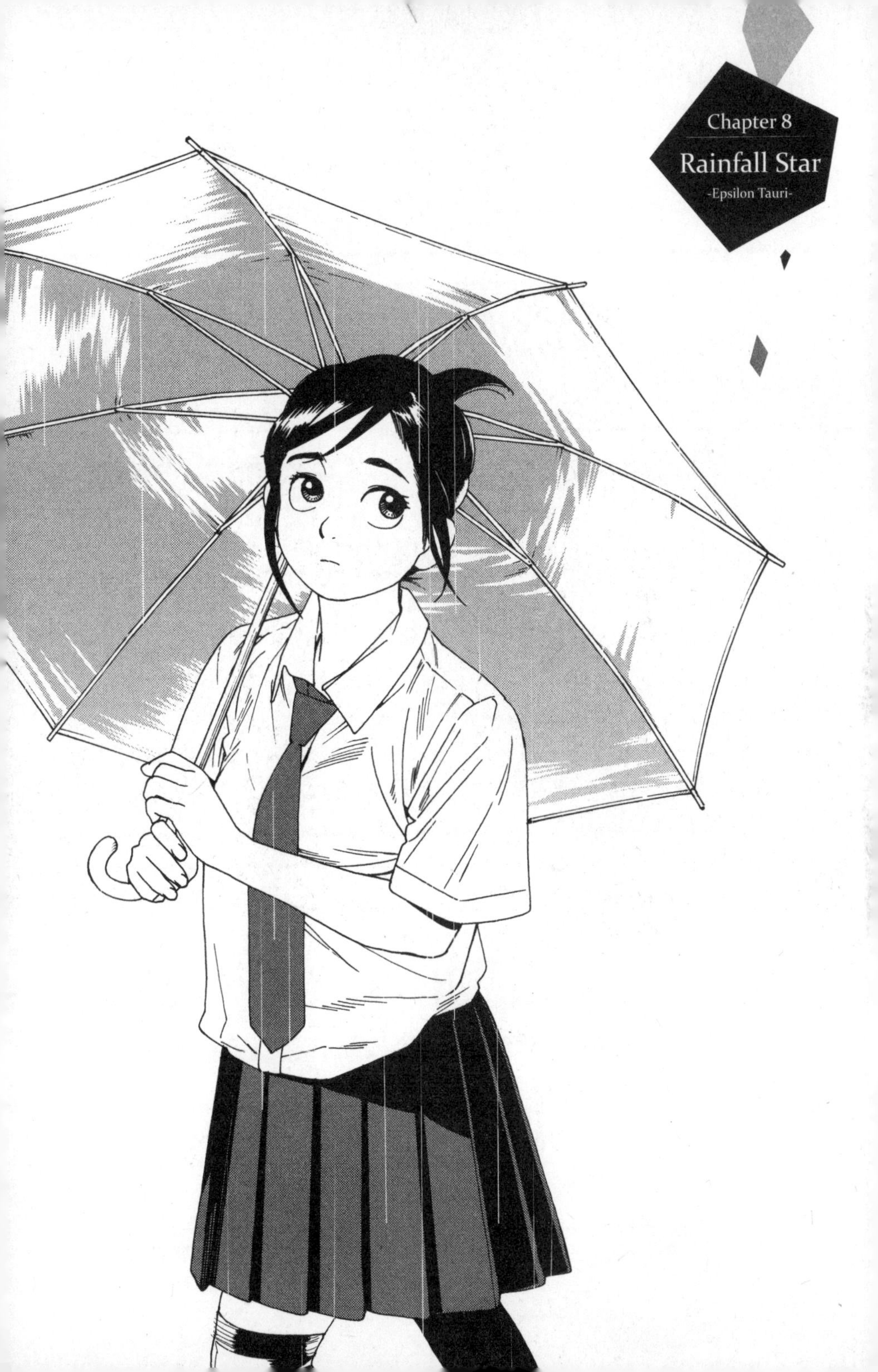
Chapter 8
Rainfall Star
-Epsilon Tauri-

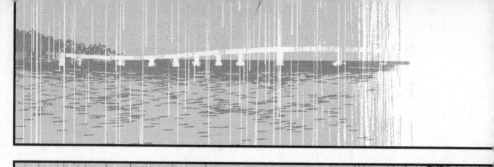

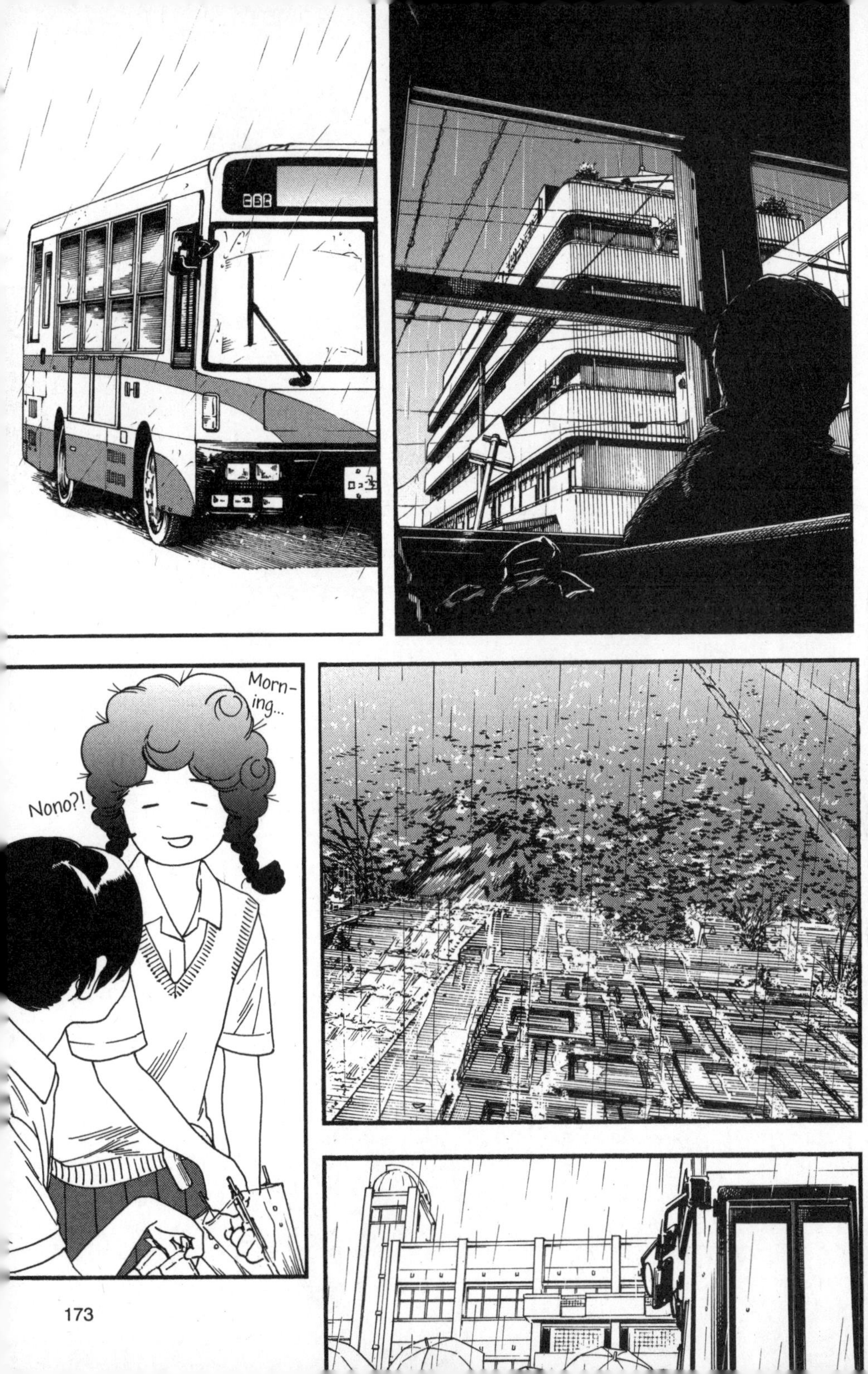
Morn-
ing...
Nono?!

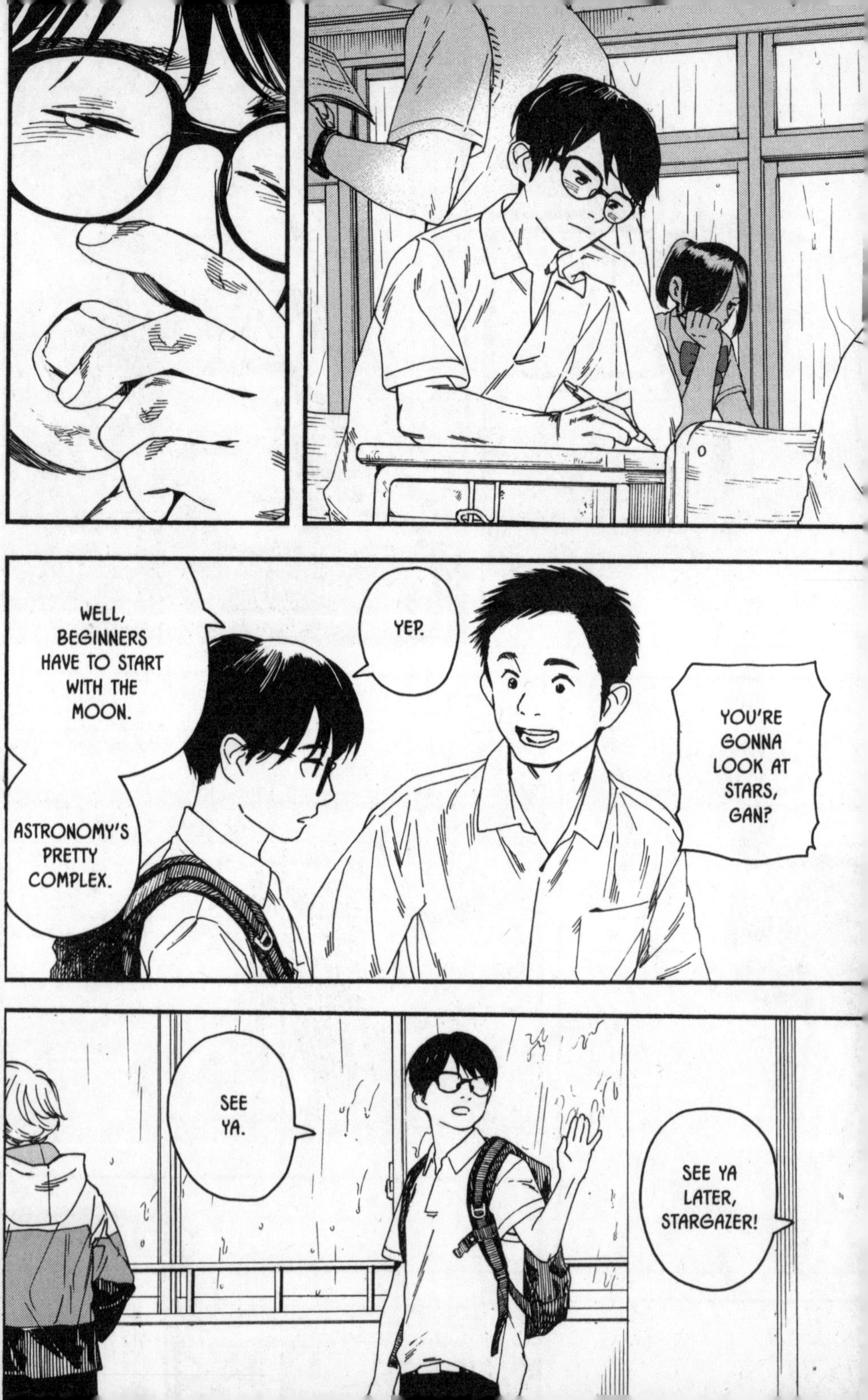
YOU'RE GONNA LOOK AT STARS, GAN?
YEP.
WELL, BEGINNERS HAVE TO START WITH THE MOON.
ASTRONOMY'S PRETTY COMPLEX.
SEE YA LATER, STARGAZER!
SEE YA.

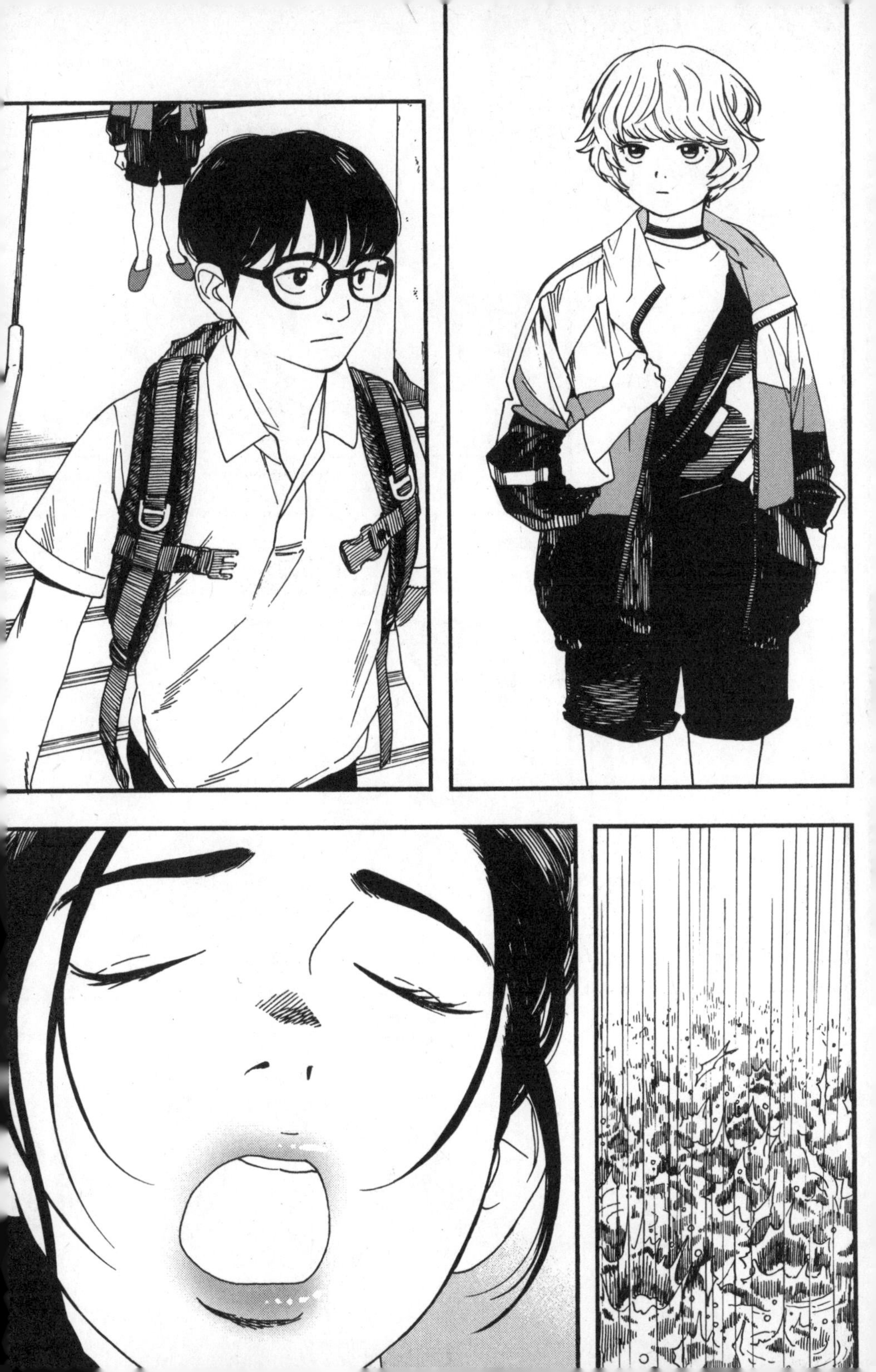

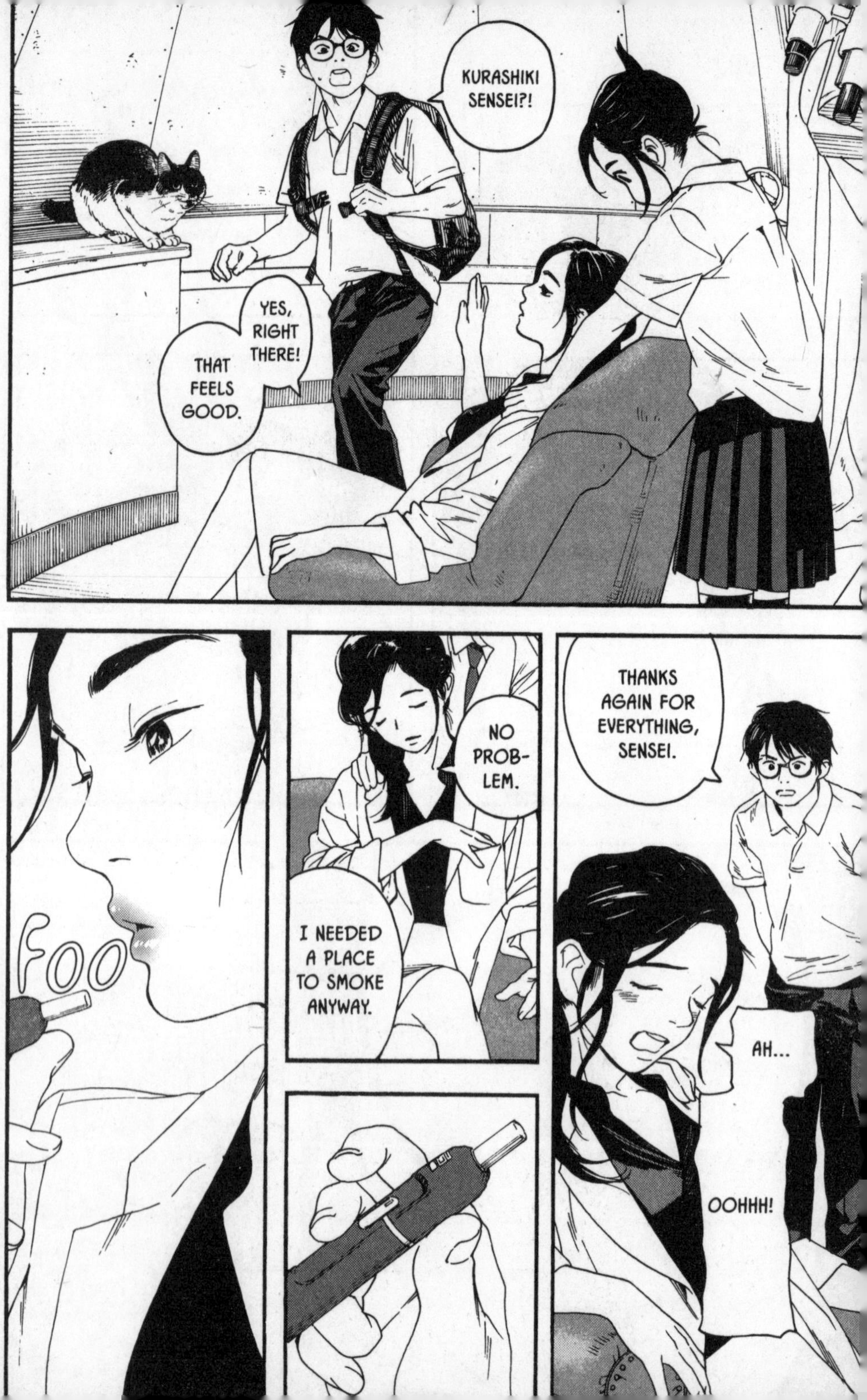
KURASHIKI SENSEI?!
YES, RIGHT THERE!
THAT FEELS GOOD.
THANKS AGAIN FOR EVERYTHING, SENSEI.
AH...
OOHHH!
NO PROB-LEM.
I NEEDED A PLACE TO SMOKE ANYWAY.
FOO

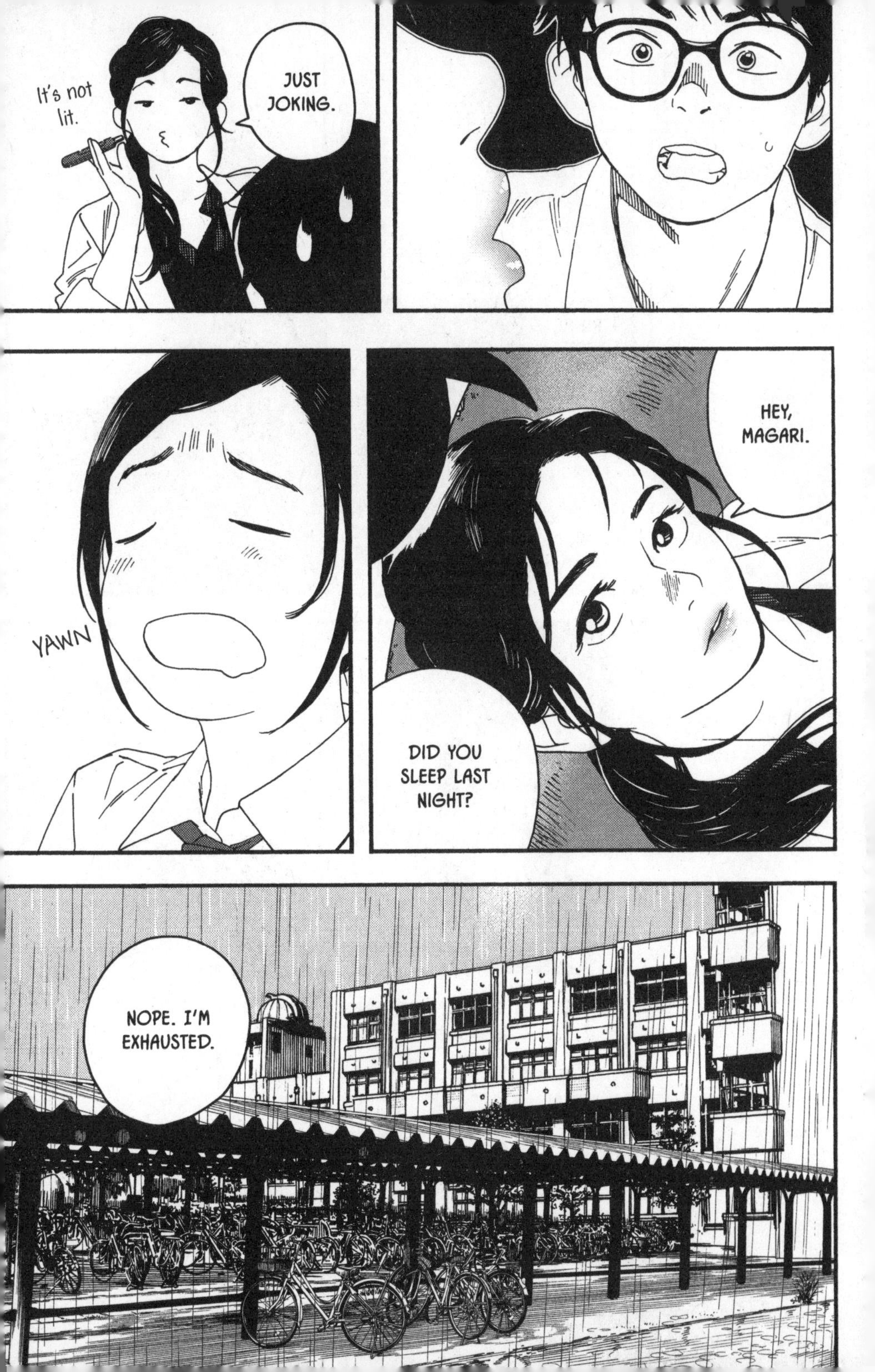
JUST JOKING.
It's not lit.
HEY, MAGARI.
DID YOU SLEEP LAST NIGHT?
YAWN
NOPE. I'M EXHAUSTED.

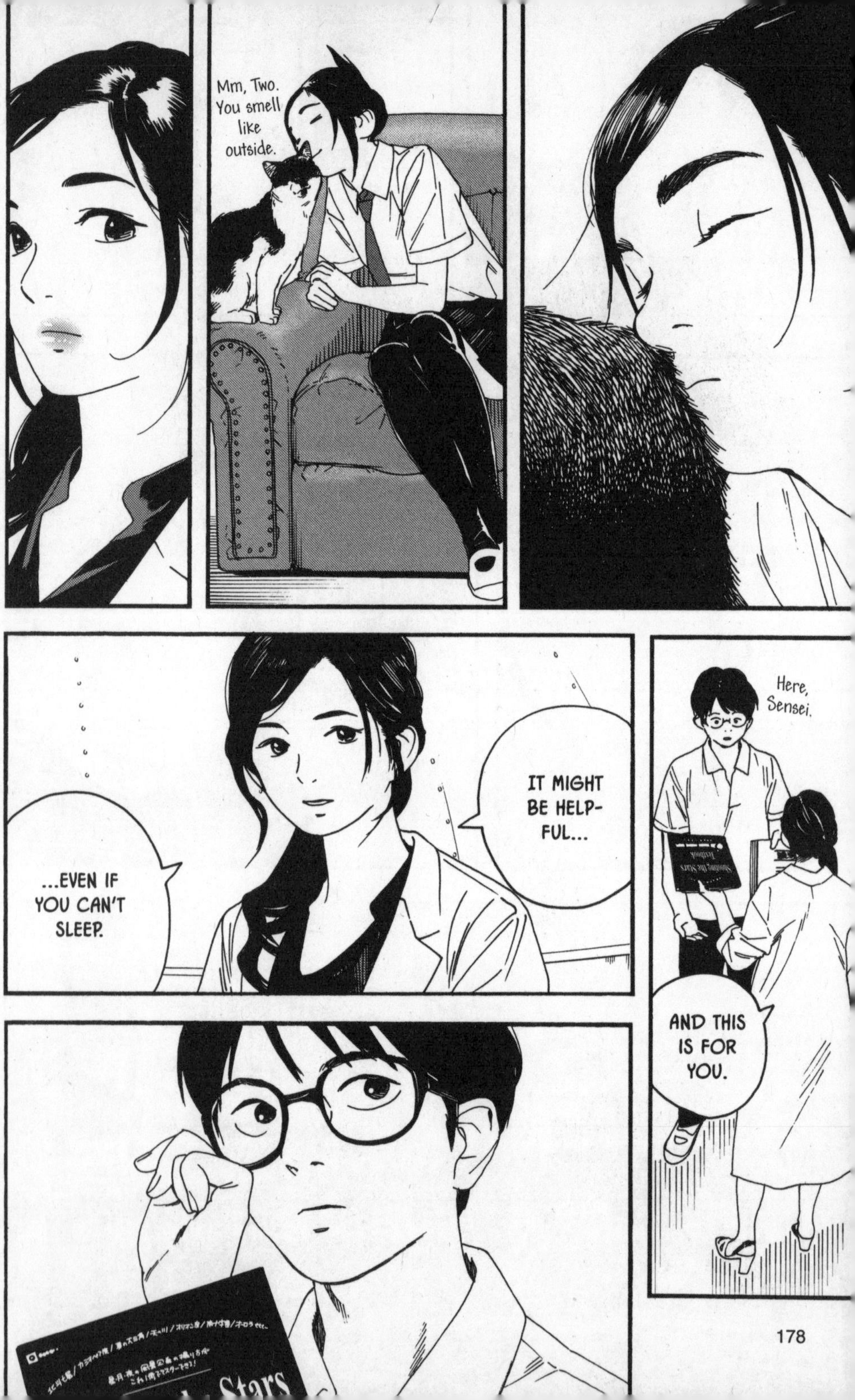
Mm, Two. You smell like outside.
Here, Sensei.
AND THIS IS FOR YOU.
IT MIGHT BE HELP-FUL...
...EVEN IF YOU CAN'T SLEEP.
Stars

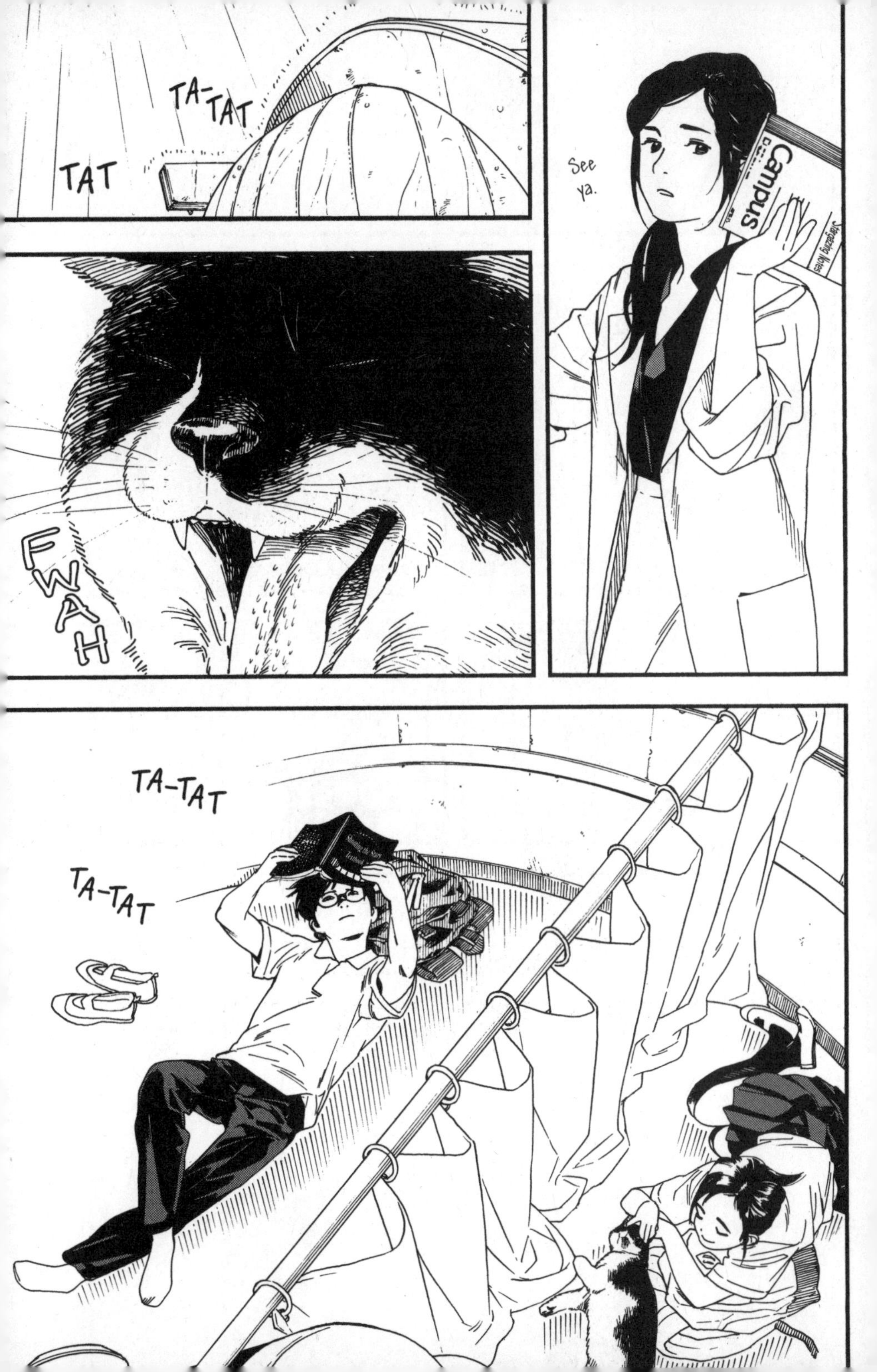
See ya.
Campus
Stargazing Notes
TA-TAT
TAT
FWAH
TA-TAT
TA-TAT

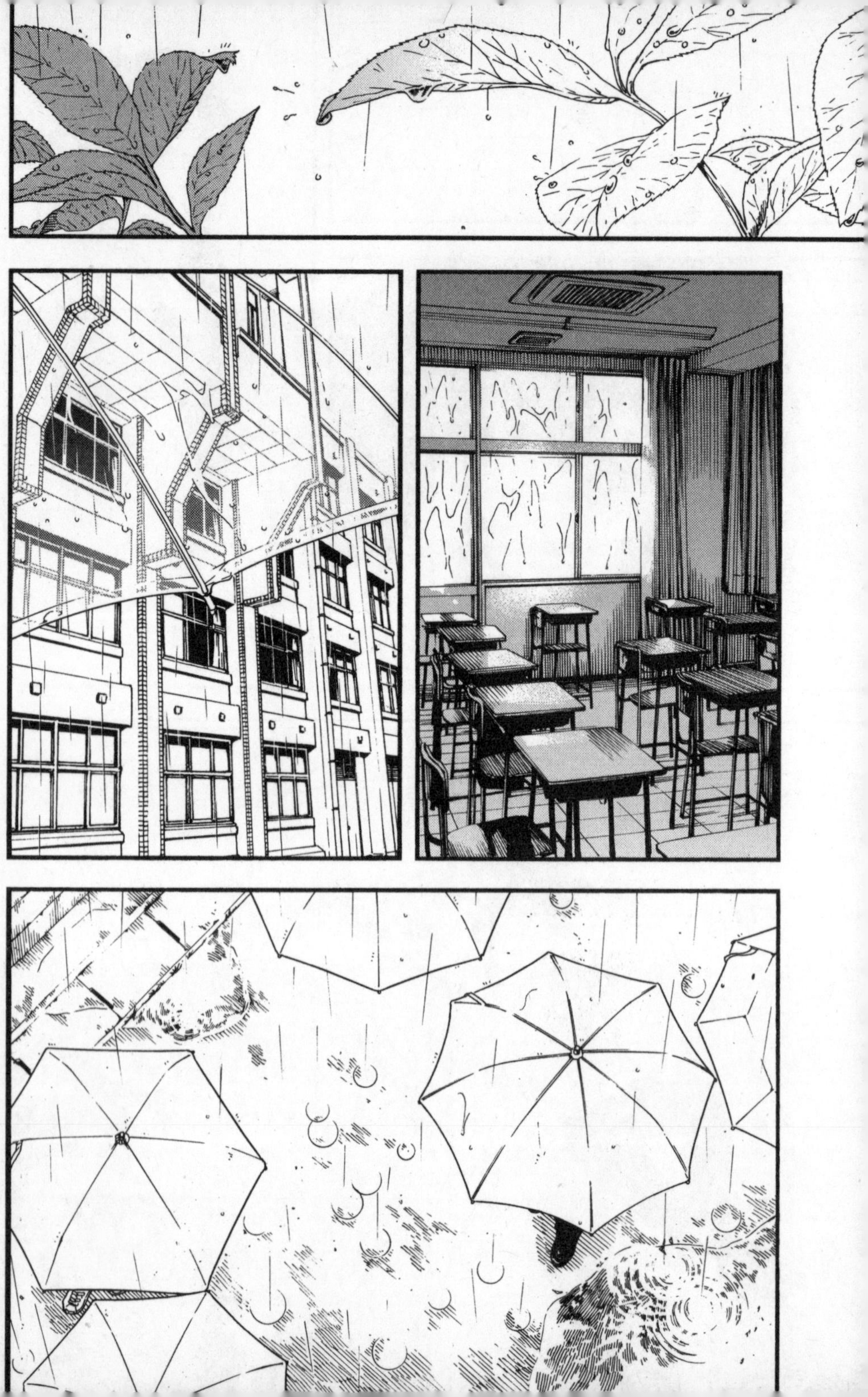

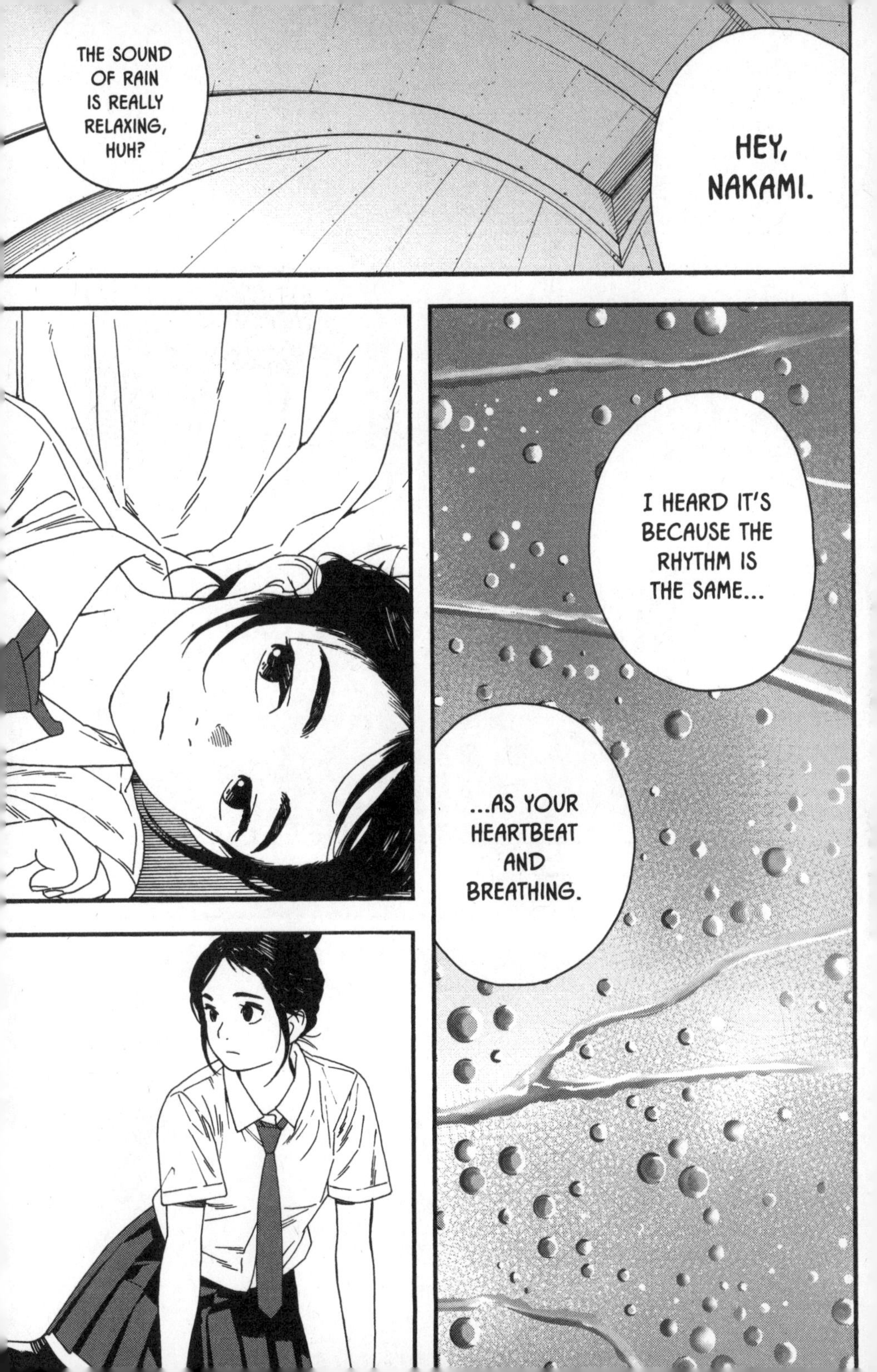
HEY, NAKAMI.
THE SOUND OF RAIN IS REALLY RELAXING, HUH?
I HEARD IT'S BECAUSE THE RHYTHM IS THE SAME...
...AS YOUR HEARTBEAT AND BREATHING.

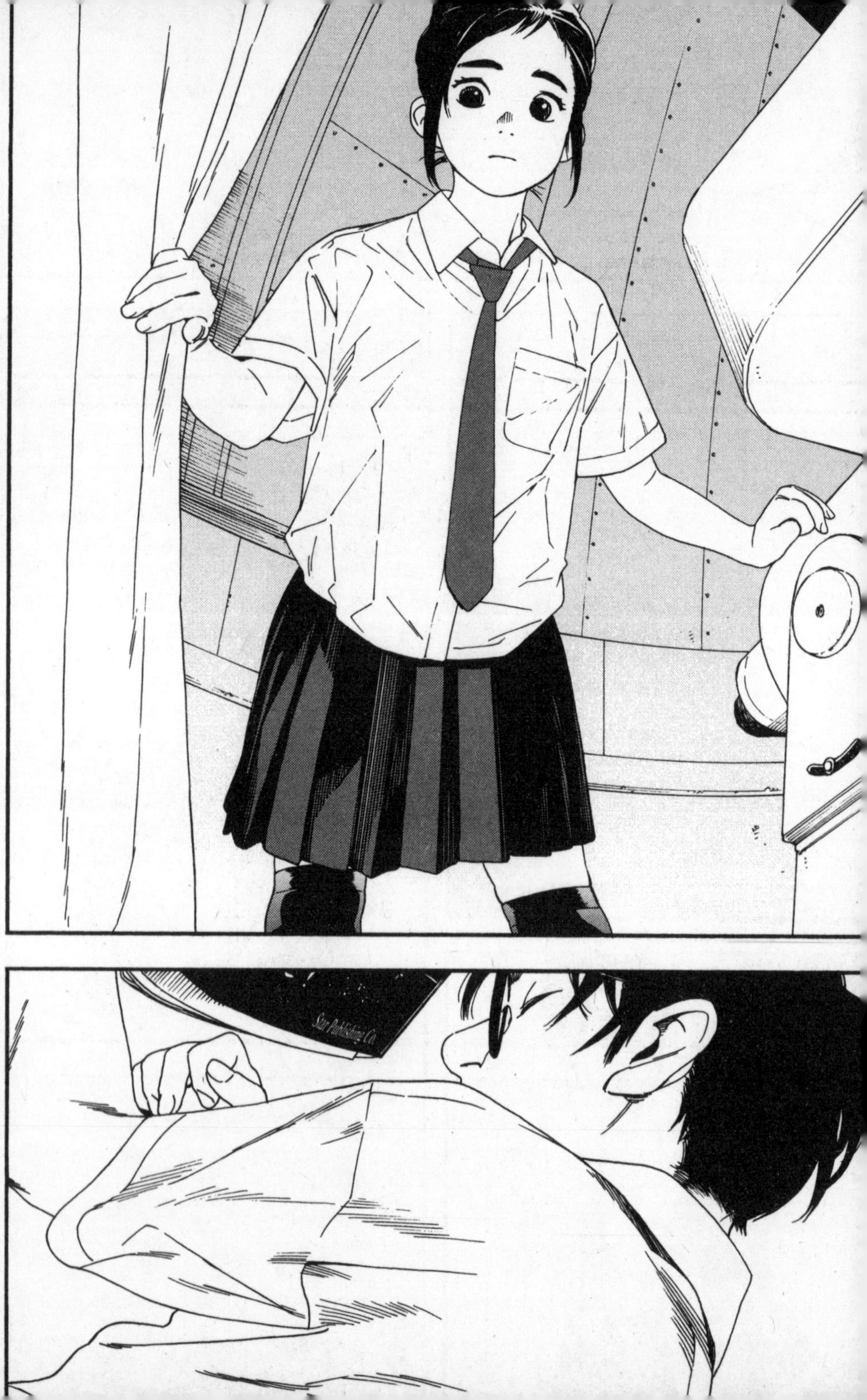
Star Publishing Co.

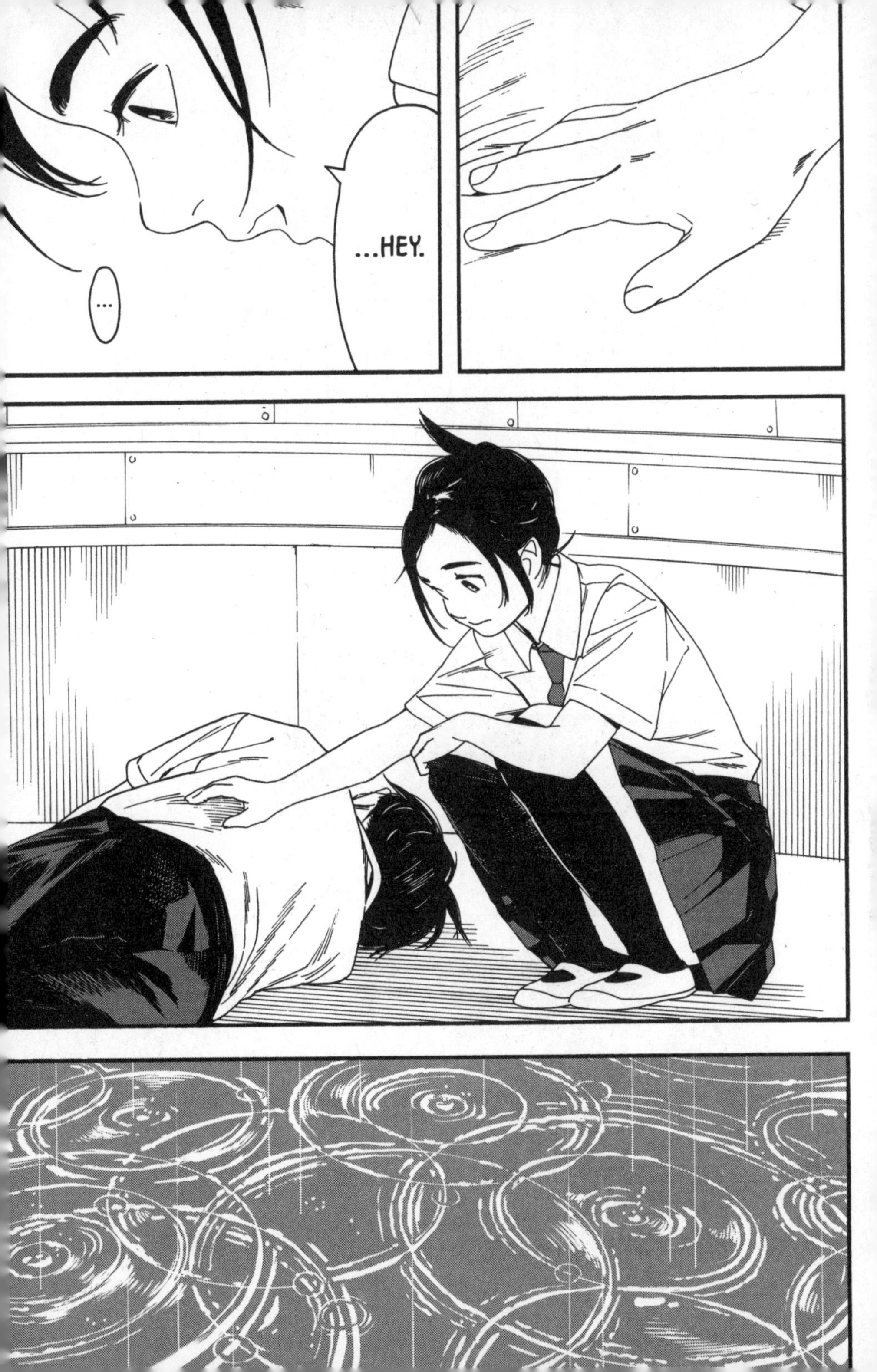
...HEY.
...

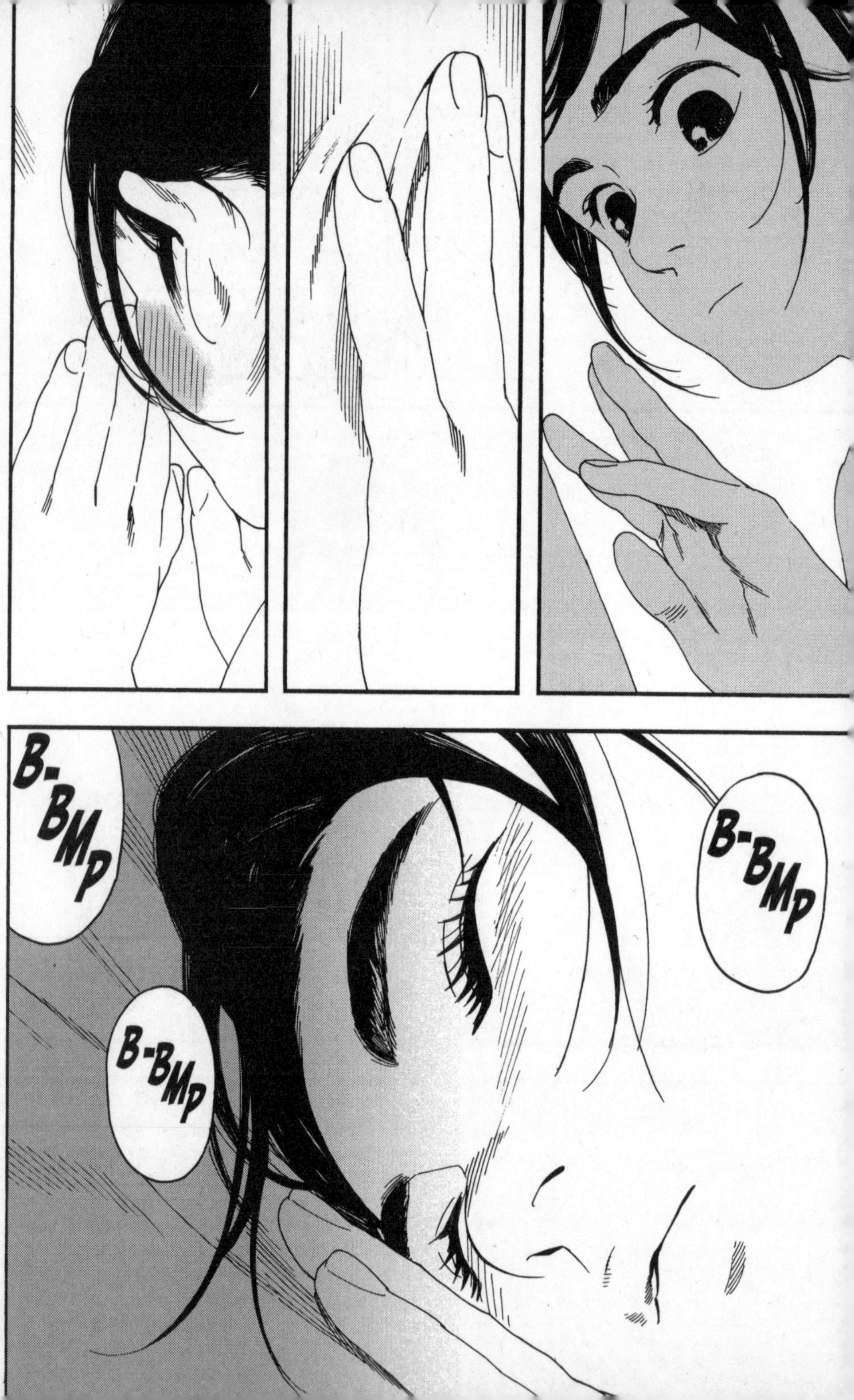
B-BMP
B-BMP
B-BMP

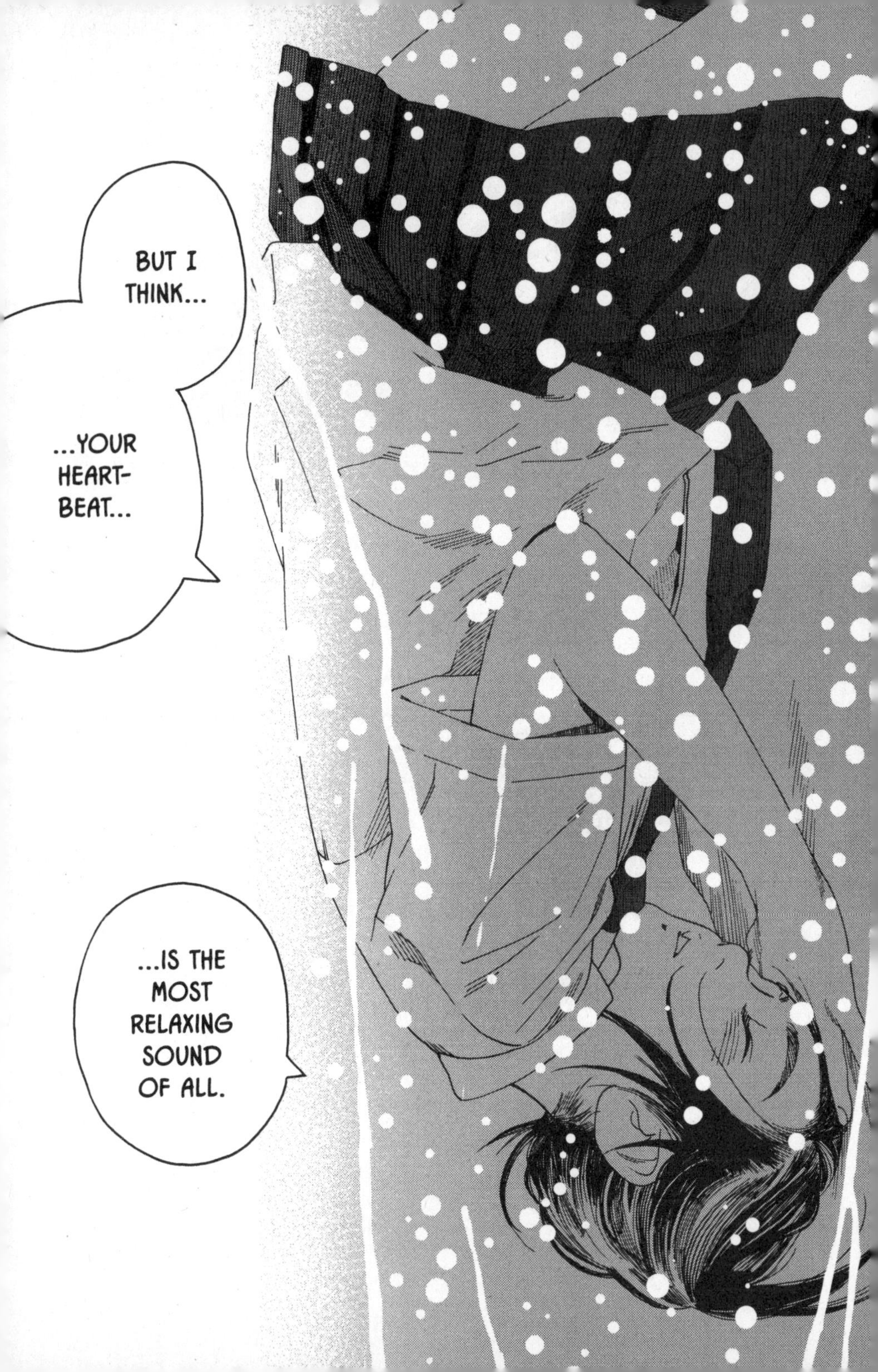
BUT I THINK...
...YOUR HEART-BEAT...
...IS THE MOST RELAXING SOUND OF ALL.

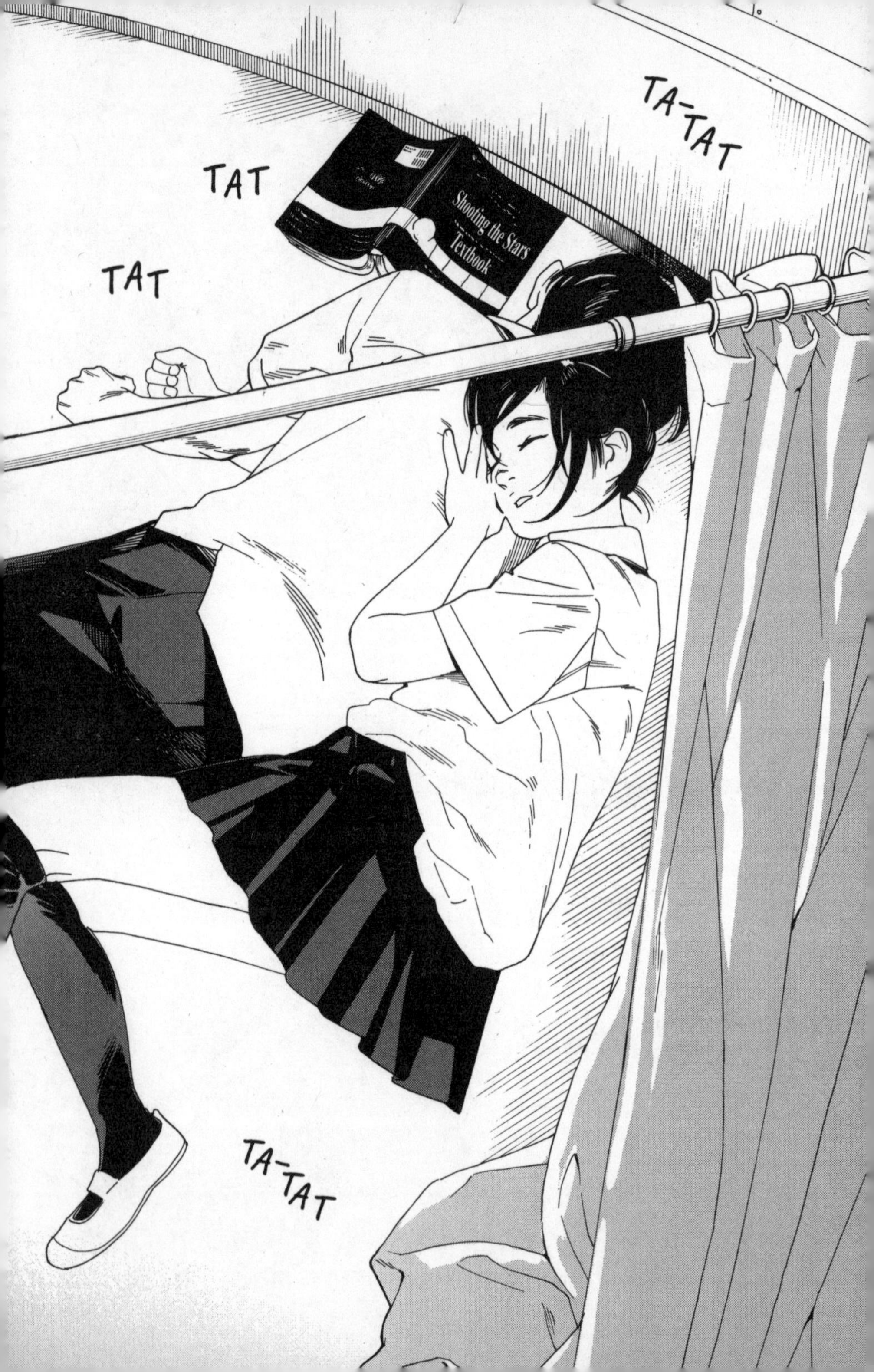
TA-TAT
Shooting the Stars
Textbook
TAT
TAT
TA-TAT

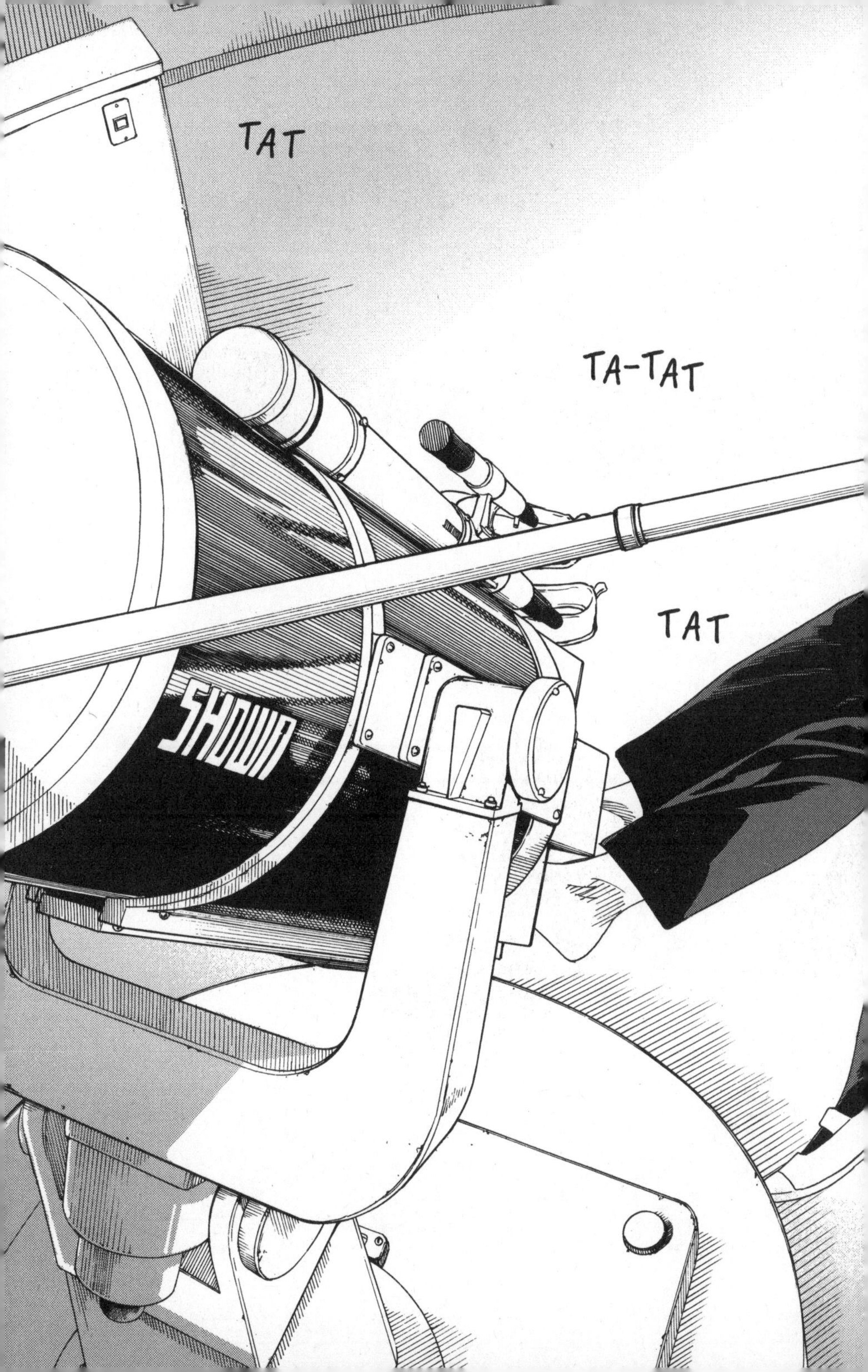
TAT
TA-TAT
TAT
SHOWA

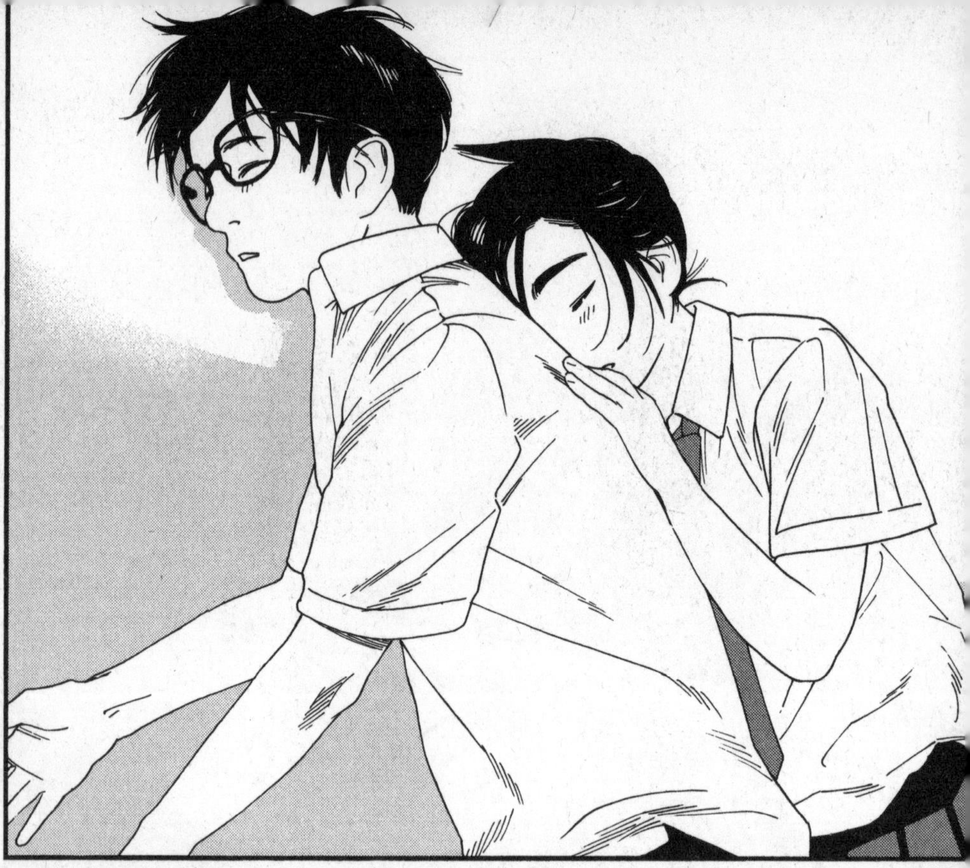
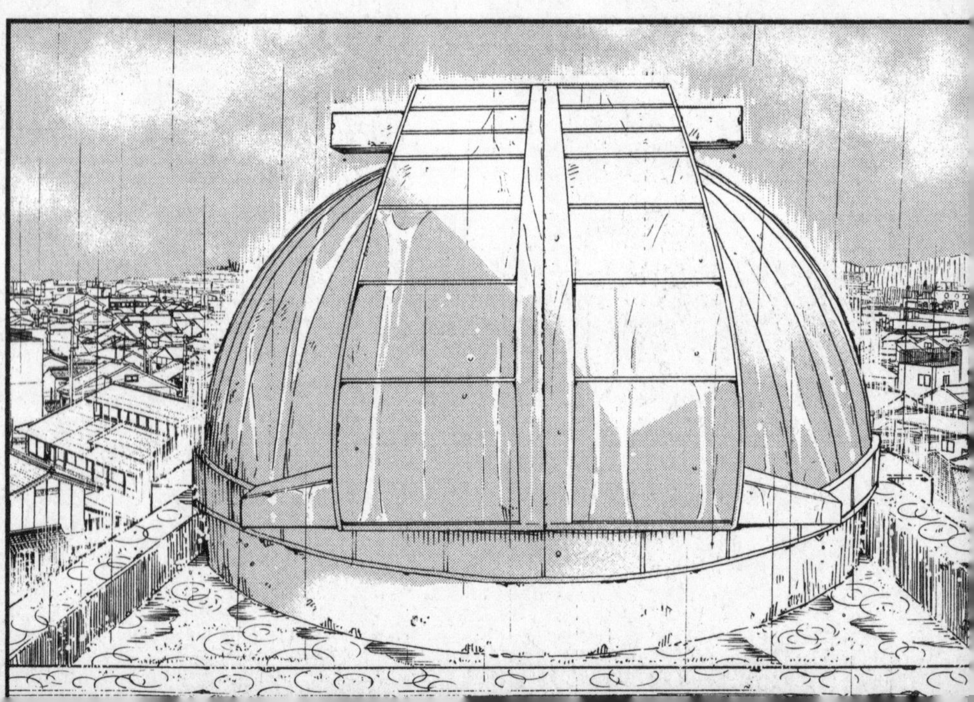

Makoto Ojiro

began her career in manga as an assistant at the age of 19. Her *Neko no Otera no Chion-san* (Cat Temple's Miss Chion) won the Bros. Comic Award in 2016. *Insomniacs After School* began serialization in 2019 and has been adapted into an anime and a live-action film.

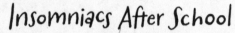

Insomniacs After School

VIZ SIGNATURE EDITION

STORY & ART BY
Makoto Ojiro

TRANSLATION
Andria Cheng

TOUCH-UP ART & LETTERING
Inori Fukuda Trant

DESIGN
Alice Lewis

EDITOR
Jennifer Sherman

KIMI WA HOKAGO INSOMNIA Vol. 1
by Makoto OJIRO
© 2019 Makoto OJIRO
All rights reserved.
Original Japanese edition published by SHOGAKUKAN.
English translation rights in the United States of America,
Canada, the United Kingdom, Ireland, Australia and New
Zealand arranged with SHOGAKUKAN.

The stories, characters, and incidents mentioned in this
publication are entirely fictional.

Original Cover Design: Kaoru KUROKI + Bay Bridge Studio

Printed in Canada

Published by VIZ Media, LLC
P.O. Box 77010
San Francisco, CA 94107

10 9 8 7 6 5 4 3 2 1
First printing, March 2023

VIZ MEDIA *VIZ SIGNATURE*

viz.com   vizsignature.com

Z
Z
Z

Cats of the Louvre
by TAIYO MATSUMOTO

A surreal tale of the secret world of the cats of the Louvre, told by Eisner Award winner Taiyo Matsumoto.

The world-renowned Louvre museum in Paris contains more than just the most famous works of art in history. At night, within its darkened galleries, an unseen and surreal world comes alive—a world witnessed only by the small family of cats that lives in the attic. Until now…

Translated by *Tekkonkinkreet* film director Michael Arias.

THIS IS THE LAST PAGE

This book reads from right to left.

Turn the book over and start reading

from the other side.

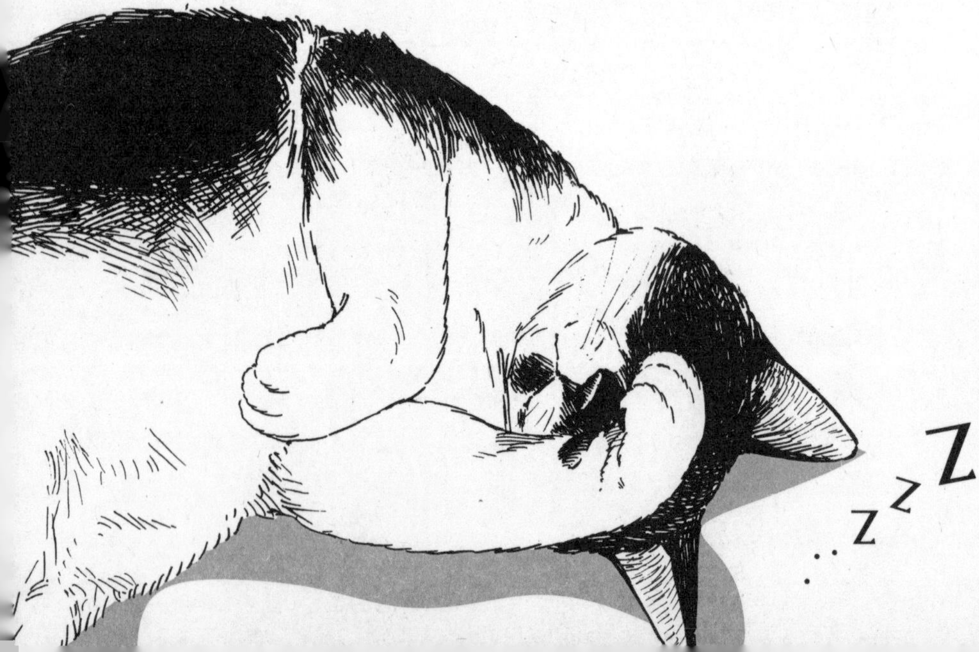
..zzZ